Promoting Human Rights in Burma

Promoting Human Rights in Burma

A Critique of Western Sanctions Policy

Morten B. Pedersen

ROWMAN & LITTLEFIELD PUBLISHERS, INC.
Lanham • Boulder • New York • Toronto • Plymouth, UK

ROWMAN & LITTLEFIELD PUBLISHERS, INC.

Published in the United States of America
by Rowman & Littlefield Publishers, Inc.
A wholly owned subsidiary of The Rowman & Littlefield Publishing Group, Inc.
4501 Forbes Boulevard, Suite 200, Lanham, Maryland 20706
www.rowmanlittlefield.com

Estover Road, Plymouth PL6 7PY, United Kingdom

British Library Cataloguing in Publication Information Available

Library of Congress Cataloging-in-Publication Data

Pedersen, Morten B.
Promoting human rights in Burma : a critique of Western sanctions policy / Morten B. Pedersen.
p. cm.
Includes bibliographical references and index.
ISBN-13: 978-0-7425-5559-4 (cloth : alk. paper)
ISBN-10: 0-7425-5559-3 (cloth : alk. paper)
1. Burma—Politics and government—1988- 2. Human rights—Burma. 3. Sanctions (International law) 4. Western countries—Foreign relations—Burma. 5. Burma—Foreign relations—Western countries. I. Title.
DS530.65.P38 2008
327.1'17—dc22

2007012386

Printed in the United States of America

∞™ The paper used in this publication meets the minimum requirements of American National Standard for Information Sciences—Permanence of Paper for Printed Library Materials, ANSI/NISO Z39.48-1992.

Contents

Foreword

Morten Pedersen is today one of the foremost students and scholars of Burmese politics anywhere outside the country. Just as importantly, he has lived and worked in Rangoon for much of the last ten years and so, as one of very few foreigners, has been able to see developments in the country firsthand. *Promoting Human Rights in Burma: A Critique of Western Sanctions Policy* not only is a product of careful research and analysis, but also reflects the perspectives and insights gained from a decade of personal discussions and observations.

This firsthand knowledge is critically important because there is in many quarters a strong tendency to make Burma exotic and to view contemporary politics in an almost mythologized way, with two-dimensional characters and a one-dimensional history. Morten Pedersen's timely study steers us firmly toward a more complex understanding of political and social change and a more rigorous assessment of Western policy.

Promoting Human Rights in Burma: A Critique of Western Sanctions Policy could not have been published at a more opportune time. Burma stands at a critical watershed. Burma's armed conflicts remain unfinished, health and education systems are severely underfunded, and there are increasing signs that the very structures and institutions on which any stable government depend are fast deteriorating. Nearly twenty years after the failed pro-democracy uprising of 1988 and the cut-off of nearly all Western aid to the country, there is an urgent need to rethink the international community's approach and, in particular, to reexamine the legacy and future of sanctions.

Burma is under one of the tightest sanctions regimes in the world, yet there is all too little discussion of its efficacy and its humanitarian consequences on one of the poorest and most war-torn societies in the world.

I hope that this book will not only help revive a serious debate about Western policy toward Burma but also lead to practical new steps forward.

Thant Myint-U

Acknowledgments

This book is at heart a joint effort to which numerous people have contributed their time, knowledge, money, or simply moral support.

I owe much to the academic institutions which have provided infrastructural and/or financial assistance for my research: most notably the Danish Research Academy and the Department of Political and Social Change, Research School of Pacific and Asian Studies, Australian National University, but also the Southeast Asian Studies Summer Institute; the Sigur Center for Asian Studies, George Washington University; and most recently the Peace and Governance Programme at the United Nations University in Tokyo.

I have benefited immensely as well from four years as senior analyst with the International Crisis Group, which stands for me as the preeminent institution of its kind—distinguished, not least, by having the courage of its opinions—as well as from shorter assignments with the United Nations, the World Bank, the European Commission, and other international organizations. I hurry to say, though, that while many people in these institutions share important parts of my view of the situation in Burma and the challenges the country faces, they are in no way accountable for or directly associated with any part of this book, which remains my sole responsibility. Indeed, this is the first time in several years that I write absolutely unfettered by the need to consider broader organizational objectives and interests.

Like all Burma analysts of my generation, I am obligated to those who in the 1950s–1980s worked, often under extremely difficult circumstances, to shed light on one of the most isolated governments and societies in the world. Without their pioneering work, this study would have lacked the historical grounding that is crucial for understanding processes of change. Several of these scholars—whom I refrain from mentioning by name only for fear of leaving someone out—were among the first to warn Western governments about the limitations and dangers of their responses to developments in Burma since 1988, a theme which is further developed in this book.

Most directly, and most deeply, I am indebted to the many people in Burma and elsewhere who during ten years of research have shared generously of their time and knowledge. I started this project in 1997, more curious than critical about the policies of the West, which from a distance looked imminently reasonable, though evidently somewhat lacking in impact. I ended up with a much less benevolent view, shaped in large part by extensive—and often intensive—discussions with Burmese from all walks of life, including dissidents, government officials, journalists, businessmen, writers, doctors, and community workers, as well as foreign diplomats and aid officials. Most must remain unnamed as their contributions would not be appreciated by their governments or the organizations they work for or belong to. But I am forever thankful to these friends, colleagues, and informants, and I can only hope that this publication, which puts their insights to work, may contribute to our shared goal of increasing international understanding of Burma and developing policies which may help that country move forward.

Last, but not least, I must express my deep gratitude to the staff at Rowman & Littlefield, who has helped put all of this into print so that it can indeed be shared and debated and agreed or disagreed with as each reader makes up her or his own mind.

Abbreviations and Acronyms

3D Fund	Three Diseases Fund
ABSDF	All-Burma Students' Democratic Front
AFPFL	Anti-Fascist People's Freedom League
AusAID	Australian Agency for International Development
ASEAN	Association of Southeast Asian Nations
BSPP	Burma Socialist Programme Party
CPB	Communist Party of Burma
DAB	Democratic Alliance of Burma
DFID	(United Kingdom) Department for International Development
DPNS	Democratic Party of a New Society
EC	European Commission
EU	European Union
GONGO	Government-organized nongovernmental organization
ICRC	International Committee of the Red Cross
IFIs	International financial institutions
ILO	International Labor Organization
IMF	International Monetary Fund
KIO	Kachin Independence Organization
KNLA	Karen National Liberation Army
KNPP	Karenni National Progressive Party
KNU	Karen National Union
MI	Military intelligence

MWAF	Myanmar Women's Affairs Federation
Na-Sa-Ka	Burmese border security force
NCGUB	National Coalition Government of the Union of Burma
NCUB	National Council of the Union of Burma
NDF	National Democratic Front
NGO	Nongovernmental (development) organization
NLD	National League for Democracy
NMSP	New Mon State Party
NUP	National Unity Party
PDC	Peace and Development Council
PNO	Pao National Organization
Sangha	Burmese monk order
SLORC	State Law and Order Restoration Council
SNLD	Shan National League for Democracy
SPDC	State Peace and Development Council
SSA-S	Shan State Army South
Tatmadaw	Burmese armed forces
UK	United Kingdom
UN	United Nations
UNA	United Nationalities Alliance
UNAIDS	Joint United Nations Programme on HIV/AIDS
UNDCP	United Nations Drug Control Programme
UNDP	United Nations Development Programme
UNHCR	United Nations Refugee Agency
UNICEF	United Nations Children's Fund
UNLD	United Nationalities League for Democracy
UNODC	United Nations Office on Drugs and Crime
U.S.	United States
USDA	Union Solidarity and Development Association
UWSA	United Wa State Army

Author's Note

Burma or Myanmar? The importance placed by political actors on the use of "Burma" or "Myanmar" as the English name for the country presents a dilemma for scholars and other observers, who wish to address all sides in the conflict. Without prejudice to the correctness of any given choice, this book adopts the preference—or most common use—of the country of publication (the United States). It therefore uses "Burma" and "Burmese" when referring to the country and its people, and "Burman" for the majority ethnic group. The capital is referred to as Rangoon, and other places, too, are called by their pre-1989 names. The exception is direct quotes and references, for which the terms used by the authors themselves are maintained. In cases where current names have gained near universal usage and old names may no longer be familiar to most readers, the former are included in parentheses after the latter; for example: Arakan (Rakhine) state, Pegu (Bago).

Introduction: The Burmese Conundrum

Since 1988, when a popular uprising catapulted Burma onto the world stage after almost three decades of self-imposed isolation, Western governments and international organizations have promoted democracy as the solution to the country's manifold development problems, from political instability and ethnic conflict to weak governance and deep-rooted, structural poverty. The scale and scope of international opprobrium facing the military regime has earned Burma the epithet "South Africa of the 1990s." Alas, nineteen years of censure and sanctions aimed at compelling the military to relinquish power to an elected government have produced no results and may have done more harm than good to the Burmese people. Greatly needed are more pragmatic, long-term efforts to help unite a long-divided country and promote socioeconomic development as the basis for a gradual process of domestically driven political reform.

The 1988 Uprising and 1990 Election

Burma first hit the international headlines in the summer of 1988 when twenty-six years of repression and economic mismanagement by General Ne Win's quixotic military-cum-socialist regime culminated in a popular uprising echoing events in the Philippines two years earlier and subsequently drawing comparisons with China and Tiananmen Square. During several months, hundreds of thousands of people from all walks of life took to the streets in cities and towns all around the country, effectively bringing the government to a standstill and demanding an end to one-party rule. Bowing to the pressure, Ne Win resigned as leader of the ruling Burma Socialist Programme Party (BSPP) and recommended a referendum on the introduction of a multiparty system. Yet, just as it looked like Burma might return to democracy, the military reasserted itself. In a move ostensibly made to save the country from disintegration, the commander-in-chief of the armed forces, General Saw Maung, assumed power as head of a nineteen-man military junta, the State Law and Order Restoration Council (SLORC)—later renamed the State Peace and Development Council (SPDC)—and the army was employed to crush the uprising and restore "order." Many protesters were killed or arrested.

The new military rulers pledged to relinquish power as soon as law and order was restored and invited political parties to form in preparation for a multiparty election. They also quickly negotiated cease-fires with four armed ethnic groups, which had been fighting the central government for decades under the banner of the Communist Party of Burma (CPB), and initiated a series of open-door, market-oriented reforms aimed at reviving the failed socialist economy. Despite continued political repression and the house arrest of Daw Aung San Suu Kyi—daughter of the country's independence hero, General Aung San, and general secretary of the National League for Democracy (NLD)—the SLORC surprised many by holding a largely fair election in May 1990. Yet, faced with an overwhelming victory by the NLD, which took 60 percent of the vote and 82 percent of the seats in parliament, the military leaders refused to step down, announcing that a new constitution would have to be put in place before the transfer of power could take place. Another clampdown on the opposition followed, which saw scores of political parties banned and hundreds of politicians and student activists jailed. Thus began a struggle, now in its eighteenth year, by the NLD and its supporters at home and abroad to get the military to recognize the election results and transfer power to a civilian, elected government.

The International Campaign for Democracy

The violent suppression of the 1988 uprising and the military's refusal to recognize the 1990 election results resonated strongly in Western countries, which were then just emerging from the shadow of the Cold War and looking to establish a "new world order" based on democratic governance. Together with the charisma of Aung San Suu Kyi, who in 1991 was awarded the Nobel Peace Prize, these developments united Western governments around a "principled" approach to Burma that elevated democracy to the primary foreign policy objective and prompted a series of actions to isolate the military regime by denying it international legitimacy, aid, trade, and investment.

Since 1988, the military has been subject to growing censure for its denial of democratic and other human rights, reinforced by diplomatic and economic sanctions to weaken the regime. Most Western governments have suspended nonhumanitarian bilateral aid, imposed an arms embargo, and denied tariff preferences to imports from Burma as well as preferential financing for trade and investments. Washington has further banned new investments by U.S. firms and blocked all imports and financial services, making it one of the tightest unilateral U.S. sanctions regimes against any country. Western governments have failed to get agreement within the UN on mandatory measures against Burma. They have, however, blocked all support from the international financial institutions, except minimal technical assistance, and restricted funding for the UN specialized agencies and international nongovernmental organizations (NGOs) to "humanitarian" programs. The United States and the European Union (EU) have also imposed a number of "smart" sanctions directly targeting the military rulers, their families, and main supporters by denying them visa rights, freezing their assets, and—in the case of the EU—selectively banning new investments in state- and military-owned companies.

Outside the machinery of government, human rights activists, Burmese exiles, and Western trade unionists have carried out extensive grassroots campaigns to stop all foreign trade, investments, and tourism. Some have worked with sympathetic lawmakers in state and local governments—mainly in the United States—to introduce selective purchasing or divestment laws targeting all companies that do business in Burma. Others have used consumer boycotts, shareholder resolutions, and lawsuits to pressure specific companies to withdraw from the country.

Although Western governments, of course, have broader concerns in Burma and, to some degree, have pursued complementary policies, this "core strategy" of promoting democracy by isolating the military regime has taken precedence over all other interests and means.

Domestic Developments

While international campaigners for democracy in Burma have drawn both inspiration and faith from the successful antiapartheid campaign in South Africa, developments since 1988 underscore how misguided such comparisons are. Far from crumbling under outside pressure, the military has further consolidated its hold on power, both in central Burma and the border regions, and the basic human rights situation has seen no fundamental improvements. Instead of progress, the Burmese people have experienced deepening poverty and deteriorating health and education systems as the government's early economic reform efforts have given way to policy paralysis and international donors shun the country. Many opportunities have been lost and important trends are in the wrong direction.

Political Transition

Save for the first few years after it took power and a short period in the early 2000s when former prime minister and intelligence chief General Khin Nyunt appeared to be engaging in a good-faith dialogue with both the NLD and ethnic armed groups, the military leadership has basically ignored the opposition. The democracy forces over time have given up their demand for the military to transfer power to the parliament elected in 1990 and today generally appear willing to consider some form of interim power-sharing arrangement to be worked out through a tripartite dialogue between the SPDC, the NLD, and ethnic minority groups, but to no avail. The SPDC has simply pushed ahead with its own transition plan and at the time of writing in early 2007 appears to be getting ready to impose a new constitution and retire control to a loyal successor regime, possibly by 2008. The army has also strengthened its control of the border regions, thus paving the way for the establishment, for the first time in the country's history, of central government institutions and authority in most, though not yet all, parts of the territory.

Despite early assurances to the contrary, the military has not allowed the representatives elected in 1990 to play any meaningful role in drafting the new constitution, a process which has been tightly controlled. Senior military officials, in fact, have become increasingly unapologetic about ignoring the original election and in recent years have openly rejected any claim by the NLD to power or legitimacy. While the future constitution, which is now essentially completed, contains some democratic features, including multiparty elections for both national and local parliaments, the unstated aim is to ensure that state power remains in the hands of the military, effectively delinked from political competition and representation of voting constituencies. The SPDC still has to get the document approved in a referendum and ensure that the opposition does not repeat its landslide victory from 1990 in the next elections. But, with the military's civilian front organizations—led by the ubiquitous Union Solidarity and Development Association (USDA)—having established a stranglehold on large parts of the countryside, this, too, may be within reach.

While the new constitution should by no means be perceived as the end of the struggle for democracy, the opposition has lost the first battle and, despite the continuing efforts of many courageous individuals, seems ill-prepared for the next phase. The contrast to the late 1980s—when Aung San Suu Kyi emerged as an icon for people fighting for democracy in Burma and around the world, prompting frequent comparisons with other liberation leaders like Nelson Mandela and Mahatma Gandhi, and the NLD seemed a formidable challenge to the military regime—is stark. The long "war or attrition" has taken a heavy toll on the main opposition party, which today seems only a shadow of its former self, its leadership aging and isolated, its membership greatly reduced and its political activities largely confined to its Rangoon headquarter.

Civil War

The travails of the political opposition are in many ways mirrored among the ethnic armed groups, which since independence have fought for local autonomy and ethnic rights, rejecting the authority of the Burman-dominated government. While the central government in 1988 had only limited control of the countryside beyond the central plains and the main valleys, the army since then—through a combination of military conquest and political negotiation—has pushed further and further into the hills, leaving less and less space for armed opposition. To many, both observers and participants, Burma's long-running civil war appears to have entered the endgame.

Since 1988, more than two dozen armed ethnic groups or factions have ceased armed struggle. Most have joined the National Convention, seeing the constitutional discussions as their best chance to get on the inside of the political process after decades in the "wilderness." The government's refusal to accommodate most of their demands has created resentment, particularly among groups such as the New Mon State Party (NMSP) and Kachin Independence Organization (KIO), which have national political objectives and strong roots in their local communities.[1] Yet, even as hopes for significant concessions from the government wane, most cease-fire leaders continue to see cooperation with the government road map as their best option. Any constitution, some reason, is better than no constitution—at least it will provide a formal framework for future negotiations.[2] Of course, they are acutely aware, too, of the backlash they would face, were they to withdraw from the National Convention. (Whether the cease-fire groups will be willing to give up their arms without stronger political guarantees is a different matter, and one bound to create strong tensions in a postconstitution period, even as the options for resistance are narrowing.)

The remaining insurgent groups, while calling for peace talks, so far have insisted that any cease-fire must be accompanied by political negotiations addressing their long-standing demand for federalism, something the government has rejected. Thus, they continue a largely defensive guerrilla war against the expanding control of the army. The Karen National Union (KNU), however—the oldest and arguably most influential of Burma's numerous ethnic armed groups—is increasingly split on the issue. Some members now believe stopping the fighting must take precedence so they can begin resettling displaced communities and rebuilding the education system, which has collapsed in large parts of Karen state during the prolonged conflict. "We missed a big opportunity," laments a KNU official, "in not reaching a cease-fire in the mid-1990s, while we were still strong militarily and had greater leverage, but we can still achieve something through a cease-fire if we eschew business and focus on helping our people."[3] Several officers from the KNU's armed wing, the Karen National Liberation Army (KNLA), in 2006 publicly rejected the authority of the Central Committee, accusing it of inefficiency and corruption,[4] and went on to negotiate a separate cease-fire deal with the government. While facing accusations themselves of simply trying to feather their own nest, many soldiers on the frontlines appear to see little prospect in continuing the fighting.

In late 2005, the army broke an eighteen-month-old "gentleman agreement" with the KNU to cease hostilities while negotiating a formal cease-fire, and launched another major offensive in northern Karen state and eastern Pegu (Bago) division. The government says this is simply a security operation to mop up elements of the KNU's 2nd Brigade, which allegedly had been attacking civilians and blowing up bombs around Taungoo.[5] Yet, the scope and nature of the offensive, which has expanded from Taungoo district into Nyaung Lay Bin and Papun districts to the east and south, suggest intent to pacify the entire area once and for all. Since April 2006, several thousand Karen refugees have arrived at the Thai border with stories of army attacks on villages, which closely resemble experiences during past "four-cuts" counterinsurgency campaigns in ethnic areas.[6] This is likely to be followed, as it has been in other border areas, by the establishment of new army bases, access roads, and central government institutions.

The Shan State Army South (SSA-S) and Karenni National Progress Party (KNPP), as well as other KNU brigades, so far, are under less pressure, but it seems inevitable that their turn will come. With a pliant government and full autonomy in internal affairs, the army will be able to continue its security operations in the posttransition phase with little interference. Indeed, should the need arise, it will be able to use the emergency clause in the new constitution to cordon off any remaining areas of rebellion and rule under martial law. This, of course, is exactly what the generals have intended to ensure.

Clearly, the military's consolidation of power does not add up to political stability, never mind legitimacy. The generals' hopes of building durable and effective structures of governance will remain unfulfilled as long as they continue to ride roughshod over the views and aspirations of the citizens. The passive resistance of the people will continue, the ethnic groups will hold on to their arms, and both domestic and international legitimacy will remain illusive. Yet, in some ways this is the ultimate tragedy: Burma remains stuck; very little has fundamentally changed over the past two decades, or seems likely to do so while everyone sticks to rigid positions and ineffectual strategies. Burma in 2007 is perhaps the most militarized society in the contemporary world, and one of the most isolated. The weakness of the country's civilian institutions, state and nonstate alike, provides a weak basis for change, whether revolutionary or more gradual.

Human Rights

The human rights situation, too, remains of serious concern. Although the prevalence of physical violence has declined in step with the waning of open political and armed antigovernment resistance, serious abuses are commonplace, particularly, in conflict-affected areas. The military regime also severely limits political and civil freedoms, and shows little respect for property rights.

While the brutality of the 1988 uprising and its immediate aftermath was exceptional for central Burma and political killings, or "disappearances," do not occur on the scale seen in some other authoritarian countries, the general political environment remains highly oppressive.[7] In order to forestall challenges to its rule, the military continues to deny its citizens basic political rights, including the freedoms to speak, organize, and assemble.[8] Since 1988, the SLORC/SPDC has added a number of repressive decrees to the existing array of security legislation from the colonial and immediate postindependence periods, which are used to sentence dissidents to long prison terms for peaceful opposition activities, usually without "due process." Censorship is extremely tight, and the administration of justice deeply problematic. The judicial system, in essence, remains a tool for protection of the powerful rather than the weak.[9]

In the border regions, the trends are similar. The spread of cease-fires has helped curtail the most severe human rights abuses, including arbitrary killings, rape, and forced portering for the army, which mainly have occurred in the context of counterinsurgency campaigns directed at ethnic minority populations suspected of supporting the insurgents.[10] Yet, serious abuses are still committed with impunity in areas where insurgent groups operate, as reflected in the regular reports of large-scale forced relocations of villages during counterinsurgency operations in Karen, Karenni, and southern Shan states and Tenasserim division.[11] Also, the growing presence of the army in areas previously under insurgent control or ungoverned has been accompanied by an increase in land confiscation, forced labor, and other compulsory contributions that threaten the livelihoods of local communities.[12] The latter problems have been compounded by the government's drive to expand the country's infrastructure beyond its financial means, as well as by the self-reliance policy of the army, which since 1998 has required local battalions to provide their own food and other necessities.

The early 2000s saw significant improvements in the government's cooperation with international human rights and humanitarian organizations, including some limited concrete progress in areas such as prison conditions and forced labor.[13] The UN special rapporteur on human rights, the International Labor Organization (ILO), the International Committee of the Red Cross (ICRC), Amnesty International, and the United Nations Children's Fund (UNICEF; on child rights) all stepped up their activities significantly. The growing willingness of the regime to discuss human rights, however, was not matched by a commitment—or ability—to redress the general climate of impunity in which the abuses take place, and since the purge of Khin Nyunt in October 2004, cooperation with international agencies has deteriorated again. The army and other security forces show few signs of changing their heavy-handed behavior toward the civilian population, particularly in remote areas inhabited by ethnic minority groups.

Economic Trends

The economy grew modestly in the early 1990s, fueled by market-oriented economic reforms which saw an expansion in the domestic private sector and foreign direct investment. Although the primary beneficiaries were a small urban elite (mainly those with government connections or access to investment capital from outside the country), many poorer households also benefited from new income opportunities, particularly in the agricultural, construction, and service sectors. The new reforms, however, stopped short of facilitating structural change, and the upswing proved to be short-lived. The government's much-publicized "Visit Myanmar Year 1996" fell far short of achieving its objectives (partly due to consumer boycott campaigns in the West), adversely affecting the hotel and tourism industry and hurting overall investor confidence. This was followed in short order, first, by a ban on all new U.S. investments in April 1997 and, then, by the Asian economic crisis which caused a sharp drop in intraregional trade and investment flows. Since then, the government has reverted to crisis management, and policy making has become increasingly ad hoc and erratic, further deterring foreign direct investment which fell to almost zero in the early 2000s before rebounding as a result of new gas and hydropower projects.

The start up of gas exports from the Yadana and Yetagun offshore gas fields in 1999–2000 provided some relief for the government. A major expansion in the garment export industry in 2000–2002 also created a large number of jobs for unskilled young women, many of whom came from impoverished rural areas to work in the new factories in the cities. Yet, the economic fundamentals remained weak and a run on the private banks in February 2003 sparked a downward spiral which disrupted trade across the country, caused widespread job losses particularly among day laborers in the construction and manufacturing sectors, and resulted in a significant contraction in overall economic activity. Many companies went bankrupt or were forced to downsize as the crisis-hit private banks cut their credit lines. New U.S. bans on financial services and Burmese imports introduced in July that year further compounded the situation, disrupting international trading arrangements based on U.S. dollar transactions and decimating the garment sector. Rising world oil prices have also hit the country hard, creating an inflationary effect across the economy as the government has increased the price of subsidized petrol and diesel nearly tenfold.

Generally speaking, rural families are less affected by shocks in the formal economy than their urban counterparts, since they are able to grow or collect more of their own food, which takes up more than 70 percent of the average family's budget.[14] Some farmers have benefited significantly from a liberalization of agricultural production and trade in some crops. Yet, the terms of trade facing the country's millions of rice farmers (i.e., the price of paddy relative to inputs such as fertilizer) have deteriorated, particularly since the government's ban on rice exports in December 2003, which forced down farmgate prices, in some cases to below production costs.[15] Growing ecological problems resulting from overuse or misuse of land, compounded by widespread deforestation, have also taken their toll, particularly on marginal farmers who struggle with deteriorating soil quality and declining yields. As people complement their incomes by gathering wood and other "free" resources, other natural resources have come under increasing pressure too.[16]

Under growing strain from declining macroeconomic trends and government interventions in local economies, households all around the country are adopting negative coping strategies such as selling assets, borrowing money from local moneylenders at exorbitant rates, cutting meals, foregoing health care, or taking children out of school, which further erode household security. Poverty is also feeding large-scale migration flows around the country and across its borders to Thailand, India, and countries further afield, which are at the same time a vital coping mechanism and a cause of social ills such a broken families, drug use, and HIV/AIDS.

The government in 2006 showed signs of renewed commitment to economic reform, but weak technical capacity and traditional economic thinking remain major impediments to the formulation of appropriate policies. Indeed, the top leaders may not fully understand that their much touted "modern, developed nation" remains largely a mirage conjured up by government officials eager to please their superiors.

Humanitarian Situation

While reliable social indicators are lacking for many parts of the country, both general surveys and case studies by international agencies from different parts of the country indicate that large segments of the population are caught in deep-rooted, structural poverty and that the situation for many people is worsening. According to calculations based on the 1997 and 2001 government household surveys, the proportion of people living under the poverty line increased from 23 percent to 32 percent over this period.[17] A joint UNDP-government survey from 2005 estimated the number at "more than 30 percent" in the country as a whole, but much higher in Chin state (70 percent) and eastern Shan state (52 percent).[18] It further indicated that, everything else equal, an increase of just 15–20 percent in food prices would push "well over 50 percent" of the total population below the poverty line,[19] a prospect that with continuing high inflation could soon become reality.

Although Burma is food self-sufficient at the national level, many people do not have sustainable access to safe food of sufficient quality and quantity. Official figures from 1997 show that only about 40 percent of households were consuming calories at or above recommended daily requirement and only 55 percent were consuming enough protein.[20] Two years later, two international agricultural economists concluded, based on studies in the Dry Zone, that the situation was worsening: "Widely scattered reports of spontaneous emergency feedings, purchase of rice water for food, and reliance on inferior cereals such as millet all suggest increasing stress. . . . The conclusion must be that consumption of many families is less than usual, less than needed, and under increasing pressure."[21] More recently, similar trends have become evident even in the peri-urban areas of Rangoon, where sale of rice water has become a normal occurrence.[22] Not surprisingly, given this situation, levels of malnutrition are very high, particularly among children. One-quarter of Burmese babies are born underweight, with long-term nutritional and health implications.[23] At the age of five, almost half are moderately to severely malnourished.[24]

With deepening poverty and minimal and declining health budgets, the health situation has become a serious concern, in particular the spread of infectious diseases. The greatest long-term threat is HIV/AIDS, which has been spreading rapidly throughout the country since the late 1980s, fueled by population mobility, poverty, and frustration that breeds risky sexual activity and drug taking, and today has become firmly established in the general population. Numbers vary between sources, but UNAIDS suggests that 620,000 people were living with HIV/AIDS in Burma in 2005. This translates into 2.5 percent of the most productive age bracket of fifteen- to forty-nine-year-olds and resulted in an estimated thirty-seven thousand AIDS deaths that year alone.[25] Malaria, traditionally the leading cause of illness in the country, is responsible for over six hundred thousand reported cases per year and at least three thousand deaths, the highest numbers of any country in Asia. Tuberculosis, too, is pervasive, with an estimated one hundred thousand cases and over twelve thousand deaths annually. For both diseases drug resistant strains are a rapidly growing problem with serious implications for the future.[26] What we are seeing for these three diseases, according to UN officials, "is an evolution of trends that we are already seeing in Africa. It could all of a sudden explode."[27]

Low educational attainment is also an increasingly serious social, economic, and political problem. More than 50 percent of children do not complete five years of basic schooling, and many of those who do take ten or more years to finish (even then, they may not be able to read and write).[28] The official literacy rate is 94 percent,[29] but a 1999 UN survey found the functional literacy rate to be only 53 percent and case studies from remote areas give figures as low as 10 percent.[30] Secondary and tertiary education is also suffering from low and falling standards.

The humanitarian situation is particularly acute in conflict-affected areas along the Thai border, where local communities suffer violence and displacement.[31] But all over the country signs of economic breakdown and social dislocation are becoming ever more evident. Increasing crime rates in Rangoon and other major cities, the continuing outflow of legal and illegal migrants in large numbers to neighbouring countries, and the many women and girls being trafficked to Thai brothels every year speak clearly to the destitution afflicting many of the country's 50 million–plus people. According to UN resident coordinator Charles Petrie, although the situation does not yet qualify as a humanitarian crisis, "there are geographic pockets of acute need in the country as well as aspects of suffering that constitute both a national and regional emergency," and conditions continue to deteriorate. The country, he warns, is not only losing the fight to stop the progression of serious health epidemics within the general population but also the skills and capacities necessary to cope with these and other development challenges.[32]

Purpose of Study

The overarching aim of this study is to evaluate Western human rights policy on Burma since 1988 and contribute to a more substantive debate about alternative strategies for promoting the freedom, security, and welfare of the country's citizens. The failure to promote political reform or substantially improve human rights, coupled with the increasingly apparent policy paralysis and resultant deepening socioeconomic crisis, raises urgent questions about the appropriateness of the core strategy, as well as the validity of the assumptions on which it rests. Broadly speaking, such questions cluster around three issues:

WHAT effect do existing policies have? While the primary goal of democracy has obviously not been achieved, further detail is needed to evaluate the usefulness of existing policies. Do they work in the right direction but have simply failed to tip the balance; are they ineffectual; or are they in fact counterproductive? Also, what are the immediate social costs for the general population which is denied international aid, trade, and investment, as well as the longer-term opportunity costs of limiting such interactions?

WHY has coercive diplomacy not worked? Whatever the net results of censure and sanctions so far, it is important to try to understand the factors that condition its impact. Is the lack of success due to weaknesses in the sanctions regime—or are there internal characteristics of Burmese politics that limit its impact? Can such obstacles be overcome, or do they constitute absolute constraints which must be worked around? This bears on the final issue of future policy.

HOW can the human rights—that is, the freedom, security, and welfare—of the Burmese people best be promoted? Ultimately, the objective of any policy study must be to help develop effective policies. If current policy is flawed, alternative approaches must be identified that maximize the probability of reaching the stated objectives. Of course, the stated objectives themselves may be questioned and alternative ones suggested.

Recent policy debates and associated research have begun to address some of these issues. Yet, the field is still characterized more by the fervor with which ideological or self-serving positions are advocated by a diversity of mainly political actors than by substantive, empirically grounded analysis, and the opposing sides remain far apart. According to proponents of the core strategy, international censure and sanctions are cause of great concern to the military leaders who supposedly are struggling to keep up morale, keep the economy afloat, and maintain the regime's support base.[33] Concrete steps by the government such as the release of Aung San Suu Kyi in 1995 and the launch of its "roadmap to democracy" in 2003 are cited as evidence that the regime is buckling under the strain of international isolation. While acknowledging that the rate of change is slower than expected, advocates of sanctions often point to South Africa where it took thirty years to defeat the apartheid regime, arguing that the pressure must be maintained until the objectives are attained. Most give short shrift to the impact of sanctions on the general population, which is claimed to be "minimal," or at least "acceptable," in light of the broader objective of regime change.

Critics, on the other hand, maintain that the core strategy is both unrealistic in its objectives and harmful in its effects on the Burmese people as well as the country's longer-term development prospects.[34] Some believe that Burma's insular military rulers are unfazed by international opprobrium and isolation, and may even prefer it. Others argue that international demands are simply too big, and the costs for the military of giving in too high, to elicit a positive response. Most critics believe that regime change will remain an illusive goal as long as the military remains obsessed with national security concerns and social and economic structures in the country remain unfavorable to effective collective action against the military state. Thus, they recommend either lifting existing sanctions altogether to maximize international exposure, trade, and investment, or at least doing more on the ground to help both the government and society move forward in areas of core concern.

Assessing these different arguments is not straight forward. Causal links between international policy and domestic developments are inherently difficult to establish in any country since multiple pressures combine to produce the latter, and even more so in Burma, where key decisions invariably are made in secrecy among a handful of insular military leaders. Different observers, meanwhile, have different assumptions, premises, and priorities, covering such fundamental issues as order versus revolution, individual rights against community rights, and the benefits of economic prosperity as compared with those of political change. Ultimately, any conclusion on the usefulness of particular policies will reflect personal value positions and theories about the process of change, past, present, and future. Such caveats aside though, some headway can be made by juxtaposing specific, observable responses to international pressure on the ground in Burma with a more general analysis of the main political forces and the challenges of transition.

Data and Sources

The study of Burmese politics, the economy, or society at large is a difficult and often thankless task. Burma remains one of the most closed societies in the world, although the post-1988 period has seen significant openings. Few foreigners have access to the military or top rungs of the government. The opposition is superficially more accessible, but working under extreme pressure, NLD leaders have been guarded in discussing the internal workings of the party or its strategies and policies. Among the general population, fear and distrust often create psychological barriers to the free exchange of information and views.

The main obstacle, though, is not so much access as it is misinformation. The struggle for state power and legitimacy has compounded the researcher's problems by politicizing data collection and analysis, resulting in strong biases in reporting on all sides of the political spectrum, including much overt propaganda. The government's censorship and manipulation of economic and other data for political purposes is matched in many ways by the well-organized and well-funded lobby networks of the democracy movement, which work actively to propagate the worst possible image of the military regime and obfuscate issues or developments that might throw doubt about the core strategy. As David Steinberg observes, "To support their respective positions, each side and their adherents have engaged in extensive media campaigns and mobilized institutions to present their actions and visions in the most favorable light, sometimes creating spurious data and information, suppressing unpleasant materials and events, and thus clouding the ability of observers to make sensitive appraisals of the internal scene."[35]

In this polarized environment, even international agencies often feel compelled to self-censor to avoid upsetting either the Burmese authorities or activists, while anyone attempting to provide a fuller picture is commonly denigrated by one side or the other, if not by both. Commentators on Burmese politics commonly joke that "you know you are on the right track when *both* the government and the opposition criticize you."

While the constraints can be daunting, the research space in Burma, however, has expanded significantly in recent years. The authorities no longer limit the activities of scholars to the extent seen during earlier periods, and many Burmese share their experiences and attitudes more openly than before. The increased presence of foreign aid officials and businessmen in the country, who interact with the government on a daily basis, has helped both to demystify the presence of foreigners and shed light on many aspects of governance. Whether this new "openness" will survive the recent consolidation of power within the army hierarchy and ascendancy of conservative views remains to be seen, but for the last several years research has been somewhat easier than in the past.

Aside from the existing literature, policy papers, human rights reports, newspaper articles, and other open sources, this study is based on several hundred semi-structured interviews conducted over seven years from 2000 to 2007, as well as countless informal conversations with participants in the processes under investigation. Sources include people from many walks of life in Burma, including the military, the civil service, the USDA, the NLD, other political parties, armed groups, private business, and a variety of civil society and exile organizations, as well as foreign diplomats, international officials, development workers, scholars, journalists, and businessmen. Research was primarily carried out in Burma, but included also policy discussions in New York, Geneva, Washington, Brussels, London, Canberra, Tokyo, Bangkok, and other capitals. In most cases, sources are identified only with a general job description, place of interview, and the month it took place. This is necessary to protect the security or reputation of informants, many of whom spoke about confidential issues or expressed views that were at odds with those of their governments or organizations. A number of confidential reports and surveys are identified as precisely as possible, typically without the author/agency, but with a title and date.

Structure

In order to address the main gaps in our knowledge and help inform international policy makers, the study covers some considerable ground, although necessarily with broad strokes. Chapter 1 provides an outline of Western policy on Burma since 1988, including the underlying assumptions and rationales. This is followed by three chapters that examine key conditions for international influence and domestic reform, specifically the priorities and perceptions of the military leaders, the balance of power between the regime and other domestic political forces, and the broader challenges of transition, including national reconciliation, good governance, democratic institution building, and economic development. Chapter 5 seeks to assess the impact and potential of existing Western policies, based on reasoned assumptions about the most likely "drivers of change" in Burma and a holistic conception of human rights that posits the equality of political, socioeconomic, and other basic rights. Finally, the conclusion provides an overall critique of the core strategy. It identifies fundamental flaws in the underlying assumptions and outlines an alternative strategy for "critical engagement" in Burma, which—arguably—better takes into account the configuration of power and interests within the country, as well as the broader, structural obstacles to political and economic development.

Notes

1. The NMSP withdrew from active participation in the National Convention in December 2005 and for the last two sessions has sent an observer mission only. Both the NMSP and the KIO have also resisted government demands on the ceasefire groups to publicly protest the adoption of Burma on the UN Security Council agenda (and have paid for their obstinacy by a blockade of trade in and out of their regions). Kachin community leader, interview by author, Rangoon, October 2006.

2. Ethnic leaders, interviews by author, Rangoon, February 2004, March 2005, and August and October 2006.

3. Interview by author, Bangkok, October 2006.

4. *Irrawaddy* (online ed.), "KNLA Commanders Accuse Unnamed KNU Leaders," 31 July 2006, www.irrawaddy.org (accessed 31 July 2006).

5. Minister of information Brigadier General Kyaw Hsan, press conference, 13 May 2006, reported in *New Light of Myanmar*, 15 May 2006.

6. For details, see Special rapporteur on the situation of human rights in Myanmar, "Situation of Human Rights in Myanmar," report to the United Nations General Assembly (A/61/369), 21 September 2006.

7. The attack by government "brown shirts" on Aung San Suu Kyi and members and supporters of the NLD during a campaign trip up-country on 30 May 2003 is a notable exception from the absence of large-scale violence against dissidents. Although claims by antigovernment groups that more than seventy people were killed remain unconfirmed, most reports suggest that extreme violence was used. See, for example, Amnesty International, "Myanmar: Justice on Trial," 30 July 2003.

8. For details, see Special rapporteur, "Situation of Human Rights in Myanmar."

9. Amnesty International, "Myanmar: Justice on Trial," 30 July 2003; "Myanmar: The Administration of Justice: Grave and Abiding Concerns," 1 April 2004; "Myanmar: Travesties of Justice—Continued Misuse of the Legal System," 12 December 2005.

10. See, for example, Special rapporteur on the situation of human rights in Myanmar, "Situation of Human Rights in Myanmar," report to the United Nations General Assembly (A/58/150), 5 August 2003.

11. See, for example, Burma Ethnic Research Group, "Forgotten Victims of a Hidden War: Internally Displaced Karen in Burma," April 1998; Amnesty International,

"Myanmar: Exodus from the Shan State," 10 July 2000; Amnesty International, "Myanmar: The Lack of Security in Counter-Insurgency Areas," 17 July 2002; and Burma Border Consortium, "Internally Displaced People and Relocation Sites in Eastern Burma," September 2002.

12. See, for example, EarthRights International, "If We Don't Have Time to Take Care of Our Fields," 24 April 2005; Amnesty International, "Myanmar: Leaving Home," 8 September 2005; Karen Human Rights Group, "Setting Up the Systems of Repression," 7 September 2006. The ethnic armed groups are not innocent of such abuses either, but there is a substantial difference of degree.

13. See, for example, ICRC, "Annual Report—Myanmar," 17 June 2005, www.icrc.org/ (accessed 28 January 2007); ILO, "Myanmar: Forced Labour Convention, 1930 (no. 29)" (report of the Committee of Experts on the Application of Conventions and Recommendations, 74th session, 2003).

14. Development consultant, interview by author, Rangoon, March 2005.

15. Many farmers benefited when the government in April 2003 liberalized the rice trade and abolished the long-standing policy of compulsory rice sales to the state at below-market prices. Six months later, however, the authorities suddenly banned the export of rice (together with five other agricultural products), causing domestic prices to crash. Unable to recover their investment, many farmers reportedly lost their land or had to cut back on inputs with detrimental effects on both yields and soil quality. The ban was modified in 2005 to allow limited exports by a few select companies, but was reimposed in 2006 when increasing prices again raised government concerns about possible social unrest. Interviews by author: rice trader, Rangoon, June 2004; agricultural economist, Rangoon, December 2004; businessman, Rangoon, March 2005 and October 2006.

16. For a detailed, qualitative study of the agricultural sector, see the World Bank, "Myanmar: An Economic and Social Assessment," internal draft, 18 August 1999. Also "Accelerating Progress among the Rural Poor in Myanmar," confidential report, 15 September 1995; "Food Security in Myanmar: A Proposal to Deal with Natural Shocks," confidential report, January 2000; and Debbie Aung Din Taylor, "Signs of Distress: Observations on Agriculture, Poverty and the Environment in Myanmar" (paper presented at Conference on Reconciliation in Burma and the Crises of Change, Johns Hopkins University, Washington, DC, 22 November 2002).

17. Development consultant, interview by author, Rangoon, March 2005.

18. This may not seem extraordinarily high in global terms, but the average Burmese household in 2001 was spending 72 percent of its budget on food. Central Statistical Organization, *Statistical Yearbook* (Government of Myanmar, 2001). This is much more than in any other Asian country and leaves very little to cover the cost of health, education, and so on. The average family in Singapore devotes 14 percent of household expenditure to food, in Thailand 32 percent, Cambodia 57 percent, and Laos 61 percent. Australian Government, Department of Foreign Affairs and Trade, *Asian Agrifood Demand Trends to 2010* (Canberra: DFAT, July 2004).

19. UN resident coordinator Charles Petrie, "Speaking Notes" (prepared for the Burma/Myanmar Forum, European Institute for Asian Studies, Brussels, 29 March 2006).

20. National Nutrition Centre, "National Nutrition Survey," 1997. Other government and UN surveys have found moderate to high iodine, vitamin A, and iron deficiencies. UNICEF official, interview by author, Rangoon, January 2005.

21. "Food Security in Myanmar: A Proposal."

22. The water used to cook rice in is normally considered a waste product, but in particularly difficult times poor families may use it to substitute for real rice. According to a local journalist, "In Lanthaia [a suburb of Rangoon], they have begun selling rice water, first for 50 kyatt, but demand was so strong it increased to 70 kyatt. The Police Special Branch was sent to investigate. They thought it was a political ploy and were told to watch the vendor and arrest him if he did not sell anything. They let him be though, once they realized that he was doing a brisk trade." Interview by author, Rangoon, December 2005.

23. UNICEF official, interview by author, Rangoon, January 2005.

24. Department of Health Planning, *Multiple Indicator Cluster Survey* (n.p.: Government of Myanmar, 2000).

25. UNAIDS official, interviews by author, Rangoon, August 2005, October 2006.

26. 3D Fund, "What Is the Proposed 3D Fund?" background briefing, 2006 [copy in author's possession].

27. Quoted in Michael Casey, "Humanitarian Crisis Looming in Impoverished Myanmar," Associated Press, 6 December 2005 (posted on *BurmaNet News*, 6 December 2005, www.burmanet.org/news [accessed 6 December 2005]).

28. UNICEF official, interview by author, Rangoon, January 2005.

29. Minister of education Dr. Chan Nyein, "Clarifications of Progress Made in the Education Sector" (presentation at government press conference, Naypyidaw, 29 November 2006; http://mission.itu.ch/MISSIONS/Myanmar/pressrelease/Press%20Release%2029%20nov%2006.pdf [accessed 27 April 2007]).

30. United Nations Country Team (Myanmar), "Country Paper," internal working paper, January 2000; UNODC, "UNCT Mission to the Wa Region" (paper presented at the Mini Dublin Group Meeting, Yangon, August 2004).

31. According to a recent report, public health indicators along the Burma-Thai border are at least twice as bad as in central Burma and "closely resemble other countries facing humanitarian disasters, such as Sierra Leone, the Democratic Republic of Congo, Niger, Angola, and Cambodia shortly after the ouster of Khmer Rouge." Backpack Health Worker Team, "Chronic Emergency: Health and Human Rights in Eastern Burma," 2006.

32. Petrie, "Speaking Notes." This assessment was echoed by UN undersecretary-general Ibrahim Gambari in his first briefing to the Security Council in December 2005. Interview by author, New York, August 2006. It is corroborated by several case studies from different parts of the country, including "Food Security in Myanmar: A

Review of Issues," confidential report, May 2004; "Kayah Needs Assessment Project," confidential report, March 2003; "Household Livelihood Security Needs in Kokang Region," confidential report, July 2003; and UNDCP, "Northern Wa Region: Report on Opium Poppy Survey with Socio-Economic Findings," June 2002.

33. Most justifications for current Western policy on Burma come in the form of statements by policy makers, newspaper editorials, website campaign commentary, and the like, as part of the superficial everyday policy debates. More substantial contributions in favor of sanctions include: Institute for Asian Democracy, "Towards Democracy in Burma," 1992; Zaw Oo and Kai Grieg, "Carrots and Sticks for Democratisation in Burma: Policies of the EU and the ASEAN," in *Human Rights in Development: Global Perspectives and Local Issues*, ed. Hugo Stokke and Arne Tostensen (The Hague/Oslo: Kluwer Law International/Nordic Human Rights Publications, October 1999); Council on Foreign Relations, "Burma: A Time for Change," report of an independent task force, June 2003; Philip S. Robertson, Jr., "Sanctions Are Working in Burma," *Irrawaddy* (online ed.), 26 August 2003, www.irrawaddy.org (accessed 26 August 2003); ALTSEAN, "Ready, Aim, Sanction," November 2003; and Alfred Oehlers, "Sanctions and Burma: Revisiting the Case Against," *Burma Economic Watch*, no. 2 (2004): 36–46. For a study supporting targeted sanctions, see Peter Wallensteen, Carina Staibano, and Michael Eriksson, "Routes to Democracy in Burma/Myanmar" (report from the Uppsala Pilot Study on Dialogue and International Strategies, Department of Peace and Conflict Research, Uppsala University, 7 April 2004).

34. See, for example, Robert H. Taylor, "External Dimensions of the Myanmar Situation," in *Myanmar and the Wider Southeast Asia—Proceedings of the International Seminar on ASEAN and the Wider Southeast Asia*, ed. Rohana Mahmood and Hans-Joachim Esderts (Kuala Lumpur: ISIS, 1991); Leon T. Hadar, "U.S. Sanctions against Burma: A Failure on All Fronts," *Trade Policy Analysis*, no. 1 (26 March 1998); Ma Thanegi, "The Burmese Fairytale," *Far Eastern Economic Review*, February 1998; Marvin C. Ott, "From Isolation to Relevance: Policy Considerations," in *Burma: Prospects for a Democratic Future*, ed. Robert I. Rotberg, 69–85 (Washington, DC: Brookings Institution Press, 1998); Mary P. Callahan, "Democracy in Burma: The Lessons of History," *NBR Analysis* 9, no. 3 (May 1998): 5–27; Ernest H. Preeg, "Myanmar: Phasing in Sanctions in Asia," in *Feeling Good or Doing Good with Sanctions*, ed. Ernest H. Preeg (Washington, DC: Center for Strategic and International Studies, 1999); David I. Steinberg, "Burma/Myanmar and the Dilemmas of U.S. Foreign Policy," *Contemporary Southeast Asia* 21, no. 2 (August 1999): 283–311; Zunetta Liddell, "International Policies towards Burma: Western Governments, NGOs and Multilateral Institutions," in *Challenges to Democratization in Burma: Perspectives on Multilateral and Bilateral Responses*, ed. International Institute of Democracy and Electoral Assistance, 131–82 (Stockholm: IDEA, 2001); Michael Aung-Thwin, "Parochial Universalism, Democracy Jihad and the Orientalist Image of Burma: The New Evangelism," *Pacific Affairs* 74, no. 4 (Winter 2001–2002): 483–505; John H. Badgley, ed., "Reconciling Burma/Myanmar: Essays on U.S. Relations with Burma,"

special issue, *NBR Analysis* 15, no. 1 (March 2004); Zarni and May Oo, "Common Problems, Shared Responsibilities: Citizens' Quest for National Reconciliation in Burma/Myanmar," a Free Burma Coalition report, October 2004; and Jeffrey Sachs, "Myanmar: Sanctions Won't Work," *Financial Times*, 27 July 2004. Also various postings by Zarni on the Free Burma Coalition website, 2005–2007, www.freeburma coalition.org/.

35. David I. Steinberg, "Contested Legitimacies in Burma/Myanmar" (paper prepared for the Myanmar Peace Initiative, Hiroshima Peace Institute, 16–18 March 2005).

CHAPTER ONE

Western Human Rights Policy

> Burma held legitimate elections and chose a leader, Aung San Suu Kyi. She has earned the right to negotiate a timetable for restoration of democracy for her people. It is our obligation as a beacon of democracy to support that effort. To make the argument that the United States should resign itself to dealing with SLORC to bring about change, compromises the very core of beliefs that define our history and guide this Nation. We do not yield to vicious dictators—we do not abandon those who strain against the barbed wire shackles of repression.
>
> —Senator Mitch McConnell[1]

During the Cold War, Burma enjoyed friendly, yet by its own choice distant, relations with the West. Despite its leftist ideology, Ne Win's military-cum-socialist government followed a policy of strict neutrality in international affairs, and at home the army was fighting a Chinese-backed communist insurgent movement. The Burma Socialist Programme Party (BSPP) shunned international investment and trade, favoring a policy of self-reliance. Japan, however, provided large-scale official development assistance, and after Ne Win, in the early 1980s under pressure from a stagnating economy, rescinded his opposition to Western assistance, West Germany and the United States became significant aid donors as well, as did the international financial institutions (IFIs).

The situation changed dramatically, however, with the army's violent crackdown on antigovernment protesters in August–September 1988 and subsequent take-over of power. Large-scale killings of unarmed demonstrators shattered widely held images of the Burmese military as a stabilizing force, and with the Cold War winding down realist priorities receded into the background in Western capitals to be replaced by idealistic notions of a new world order based on democracy and human rights, placing Burma on the "wrong" side of the redrawn lines of international politics. The State Law and Order Restoration Council (SLORC) might still have avoided the international opprobrium that was to follow, as it moved to dismantle the socialist one-party system and command economy and quickly negotiated a cessation of fighting in the war-torn northeast. The military leadership, however, made a serious miscalculation by holding an election in 1990 only to refuse to respect the result and generally proceeded to handle its international relations with all the sophistication of the proverbial bull in the china shop. This, together with the emergence of Aung San Suu Kyi as an international democracy icon after being awarded the Nobel Peace Prize in 1991, made Burma a one-dimensional issue in the West, which had no significant strategic or economic interests in the country. Buoyed by victories in Eastern Europe and South Africa, many in the growing global human rights movement came to see the country simply as a case of "democracy denied." That it was also a war-torn state emerging from decades of armed conflict and a "least developed country" transitioning from a socialist to a more market-oriented economy in the midst of a serious humanitarian crisis was largely ignored.

While some adjustments have been made to Western policy over the years as understanding of the complex social, political, and economic situation in Burma has improved, most governments and organizations have given priority to promoting democracy and for that purpose have sought to isolate the military government by denying it international legitimacy, aid, trade, and investment. This core strategy—which assumes that the military's stranglehold on power can be broken by denying it external reinforcement and that all human rights concerns in the country, including basic human rights, peace building, and poverty alleviation, are hostage to democratic reform—has been pushed forcefully by a transnational advocacy network linking the pro-democratic opposition inside Burma with influential Western policy makers, international solidarity groups, and the mainstream media. Symptomatically, Burma today is the only country in the world where the first priority of the UN is to promote democracy,[2] and receives less international assistance than any other least developed country.

This chapter traces the implementation of the core strategy since 1988 through a historical account of the policy process in key countries and organizations. It also considers tensions within the core strategy that have led to limited complementary initiatives, but demonstrates that these have failed to materialize as serious policy initiatives due to the overriding imperative of isolating and weakening the military regime.

The Core Strategy

The lead actors in the campaign for democracy and human rights in Burma are Western governments, led by the United States. Yet, significant efforts have been made to develop a multilateral front, working through international organizations such as the UN and the IFIs, as well as to get countries in the region to increase pressure on the military regime. In addition, single-issue advocacy groups, human rights organizations, individual parliamentarians, and other nongovernmental actors committed to bringing about a regime change in Burma (hereafter referred to collectively as "the Free Burma movement") have lobbied governments and international organizations to close perceived "gaps" in existing policy, while also pursuing more direct forms of "people's diplomacy." In the area of trade and investment, consumer boycotts have been equally as disruptive as government sanctions, if not more. The sum of Western human rights policy thus reflects a complex interplay amongst a diverse set of actors working at different levels of the international system.

The United States

The U.S. government has been the most virulent in its condemnation of Burma's military rulers, and the most uncompromising in its demand that they relinquish power immediately and unconditionally. Since the 1990 election, it has been a matter of principle for many U.S. policy makers to reverse the injustice done by the military in denying the victorious party government office. Their first, and at times seemingly only, commitment has been to Aung San Suu Kyi, who has been described respectively as a "statue of liberty,"[3] and a "heroine of freedom" battling an "evil empire,"[4] reflecting a perception of Burma as a moral issue on which no compromise is possible. Thus, while Washington officially has three broad priorities in Burma—democracy, human rights, and narcotics—U.S. statutory policy, driven by Congress, effectively has had a single overriding purpose: to support Aung San Suu Kyi and bring the National League for Democracy (NLD) to power. The State Department has maintained some discretionary space to pursue complementary objectives but has used it only sparingly. Indeed, U.S. officials have remarked in private that they cannot do anything without first conferring with

Aung San Suu Kyi, who for most intents and purposes has been given a veto over U.S. policy.[5]

The administration initially resisted calls from Congress for sweeping unilateral sanctions, arguing that they would be ineffective and harm broader U.S. interests. Yet, a proactive engagement strategy—like the one pursued by the United States in other Asian countries such as China, Vietnam, and Indonesia—was never seriously considered, and since the mid-1990s Washington has stepped up the pressure, putting in place one of the strongest U.S. sanctions regimes against any country in the world (see box 1.1 for an overview of U.S. sanctions on Burma, 1988–2007). While the European Union (EU) and Australia, concerned about the continuing political deadlock and deteriorating socioeconomic conditions inside Burma, have been exploring complementary policies, the U.S. position has only hardened over time. Washington has also made significant efforts to persuade or cajole other governments and international organizations to follow its lead and isolate the military regime.

The U.S. government responded to the military's take-over of power in 1988 by suspending all bilateral aid, noting its opposition to any further assistance or loans to Burma from the IFIs, and banning sales of U.S. military

Box 1.1. Overview of U.S. Sanctions

- Ban, in September 1988, on arms exports
- Suspension, in September 1988, of all nonhumanitarian aid
- Blocking, since 1988, of all assistance from the International Monetary Fund, the World Bank, and the Asian Development Bank
- Withdrawal, in 1989, of Generalized System of Preferences (GSP) preferences for imports from Burma, as well as Export-Import Bank preferential financing for U.S. exports to Burma and Overseas Private Investment Corporation (OPIC) financial services for investments in Burma
- Termination, in 1991, of a U.S.-Burma bilateral textile agreement
- Ban, in October 1996, on entry visas to the United States for Burmese military and government officials and their families (further expanded in July 2003)
- Ban, in May 1997, on all new U.S. investments in Burma
- Ban, in July 2003, on all imports from Burma
- Ban, in July 2003, on export of financial services to Burma
- Freeze, in July 2003, on all assets of Burmese military and government officials and institutions held in the United States

equipment. It also withdrew Generalized System of Preferences (GSP) benefits for Burmese exports to the United States under labor rights provisions of the 1974 Trade Act. Most of these measures were later confirmed, and further measures added, when President Bush in 1989 denied Burma certification for cooperation in drugs eradication, a step which legally requires Washington to withhold assistance under the Foreign Assistance Act of 1961 (except for specified humanitarian and counternarcotics assistance); to vote against proposed loans from six multilateral development banks; to deny sales or financing under the Arms Export Control Act; and to deny financing by the Export-Import Bank.

These initial measures reflected a broad consensus within policy-making circles in Washington that the SLORC was an illegitimate government. Yet, having clearly expressed its opposition to the new regime, the U.S. government was divided over how to proceed. While the administration wanted to keep the lines of communication with Rangoon open in order to maximize U.S. leverage on all issues of national concern, hard-liners in Congress argued that any international activities in Burma legitimized the military regime and undermined the position of the pro-democracy forces. This schism persisted through the first half of the 1990s, which saw members of Congress block the appointment of a new U.S. ambassador to Burma, as well as a planned resumption of limited antinarcotics assistance, but fail to build sufficient support for unilateral trade and investment sanctions. Since then, hard-line views have won out and today are rarely challenged.

The issue of appointing a new ambassador arose when Ambassador Burton Levin retired in 1990. The Bush administration, after some delay, appointed a replacement, but while approving the candidate, the Senate Foreign Relations Committee stated its view that

> the full Senate should consider [the nomination of a new ambassador] only if the administration has taken the following actions: Issued a strong statement condemning the SLORC and stating that the decision to send an ambassador to Burma does not in any way constitute acceptance of the regime, removed the current military attaches from the U.S. Embassy in Rangoon, suspended its contacts with Burma's military attaches in Washington, agreed to support a UN arms embargo against Burma, and opposed further UNDP [United Nations Development Programme] funding for Burma. . . . We do not want to send an ambassador to Burma at a time when such an action would grant unwarranted legitimacy on this brutal regime.[6]

State Department officials sought to persuade Congress that "if the United States is to speak out appropriately to Burma's rulers, then we should have an ambassador in place who can speak with authority as the President's personal representative."[7] Yet, the critics carried the day, and the United States since then has been represented in Burma at a technical level only, by a chargé d'affaires.

Antinarcotics assistance has been another contentious issue. In the early 1990s, 60–70 percent of the heroin on American streets originated from Burma.[8] The U.S. administration therefore was keen to maintain maximum flexibility to respond to opportunities for cooperation with the Burmese government, illegitimate or not, on drugs eradication. This was vehemently rejected, however, by some members of Congress:

> There are suggestions in some quarters that our government establish limited ties with the Burmese dictatorship for drugs eradication. Establish official ties? Extend aid to the bloodiest gangsters in Southeast Asia? What planet are the advocates of this policy living on? . . . The suggestion of resuming assistance to the Burmese government is repulsive, repugnant, and an insult to the values of our country. If we want to have a long-term impact on the drug traffic and the production of opium in Burma, we should use our resources to support those who are fighting the dictatorship. When democracy comes, the ethnic groups who have been driven into the drug trafficking will have an incentive to earn an honest living and live in a civilized and democratic society.[9]

The issue came to a head in 1995 when a proposal supported by both the State Department and the Drug Enforcement Agency to expand in-country training of antidrugs enforcement units and funding for United Nations Drug Control Programme (UNDCP) crop substitution activities was blocked by Congress, which narrowly passed a bill explicitly prohibiting any U.S. funding for narcotics control in Burma. Although the relevant legislation was overturned again the following year, U.S. antinarcotics cooperation with the Burmese government has remained limited to intelligence exchange.

While the hard-line view prevailed on these lesser issues, the administration initially resisted pressure from Congress to impose wider economic sanctions. The Customs and Trade Act of 1990 called on the president to impose "such economic sanctions as he determines appropriate" unless he could certify to Congress before 1 October 1990 that Burma "has satisfied the certification requirements of the Narcotics Control Trade Act, national government legal authority in Burma has been transferred to a civilian government, martial law has been lifted, and political prisoners have been released."[10] Yet, the Bush administration did only the minimum necessary by terminating a textile agreement between the United States and Burma, a largely symbolic measure that did nothing to hinder a large increase in garment imports from

Burma over the following decade. Further resolutions from Congress, calling for economic sanctions, in particular, on U.S. imports of teak and marine products were also basically ignored. The assistant secretary of state for the Bureau of East Asian and Pacific Affairs, Richard H. Solomon, later explained the position of the administration: "To be meaningful, trade sanctions would have to be multilateral and comprehensive, including Burma's major trading partners, particularly China. . . . Our own commercial relations with Burma are miniscule. . . . Curtailing this small volume of commerce would have no practical effect on Burma, but it could well do some damage to U.S. business interests and cost American jobs at home. . . . In addition, the imposition of trade restrictions would be inconsistent with our GATT obligations and ill-timed as we attempt to bring the Uruguay Round to a successful close."[11]

The first Clinton administration, which took over in 1993, continued to oppose economic sanctions, supposedly due, among other things, to concern that any new sanctions against Burma would look hypocritical in light of its move to grant most favoured nation (MFN) status to China whose government was guilty of many of the same injustices.[12] Nonetheless, it adopted a somewhat harder and more proactive line. After an interagency policy review, the deputy assistant secretary of state for Asia and the Pacific, Thomas Hubbard, in November 1994, went to Rangoon—the highest ranking U.S. official to do so since the SLORC took power—where he warned the Burmese leadership that while the United States would respond positively to progress in democratization, human rights, and counternarcotics, continued intransigence would have serious consequences. In press interviews, he emphasized, "We want to move forward on all our objectives simultaneously—we will not allow the SLORC to pick and choose the issues it finds less controversial."[13] This was followed by a visit by the U.S. ambassador to the UN, Madeleine Albright, who in September 1995 went to Rangoon to meet Aung San Suu Kyi after her release from six years of house arrest a few months earlier. In addition, President Clinton appointed two special envoys on Burma, who in June 1996 toured Japan and Southeast Asia, officially to seek "a coordinated response to ongoing developments in Burma,"[14] but unofficially to persuade Association of Southeast Asian Nations (ASEAN) leaders not to admit Burma into the grouping.

In December 1995, Senator Mitch McConnell introduced the Burmese Freedom and Democracy Act in Congress. According to the proposed text, it was the policy of the United States to "support actively the prompt transition from a military dictatorship to a democratic government in Burma" and "recognize the individuals who won the 1990 election as the legitimate representatives of the Burmese people." It called for a mandatory ban on all U.S. investments and assistance to Burma, as well as a ban on entry visas for Burmese officials to the United States, "until such a time as an elected government of Burma has been allowed to take power" and further authorized the administration to prohibit all imports from Burma, as well as the use of American passports for travel to Burma, and to "withhold from each international organization that funds activities in Burma other than humanitarian activities an amount equal to the United States' proportionate share of that funding."[15] In an attempt to ram it through the Senate, the bill was referred to the Senate Committee on Banking where, after a brief hearing involving only three "friendly" witnesses, it was incorporated into the annual appropriations bill. The chairman of the committee, Senator Alfonso D'Amato, a cosponsor of the bill, berated the administration for failing to "exercise leadership" by not pursuing "a more aggressive and activist policy."[16] McConnell himself further explained the rationale for sanctions: "The fact that [the NLD] was robbed of the reward of free and fair elections defines America's opportunity and obligation. . . . Since her release from six years of house arrest, Aung San Suu Kyi has emphatically opposed foreign investment and repeatedly called upon the international community to take firm steps to implement the results of the 1990 elections. The bill before your committee responds to her calls."[17] In the House of Representatives, which was considering an identical bill, Dana Rohrabacher echoed these sentiments: "Aung San Suu Kyi, this heroine of freedom, this woman who in our time has shown us what we should be like as Americans, champions of freedom, has asked us to put economic sanctions on this regime because it now has shown its true colors. The SLORC does not want reform. It instead is seeking further repression and will grasp on to power until . . . they are forced from power by pressure from the outside or perhaps by revolution from their own people."[18]

Concerned about being painted into a corner, the administration countered with an alternative amendment, developed in cooperation with Senators William Cohen and Dianne Feinstein, which incorporated McConnell's proposed ban on entry visas for Burmese officials but limited any future investment sanctions to new investments and left it at the president's discretion to impose them if "the Government of Burma has physically harmed, rearrested or exiled Aung San Suu Kyi or has committed large-scale repression or violence against the democratic opposition." It also gave the president authority to resume aid if he determined that there had been "substantial progress in improving human rights practices and implementing democratic government," a weaker test than McConnell's bill which required an elected government. Finally, humanitarian and counternarcotics assistance was explicitly permitted, although in the latter case subject to certification of full Burmese cooperation and consistency with U.S. human rights concerns.[19] During the ensuing debate on the Senate floor in September 1996, Cohen criticized McConnell's bill for limiting the United States' ability to foster change in Burma by taking away from the administration "those tools of diplomacy—incentives in both a positive and negative sense—which are crucial if we are ever going to hope to effect change in a nation where our words and actions already carry diminished clout."[20] The rest of the Senate was divided. Those in favor of investment sanctions presented it as a moral choice, which they argued might further create momentum for a global sanctions regime that would force the military government from power. Most of those opposed, however, saw no prospect of Burma's neighbors joining in and rejected unilateral sanctions as futile or damaging to U.S. interests. Some argued that American engagement and trade would be a more powerful force of change than isolation. Ultimately, the skeptics carried the vote by fifty-four to forty-five and the Cohen-Feinstein amendment was signed into law on 30 September 1996. Accordingly, the only immediate step was a proclamation issued by President Clinton a few days later, suspending "the entry into the U.S. of Burmese nationals, who formulate, implement, or benefit from policies that impede the country's transition to democracy, or who benefit from such policies."[21] The ground was moving, however. Aung San Suu Kyi, at this time, was openly calling for international sanctions to force the generals to the negotiation table and had criticized major U.S. investments in the oil and gas sector, which made the United States the fourth largest investor in Burma. In the United States, popular pressure for sanctions was also building, culminating with the adoption of a series of local selective purchasing and divestment laws in 1995–1997.

Until this point, no U.S. administration had paid serious attention to Burma, but the turning point came in 1997 under the second Clinton administration. The new foreign policy team—with Madeleine Albright as secretary of state, Sandy Berger as head of the National Security Council, and Bill Richardson as U.S. ambassador to the UN—were all outspoken supporters of Aung San Suu Kyi. Albright, in particular, had formed a close personal attachment to the Nobel Peace laureate since her visit to Rangoon in September 1995 and now took on her cause with a vengeance. With external pressure on Washington to act growing, this provided the necessary catalyst to overcome any residual resistance within the government to unilateral measures, and on 20 May 1997, the president issued an executive order prohibiting all new U.S. investments in Burma: "I, William J. Clinton, President of the United States of America, hereby determine and certify that, for the purposes of [the Foreign Appropriations Act of 1997], the Government of Burma has committed large-scale repression of the democratic opposition in Burma after September 30, 1996, and further determine that the actions and policies of the Government of Burma constitute an unusual and extraordinary threat to the national security and foreign policy of the United States and declare a national emergency to deal with that threat."[22]

The ban was targeted at the development of economic resources located in Burma, and explicitly exempted trade and service contracts, as well as nonprofit educational, health, and other humanitarian programs. Still, this was by far the strongest measure adopted by any government against the military regime and marked a closing of the long-standing schism between hardliners in Congress and administration officials. In a radio program in May 1997, deputy assistant secretary of state for the Department of Democracy, Human Rights, and Labor Gare Smith now argued that, for the sanctions to be removed, the SLORC would have to recognize the 1990 election, a yardstick that clearly elevated democracy over all other U.S. objectives in Burma, including broader human rights.[23] Echoing this view, deputy assistant secretary of state for the Bureau of International Narcotics and Law Enforcement Jonathan Winer further stated, "The world community has a responsibility to push [the military regime] into the dustbin of history sooner rather than later by making it impossible for them to sustain the illicit control they have of their country."[24] The executive order itself did not contain any specific conditions for lifting the ban, but the president emphasized that "Burma's international isolation is not an inevitability" and called on the military government "to lift restrictions on Aung San Suu Kyi and the political opposition, to respect the rights of free expression, assembly and association, and to undertake dialogue that includes leaders of the NLD and the ethnic minorities and deals with the future of Burma."[25] The order has been renewed every twelve months since then, without any significant debate.

Following the imposition of the investment ban, the pressure in Washington for further action against the military regime abated somewhat. An attempt by Rohrabacher in October 1998 to get a resolution through the House, which called on the U.S. government to work for the removal of the junta from Burma's seat in the UN and its replacement by representatives of the elected parliament,[26] died in committee. The following year, the State Department found that the Burmese government had "engaged in or tolerated particularly severe violations of religious freedom" and thus was noncompliant with the International Religious Freedom Act of 1998 (a designation which offers a menu of fifteen discretionary policy responses). The department, however, decided not to impose any new sanctions, although a spokesman pointed out that the designation might justify the upholding of existing sanctions even if the original reason for them should not apply anymore.[27] In May–June 2001, Senator Tom Harkin and Representative Tom Lantos made a renewed attempt to assert U.S. authority, targeting the rapidly growing import of garments. In introducing in the Senate a joint bill to ban U.S. import of all articles produced, manufactured, or grown in Burma, Harkin argued,

> Due to rising U.S. imports of apparel and textiles from Burma, more than 400 million dollars are now flowing into the coffers of the Burmese military dictatorship [this figure represented total export revenue in 2000, not—as indicated by Harkin—the government's share of the profits, which was much smaller; see chapter 5]. These ruthless military dictators and their drug-trafficking cohorts are spending this hard currency to purchase more guns from China and to buy loyalty among their troops to continue their policy of extreme repression and human cruelty. . . . A trade ban with Burma will signal American readiness to join in a new and stronger course of coordinated, multilateral action that is designed to force the Burmese generals from power once and for all.[28]

This initiative, too, stalled, however, supposedly after a personal request from Aung San Suu Kyi to the U.S. government to withhold for the time being further sanctions, which she feared could disrupt ongoing sensitive talks with the government.[29]

The release of Aung San Suu Kyi from house arrest in May 2002 improved the overall political atmosphere and, at first, seemed to facilitate a rapprochement between Washington and Rangoon, focusing particularly on the contentious issue of drugs. In July 2002, Brigadier General Kyaw Thein, head of military intelligence's Department of Ethnic Affairs and Drugs, was invited to Washington, the first visit by a high-ranking Burmese official in more than five years. U.S. officials also began commenting publicly, and positively, on Burma's counternarcotics efforts.[30] Yet, by the time the annual decision on certification was to be made in January 2003, renewed tensions had emerged between the NLD and the authorities and those supporting certification were ultimately overridden by hard-liners in Congress and the administration, thus blocking any further improvement in U.S.-Burma relations, which instead reverted to the familiar pattern of strident rhetoric and mutual acrimonious accusations.

The next turning point came in May 2003, when Burmese government "brown shirts" attacked Aung San Suu Kyi and members and supporters of the NLD at Depayin in Upper Burma, killing an undetermined number of people. This violent development caused a massive backlash in Washington where an outraged Congress now moved at exceptional speed to impose several new measures, including the import ban first proposed by Harkin and Lantos two years earlier. The Burmese Freedom and Democracy Act of 2003, which was introduced by Mitch McConnell in the Senate on 4 June 2003 and adopted less than six weeks later with an overwhelming majority of ninety-seven to two, included a new import ban on any article "produced, mined, manufactured, grown or assembled in Burma," as well as a freeze on any assets held in the United States by the State Peace and Development Council (SPDC) or senior officials. It also extended the existing visa ban to encompass more high-level officials from the military and associated institutions, and for the first time enshrined in specific country legislation the long-standing U.S. practice of opposing any assistance or loans from the IFIs to Burma. The conditions for lifting the import ban and legislation on multilateral lending were specified as "substantial and measurable progress to end violations of human rights, implementing a democratic government and combat narcotics," with further detailed definitions of each of these objectives.[31] Going even further, the administration, on its own initiative, added a prohibition on "the exportation or reexportation, directly or indirectly, to Burma of any financial services either from the U.S. or by a U.S. person, wherever located."[32] Both measures were signed into law by President Bush on 28 July 2003, making the U.S. sanctions regime on Burma one of the most comprehensive against any country.

Since these events, a broad consensus has emerged within most parts of the U.S. government on making Burma a priority in its Asia policy and stepping up the pressure further. With little left to sanction, Washington during the second Bush administration (2005–2008) has focused on persuading other actors, notably the UN Security Council (see later in this chapter) and ASEAN, to join the U.S. campaign. In 2005, ASEAN was told in no uncertain terms that Burma's scheduled chairmanship of the grouping in 2006 was unacceptable and would have negative implications for overall U.S.-ASEAN relations. In August 2006, disagreement over Burma saw the United States back away from a planned binding formal trade and investment agreement with ASEAN, agreeing only to a nonbinding "framework arrangement." According to observers in Washington, the administration "has mounted a diplomatic offensive against the military government of Burma, suggesting to nations in the region that it is a 'test case' for whether they hold the same values and standards as the United States."[33]

Hard-line members of Congress, meanwhile, continue their long-standing efforts to force international organizations to get in line with U.S. sanctions policy. An early version of the 2006 Foreign Operations Act, reported in the Senate in June 2005, targeted not just the IFIs, but also the Global Fund for HIV, Tuberculosis, and Malaria (hereafter the "Global Fund"), the UNDP, the United Nations Office on Drugs and Crime (UNODC), ASEAN, and all countries that sell "weapons or defense-related equipment" to the SPDC, all of which were threatened with American funding cuts if they did not comply with specific restrictions on their activities.[34] Most of these clauses were dropped from the final act—those on the UNDP and ASEAN though, only after they had had the intended effect—but Mitch McConnell, the lead proponent of this strategy, has made it clear that U.S. pressure on international organizations will be maintained: "Sanctions worked in South Africa, and they will in Burma too. They strike at the junta's lifeblood, namely its monopoly on all investments and total dominance of Burma's licit and illicit economies. Sanctions are a tremendous loss of face for the SPDC, a scarlet letter, particularly in the international arena. More important, sanctions empower those in Burma on the frontline of the struggle. The fact that the elected leaders in Burma support sanctions should be enough for democratic nations to impose them."[35]

The European Union

The EU and its member states, too, have prioritized democracy in their relations with Burma and have worked closely with the United States to forge a strong international front against the military regime through a combination of censure and gradually escalating sanctions. Since the early 2000s, a gap has opened up between the two sides of the Atlantic as the EU has rejected sweeping trade and investment bans in favor of measures directly targeting the military regime and its main support base. European aid agencies have also moved more proactively to address the emerging humanitarian crisis in Burma, having decided in 2002 essentially to separate its "political" and "humanitarian" strategies. Yet, while overall EU policy today is more balanced than the U.S. position, it remains well within the parameters of the core strategy and pressure for wider sanctions persists, particularly in the UK, which traditionally has been one of the most hard-line countries in Europe, along with Denmark, Sweden, and Holland (see box 1.2 for an overview of EU sanctions, 1988–2007).

The military's take-over in 1988 provoked strong words of condemnation from all European capitals, which immediately suspended nonhumanitarian aid and joined Washington in opposing any new assistance from the IFIs.[36] Two years later, the European Parliament awarded Aung San Suu Kyi the 1990 Sakharov Prize for Freedom of Thought, while Sweden and France took

Box 1.2. Overview of EU Sanctions

- Suspension, in September 1988, of all nonhumanitarian aid (modified in October 2004 to allow some forms of development assistance)
- Imposition, in July 1991, of an arms embargo
- Severance, in 1992, of defense links (withdrawal of European military attachés from Rangoon)
- Ban, in October 1996, on visas for high-ranking military officers and government officials, and their families (further expanded in October 1998 to include tourist and transit visas, and in June 2003 and October 2004 to include lower-level officials and those in regime-affiliated organizations respectively)
- Moratorium, in October 1996, on high-level bilateral visits to Burma
- Withdrawal, in March 1997, of preferential trade tariffs for Burmese agricultural and industrial exports
- Ban, in April 2000, on export of "dual purpose" goods
- Freeze, in April 2000, on assets held in Europe by Burmese officials and regime supporters included on the visa ban list
- Ban, in October 2004, on new investments in state- and military-owned companies

the lead in pushing for strong human rights resolutions against the military regime in the UN General Assembly and the UN Commission on Human Rights, respectively. Further sanctions followed with a ban on arms exports in 1991 and suspension of defense links in 1992.

In 1993, following the retirement of SLORC chairman General Saw Maung, the EU attempted to initiate a "critical dialogue" with the military regime based on several benchmarks: release of Aung San Suu Kyi and all other political prisoners, meaningful dialogue between the SLORC and the NLD, free access to Burma for foreign nongovernmental development organizations (NGOs), liberalization of the economy, and progress on the creation of democratic institutions. In return, EU member states offered to increase support for humanitarian relief through NGOs, resume bilateral assistance to the government, and encourage investment by European companies.[37] This reexamination of EU policy, which echoed similar reviews in Washington and Canberra around the same time, reflected new hope that the change in leadership in Rangoon, along with the lifting of martial law and convening of a constitutional assembly in January 1993, signaled a new beginning. Yet, there may also have been a wish to position European companies for commercial profit in Burma's growing economy. Notably, British foreign secretary Douglas Hurd in March 1994 attempted to separate human rights and economic concerns when he welcomed a decision by British businessmen to send a trade mission to Burma: "We are strongly critical of the abuse of human rights by the SLORC and, in particular, of the election results and the treatment of the leaders of the winning party. But that should not impede or prevent trade, and indeed, in certain circumstances, trade can actually have a useful effect in opening up and showing the need for change in the country."[38]

In any case, the détente was short-lived. The European initiative was met with silence from Rangoon, and after the arrest and death in detention of its honorary consul in Burma, Jack Nichols, in June 1996, Denmark took the lead in pushing for stronger punitive measures. In July, Danish foreign minister Niels Helveg Petersen traveled to Washington and Dublin (which held the EU presidency at the time) to discuss the possibility of economic sanctions. The European Parliament went a step further still and called for a comprehensive European embargo on Burma covering trade, tourism, and investments by European companies, a call which it since has repeated regularly.[39] The big three—Britain, Germany, and France—all resisted further "unilateral" sanctions. According to British foreign secretary Malcolm Rifkin, "Any decision to impose economic sanctions against the military government in Burma should be made by the UN Security Council."[40] Yet, with new crackdowns on the NLD following the party's walk-out from the military-controlled constitutional assembly in November 1995 and moves toward investment sanctions underway in the United States, the ground was shifting in Europe, too.

In October 1996, the EU adopted its first common position on Burma, intended to promote "progress towards democratization and securing the immediate and unconditional release of detained political prisoners." The new policy reaffirmed the sanctions already in place and added a ban on entry visas for members of the SLORC, as well as senior members of the military or the security forces "who formulate, implement, or benefit from policies that impede Burma's transition to democracy," and their families. It also suspended high-level bilateral visits by member state governments to Burma (ministers and officials at the level of political director or above).[41] No agreement was reached on economic bans, but the new common position foreshadowed the possibility of further unspecified sanctions if the situation did not improve, and in early 1997 the EU withdrew GSP privileges for Burmese industrial and agricultural exports. Although the latter step technically was prompted by a specific complaint from the International Confederation of

Trade Unions (ICTFU) over the situation of forced labor in Burma, the broader political campaign against the military government provided the context for what was an unprecedented action (as it has done for subsequent actions by the International Labor Organization [ILO] on this issue). Indeed, this was the first time ever the EU had linked workers' rights to trade, and there were great concerns in some European capitals that it could unleash a host of union calls for trade sanctions on other countries accused of forced labor or child labor. In economic terms, the withdrawal of GSP was insignificant since it only affected goods worth around $30 million and no change in trade flows could be discerned afterward.[42] The symbolic value, however, was significant as the Burmese regime had now been singled out as *uniquely* abusive and thus deserving of differential treatment.

The hardening attitude within the EU became all the more evident over the following years as the grouping made Burma a major issue in its relations with ASEAN, at significant costs to interregional cooperation. Having failed to persuade Burma's neighbors not to admit it into ASEAN in July 1997, the EU demanded that Burma be excluded from future interregional meetings. ASEAN member states accepted this in the case of the biannual Asia-Europe Summit meetings (ASEM), supposedly because countries participate in this framework as individual states. They insisted, however, that no discrimination be made in the case of bloc-to-bloc meetings. The ensuing diplomatic crisis saw the cancellation of several consecutive ASEAN-EU Ministerial and Joint Cooperation Committee meetings between 1997 and 2000, which delayed a number of mutual development programs. The EU eventually backed down and the first foreign ministers meeting with Burmese participation went ahead in December 2000 in Vientiane, although several European countries sent lower-level representation. Yet, the EU has continued to deny Burma accession to the 1980 ASEAN-EU Economic Cooperation Agreement, which would give the country access to various EU development assistance programs (this despite having accepted the two other recent members of ASEAN, Cambodia and Laos, whose political record is hardly inspiring either). In July 1997, EU president Jaques Poos told reporters that "the EU will agree to extend assistance to Burma under the ASEAN framework only if five conditions are met—release political prisoners, restore democratic dialogue, stop arresting political dissidents, fix a date for democratic elections, and allow freedom of democracy and movement."[43]

The UK elections in May 1997 prompted another turning point in European policy debates on Burma, in which Britain as the former colonial power always has taken the lead. Having pledged to make human rights a centerpiece of its foreign policy, the new Labour Party government moved fast to make an example of Burma and in June 1997 suspended financial support for British companies trading with Burma. London also took steps to discourage tourism and stepped up it efforts within the ILO to increase pressure on the Burmese government concerning forced labor. On the former issue, a British member of the European Parliament later stated,

> The NLD has made very clear policy decisions, specifically asking foreign visitors to stay away. . . . Whilst you may be able to give a few dollars to benefit someone working in the tourism industry, the scales do not quite balance when tourism is simultaneously helping to prop up a regime that keep 48 million people in the most desperate poverty. . . . Wild claims from some in the industry that the "overwhelming majority" want tourism are pure fantasy. The fact is that the NLD is the only party mandated to represent the interests of Burma's people. . . . I have been fortunate enough to meet Suu Kyi, after travelling into her country under the cover of a tourist visa obtained in Bangkok. Her courage and heroism is breathtaking, and her grace and composure and dignity affected me deeply. . . . She has asked for sanctions so that the junta will be starved out of existence.[44]

Subsequently, as the debate intensified before the renewal of the Common Position in October 1998, both Britain and Holland joined Denmark and new EU country Sweden in pushing for economic sanctions. British foreign office minister Derek Fachett argued,

> Outrage is necessary but not enough. We need, among other things, to have measures which make it clear to the regime that Burma will not be integrated into the world until its government changes its ways. . . . We have urged our colleagues to adopt the same national measures as the UK has taken on trade, investment and tourism. . . . We argue for a strengthening of the Common Position. One step would be to include transit visas. Why should European airports or capitals be open to SPDC officials as convenient stopping points—and shopping or tourism havens—on the way to meetings in New York or Geneva? But we are also trying to build consensus for further measures. . . . There are those in the EU who are reluctant to move forward in these ways. We continue to work . . . to persuade them that it cannot be in the wider interests of the EU to fold our hands and watch events in Burma take their course; that we must act, and continue to act to ensure that our friends in Burma know we remain with them.[45]

Holland up till this point had been relatively passive in EU Burma policy discussions, but in October 1998, the minister of foreign affairs, J. J. van Aartsen, and the minister of development cooperation, E. L. Herfkens, sent a joint letter to the chair of the Commission on Foreign Affairs in the European Parliament stating their support for economic sanctions:

> The Netherlands will plead for economic sanctions like an investment ban by the EU. Extending the EU sanctions regime, which the NLD and NCGUB [National Coalition Government of the Union of Burma] are also urging, is the next, logical phase in the approach that the EU decided to take in October 1996. In the first instance the emphasis was on lighter sanctions, to prevent direct isolation of Burma and to leave room for increasing the political signal in case the human rights situation would worsen further. Now the lighter sanctions have had no effect. . . . An investment boycott by the EU would hit Burma hard: in 1997 more than 60 percent of foreign investments in Burma came from the EU. These investments are concentrated in the oil and gas industry of which the profits are an important pillar of support for the regime.[46]

The call for investment sanctions failed to sway opposition from Germany and France, in particular. French cooperation minister Charles Josselin publicly stated that Paris would oppose any proposal for the EU to impose economic sanctions on Burma which, he argued, would fail to achieve their political objectives and harm the civilian population.[47] But Britain continued to lead by example. In a highly unusual move in April 2000, the Labour Party government privately requested that Premier Oil sell its $200 million stake in the Yetagun gas project, thus lending support to grassroots campaigns underway against the company. It also put pressure on British American Tobacco (BAT). Both companies subsequently withdrew from Burma.

Over time, the persistent pressure from London and elsewhere has elicited a series of concessions from more engagement-oriented European governments, which have agreed to a gradual strengthening of the common position, mainly in the form of "targeted sanctions" aimed at the military leadership and regime supporters. In October 1998, the EU extended the visa ban on Burmese government officials to cover transit visas and tourist officials.[48] In April 2000, it strengthened its arms embargo by prohibiting the sale, supply, and export of any "dual purpose" goods, and decided also to freeze any funds held in Europe by Burmese officials included on the visa ban list, who now for the first time were mentioned by name.[49] In May 2001, Burma was excluded (as the only country) from the Everything but Arms initiative, which has given full duty-free and quota-free EU market access for all products except arms originating from the world's forty-nine least developed countries. In June 2003, the EU further extended the scope of the visa and asset freeze to include senior officials of the Union Solidarity and Development Association (USDA), who were reported to have been responsible for the violent attack on Aung San Suu Kyi and other NLD members and supporters a few weeks earlier.[50] Finally, in September 2004, a limited investment ban was added, covering new investments by European companies in Burmese military-owned economic enterprises, together with a further expansion of the visa ban and asset freeze to include all military officers at the level of brigadier general and above, and their families.[51]

The EU has yet to impose the type of sweeping economic sanctions seen in the United States. Indeed, since the imposition of the U.S. import ban in July 2003, even the most hard-line European governments have backed away from this option, the general feeling being that it has done more harm than good. An autumn 2003 internal review of EU policy by the EU Commission concluded that a general trade ban would be both illegal under international law and detrimental to the welfare of the Burmese people:

> Since Burma is a member of the WTO [World Trade Organization], the possibility of imposing sanctions in the field of trade in goods and services is subject to the rules of those agreements falling under the WTO to which Burma is a party, namely the General Agreement on Tariffs and Trade (GATT) and on Trade in Services (GATS). . . . The GATT allows for trade restrictions only with respect to arms and military equipment, or if imposed in pursuance of obligations under the United Nations Charter for the maintenance of international peace and security (i.e., based on a mandatory decision of the Security Council). . . . Future EU policy in the field of restrictive measures will have to take into account the international commitments of the EU, in particular WTO agreements, and have to be in accordance with international law and common principles on the rule of law. It is also important that the legal instruments make provision for appropriate exemptions to take account of humanitarian needs of targeted persons. . . . The Commission would also argue that the humanitarian effects of a general trade ban on the Burmese population will be much greater than the economic effects on the Burmese regime.[52]

While the commission warned against easing restrictions on the Burmese regime at a time when the democratic forces were under strong pressure, it recommended that the EU and its member states instead step up efforts to get ASEAN to increase its pressure on Rangoon.

The pressure for wider EU sanctions continues though, mainly in the UK. In October 2006, the British All-Party Parliamentary Group for Democracy in Burma and the Conservative Party Human Rights Commission joined with the Burma Campaign UK, Christian Solidarity Worldwide, and the Trade Union Congress in calling on the government to unilaterally ban investments in Burma. "I am appalled," said chairman of the All-Party Parliamentary Group John Bercow on that occasion, "that the government continues to act as if nothing needs to be done to stop companies investing in Burma. . . . Britain should be straining every muscle to starve the Burmese tyrants of the money they need. We should use our political and economic influence to turn the screws on the Government of Burma and promote the speedy transition to democracy."[53] The coalition, which is also demanding more British aid for Burmese democracy groups, claims that major investments by UK firms or through British territories are propping up the regime and fueling human rights abuses. Ultimately seeking an EU-wide investment ban, they want the British government to set an example.[54]

Other Governments

Few other Western countries have any significant links with Burma. Yet, non-EU governments in Europe, such as Switzerland and Norway, are formally associated with the EU common position. Canada also has a range of sanctions in place, similar to the EU. New Zealand has taken fewer legal steps, but has almost no exchange with Burma to begin with. The only Western country that has deviated substantially from the core strategy is Australia, which—while working closely with the United States and the EU to maintain pressure on the military regime in the UN and other multilateral forums—has explicitly rejected the policy of isolation, including visa bans and economic sanctions. In the words of Foreign Minister Alexander Downer,

> Economic sanctions are unlikely to be effective and will instead likely harden the attitude of the regime very substantially. . . . We want a practical policy that produces practical results. . . . We are not into the game of seeking newspaper headlines for the sake of self-aggrandisement.[55]

> We haven't always entirely agreed with the approach taken by the United States, or for that matter from time to time by the British government. . . . Obviously we don't want to embrace the SPDC . . . but at the same time we take the view that some sort of engagement with them is better than none. We doubt very much whether much will be achieved by stamping our feet and having nothing to do with them, and putting out angry press releases all the time.[56]

Australia's long-standing conservative government has sustained sharp criticism for this stand from the NLD, as well as its own opposition,[57] but has consistently maintained that a strong principled stand on human rights is best complemented by direct, critical engagement with the government. As Australian human rights commissioner Chris Sidoti stressed in 1999, responding to NLD criticism of Australia's new human rights training program, "Whether the NLD likes it or not, the simple fact is that it is not presently in a position to do very much at all about protecting the human rights of the people of Burma. The government on the other hand, however illegitimate the process by which it assumed power may be, is. . . . If the government has expressed a wish to do something about human rights, we should be willing to enter into dialogue to see whether that is possible."[58]

Canberra favors an approach that not only pays attention to the overarching political issues, but seeks to promote progress in core policy areas. Since the late 1990s, the Australian Agency for International Development (AusAID) has thus engaged directly with the relevant authorities on human rights, nutritional issues, and agricultural research, apart from funding humanitarian projects through the UN and international NGOs. Its high-profile human rights training program was suspended after the Depayin attack in May 2003, though, and the unofficial Australian position today seems to be, as far as possible, to quietly ignore Burma.

Supranational Organizations

Unsurprisingly, given the general consensus among Western governments, key supranational organizations generally have been "enlisted" in support of the core strategy. The United States has taken the lead together with European countries in pushing for strong human rights resolutions and, to a lesser extent, action on Burma within the UN system. Western countries have also blocked all new loans and financial assistance to Burma from the IFIs, including even most technical cooperation.

The United Nations

The UN General Assembly (UNGA) and the UN Commission on Human Rights (UNCHR) since 1991 each has passed fifteen consecutive consensus resolutions on Burma deploring the human rights situation in the country and calling for democratic change. The resolutions, which traditionally have been drafted by European governments based on the reports of the special rapporteur on the situation of human rights in Burma,[59] have grown progressively stronger—and longer—over time, reflecting growing frustration with the lack of progress, as well as increasingly effective lobbying by pro-democracy groups. Demands for an immediate transfer of power to the elected parliament were replaced in 1997 by calls for tripartite dialogue between the military, the NLD, and ethnic minority groups, but the underlying premise remained unchanged—as the most recent resolutions state: "The establishment of a genuine democratic government is essential for the realization of all human rights and fundamental freedoms," as well as for "achieving sustainable development and economic growth."[60] Accordingly, the UN secretary-general, who since 1993 has been charged with helping implement the General Assembly resolutions through his "good offices," has focused on democratization ahead of any other objectives (on these efforts, see later in this chapter).

Burma has also come under scrutiny by several thematic human rights bodies within the UN, including the ILO, the Committee for the Elimination of Discrimination against Women, the Committee on the Rights of the Child, and the Working Group on Arbitrary Detention, as well as various special rapporteurs. The ILO, in particular, has become a forum for intense pressure. A case against Burma for widespread use of forced labor was first brought in the early 1990s, but took a serious turn in 1999 when the government's lack of cooperation with an official Commission of Inquiry led the International Labor Conference to suspend its rights to participate in ILO activities (except for the purpose of "direct assistance to implement immediately the recommendations of the Commission of Inquiry").[61] This was the first time in its history that the ILO had taken such a dramatic step. The following year, the conference went a step further, adopting a resolution that recommended to all ILO constituents—governments, employers, and workers—to "review their relations with Burma and take appropriate measures to ensure that such relations do not perpetuate forced labour," essentially a call for sanctions.[62] Implementation of the resolution was suspended before any action could be taken when the Burmese government showed signs of cooperating, but was reactivated in March 2005 after the ILO had failed to make more substantial progress.[63] Throughout this process there have been tensions between ILO officials who have stressed the need for patience and diplomacy and, in particular, Western government and worker representatives who have pressed for earlier and stronger punitive measures.[64] By November 2006, however, the deadlock with the Burmese government had become so apparent that the ILO Governing Body decided to refer the issue of forced labor to the Security Council, the International Court of Justice, and the International Criminal Court, yet another unprecedented step.

The Security Council, the highest organ within the UN system and the only one with the authority to issue and enforce binding resolutions, steered notably clear of Burma through the 1990s and early 2000s. While activists, from time to time, sought to raise it, none of Burma's neighbors supported further internationalization of the issue, preferring to deal with it bilaterally, and Western governments—unwilling to force a showdown in the Security Council and perhaps also still unsure about the relevance of Burma to its mandate of securing "international peace and security"—did not push it. By 2005, however, the United States had run out of options for escalating pressure on the military regime unilaterally, and with growing recognition that Western sanctions were undermined by the rapidly expanding links between Burma and its immediate neighbors, Washington turned to the Security Council in an attempt to draw in China.[65] In December 2005, the fifteen members of the council agreed to an informal briefing on Burma by UN undersecretary-general Ibrahim Gambari, and on 15 September 2006, they voted ten to four, with one abstention, to adopt the issue on the formal agenda.[66] China and Russia voted against, along with Congo and Qatar, but Japan and the Philippines joined the "Western" camp, the former after a last minute turnaround that U.S. officials credit to a personal intervention from President Bush.[67]

To date, this is as far as it has gone. The United States worked hard through the remainder of 2006 to push through a binding resolution, which would have called, among other things, on the military regime to "begin without delay a substantive political dialogue, which would lead to a genuine democratic transition, to include all political stakeholders . . . take concrete steps to allow full freedom of expression, association and movement . . . and cease military attacks against civilians."[68] Yet, despite numerous compromises by Washington to make it as palatable as possible to other members—notably by abandoning any push for multilateral sanctions in favor of strong support for the UN secretary-general's "good offices" and other UN agencies—the resolution in January 2007 was defeated by vetoes from both China and Russia, the first double-veto in the Security Council since the end of the Cold War.[69] While acknowledging that Burma faces serious internal problems requiring urgent reform, the two veto-bearing permanent members flatly rejected the underlying claim that the country constitutes a threat to international peace and security, arguing that the matter should be dealt with by other UN organs. South Africa, Indonesia, Congo, and Qatar offered similar objections, all emphasizing that none of Burma's neighbors considered the country a threat to peace.[70] The failure to get a resolution is not the end of Security Council action on Burma, though. Once on the formal agenda, an issue can be raised by any member at any time. The UN Secretariat will also be required to provide regular formal reports to the council on developments in the country.

While the impact of UN human rights resolutions and related debates is diminished by the absence of enforcement measures (even the 2000 ILO resolution, which implicitly calls for punitive measures to be implemented, relies on voluntary implementation by member states and organizations), they have formed a symbolic focal point for international pressure and put Burmese officials on the defensive in international forums, forcing them to personally defend their country's human rights record. The discussions among member states to find consensus language have also put pressure on Burma's neighbors, who have found it increasingly difficult to openly align themselves with the regime. The consent of the latter with the resolutions has, until recently, been mainly pro forma, the result of unwillingness to unnecessarily upset relations with the United States and other Western governments rather than agreement with the underlying agenda. Yet, the formal consensus has been important, for example, in legitimizing and shaping the role of the UN secretary-general through his personal envoys. This is likely to continue despite the failure to get a Security Council resolution, since even China and Russia support a strong role for the secretary-general's "good offices," and indeed favor it as the most appropriate venue for dealing with Burma.

International Financial Institutions

U.S. and European executive directors on the boards of the International Monetary Fund (IMF), the World Bank, and the Asian Development Bank (ADB), as noted, have been required since 1988 to vote against any loans or financial assistance to Burma. The IMF has continued its mandatory Article IV missions, and the World Bank has published two substantial reports on the Burmese economy, one in 1995 and another in 1999. The IMF has also provided some minimal technical assistance for statistical work. But without any prospects for new programs while the military remains in power, there has been no sustained policy dialogue. Indeed, when the World Bank in 1999 sought to initiate discussions with the Burmese government based on its report on the poverty situation in the country, the U.S. Treasury Department threatened to cut all funding for the bank worldwide if it sent senior level officials to Rangoon.[71] This threat, which was repeated by Senator Mitch McConnell personally in 2004,[72] has paralyzed the World Bank, leaving it unable to maintain even minimal appropriate relations with Burma as a founding member or to keep up a proper Watching Brief.

The ADB has been somewhat more active, reflecting the fact that Western control of this regional institution is less pronounced. Burma is part of the Greater Mekong Subregion (GMS) economic cooperation scheme, which is supervised and partially funded by the ADB, and has benefited from some technical assistance programs under this initiative. Following the release of Aung San Suu Kyi from house arrest in May 2002, ADB officials undertook three detailed sector reviews, normally a precursor for identification of specific assistance projects and programs. No new loans, however, have been provided since 1986, and when the ADB—also in 2002—proposed to provide funding for Burma under a regional GMS drug control project, objections were raised by both the United States and European countries before the "parent" proposal was withdrawn for other reasons.[73]

It is likely that the IFIs would deny Burma any significant support even if the political conditionalities were lifted. Major lending from any of the three institutions is conditional on a proven commitment to economic reform, which is currently lacking in Burma. Yet, by blocking even policy dialogue and technical assistance, Western governments have indicated that they have no interest in facilitating economic reform under the present government. Burma has also been denied access to the World Bank's Low Income Countries under Stress (LICUS) and postconflict programs, despite the fact that these are specifically designed to help countries that do not fulfill the requirements for mainstream programs.

UN Funds and Programs

The UN agencies are under less stringent restrictions than the IFIs. Yet, Western pressure was behind the decision by the UNDP Governing Council in 1992 to impose an extraordinary mandate on UNDP/Burma, which since then has been required to focus on "activities with grassroots level impact in the areas of health, education, food security, HIV/AIDS and the environment."[74] A year later, the U.S. Congress placed Burma on the list of "outlaw states" (along with Libya, North Korea, and Iraq), which under the provisions of the Foreign Assistance Act of 1961 mandates that voluntary U.S. funding for any UN agency be automatically reduced if the agency conducts programs in Burma. Accordingly, the 1994/1995 Foreign Relations Authorization Act stated, "Of the funds made available for the UNDP for fiscal year 1995, $26m may only be payable if the President certifies to the Congress that the UNDP has initiated no new programs and no new funding for existing programs in or for Burma since the UNDP Governing Council meeting of June 1993; that such programs address unforeseen urgent humanitarian concerns; or that a democratically elected government in Burma has agreed to such programs."[75]

U.S. funds for the UNDP were eventually released when the State Department certified that there had been no new programs *beyond* those contemplated in the UNDP Governing Council mandate, but this happened only after a heated row with hard-liners in Congress, who apparently had intended to cut UNDP funding altogether.[76] Since then, all UNDP programs have been carefully scrutinized by Washington, thus forcing UNDP officials to balance their responsibility to the people of Burma against the risk of upsetting the U.S. government. The U.S. Foreign Affairs Reform and Restructuring Act of

1998 makes further explicit the criteria on which U.S. funding for UNDP is conditional:

> Of the amounts made available for fiscal years 1998 and 1999 for United States voluntary contributions to the United Nations Development Program an amount equal to the amount the United Nations Development Program will spend in Burma during each fiscal year shall be withheld unless . . . all programs and activities of the United Nations Development Program (including United Nations Development Program—Administered Funds) in Burma—
>
> (1) are focused on eliminating human suffering and addressing the needs of the poor;
> (2) are undertaken only through international or private voluntary organizations that have been deemed independent of the State Law and Order Restoration Council (SLORC) . . . ;
> (3) provide no financial, political, or military benefit to the SLORC; and
> (4) are carried out only after consultation with the leadership of the National League for Democracy and the leadership of the National Coalition Government of the Union of Burma.[77]

The Global Fund

In 2004–2005, the Global Fund came under similar pressures over a planned $98 million five-year program to fight HIV/AIDS, malaria, and tuberculosis in Burma and eventually withdrew. There has been some controversy over the intentions behind these pressures and the exact role they played in the decision by the fund in August 2005 to terminate its programs, a decision which UN officials criticized for putting thousands of lives at risk.[78] Yet, it seems clear that members of Congress, together with other U.S.-based groups and individuals, first, sought to stop or restrict the planned programs and, ultimately, contributed to making them unworkable in an already difficult operational environment.

Soon after the Global Fund signed its first grant agreement with Burma in August 2004 (for tuberculosis), three senior U.S. senators, including Mitch McConnell, wrote jointly to its executive director requesting that the fund "withhold the disbursement of additional funds to Burma." The fund, they protested, "seemingly fails to recognize that the SPDC is solely responsible for creating the myriad humanitarian crises faced by Burma today."[79]

In early 2005, members of Congress further upped the pressure on the Global Fund by including a provision in the 2006/2007 Foreign Operations Bill, cautioning the Global Fund that U.S. funding for the fund could be reduced if any money was given "to the SPDC in Burma, directly or through groups or organizations affiliated with the Global Fund."[80] The same bill also threatened to withdraw about $50 million—roughly half—of U.S. core funding for UNDP, which had been appointed "principal recipient" of the Global Fund money, if it failed to certify that all its programs in Burma, including those it administered for others such as the Global Fund, provided "no financial, political, or military benefit, including the provision of goods, services, or per diems, to the SPDC or any agency or entity of, or affiliated with, the SPDC."[81]

Against the backdrop of these legislative efforts, congressional staffers, together with representatives of the Open Society Institute (OSI) and other U.S.-based groups, put pressure on the Global Fund to institute extra safeguards on its Burma programs. The OSI, in an internal memo to the fund, emphasized that it had "no objection to funding HIV/AIDS, TB and malaria programs in Burma, per se," but insisted, among other things, that "none of the programs should be conducted by or with financial assistance to the ruling military junta or government-organized NGOs (GONGOs)." "The junta," OSI argued, "has a long history of using international aid to serve its own purposes and to advance its claims to legitimacy. . . . [It] is not in a position to deliver programs effectively and equitably . . . there will be no meaningful way to monitor programs or the use of funds." It suggested that the programs instead be implemented through international NGOs.[82]

As a result of these various pressures linking its funding to the nature of its programs in Burma, the Global Fund introduced a series of ever tightening restrictions on use of its funds, to a point that not only compromised program effectiveness, but also seemed in breach of its own regulations.[83] These "additional safeguards" were not all formally announced but reportedly included (a) zero cash flow to the government and affiliated entities; (b) all project personnel of national entities to be contracted by the UNDP and, if government officials, requiring proof of separation from the government; and (c) no project signing ceremony pictures with government officials or affiliated agencies. As a result of the "zero cash flow" policy, UNDP staff had to travel all over the country to personally pay out subsistence per diems to each individual participant in government-hosted workshops, wasting much time and money. Similarly, all program vehicles had to have UN drivers and be parked on UN premises overnight. Capacity building for government departments was also effectively blocked.[84] A study commissioned by the UK Department for International Development (DFID) concluded, "The measures will complicate the implementation in a context where considerable logistical difficulties already exist. . . . It is also questionable whether the safeguards are developmentally sound."[85] Additional safeguards are a standard mechanism used by the Global Fund secretariat to ensure accountability in perceived problem countries. In this case, however, they crossed a conceptual line and became political conditionalities. Blocking capacity building and project signings involving government officials, for example, was not about ensuring accountability, but was an attempt to minimize any political capital the government might gain from the programs.

The decision in August 2005 to terminate the Global Fund programs altogether was made after the Burmese government announced new travel and import clearance procedures (notably a requirement that travel of international officials to project sites had to be approved six weeks in advance), which, according to fund officials, "would effectively prevent the implementation of performance-based and time-bound programs in the country, breach the government's commitment to provide unencumbered access, and frustrate the ability of the Principal Recipient to carry out its obligations."[86] Aid officials on the ground in Burma, however, point out that the new government restrictions were themselves a reaction, in part at least, to the politicization of the programs by external groups, which raised the ire of the authorities: "The fact," says one, "that these measures were introduced with increasing severity while the Global Fund supported interventions themselves had in effect yet to really commence on the ground meant that obtaining government concurrence became increasingly more complex and problematic, as these conditions were perceived by the authorities to be part of a wider strategy by political groups to terminate the grant."[87]

Aid officials also question the basic premise on which the Global Fund decision was allegedly made: that the new government regulations made it impossible to implement the planned programs. The least the fund could have done, many say, was to suspend the programs and go back to the government to renegotiate. "That it failed to do so suggest[s] that it felt under political pressure to get out of Burma."[88] As it was, the relevant restrictions were in fact partially lifted soon after and most agencies addressing the three diseases have continued to expand their activities during 2005–2006, suggesting that the Global Fund programs, too, were viable. A senior UN official concludes,

> The continuous scrutiny and growing influence of humanitarian operations by a small group of Washington and Thailand-based advocates is making it almost impossible for the assistance community in Myanmar, especially the UN, to resist the State Peace and Development Council's (SPDC) attempted closure of humanitarian space. In a very strange way these lobbyists and the harder-line elements of the regime seem to have developed a common agenda: the departure of the assistance community from Myanmar. . . . The reason for the ter-

mination of the Global Fund grants is basically the inflexibility arising from a range of special safeguards applied to the funding mechanism in the Myanmar context. The additional conditionalities combined with the usual applicable strict adherence to a time bound and performance based schedule by the Global Fund meant that practical implementation options were so significantly limited that delays in implementation were inevitable in an already complex operating environment. Rather than temporarily suspending the grants, to attempt to identify more appropriate parameters for the Myanmar situation ensuring not only accountability but also workable implementation arrangements to get the assistance to those in need, the Secretariat decided to immediately terminate the three grants, even before the actual programme implementation had started.[89]

Nongovernmental Actors

While governments and international organizations tend to grab the headlines, Western Burma policy bears a major imprint from the efforts of nongovernmental actors, including exile groups, student activists, human rights organizations, and other solidarity groups, which have worked ceaselessly to put the country on the international agenda and isolate the military regime.

The Free Burma movement originated from a core of single-issue NGOs, mainly established by Burmese exiles or young, idealistic Westerners who discovered Burma through personal encounters with Burmese refugees in Thailand.[90] Yet, starting from a small base of committed individuals, mostly working voluntarily and with little training or experience, the movement has grown to become a multimillion dollar advocacy industry, funded by Western governments and foundations and reinforced by professional human rights advocates and more established organizations, like trade unions and social investment funds. Core members include organizations as diverse as the exile National Coalition Government of Burma (NCGUB), the Shan Women's Action Network (SWAN), the OSI, the Free Burma Coalition,[91] Trillium Asset Management, Burma Campaign UK, Christian Solidarity Worldwide, Human Rights Watch/Asia, and the International Committee of Free Trade Unions. There are also a number of active Asian NGOs, including Forum Asia and Alternative ASEAN Network on Burma (ALTSEAN).

Like other transnational advocacy networks, the Free Burma movement has made extensive use of the internet to organize and publicize its activities, and has formed close links with sympathetic journalists, parliamentarians, Nobel Peace Prize laureates, rock musicians, and other celebrities, who have helped bring its message to the attention of the highest level of governments as well as the broader public. Its work has been facilitated by the moral authority and global recognition of Aung San Suu Kyi, as well as by prior experience from the antiapartheid campaign in the 1980s that has provided both seasoned advocates and strategic models for the Burma campaign. Symptomatically, apart from Aung San Suu Kyi herself, the individual most often quoted by politicians and advocacy groups in favor of sanctions and isolation is Archbishop Desmond Tutu, who has repeatedly called on the world to "do for Burma what it did for South Africa."[92]

The instrumental role of the Free Burma movement in shaping Western human rights policy is evident in four overlapping areas. First, it has played a critical function in *exposing* human rights violations in Burma and drawing international attention to the plight of the Burmese people. Political organizations linked to the NLD or insurgent groups inside Burma have joined with single-issue NGOs and more established human rights organizations like Amnesty International and Human Rights Watch to produce a wealth of reports detailing human rights abuses ranging from extrajudicial killings and rape to forced relocations, the denial of political freedoms, and economic exploitation. Such reports vary from the comprehensive annual Human Rights Yearbook produced by the exile government to more analytical, thematic reports focusing, for example, on rape or forced relocations, and regular newsletters or websites reporting on individual cases. Thematic reports, such as the "Shan Rape Report" published in 2002, which listed more than five hundred rapes by Burmese army soldiers of ethnic minority women,[93] in particular, have been instrumental in galvanizing international outrage and keeping Burma on the agenda of international policy makers who have many competing claims on their time.

Second, the Free Burma movement has used human rights information strategically in *framing* the political struggle in Burma as a moral struggle and supporting its call for international action to remove the military government from power. Many human rights reports on Burma are written by groups directly associated with the main opposition groups, others by international solidarity groups, but most give priority to demonizing the military government (as opposed to providing objective and comprehensive coverage of the issues).[94] Little attention has been paid, for example, to the progress made in improving prison conditions or the decrease in severe human rights abuses in the cease-fire areas—issues that would be relevant for identifying opportunities for alleviating abuses in other areas, but could weaken the call for isolation of the military regime. Nor has anything substantive been written about the human rights abuses committed by armed antigovernment groups, which similarly could muddle the presentation of the struggle in Burma as a battle between "good" and "evil." The political purpose of much of the human rights reporting is evident, too, in the attempts to invoke concepts such as "genocide" and "use of rape as a weapon of war," the application of which to the situation in Burma is questionable, but which have powerful resonance in international human rights discourse and potentially could justify armed humanitarian intervention.[95] Symptomatically, the majority of Burma-related human rights organizations call first and foremost for punitive measures against the military government, often at the expense of policies that might address the complex historical and structural context of armed conflict and poverty in which many abuses take place, or at least could provide immediate protection for vulnerable communities. None of this is to say that the Burmese government and its security forces are not guilty of serious human rights abuses, but simply to point out that human rights reports often are used deliberately to advance a broader political agenda.

Third, members of the Free Burma movement have engaged directly in *lobbying* governments and international organizations to condemn or impose sanctions on the military government. The Burmese exile government, for example, has been instrumental in securing tough human rights resolutions in the UNGA and UNHCR, as have international trade unions in pushing ILO and other action on forced labor. Moreover, local activists in the United States, Britain, Holland, and the Scandinavian countries, in particular, have lobbied for national and international sanctions legislation, using personal relations with sympathetic policy makers as well as Amnesty International–style telephone and letter campaigns ahead of crucial decisions. The most dramatic example of this was the successful promotion of local government action in the United States in the late 1990s when two states and twenty-four cities, including New York, Los Angeles, and San Francisco, introduced selective purchasing and/or divestment laws aimed at forcing private companies out of Burma, in most cases after intensive grassroots pressure. The movement, which was modeled on similar campaigns against South Africa in the 1990s, was stopped in 2000 when the Supreme Court struck down a Massachusetts State selective purchasing law on grounds that it was unconstitutional as it undermined the authority of the president and Congress to define U.S. foreign policy.[96] By this time, however, activists were well underway to achieving their primary goal of federal sanctions. The U.S. investment ban was already in place and a total import ban was being considered in Congress. No comparable action has been possible in Europe where no similar culture of local government foreign policy action exists, yet European activists have certainly been active throughout the 1990s and 2000s in pushing their governments to adopt further sanctions. In 2002 a broad alliance of British campaign groups, trade unions, and businesses launched the Burma Sanctions Coalition to press the UK government to impose investment sanctions on Burma and work for similar measures within the EU. Two years later, the EU under pressure from London imposed its ban on new investments in Burmese state-owned companies. As noted, the pressure continues on Whitehall to institute a total, unilateral investment ban.

Finally, campaign groups have played a crucial role in their own right in denying the military regime the benefits of international trade and investments, parallel to and beyond the official sanctions regime. This has involved a wide range of actions from negative publicity campaigns and the threat of consumer boycotts to shareholder resolutions, divestment, and lawsuits aimed at forcing companies doing business with or in Burma to pull out. The boycott campaign started in North America in the early 1990s as a series of ad hoc efforts by local campaign groups aimed mainly at oil companies like Texaco, Amoco, and Petro-Canada, which had entered into oil and gas exploration deals with the SLORC, involving substantial signature bonuses. The movement, however, soon gained more structure and scope. In 1993, Trillium Asset Management, a socially responsible investment firm based in Boston, organized a number of like-minded investors to begin filing shareholder resolutions with companies doing business in Burma. The firm also became a driving force behind the push for local government sanctions described above. The defining moment, though, was probably the creation in 1995 of the Free Burma Coalition (FBC), founded by a Burmese exile student activist, which—using the Internet—launched a hugely successful effort to coordinate both American and international actions against companies involved in Burma. The FBC first mobilized around the Boycott PepsiCo Campaign, targeting the world-renowned American soft drink and snacks producer, which ultimately sold its bottling plant in Burma after facing protests and consumer boycotts at universities all around the United States. This led to similar campaigns against a wide range of companies, including some of America's largest retail stores, as well as international companies such as Suzuki that had high market exposure in the United States. By 2002, the FBC had local chapters at more than one hundred North American universities and was working closely with social investment funds, labor organizations, religious institutions, and other advocacy groups. It also had grassroots member groups or affiliates in twenty-eight countries. The boycott movement in the United States appears to have run out of steam after the 2003 import ban, which left international companies as the only remaining targets. It continues, however, in Europe where groups such as Burma Campaign UK and Burma Centre Netherlands have led high-profile campaigns against investors like UNOCAL, Premier Oil, British Tobacco, and Triumph, as well as a number of clothes stores and travel companies sourcing from Burma.

The message in all of these campaigns has been simple, yet effective: Since the military is heavily involved in the economy, the profits from foreign trade and investments are said to simply prop up an illegitimate regime and pay for the soldiers and guns that oppress the Burmese people. A number of companies and sectors have been linked directly to human rights violations, mainly in the form of forced labor and displacement of local populations.[97] For many companies, the "other market" risks of being associated with this narrative have been too large to ignore. The Burma Campaign UK thus lists 63 companies, which supposedly have withdrawn from Burma or made a principled decision not get involved in the country as a result of grassroots pressure (compared to 133 that still operate there).[98]

The main focus of the Free Burma movement has been business links, since these have been least affected by government sanctions. The overarching aim, however, has been to block nearly all international exchanges with Burma. In the 1990s, exile members of the NLD and solidarity groups in the United States, Europe, and Australia campaigned also to uphold and expand the aid boycotts. UN agencies that continued their activities in Burma, although at reduced scope, were subject to heavy criticism, as were international NGOs, the first of which entered Burma in 1991–1992 after the SLORC withdrew a three-decades-old ban on such activities. The Australian government also became subject to widespread criticism in 1999 when it initiated a program of human rights training for midlevel government officials, as did the World Bank when it took initiative to reestablish an economic policy dialogue with the government in 1999 and the International Committee of the Red Cross (ICRC) when it reentered Burma in 2000, initially to work in the country's prisons. All of these initiatives—although evidently aimed at improving human rights—were seen by supporters of the core strategy as providing the regime with international legitimacy and thus diluting the primary push for regime change.[99] The Global Fund debacle presents only the most recent example.

Contentious Issues and Complementary Initiatives

As indicated, there have been tensions in the core strategy, linked mainly to concerns by some policy makers that opportunities for influence were being missed and the costs imposed on the Burmese people as a result of the efforts to isolate the military government were too high. This has led to some complementary initiatives, including sporadic efforts to initiate a face-to-face dialogue with the military rulers and, since the early 2000s, a significant increase in humanitarian assistance. There have also been attempts to provide technical and financial support for the opposition, which has been isolated too by measures aimed at the regime. Each of these efforts is part of a comprehensive picture of Western human rights policy on Burma, yet all of them have been constrained and significantly weakened by the overarching strategy of isolation.

Political Dialogue

The appropriate level and purpose of diplomatic engagement with the military government has been a contentious issue and the subject of several policy adjustments over the years. The most hard-line advocates of the core strategy, such as former U.S. secretary of state Madeleine Albright, have viewed diplomatic isolation as an integral part of the sanctions package and have rejected any kind of dialogue with the government in Rangoon.[100] Most governments, however, have been uneasy about this strategy, which has left their foreign ministries as bystanders in a "war of words" between Western politicians and Burmese officials, amounting to little more than name-calling and the exchange of acrimonious accusations. In 1994–1995, the United States, Britain, and Australia all sent special envoys to Rangoon to clarify their positions directly to the military leadership, including specific benchmarks for progress. This was followed in 1999–2002 by three EU troika missions, as well as a visit by Australian foreign minister Alexander Downer. Both times, such visits were facilitated by an apparent thaw in relations between the regime and the opposition, which gave international actors hope that change was underway and provided cover against criticism from advocacy groups at home who were against any form of engagement. Yet even then, the contacts were at a relatively low level—no Western heads of states have visited Burma since 1988 and Downer's visit in 2002 was the first and last by a Western foreign minister. Further, Western officials on these occasions seem to have been primarily concerned about reiterating their demands for political reform (and meeting Aung San Suu Kyi), while the Burmese government has responded defensively with hour-long expositions on Burmese history and the critical role of the army in protecting and building the union. No real dialogue has ever been established or progress made in finding common ground. Indeed, such brief contacts seem to mainly have reinforced preexisting prejudices between the different sides.

In the absence of active bilateral relations, the UN secretary-general since 1993 has been given a mandate by the General Assembly to engage with the military government.[101] Boutros Boutros-Gahli and Kofi Anan both on occasion met personally with Burmese leaders and officials on the sidelines of international meetings, but the heavy lifting has been done by special envoys. The UN assistant secretary-general for political affairs, Alvaro de Soto, made a total of eight visits to Burma from 1995 to 1999, meeting with government officials, political leaders, and civil society groups. He was replaced by former Malaysian representative to the UN Razali Ismail, who made another ten visits from April 2000 to March 2004, before being denied further access and retiring his position in early 2006. In 2006, UN undersecretary-general Ibrahim Gambari took over and made two visits to Burma, in May and November, before the change of guards in the UN Secretariat in New York.[102]

The "good offices" approach has allowed some form of dialogue to take place, while saving national officials from having to engage in face-to-face meetings with the generals that inevitably would become the subject of criticism and embarrassment at home. The envoys, however, have been significantly constrained both directly by Western governments and the Free Burma movement, and indirectly through their close association with the Western-imposed democracy agenda of the UN. In 1998–1999, de Soto made a joint approach with the World Bank to motivate the Burmese government to speed up reforms by dangling the carrot of multilateral assistance for economic development. The plan, however, was leaked to the International Herald Tribune, which (mistakenly, as it were) reported that the UN and World Bank were offering $1 billion in return for political reform, causing outrage among democracy groups who were against any form of nonhumanitarian assistance under the present regime (as well as by Burmese government officials who resented the implication that they could be "bought"). In reality, no such concrete offer was ever made (or planned). The idea was simply to show the government what would be available if it went ahead with political and economic reform (i.e., to create a win-win scenario).[103] Yet, faced with criticism from all corners, the political will to follow up quickly evaporated in the UN and Western capitals, leaving the envoy (and the World Bank) without cover. De Soto withdrew soon after, complaining of a lack of support for his efforts.

Razali, who had the advantage of being associated with Malaysian prime minister Mahathir, initially seemed to make good progress and was able, for a while, to facilitate talks between the SPDC and Aung San Suu Kyi. Yet, his efforts were eventually frustrated by his intimate association with the democracy agenda of the UN, which essentially required him to work for the aims of the West and the NLD, not a sustainable position for a facilitator. According to a Burmese diplomat, the military leadership lost trust in Razali "due to his frequent visits to Washington and London." In November 2002, this sentiment turned to hostility when he arranged to meet with Aung San Suu Kyi in Shan state, a plan that the generals "saw as being politically motivated."[104] Ultimately, Razali—like the United States and EU envoys—was unable to break out of the mould of the core strategy and serve a genuinely "mediating" role. He may also—like them, as well as de Soto—have been too low level to get sufficient traction with the Burmese military leaders for whom rank and protocol matter a great deal.

Gambari has overcome some of the weaknesses of the former envoys (or rather of the conditions they operated under). His rank as UN undersecretary-general has helped secure him access, twice, to Senior General Than Shwe as well as Aung San Suu Kyi. He has also deliberately sought to initiate a broader dialogue with the regime, including not just political issues, but also broader human rights, economic reform, and humanitarian space (which, when they were raised in the past, were mainly used as means to an end). Recent developments within the Security Council suggest that this approach could continue. The secretary-general today has near universal support for his good offices efforts, including from China and Russia, and the U.S. draft resolution, for the first time, elevated "nonpolitical" issues to some level of equality with political ones (not because Washington agrees with this, but as a way to gain support from other member states). Still, Gambari—or whomever may succeed him—faces an uphill struggle. While their support is crucial, many governments seemingly see the UN's good offices role as a convenient excuse for not getting involved diplomatically themselves. There is no will in the international community to elevate the dialogue with the Burmese regime to the level seen in places like North Korea or the Middle East. Moreover, the continuing demands from governments, advocacy groups, and the media alike for immediate political results make it impossible for the envoys to engage in the kind of long-term trust building and give-and-take discussions which are minimally required to make progress with a deeply insular and intransigent regime.

Humanitarian Aid

The humanitarian situation presents another dilemma for supporters of the core strategy. Burma being one of the poorest countries in the world, not everyone has agreed with the aid boycotts. Already in 1992, the United Nations Children's Fund (UNICEF) made a fervent plea for international attention to what it called the "silent emergency" in Burma.[105] The same case has been made by local people and organizations, particularly but not exclusively from the ethnic minority areas. In 1998, at a conference in Germany, a prominent Kachin community leader, for example, made a passionate call for international assistance to help rebuild local communities ravaged by war:

> The government and the ceasefire groups have agreed upon the institution of development projects as one of the most vital ways to stabilise the peace and foster reconciliation. . . . Many ethnic minority groups feel extremely disappointed that, in general, foreign governments are not responding to the progress of these ceasefires or indeed even understand their significance or context. . . . It seems that certain sectors of the international community have the fixed idea that none of the country's deep problems, including ethnic minority issues, can be addressed until there is an overarching political solution based upon developments in Rangoon. In contrast, the ceasefire groups believe that simply concentrating on the political stalemate in Rangoon and waiting for political settlements to come about—however long this takes—is simply not sufficient to bring about the scale of changes that are needed. It ignores realities on the ground in areas long affected by war. To revitalise these communities and bring about real reform, health, social and economic development must run in tandem with political progress.[106]

Calls for immediate international action to address the acute vulnerabilities of Burma's impoverished population, however, were for a long time rejected by the pro-democracy movement. In the early 1990s, the NCGUB called for a total aid boycott. The government-in-exile was adamant that no international aid organizations, including UN agencies and international NGOs, should be in Burma. Their presence, it argued, merely serves to "legitimise an illegitimate regime"—they are "manipulated by the government" and "unable to reach the intended beneficiaries"; they should "focus instead on helping Burmese refugees in neighbouring countries and developing cross-border programmes in areas outside government control."[107] This position was embraced by exile groups and pro-democracy activists around the world, who accused—and in some cases still accuse—aid organizations working on the ground in Burma of not understanding "the real situation" in the country.[108] Aung San Suu Kyi sought to outline a more nuanced position, which rejected "aid to the government" but supported "aid to the people." Soon after her release from house arrest in July 1995, the opposition leader put forward two main principles for foreign aid: (1) International aid agencies have an obligation to work in close cooperation or consultation with the elected NLD leadership. (2) Aid should be delivered to "the right people in the right way."[109] In later interviews, she expanded on this theme, arguing that the NLD is not against aid as long as it is not channeled through government structures, is properly monitored, and is distributed equally to all those in need, irrespective of their political views.[110] Yet, while these statements differed from the early hard-line position of the NCGUB, Aung San Suu Kyi in private conversations with diplomats and aid officials in the 1990s expressed strong concern that it might in fact not be possible to distribute aid according to the minimal criteria. She was particularly worried that the government would use international assistance to reinforce the state's control structures and help pacify opposition to the regime by directing it to government supporters.[111] Commenting on this in an interview in 1998, the opposition leader concluded, "We don't think it is time for NGOs to come in. . . . Why don't they go to the Karen refugees on the border. There is plenty of need there. We inside really have to help ourselves."[112]

Western aid boycotts, in principle, have exempted humanitarian aid. But faced with an often uncooperative government and resistance from the main opposition party as well as activists in their own countries, international donors throughout the 1990s were reluctant to commit funding to any programs beyond emergency relief. The U.S. Congress, again, was the most hard-line, generally opposing the distribution of *any* aid inside Burma. The U.S. State Department and Agency for International Development (USAID) for a while in the 1990s provided limited funding for two U.S. INGOs working on community development, but were stopped—according to a USAID official—by "forces coming out of the woodwork [a veiled reference to congressional hard-liners]."[113] In January 1999, following a visit to Rangoon where he met with both Khin Nyunt and Aung San Suu Kyi, Representative Tony Hall briefly broke ranks. Calling for more humanitarian aid to Burma, the congressman publicly criticized the opposition leader for being out of touch with the real problems facing the country.[114] Yet, he later withdrew—under strong grassroots pressure—a planned bill, which would have eliminated the existing restrictions on U.S. funding for UNDP programs in Burma.[115] Although Australia and several European countries provided funding windows designed to help the most vulnerable sections of the Burmese population, they also generally kept within the boundaries set by the NLD, channeling only limited assistance through UN agencies and INGOs working at the grassroots level and emphasizing primary health projects.[116] These criteria were so closely adhered to that aid organizations had difficulties getting funds even for obviously people-centered programs such as safe water and sanitation, and education.

After the withdrawal of most of the big bilateral donors and multilateral lending agencies, the UN system emerged as the most important development cooperation partner in Burma.[117] Yet, concerns expressed by the international community through various UN General Assembly resolutions greatly constrained its activities as well (and continue to do so). Of the eight UN agencies active in the country in 2001, only the UNDP and UNICEF had annual budgets over $10 million and all were struggling to attract funding beyond their core budgets to meet specific project requirements.[118] The extraordinary mandate imposed on the UNDP blocked it (and still does) from engaging in policy dialogue and administrative capacity building, normally two of its primary responsibilities in weak states.[119] It also obstructed a concerted and cohesive UN approach to addressing human development needs in the country as different agencies were working under different mandates. The nongovernmental sector, too, remained very small. Many international NGOs shied away from entering Burma altogether due to the political controversies, some opting instead for refugee programs and cross-border activities. The few who came typically spent inordinate amounts of time and administrative resources chasing illusive funding windows and fulfilling extraordinary demands on monitoring. By the end of 2001, there were thus fewer international NGOs active inside Burma (thirty) than on the Thai-Burma border (fifty), and their total annual budget was only $15–20 million.[120]

The figures speak for themselves. From 1991 to 2000, Burma received only $78 million per year in official development assistance (much of which was Japanese debt relief).[121] Specifically in the area of HIV/AIDS, the combined budget of all national and international organizations in 2000 was approximately $3 million, or just 2.5 percent of the budget in Thailand which had a similar epidemic.[122]

The past five years or so have seen an emerging shift. In June 2001, the heads of eight UN agencies operating in Burma, in an open letter to their head offices overseas, described the situation as being "on the brink of a humanitarian crisis" and called for "a dramatic overhaul of budget allocations to Myanmar." Under the circumstances, they argued, "humanitarian assistance is a moral and ethical necessity . . . the nature and magnitude of the humanitarian situation does not permit delaying until the political situation evolves."[123] This helped prompt a reassessment of aid policy, particularly within the EU and its member states, which have since significantly expanded their aid commitments. In October 2001, the common position was modified, paving the way for large-scale EU and bilateral funding in support of HIV/AIDS programs. Two years later, EU commissioner for humanitarian aid Poul Nielson made it clear that the EU no longer would link humanitarian aid to the political situation: "We do not know when democracy will return to Burma. And we cannot wait for this moment to act. The human costs of social deprivation are much too large to be left aside. The international community needs to be able to continue humanitarian operations without conditionalities and benchmarks."[124] This was followed up in October 2004 with further amendments to the common position, which now explicitly states that the suspension of nonhumanitarian aid and development programs is exempted for (a) human rights, democracy, good governance, conflict prevention, and building the capacity of civil society; (b) health and education, poverty alleviation, and in particular the provision of basic needs and livelihoods for the poorest and most vulnerable populations; and (c) environmental protection, and in particular programs addressing the problem of nonsustainable, excessive logging resulting in deforestation.[125] At the time of writing, in January 2007, the European Commission (EC) is finalizing its first ever Country Strategy paper for Burma, which will commit substantial new funding over the next seven years (2007–2013), primarily for health and education, but potentially also livelihoods.[126] The EU countries have also taken the lead in setting up the new Three Diseases Fund (3D Fund) to replace the Global Fund,[127] thus openly rejecting the position of mainly U.S.-based groups that have been strongly critical of such engagement. According to EC officials, the new programs are intended "to launch a serious dialogue with the Myanmar government aimed at accomplishing longer-term policy change, while also strengthening efforts to build social capital and civil society."[128] As the EC director general for external relations explains,

> We want to avoid a lost generation in Burma/Myanmar. If the young generation who should be the agents for change, are enfeebled by bad health, lack of education and no livelihood prospects, this is highly likely. . . . We have to recognise that in Burma/Myanmar, there is still a functioning education system, market economy and civil society. We cannot abandon these. Instead, we should seek to find ways to reinforce these positive elements in the country. . . . We want to expand our ongoing political dialogue to include a wider spectrum of individuals and agencies that have a stake in building the future of Burma/Myanmar—the education, health and economic authorities, for example.[129]

Individual EU member states, too, have expanded their aid programs in Burma, notably the UK. DFID, which restarted its bilateral aid program in 2002, has since put an aid officer back in the embassy in Rangoon and taken the lead in exploring and defining appropriate uses of aid in Burma under the current difficult circumstances. Several other governments, including Sweden, Denmark, and the Netherlands, which like the UK have traditionally taken a tough political line against the military regime, are also gearing up for new programs, focusing on health and education, as is non-EU member Norway.

Increasing donor commitments since 2001 have allowed aid agencies on the ground to significantly broaden and scale-up their programs. The UNDP, for example, has expanded its Human Development Initiative from $8 million per year in phase three to $24 million in phase four, increasing the number of townships covered from 24 to 66 (out of 324),[130] while the World Food Program (WFP) and the UN Population Fund (UNFPA) have started entirely new programs. Many large international NGOs, including World Vision, Population Services International (PSI), and Médecins Sans Frontières (MSF)-Holland, have also expanded their programs several-fold.[131] Nonetheless, Burma remains greatly underfunded by any needs-based or efficiency-related criteria. Although annual official development assistance has increased to about $120 million,[132] this is still less than $3 per capita per year, much lower than most comparable countries.[133] Similarly, although the total budget for INGOs has nearly doubled to $30 million, this still only amounts to about 10 percent of the activity per capita in countries like Nepal and Cambodia, which face similar socioeconomic problems.[134]

Many governments and organizations are committed to do more. The political opposition in Burma has also significantly moderated its objections to aid.[135] But the United States maintains its position of "no development aid before democracy"—as do some opposition and solidarity groups—and thus blocks a broader shift at the multilateral level.[136] As amply demonstrated by the events leading to the termination of the Global Fund programs, even micro decisions about the appropriate use of aid in Burma are still made in the political arena, dictated by the overarching imperative of isolating the government. The aid agencies in Burma thus continue to operate in a highly politicized and often hostile international donor environment (in addition to the problems they face with the government, which suspects them of acting a Trojan horse for Western political agendas).

Political Aid

While the core strategy has been to weaken the military government, some complementary efforts have been made to support the pro-democracy movement through aid for opposition groups. The U.S. Congress since the mid-1990s has provided substantial assistance for democracy-building activities ($6 million in 1996, increasing to $11 million in 2006), the majority of which has been distributed by the National Endowment for Democracy and other quasi-governmental institutions like the International Republican Institute. The EC, along with European governments and the German political foundations, have also provided some support for advocacy, media, and other civil society groups associated with the democracy movement.

The model for this type of assistance is Eastern Europe in the 1980s, where Western governments helped support democrats who later became drivers for the cataclysmic upheavals at the end of the decade (and, in some cases, leaders of postcommunist governments). The basic idea is to strengthen the prodemocracy movement and prepare it for taking over a future democratic government. Yet, since very little space exists inside Burma for overtly political activities, almost all the funding has gone to exile groups, including the exile government, various umbrella groups on the Thai-Burma border, and a plethora of small human rights organizations headed by dissidents. These groups, generally, have only weak linkages with the opposition inside the country and seem destined to remain marginal players in the struggle for power. Judging from the experience in Cambodia, even if there was a major rupture in the future, it is questionable whether exiles would be able to return to take up key positions which more likely would be claimed by those who have stayed behind and suffered through years of repression and harassment.

Some exile groups, particularly on the Thai-Burma border, have been working to establish underground networks or support broader capacity-building activities inside Burma. In the late 1990s, for example, the United States supported the establishment of so-called political defiance groups, which were supposed to build support for nonviolent action among the general population.[137] The limitations of this work, however, were revealed when a planned "uprising" on 9 September 1999 failed to generate any significant protest activity inside the country. Instead, the majority of Western-funded work by exile groups has been information related and aimed mainly at constituencies overseas. This has created an unhealthy dynamic whereby exile groups are funded by Western donors essentially to provide human rights information for international condemnation of the military government, which then elicits further funding for themselves, but with few direct links to groups or developments inside the country.

Assistance to exiled opposition leaders, activists, and political refugees has significant humanitarian merits. Certainly, it is appropriate to help people who in many cases have suffered greatly for a worthy cause and provide them with the means to reestablish their lives and build new careers. Some may return to Burma at a future date and contribute to its rebuilding. Broader education and training programs, particularly on the Thai-Burma border, are also of obvious value and hopefully long-term benefit for the country. Yet as long as political aid is concentrated outside the country, its primary effect is to feed the existing cycle of human rights reporting, Western condemnation, and sanctions, and therefore does little to complement the core strategy. In fact, it may be counterproductive. Since grants overwhelmingly go to those who most convincingly speak the language of Western democracy promoters, Burmese groups are encouraged to adopt Western-defined agendas rather than offer local perspectives and solutions.[138] The competition over assistance has also contributed to splits within and among exile groups, and between them and groups inside the country who often feel left out.[139]

Output

Overall "Western" policy has emerged through a series of negotiations within and between key policy-making communities; it is constantly evolving and many aspects have been and remain contested, creating ambiguities and internal contradictions. The United States has the most hard-line position, reflecting traditional foreign policy orientations in that country, but the rhetoric in the UK, Denmark, Sweden, and Holland in the 1990s was very similar and it is only since the early 2000s that significant differences have opened up. European parliamentarians even today often use language which echoes that of their counterparts in the U.S. Congress, although they have relatively less influence on foreign policy, particularly in the EU context where, now, twenty-five countries have to agree.

Whatever differences exist, all Western governments, with the partial exception of Australia, have remained faithful to the central tenets of the core strategy: that democracy (regime change) is the immediate priority and best advanced through a combination of censure and sanctions aimed at isolating the military regime from the international community and global economy. The Free Burma movement, generally speaking, has been pushing for even harsher measures, including expulsion of Burma from the UN (and ASEAN) and universal economic sanctions enforced by the Security Council. Most international organizations have resisted the path of isolation but have to a large extent been forced to go along with U.S. and European policy. This Western position, though, contrasts sharply with the bilateral policies of most of Burma's regional neighbors, which—despite growing impatience with Rangoon in recent years—remain committed to expanding both political and economic links whatever the regime in power and drawing it into regional affairs. Among Asian governments, only Japan and South Korea have some limited "sanctions" in place (on aid and arms sales) or have been willing, at times, to cosponsor UN resolutions. The Philippines, though, joined Japan in voting for discussions on Burma at the Security Council, and ASEAN parliamentarians, like their counterparts in the United States and Europe, have taken much more hard-line positions than their governments.

The core strategy is defined most fundamentally by its prioritization of democracy (regime change) ahead of all other objectives, including peace building, economic development, and even basic human rights and humanitarian concerns. The latter two issues have been used extensively in making the case for isolating the regime, but efforts to address them directly—despite their urgency—have been greatly circumscribed and often implemented against the will of the strongest proponents of the "democracy paradigm." It is not that Western policy makers do not care about peace and development. Some believe nothing can be accomplished while the regime remains in power; others have moral concerns about engaging with a "pariah" regime. But mainly, efforts in these areas have been sacrificed on the altar of isolating and weakening the regime to bring about the core objective of regime change.

Advocates of sanctions sometimes claim that sanctions have only really been in place since the U.S. Burmese Freedom and Democracy Act of 2003,[140] or even that there are no real sanctions yet. Far from it, the deliberate isolation of the military regime (and by extension often the wider society), which forms the second key tenet of the core strategy, has been in place since 1988 and, despite some attempts to modify it, has generally been growing. The regime has never been accorded political recognition beyond the formality of basic diplomatic relations. Indeed, it has been shunned and demonized since the day it took power on 18 September 1988 (which is not to say it did not bring this on itself). Nearly all assistance normally offered to least developed countries has been suspended, too, since 1988, *including* most humanitarian aid that according to basic humanitarian principles should be provided purely based on need, without consideration for regime type or the political affiliation of the victims. Until just a few years ago, many proponents of the core strategy insisted that aid should only be provided across the border (from Thailand in particular) to avoid any cooperation with the regime, disregarding that only a fraction of the country's poor can be reached in that way. Although this view is rare today, attempts to ensure that absolutely no benefits are derived by the regime continues to block many important programs and in 2005 resulted in the withdrawal of the Global Fund. Clearly, these are serious sanctions—even more "isolating," in fact, than the U.S. trade, investment, and financial bans. The attempt to weaken the military regime has been so pervasive that almost no assistance has been forthcoming even for cross-cutting programs normally considered essential to democratization, as well as peace and development, such as administrative and economic reforms, civil society support, or education (never mind crucial, live-saving humanitarian efforts).

The general view in Washington is that nothing can be achieved while the military remains in power. Conversely, many U.S. policy makers and officials appear to pay little attention to the broader, structural development challenges facing the country. While U.S. official statements and sanctions legislation call for improvements in a number of areas, these are generally seen as part of a whole, with regime change viewed as the primary criterion for progress. The political reality in Washington is such that anything short of a handover of power to a democratic government is likely to be rejected by hard-liners in Congress—and, under the current administration, probably by the White House as well—as insufficient for relaxing sanctions or significantly expanding U.S. engagement in other areas. The multiple layers of legislation further complicate the situation, as Burmese compliance with any single measure may still stop short of satisfying conditions in other areas. It is not that all U.S. policy makers agree with Mitch McConnell that victory is in sight. The optimism of the late 1980s and early 1990s when Burma was thought to be on the brink of revolutionary change has largely dissolved and State Department officials, especially from the regional branch, have long taken a more sanguine view of American influence and the prospects for change. Nonetheless, Washington seems intent on staying the course, for reasons of principle—and perhaps political expediency—if nothing else. In the words of assistant secretary of state for the Department of Democracy, Human Rights, and Labor Lorne W. Craner, in March 2004,

> This Administration will maintain its unwavering commitment to support the long-suffering people of Burma until each is free to participate fully in the governance of their country by once again electing their leadership through a free and fair democratic process as they did in 1990. We will not end the pressure until every political prisoner is free, offices of political parties are open and active, and ethnic groups are at peace and represented in any discussions of Burma's political future. There has been unprecedented agreement within both the executive and legislative branches of the U.S. government to intensify pressure on the regime, and we cannot back down until the pressure yields results. To quote another Nobel Laureate familiar with the struggle for freedom, Archbishop Desmond Tutu: "If the people of South Africa had compromised the struggle against apartheid, we may never have gained our freedom." In Burma to settle for anything less than freedom and justice, for the democratic participation of all people, would be to accept the presence of oppression and to dishonor our brave brothers and sisters who have dedicated themselves to the future of a democratic government.[141]

The EU has been more careful to keep a door open for the Burmese regime. The common position notes that "in the case of a substantial improvement in the situation in Burma, not only the suspension of existing measures, but also the gradual resumption of cooperation will be considered."[142] Still, while many European officials openly question the usefulness of isolation, without any signs of significant progress in Burma few ministers—not to mention parliamentarians—are prepared to do anything that might be interpreted as weakening international demands or pressure. This was evident at the time of the decision in 2004 to allow Burma into ASEM, which was of critical importance to broader Europe-Asia relations and in principle supported by all governments, yet only became possible after an internal compromise that gave traditionally hard-line governments a "cover" in the form of a parallel strengthening of sanctions. There is no doubt that the EU is more inclined than the United States to respond positively to partial reforms in Burma or explore complementary measures aimed at improving the welfare of the Burmese people. Yet, the legacy of years of condemnation and confrontational policies is difficult to put aside and the campaign groups maintain significant influence, particularly in Britain, Holland, and the Scandinavian countries, helped by nearly two decades of largely one-sided, headline-driven media coverage, which has "conditioned" the public to view Burma as a struggle between "good" and "evil" and has reinforced a perception that punitive measures are a moral choice *whatever* their practical implications.

On the other hand, there is little prospect of significantly greater coercive pressure on the military regime. For the United States, the only unilateral step left is military action, something which U.S. officials have made clear is out of the question.[143] The EU could conceivably move to impose a comprehensive investment ban, if for no other reason than a political need to "do something" in response to the continued recalcitrance of the military regime, but existing and potential future EU investments are extremely limited. Western governments, along with human rights groups in the region, have long sought to persuade, cajole, and embarrass Asian countries to join the campaign. But as the events surrounding the Security Council show, while there is growing consensus on the need for reform in Burma, views continue to differ widely on how to bring it about. ASEAN countries may have become more critical of the military regime but ultimately are constrained by the modus operandi of the grouping, which emphasizes consensus decision making and noninterference in the internal affairs of its members. There is also a deep-rooted ideological commitment among governments in the region to the idea of growth (and, by extension, economic integration) as the best path to security, stability, and sociopolitical reform. While some hope work underway on a new ASEAN charter will pave the way for a new, more proactive approach to issues such as Burma, including sanctions against members which fail to live up to group norms, this seems unlikely given the serious political and human rights problems facing several countries in the region. As for Burma's immediate neighbors, China has made it abundantly clear that it remains strongly opposed to any form of coercive international measures. Beijing, of course, does not want to see international—and particularly American—interference in a strategically important neighbor. Moreover, China, India, and Thailand all have important geostrategic and economic interests in the country, which require them to stay on reasonable terms with whatever regime is in power.

These realities form the parameters within which current Western human rights policy must be assessed and any alternatives developed.

Notes

1. Senator Mitch McConnell, statement on the floor of the Senate, 8 December 1995.
2. UN official, interview by author, Bangkok, 9 December 2004.
3. Senator Tom Harkin, statement in the Senate on introduced bills and joint resolutions, 22 May 2001.
4. Representative Dana Rohrabacher, statement on the floor of the House of Representatives, 23 May 1996.
5. Interviews by author: U.S. diplomat, Rangoon, January 2002; U.S. congressional staffer, Washington, DC, July 2000.
6. Senator Alan Cranston, statement on the floor of the Senate, 12 March 1992.
7. Assistant secretary of state for the Bureau of East Asia and the Pacific Richard H. Solomon, testimony before the House Foreign Affairs Subcommittee for Asian and Pacific Affairs, 20 May 1992.
8. Assistant secretary for the Bureau of International Narcotics and Law Enforcement Affairs Robert Gelbard, testimony before the Senate Subcommittee on Foreign Operations, 24 July 1995.
9. Representative Dana Rohrabacher, statement before the House Subcommittee on Asian and Pacific Affairs, 8 May 1990.
10. U.S. Congress, 101st, 2nd session, H.R. 1594, *Customs and Trade Act of 1990*, n.d.
11. Solomon, testimony before the House.
12. U.S. government official, interview by author, Washington, DC, 24 July 2000.
13. Deputy assistant secretary for the Bureau of East Asian and Pacific Affairs Thomas C. Hubbard, testimony before the House Subcommittee on Asian and Pacific Affairs, 28 November 1994.
14. White House, "Special Envoys on Burma" (statement by the press secretary, Office of the Press Secretary, 7 June 1996).

15. According to an American journalist specializing in Burma at the time, Mitch McConnell, a right-wing Republican who had taken over the chairmanship of the Senate Appropriations Subcommittee on Foreign Operations earlier in the year, was persuaded by a member of his staff that taking a tough line on Burma would be a good way to embarrass President Clinton. Interview by author, Rangoon, September 2004.

16. Senator Alfonso D'Amato, introduction of the *Burma Freedom and Democracy Act* before the Senate Banking Committee, 22 May 1996.

17. Senator Mitch McConnell, testimony on the *Burma Freedom and Democracy Act* before the Senate Banking Committee, 22 May 1996.

18. Rohrabacher, statement on the floor of the House.

19. U.S. Congress, 104th, 2nd session, H.R. 3540, *Foreign Operations Act of 1997* (Engrossed Senate Amendment), n.d.

20. U.S. Senate, 104th Congress, 2nd session, Senate floor discussion of H.R.3540, *Foreign Operations Act, 1997*, Amendment No. 5019, 25 July 1996.

21. The stipulated conditions for lifting the ban, "in whole or in part," included "release of NLD leaders and other pro-democracy activists," initiation by the government of a "genuine dialogue with the democratic opposition," or "significant progress toward improving the human rights situation." White House, "Suspension of Entry as Immigrants and Nonimmigrants of Persons Who Formulate or Implement Policies That Are Impeding the Transition to Democracy in Burma or Who Benefit from Such Policies" (proclamation by the president of the United States of America, Office of the Press Secretary, 3 October 1996).

22. White House, "Executive Order Prohibiting New Investment in Burma," Office of the Press Secretary, 20 May 1997.

23. Voice of America, "Crackdown in Burma," *On the Line*, hosted by Robert Reilly, aired in May 1997 (transcript posted on BurmaNet List, 31 May 1997).

24. Voice of America, "Crackdown."

25. White House, statement by President Clinton to the United States Congress on Burma sanctions, Office of the Press Secretary, 20 May 1997.

26. U.S. House of Representatives, H.R. 603, 15 October 1998.

27. Reuters, 23 December 1999.

28. Harkin, statement in the Senate.

29. Mike Jendrzejczyk (director of Human Rights Watch/Asia), interview by author, Washington, DC, 21 September 2001.

30. See, for example, assistant secretary of state for the Bureau of East Asia and Pacific Affairs James A. Kelly, "U.S. and Burma" (dinner talk given at the Paul H. Nitze School of Advanced International Studies Conference on Burma, Washington, DC, 21 November 2002).

31. U.S. Congress, 108th, 1st session, S. 1215, *An Act to Sanction the Ruling Burmese Military Junta, to Strengthen Burma's Democratic Forces and Support and Recognize the NLD as the Legitimate Representative of the Burmese People*, n.d.

32. White House, "Executive Order Blocking Property of the Government of Burma and Prohibiting Certain Transactions," Office of the Press Secretary, 28 July 2003.

33. Glenn Kessler, "U.S. Sees Burma as a 'Test Case' in Southeast Asia," *Washington Post*, 3 January 2006.

34. U.S. Congress, 109th, 1st session, H.R. 3057, *Foreign Operations Act, 2006* (reported in Senate), n.d.

35. Mitch McConnell, "Sanctions Are the Most Effective Weapon against Burma's Military Regime," *Times Asia*, 23 January 2006 [op-ed].

36. West Germany at the time was Burma's second largest source of development aid after Japan, providing around $75 million in annual assistance. Aung Lwin, "The German Connection," *Burma Issues*, January 1994.

37. Zunetta Liddell, "International Policies towards Burma: Western Governments, NGOs and Multilateral Institutions," in *Challenges to Democratization in Burma: Perspectives on Multilateral and Bilateral Responses*, ed. International Institute of Democracy and Electoral Assistance, 139 (Stockholm: IDEA, 2001).

38. Quoted in *INEB Reader*, Bi-Monthly Newsletter of the International Network of Engaged Buddhists (September/October 1994), 7.

39. *Agence France Presse*, 24 October 1996.

40. *The Nation*, 30 October 1996.

41. Council of the European Union, *Common Position of 28 October 1996* (96/635/CFSP).

42. Stephan Colignon, "The Burmese Economy and the Withdrawal of European Trade Preferences" (Briefing Paper No. 97/02, European Institute for Asian Studies, April 1997).

43. *The Nation*, 26 July 1997.

44. Glenys Kinnock, "Travellers Should Boycott Burma," *Times*, 9 May 2001. The representation of Aung San Suu Kyi's views in this article is misleading (as is the implicit claim that the Burmese people at large are against tourism). Burma's opposition leader sees external pressure as *supportive* of domestic action only and, in recent years, has explicitly offered to share power with the military (see chapter 3 in this volume for further details). The quote, however, reflects a common strand of thinking among the more radical parts of the Free Burma movement who perceive sanctions in terms of economic warfare.

45. Foreign Office Minister Derek Fachett, "Burma" (speech at the Christian Aid/Burma Action Group Conference on Burma, Regent's College, London, 15 October 1998).

46. J. J. van Aartsen and E. L. Herfkens, letter to the chair of the Commission on Foreign Affairs in the European Parliament, dated 16 October 1998 [copy in author's possession].

47. *Agence France Presse*, 3 October 1998.

48. Council of the European Union, *Decision 98/612/CFSP Concerning Extension of Common Position* (96/635/CFSP), 26 October 1998.

49. Council of the European Union, press release no. 101-7533/00, 10 April 2000.

50. Council of the European Union, "Council Conclusions," 16 June 2003, http://europa.eu.int/comm/external_relations/myanmar/intro/gac.htm (accessed 15 March

2005). Derek Tonkin points out that by June 2004, there were more individuals subject to EU financial sanctions in Burma (379) than in Al Qaeda and the Taliban (309) and Iraq (224), including several children. Personal communication, 15 June 2004.

51. Council of the European Union, *Common Position of 25 October 2004* (2004/423/CFSP).

52. European Commission, "Report on Myanmar," internal document, November 2003.

53. Quoted in *Mizzima News*, "British MPs, Activists Urge UK to Ban Investments," 3 October 2006, www.mizzima.com/MizzimaNews/News/2006/Oct/index.html (accessed 3 October 2006).

54. See Conservative Party Human Rights Commission, "Conservative MP's Call for Debate on Burma," 30 October 2006, www.conservativehumanrights.com/news/october06/30.10.06_burmandebate.htm (accessed 14 December 2006); Christian Solidarity Worldwide, "CSW Calls on UK Government to Ban Investment in Burma," www.csw.org.uk/latestnews/print.php?id+552 (accessed 12 December 2006).

55. Quoted in *The Nation*, "Canberra Coalition Will Maintain Burma Policy," 23 April 1996, shortly after the conservative government first took office.

56. Australian Embassy Yangon, "Comments by Australian Foreign Minister, the Hon Alexander Downer, MP on Myanmar Made at Media Conferences in Hanoi," press release, 1 August 2001.

57. See, for example, *Asiaweek*, "Suu Kyi Says Australia Hampers Myanmar Democracy," 23 September 1999, for critical comments by Aung San Suu Kyi and the Australian Labour Party foreign affairs spokesman on Canberra's attempts to engage the military government in a human rights dialogue.

58. Quoted by Reuters, "Australia Defends Rights Visit to Myanmar," 5 August 1999.

59. The UNCHR already in 1989 appointed an "independent expert" to assess the human rights situation in Burma, but for the first two years treated this as an internal review. Its first resolution in 1992 formally established a special rapporteur on human rights in Burma, who since then has submitted annual reports to both the UNGA and the UNCHR.

60. United Nations Commission on Human Rights, 61st session, "Resolution on the Situation of Human Rights in Myanmar," 11 April 2005. The stated assumption that democracy is a precondition for economic growth, which directly contradicts prevailing notions of modernization among most East Asian governments as well as their official rationale for rejecting sanctions as a means for change in Burma, indicates that the resolutions, despite their formal status as approved by consensus, essentially are tools of Western human rights diplomacy. When the resolution on Burma for the first time was brought to a vote in the UN General Assembly in 2006, all of its neighbors voted against it, except Thailand, Singapore, and the Philippines, which all abstained. UN General Assembly, 61st session, item 67(c), *Recorded Vote* (A/C.3/61/L.38/Rev.1), 22 November 2006.

61. ILO, "ILO Concludes 87th Conference," press release, 17 June 1999.

62. ILO, "International Labor Conference Adopts Resolution Targeting Forced Labour in Myanmar," press release, 14 June 2000.

63. ILO, "ILO Governing Body Concludes 292nd Session," press release, 24 March 2005.

64. ILO officials, interviews by author, Rangoon, 2003–2006.

65. The decisiveness of the United States move to get Burma on the Security Council surprised even seasoned observers in New York, who had thought it unlikely that Washington would risk upsetting relations with China over a relatively "minor" issue such as Burma. They may, however, have underestimated the internal political imperatives in Washington, particularly the involvement of President George W. Bush and First Lady Laura Bush, both of whom took a personal interest in the case and thus helped rally the administration behind it. U.S. ambassador to the UN John Bolton is said to be have been particular keen to "deliver Burma" to the president who had appointed him over congressional opposition. Former U.S. State Department official, interview by author, Bangkok, October 2006. The U.S. campaign received a further boost with the release by former Czech president Vaclav Havel and South African bishop Desmond Tutu of the report "Threat to the Peace: A Call for the Security Council to Act in Burma" in September 2005, which immediately became a rallying point for a rapidly growing list of parliamentarians, human rights groups, dignitaries, and even Hollywood stars calling for Burma to be addressed at the Security Council.

66. Since the adoption of an issue on the Security Council agenda is considered a procedural matter, it only needs nine votes in favor and permanent members cannot use their veto. Any further action, such as a resolution, is a matter of substance; it, too, requires a nine-vote majority, but the five permanent members can veto.

67. Kessler, "U.S. Sees Burma as a 'Test Case.'"

68. For the text of the draft resolution, which was presented for a vote in January 2007, see United Nations Department of Public Information, "Security Council Fails to Adopt Draft Resolution" (SC/8939), 12 January 2007.

69. The resolution received nine votes in favor (primarily Western countries, but including also Ghana and Panama), with three against (China, Russia, and South Africa) and three abstentions (Congo, Indonesia, and Qatar).

70. United Nations Department of Public Information, "Security Council Fails to Adopt Draft Resolution."

71. The Treasury reportedly took this dramatic step under pressure from Senator Mitch McConnell. Former World Bank official, interview by author, Bangkok, May 2003.

72. Mitch McConnell, "Statement on the State Department FY'05 Budget Request," press release, 8 April 2004.

73. UNODC official, interview by author, Rangoon, January 2004.

74. United Nations Development Programme (UNDP) Governing Council, "Assistance to Myanmar" (Decision 92/26), 26 May 1992.

75. U.S. Congress, 103rd, 2nd session, *Foreign Relations Authorization Act, Fiscal Years 1994 and 1995*, 28 April 1994.

76. Liddell, "International Policies," 159.

77. U.S. Congress, 105th, 2nd session, H.R. 1757, *U.S. Foreign Affairs Reform and Restructuring Act of 1998*, sec. 1106, "Limitations on the United States Voluntary Contributions to the United Nations Development Program," n.d.

78. UN resident coordinator Charles Petrie was quoted as saying, "Without exaggeration, people are going to die because of this decision. People who survived the regime are going to die because we are not able to provide the humanitarian aid to help them survive the diseases." *Los Angeles Times*, 27 December 2005. UNAIDS Resident Representative Brian Williams expressed similar sentiments, likening the withdrawal to stopping feeding people in a refugee camp. Interview by author, Rangoon, March 2006.

79. Chairman of the U.S. Senate Committee on Health, Education, Labor, and Pensions Judd Greg; chairman of the U.S. Senate Subcommittee on Foreign Operations Mitch McConnell; and chairman of the U.S. Senate Subcommittee on East Asia and Pacific Affairs Sam Brownback, letter to Richard G. A. Feachem, executive director of the Global Fund, dated 28 September 2004 [copy in author's possession].

80. U.S. Senate, 109th Congress, 1st session, H.R. 3057.RS, *Foreign Operations Act, 2006* (reported in Senate), 24 June 2005.

81. As noted, the UNDP since the mid-1990s has operated under similar restrictions from Congress, but the new provisions went further by further specifying the nature of the actions to be forbidden and including a wider range of allegedly government-affiliated agencies. The text did not explicitly refer to the Global Fund programs, but the organizations specified in the bill as affiliated with the government were the same as those named as implementing partners in Global Fund documents (including the Myanmar Council of Churches, which is a genuine NGO, and the Myanmar Medical Association, which while under government influence is generally judged by aid officials to be a competent and useful professional organization). International aid officials, interviews by author, Rangoon, December 2005, March 2006. The UNDP provision was omitted from the final act after the withdrawal of the Global Fund from Burma in August 2005.

82. Aryeh Neier (OSI), memorandum to Brad Herbert (Global Fund), 24 September 2004 [copy in author's possession].

83. The Global Fund had already, before approving the grants, put in place several safeguards, notably by appointing the UNDP as principal recipient of all fund money to secure maximum oversight on the ground.

84. International aid officials, interviews by author, Rangoon, February and October 2006.

85. Adeze Igboemeka, "Aid Effectiveness in Burma/Myanmar," August 2005, www2.dfid.gov.uk/mdg/aid-effectiveness/newsletters/burma-report.pdf (accessed 2 December 2006).

86. Global Fund, "Fact Sheet: Termination of Grants to Myanmar," 18 August 2005, www.theglobalfund.org (accessed 29 January 2007).

87. Internal UN memo, n.d. [copy in author's possession].

88. International NGO representative, interview by author, Rangoon, March 2006.

89. Internal UN memo, n.d. [copy in author's possession].

90. Liddell, "International Policies."

91. The founder of the Free Burma Coalition, Maung Zarni, who was instrumental in popularizing the international boycott campaigns in the 1990s, has since rejected this approach as ineffectual and harmful. While the organization retains its name, it is thus no longer part of the Free Burma movement (although it continues to pursue democracy through different means). Several former members, who disagreed with the shift, have founded the U.S. Campaign for Burma instead.

92. See, for example, Desmond Tutu, "Foreword," Burma Sanctions Coalition briefing, March 2002, www.burmacampaign.org.uk/sanctions_briefing.html#foreword (accessed 21 January 2007).

93. Shan Human Rights Foundation and Shan Women's Action Network, "License to Rape," 2002.

94. Notable exceptions are Amnesty International and the International Coalition against Landmines, both of which provide objective, solution-seeking reporting and carefully avoid taking sides in the political struggle.

95. Judgment on these issues is difficult and perhaps best left to lawyers, but claims that the military regime is guilty of genocide or using rape as a weapon of war are not, generally, supported by international human rights officers on the ground in Burma. Interviews by author, Rangoon, 2000–2006. This assessment is echoed by Raluca Enescu from the International Campaign to Ban Landmines, an organization that has also done work in the relevant areas of the country. While emphasizing that "atrocities and/or severe and condemnable violations of International Humanitarian and Human Rights Law are certainly taking place," he argues that they are "not at the level that justify the use of the term genocide. . . . While some atrocities are common, especially in prisons, they are not systematic enough to justify the use of the legal concept of genocide. Some atrocities which occur during military operations halt once the military operation halts, and if genocide was taking place we would expect to see the atrocities continue even after the reason for the military operation ceases." *Burma Digest*, "Interview with Raluca Enescu," 26 September 2006, www.burmadigest.wordpress.com/ (accessed 10 January 2007).

96. Some local governments responded by replacing their selective purchasing laws with directives requiring public pension funds to divest their stock in any company involved with Burma, but the momentum of the grassroots movement was lost after the Supreme Court decision and subsequent federal action.

97. See, for example, the Burma Campaign UK website, www.burmacampaign.org.uk; International Confederation of Free Trade Unions, "Doing Business with Burma," January 2005; EarthRights International, "Destructive Engagement: A Decade of Foreign Investment," October 1999.

98. Burma Campaign UK, "Companies Not Supporting the Regime in Burma," n.d., www.burmacampaign.org.uk/dirty_list/clean_list.html (accessed 22 January

2007). Although the list appears to include also companies that left for reasons unrelated to the boycott campaigns, there is no doubt that the latter have been generally successful in their objective of forcing companies out of Burma.

99. The campaign against aid largely dissolved in the early 2000s as recognition of the dire humanitarian situation in Burma and the work of aid agencies improved. The recent pressures on the Global Fund and the UNDP, however, suggest that some lobby groups were simply biding their time, although their strategy has shifted to more subtle, behind-the-scenes efforts.

100. In the words of a U.S. official, "Madeleine Albright's 'dialogue' with the regime was, literally, limited to shouting at them at ASEAN post-ministerial meetings." Interview by author, Washington, DC, June 2000.

101. The mandate of the secretary-general derives from a 1993 request by the General Assembly that he "assists in the implementation of the present resolution," which has been reiterated annually since then. United Nations General Assembly, 48th session, *Resolution on the Situation of Human Rights in Myanmar* (A/RES/48/150), 20 December 1993. Since the special rapporteur on human rights was already mandated to report on the human rights situation, Boutros Boutros-Ghali interpreted his role as being one of "good offices," a definition which was subsequently embraced by the General Assembly and its member states.

102. The special envoys have received technical support from the Political Affairs Department in New York, but cooperation and coordination with other parts of the UN system, including the special rapporteurs and the resident coordinator in Rangoon have been largely ad hoc. Instead, Razali from 2002 to 2005 worked closely with the country representative of the Centre for Humanitarian Dialogue in Rangoon, Leon de Riedmatten, who maintained contacts with key domestic actors in between the visits of the special envoy.

103. World Bank official, interview by author, Washington, DC, July 2000.

104. Interview by author, Rangoon, March 2006.

105. UNICEF, "Possibilities for a United Nations Peace and Development Initiative for Myanmar," draft letter to the UN secretary-general, 16 March 1992 [copy in author's possession].

106. Seng Raw, "Views from Myanmar: An Ethnic Minority Perspective," in *Burma: Political Economy under Military Rule*, ed. Robert H. Taylor, 161–62 (London: C. Hurst & Co., 2001).

107. See, for example, NCGUB, "Statement on U.S. Aid Policy," Council of Foreign Relations, 28 October 1992; NCGUB, "Bommersvik Declaration," Convention of Elected Representatives, 27 July 1995.

108. For further details on these claims, see Marc Purcell, "Axehandles or Willing Minions? International NGOs in Burma," in *Strengthening Civil Society in Burma: Possibilities and Dilemmas for International NGOs*, ed. Burma Centre Netherlands, 73 (Chiang Mai, Thailand: Silkworm Books, 1999).

109. Aung San Suu Kyi, letter to Gustave Speth, UNDP administrator, dated 14 January 1996 [copy in author's possession]; Aung San Suu Kyi, message to the Briefing on Burma, 25 May 1997.

110. See, for example, interview with Aung San Suu Kyi, *Asiaweek*, 11 June 1999.

111. U.S. congressional staffer, interview by author, Washington, DC, 27 July 2000.

112. Quoted in Purcell, "Axehandles," 94.

113. Interview by author, Washington, DC, March 2004.

114. *South China Morning Post*, "US Lawmaker Rejects Opposition Veto," 18 January 1999.

115. New England Burma Roundtable, "Action Update: Hall Plans Not to Offer Pro-Junta Amendment," 16 July 1999 (posted on BurmaNet List, 16 July 1999). According to a U.S. embassy official in Rangoon, "The boycott of humanitarian aid has been part of a broader policy strategy and was never really an issue until the late 1990s; when it did become an issue, we conferred with the NLD which requested that we maintain our policy." Interview by author, January 2002.

116. Australia, in the late 1990s, provided around $500,000–750,000 per year for international NGO projects in the areas of primary health care and poverty alleviation. The embassy also has a small Direct Assistance Programme managed by the embassy in Yangon. AusAID, "Country Information," www.ausaid.gov.au (accessed 20 March 2005). The British government had similar, but slightly larger programs. DFID, "Burma: Country Strategy Paper," July 2000.

117. Japan did provide substantial bilateral assistance to Burma throughout the 1990s, mainly in the form of debt relief.

118. UNODC was particularly badly affected by this (despite the massive drugs problems in Burma), as 90 percent of its funding comes from supplementary funds, which are highly vulnerable to political exigencies. UNODC official, interview by author, Wa Special Region, March 2003.

119. UNDP's scope for addressing policy issues was increased informally at the annual General Council meeting in September 2001. UNDP official, interview by author, Rangoon, December 2002.

120. This figure includes INGO projects funded by bilateral and multilateral donors; the "added" contribution of INGOs from private contributions is much lower.

121. UNESCAP, "Statistical Yearbook for Asia and the Pacific 2001," October 2001.

122. UNAIDS, "The United Nations Joint Action Plan on HIV/AIDS," 2001–2002.

123. United Nations Country Team, "A Silent Humanitarian Crisis in the Making," letter to head offices, dated 30 June 2001 [copy in author's possession].

124. Commissioner Poul Nielson, "Advocating the Needs of the Vulnerable" (keynote address, Open Burma Day, Brussels, October 2003).

125. Council of the European Union, *Common Position of 25 October 2004* (2004/423/CFSP).

126. European Commission. "EC-Burma/Myanmar Country Strategy (2007–2013)," draft, November 2005.

127. The 3D Fund has drawn total pledges of $99.5 million for 2007–2011. DFID has committed £20 million and Australia $11 million to the new fund, while the EC

together with Sweden, Norway, and the Netherlands have pledged the remainder and were processing proposals at the time of writing. Funding was available from November 2006 to carry over programs initiated under the Global Fund. UNAIDS official, interview by author, Rangoon, October 2006.

128. EC official, interview by author, Rangoon, July 2005.

129. EU director general Eneko Landaburu, "Supporting People—Assisting Transition" (paper presented at the Burma/Myanmar Forum, European Institute for Asian Studies, Brussels, 29 March 2006).

130. UNDP official, interview by author, Rangoon, July 2006.

131. World Vision grew from $2 million in 1999 to $8.5 million in 2005 (and foresees a further doubling by 2010). PSI and MSF-Holland have both doubled their staff since 2002 and substantially expanded most aspects of their work. Country representatives, interviews by author, Rangoon, March 2006.

132. OECD, "Geographical Distribution of Financial Flows to Aid Recipients," January 2006. The figure of $120 million is from 2004.

133. Laos per capita is $50; Cambodia, $35; Nepal, $15; and Bangladesh, $7. UNDP, "Human Development Report 2004," n.d.

134. Nepal, with a population of 25 million, has about 275 international NGOs with a budget of $175 million; Cambodia, with a population on 15 million, has about 115 with a budget of $110 million. Guy Stallworthy, "A NGO Perspective on Assistance in Myanmar" (paper presented at the European Commission's Burma Day 2005, Brussels, 6 April 2005).

135. According to NLD spokesman U Lwin, Aung San Suu Kyi told Japanese foreign minister Yoriko Kawaguchi in August 2002 that she would no longer oppose foreign aid provided it fell within strict guidelines: "She is not going to object to that which will benefit the people. . . . She will support development proposals including infrastructure projects which will benefit the people, like hydro-electric projects, mainly in energy and electricity." Europe-Burma Office, "Aung San Suu Kyi Raises the Stakes for Dialogue," general release, Brussels, 6 August 2002. In a public statement in 2006, the NLD further explained, "Because of the insufficiency of financial resources . . . the situation is reached whereby humanitarian assistance from international organisations . . . is urgently required." NLD, "Special Statement," 20 April 2006. See also 88 Generation Students, "Statement on Humanitarian Assistance to Myanmar," 6 September 2005; and Burma Campaign UK, "Pro-Aid, Pro-Sanctions, Pro-Engagement: A Position Paper on Humanitarian Aid," July 2006. The latter paper, which is endorsed by nineteen exile and pro-democracy advocacy groups, including NCGUB and the Ethnic Nationalities Council (ENC), expresses support for humanitarian assistance in parallel with targeted sanctions and diplomatic efforts.

136. According to a U.S. State Department official, some in the U.S. government still argue that aid would undermine the people's thirst for freedom and thus postpone "the revolution" that would usher in a new era of democracy. Interview by author, Washington, DC, March 2004.

137. For information on this "covert" work, see Gene Sharp, "Exploring Non-Violent Struggle in Thailand and Burma," *Nonviolent Sanctions: News from the Albert Einstein Foundation* IV, no. 2 (Fall 1992); Jonathan Mowat, "The New Gladio in Action?" *Online Journal*, 19 March 2005, www.onlinejournal.com (accessed 20 January 2007).

138. The problem of bias in funding, not surprisingly, is mainly commented on by critics of border politics, including both Burmese and foreigners. For a sympathetic reflection on this problem, see Christina Fink, "An Independent Evaluation of Endowment-Funded Ethnic Nationality-Related Projects in Burma" (report prepared for the National Endowment for Democracy, Washington, DC, May 2000), 77.

139. See, for example, David O'Hanlon, "Whatever Happened to the ABSDF?" *Irrawaddy* (print ed.) 9, no. 9 (December 2001); also Liddell, "International Policies," 170–73.

140. For example, Kyi May Kaung, "Sanctions and Burma: Shades of Grey," *Foreign Policy in Focus: Strategic Dialogue*, 18 January 2007, www.fpif.org/fpiftxt/3917 (accessed 25 January 2007).

141. Assistant secretary of state for the Department of Democracy, Human Rights, and Labor Lorne W. Craner, testimony before the House International Relations Committee, Subcommittee on Asia and the Pacific, 25 March 2004.

142. Council of the European Union, *Common Position of 25 October 2004*.

143. "We are not going to attack Burma, never." Deputy Assistant Secretary of State Eric John, quoted in *Irrawaddy* (online ed.), "The New Word from Washington," 1 May 2006, www.irrawaddy.org (accessed 1 May 2006).

CHAPTER TWO

Regime Priorities and Perceptions

> Today our armed forces are engaged not only in the task of defending the state, but as part of their historical duty, are performing other duties in the political, economic and social sectors. Since we have been given, through circumstance, the opportunity of shouldering the responsibilities of State at this time, we have pledged with pure goodwill to make every endeavour to build a modern developed nation where peace prevails.
>
> —Senior General Than Shwe[1]

Since 1988, numerous studies, advocacy reports, and newspaper articles have been published, detailing the repressive behavior of the Burmese military government and its security agencies. Little systematic attention has been paid, however, to the subjective basis of such behavior. Why does the State Law and Order Restoration Council/State Peace and Development Council (SLORC/SPDC) insist on maintaining military leadership of the state? What are the generals' fears concerning political and economic liberalization? How do they perceive international influence attempts? In order to develop effective international strategies to effectuate change, it is imperative to understand the target's perspective.

Since Western countries have neither the authority to evoke a sense of obligation on part of Burma's military rulers to comply with their demands, nor the resolve to force them to do so, their influence depends on affecting the regime's internal decision-making process in the desired direction. Censure and sanctions are ways to impose costs on the regime for continuing its offensive behavior. Yet, a decision to comply or not comply with particular demands does not depend on the costs of resisting alone. It is influenced equally by the perceived costs of complying with the demands, which may arise from giving up intrinsic benefits of current behavior or from the act itself of giving in to external pressure.

There is, of course, no way to properly quantify human decisions, which are wholly subjective. The expected costs and benefits to the regime of any given course of action depend on how it values particular "consequences," as well as on its assumptions about the probability of such consequences occurring. Nonetheless, by identifying the national objectives and priorities of the top leaders (i.e., those partaking in the core decisions of the regime), as well as their underlying attitudes and beliefs, we can at least gauge their general psychological disposition to comply with certain kinds of demands under particular sets of circumstances. This, in turn, forms an important basis for assessing the impact of current international policies, as well as for developing an optimal strategy for promoting the desired changes in governance.

The aim of this chapter is a modest one: to elucidate certain basic outlooks that guide the collective behavior of the military regime. An attempt, however, is made also to trace diverging views within the military hierarchy and assess their implications for action.

National Objectives and Priorities

The basic program of the SLORC/SPDC was sketched out in several early policy proclamations, the sum of which is a series of core values, strategic concepts, and specific national objectives that continue to form the basic framework for military rule today.

Immediately upon taking power in September 1988, the SLORC issued a declaration outlining four objectives:

1. Restoration of law and order
2. Rehabilitation of transport and communication
3. Alleviation of the socio-economic crisis
4. Preparation for multiparty elections to be held at completion of the aforementioned tasks[2]

This was a short-term program, focusing on crisis management. The SLORC, it indicated, would be a caretaker government only, set up to restore normal government functions that had collapsed during the upheaval and to oversee an orderly political transition. The new ruling council, however, also laid out a broader program for the armed forces in the form of three "main national causes," which since the 1990 election have been used to justify the extension of military rule beyond its original time frame:

1. Nondisintegration of the union
2. Nondisintegration of national solidarity
3. Consolidation of sovereignty

The significance of the main national causes was highlighted in 1992 when they were included among six "guiding principles" for a new constitution, which was to be deliberated at the National Convention starting the following year:

1. Nondisintegration of the union
2. Nondisintegration of national solidarity
3. Consolidation of sovereignty
4. Multiparty democracy
5. Justice, liberty, and equality
6. Leading role for the military in national politics

The fourth and fifth principles reiterated the SLORC's supposed commitment to restoring democracy, but were circumscribed by the sixth which revealed the intention of the military leadership to maintain control of the government indefinitely. This was subsequently confirmed in a semiofficial document entitled *Destiny of the Nation*, published in 1995, which discussed the substance of the three main national causes in detail and further laid out a longer-term, strategic framework for military rule in the form of twelve "national objectives," thus laying to rest any notion of the military as a temporary "caretaker" government:

Political objectives

1. Stability of the state, community peace and tranquility, prevalence of law and order
2. National reconsolidation
3. Emergence of a new enduring state constitution
4. Building of a new modern developed nation in accord with the new state constitution

Economic objectives

1. Development of agriculture as the base and all-around development of other sectors of the economy
2. Proper evolution of a market-oriented economic system
3. Development of the economy inviting participation in terms of technical know-how and investments from inside the country and abroad
4. Initiative to shape the national economy must be kept in the hands of the state and the national peoples.

Social objectives

1. Uplift of the morale and morality of the entire nation
2. Uplift of national prestige and integrity, and preservation and safeguarding of cultural heritage and national character
3. Uplift of dynamism of patriotic spirit
4. Uplift of health, fitness and education standards of the entire nation[3]

Since they were promulgated, the national objectives have become the standard frame of reference for official speeches and publications concerned with the state of the country and the development efforts of the government. An eclectic mixture of government aspirations and general policy statements, they define a broad development agenda, including political, economic, and foreign policy objectives. Yet, the underlying themes of stability, unity, and patriotism show how closely wedded this development program is to the military's overarching national security objectives.

Core Values

The military government is officially committed to building "a modern, developed nation," but this abstract agenda veils a clear prioritization between certain "core values" of national security and other "lesser values" linked to a more progressive political and economic development agenda. As one government publication stresses, "Security is the most basic and the most important requirement of the country. . . . A nation without security is incapable of doing anything. Economic activities are impossible. Social welfare is jeopardised. Governments as well as the people must first ensure security to enable them to pursue their objectives."[4]

The core values of the government are encapsulated in the three main national causes of *national sovereignty*, *territorial integrity*, and *national solidarity*, which are intrinsically linked. Since 1988, this national security program has replaced socialism as the official "ideology" of the state, establishing goals, evaluative criteria, and justifications for action, while also providing the military government with an identity and a raison d'être.[5] As such, it is a major influence on the perceptual processes of military officers and government officials who, in turn, are trying to inculcate it into society. "In marching towards these goals, the Tatmadaw [Burmese for 'armed forces'] needs to be helped by the entire mass of the people including political parties. . . . The SLORC has laid down these objectives with a sincere desire for the well-being of the State and of the people. . . . Any opposition to these objectives will only hurt the masses. . . . All those who love the State and its people will join hands in implementing these objectives."[6]

It is this aspect of SLORC/SPDC rule, together with the council's peculiar conceptions of "national sovereignty," "territorial integrity," and "national solidarity," which distinguishes it from many other authoritarian regimes around the world, yet reveals its close kinship with the Revolutionary Council (1962–1974) and the Burma Socialist Programme Party (BSPP) government (1974–1988) for whom socialism always seemed mainly a convenient cover for more fundamental national security interests.[7]

National Sovereignty

The idea of national sovereignty has strong emotional appeal to Burma's military rulers, who are deeply influenced by the historical memory of British subjugation of the once powerful Burman kingdoms in the nineteenth century and since independence in 1948 have faced continuous internal conflict and interference by external powers. In the words of former foreign minister Ohn Gyaw, "Independence in Myanmar was regained only after great sacrifices in lives and property by the Myanmar people. Having encountered the bitter experiences of over a hundred years of colonialism, we greatly cherish our independence and are determined never to be subjected again to the domination by foreigners. We will never let outsiders dictate our destiny and shape our future."[8]

The implicit aim of successive military governments since 1962 has been to restore the "golden age" of Burma's monarchical past when the Burmese (or rather the Burmans) were feared and respected in the region, and in full control of their own destiny and resources. The late senior general Saw Maung minced no words about this: "The nation should be one in which only Myanmars reside and which Myanmars own. We will have to be vigilant against Myanmar, the home of Myanmar nationals, being influenced by anyone. And it is important that Myanmar does not become the home of mixed bloods influenced by alien cultures though it is called Myanmar."[9] In practical terms, this implies not only a natural resolve to defend Burma against military conquest, but also a more peculiar obsession with maintaining *total* national control of all details and affairs of Burmese life. The military leaders perceive it to be their national and professional duty to counter *any* form of external influence, not just politically, but also in the economic, social, and cultural spheres: "Seen from our perspective, security entails non-interference in internal affairs and freedom from external pressure. Security is synonymous with the basic right to freely choose one's own political, economic and social systems and to determine one's future at one's own pace and in accordance with cherished values and ideals."[10]

To outside observers, such stridently nationalistic rhetoric may seem anachronistic. It would be a mistake, however, to underestimate the continuity in military thinking since the immediate postindependence period and the deep sense of insecurity that continues to drive the current government's priorities and behavior. Fear of foreign aggression has been vividly reflected in Burma's foreign policy orientation since the 1950s, reflecting internal as well as external conditions. Unable for economic reasons to build a strong conventional army—and unwilling, for ideological reasons, to join the Commonwealth—the first government of independent Burma developed a foreign policy based on strict neutralism and the "five principles of peaceful coexistence." As the Cold War heated up and Burma's internal conflicts continued, this policy played a vital role in balancing off the contending superpowers and avoiding being dragged into another Vietnam or Korean War. Indeed, after the military took power in 1962, the Revolutionary Council carried "neutralism" to the extreme of "isolationism" by closing its borders and generally withdrawing from world affairs.[11]

The end of the Cold War has significantly improved the security climate in the region, allowing the SLORC/SPDC to roll back the policy of isolationism. Yet, the military leaders continue to exhibit a keen sense of physical vulnerability owing, in part, to Burma's sensitive geostrategic location between two major powers, China and India,[12] but particularly to the strident rhetoric by Western governments and organizations which—however far-fetched this may seem—has raised the specter of a U.S. or U.S.-led invasion to overthrow the regime. As one government publication warns: "The West Bloc countries, in waging its Cold War against its adversary the East Bloc, had adopted a pattern of democratic warfare. The grand strategy of the West Bloc is to eliminate dictatorial systems and establish democratic states. Some countries in the West Bloc consider Myanmar a dictatorial regime."[13] These fears have spurred major efforts to upgrade the country's ground-to-air defenses and other conventional defense capabilities, as well as renewed preparations for a "total people's war." The SLORC/SPDC has also built a number of new roads and bridges in the delta region, reportedly "to secure access for tanks in the case of a foreign invasion," and enforces a policy of rice self-sufficiency in each state and division "to ensure that the army can rely on local supplies during extended guerrilla warfare against an occupying force."[14] While some of this may simply be long-term contingency planning, more immediate fears have surfaced at times of national crisis, such as during the 1988 uprising when the arrival of a U.S. Navy vessel in Burmese waters caused panic in the War Office, as well as in connection with American military interventions elsewhere in the world.

Military concerns over subtler forms of external influence, partly linked to perceived neocolonialist designs by Western countries, also have impacted policy greatly over the years and continue to do so. In an attempt to secure national political and economic control and protect the country against Western cultural influences, the Revolutionary Council in the 1960s nationalized most industries and commerce, discontinued foreign aid programs, closed down Western cultural agencies, and banned English language teaching. Subsequent governments have felt compelled to ease the country's isolation to salvage a stagnating economy and counter the risk of social unrest, which could threaten their hold on power and invite more direct foreign intervention.[15] Yet, perceptions change more slowly than policy, and since 1988, Western pressure for democracy and human rights, compounded by the new influx of foreign capital, organizations, and cultural influences, has raised new fears among conservative military leaders. Although the SLORC/SPDC has significantly relaxed the long-cherished notion of territorial sanctity, the ideal of absolute sovereignty remains. "In some countries," writes one military publication, "when a market economy is given a free reign, the economy falls into the hands of foreigners. When foreigners become affluent, they begin to interfere and influence national politics. Own nationals become hirelings. This is a neo-colonial pattern based on the economy. Myanmar cannot be allowed to follow this pattern."[16]

Ongoing openings to the world have thus been cautious and accompanied by strong warnings about foreigners and measures to strengthen national resilience to foreign influences (see later in this chapter for further details).

Territorial Integrity

The need to safeguard the union has been another leitmotif of Burma's military governments since 1962 when General Ne Win justified the military coup as necessary to prevent national disintegration in the face of civilian government failures.[17] It remains a paramount concern today, closely linked to external threat perceptions.

Burma's long-running ethnic insurgencies have not only invited foreign interference in the border regions, but have also deprived the state of vital human and natural resources, thus diminishing national power (not to mention being a sore point for military national pride and professional self-esteem). Indeed, until 1988, the Union of Burma existed in name only, as the central government had no control over large areas of the country, which for most intents and purposes constituted independent territories with their own (rudimentary) administrations, health and education systems, and foreign relations. Not surprisingly perhaps, military officials frequently refer to the specter of social and economic disintegration presented by the breakup of the Soviet Union and Yugoslavia to rationalize their insistence on maintaining control of the political transition process.[18]

Although all but a few fringe ethnic minority organizations today have abandoned calls for independence and instead seek greater autonomy within a federal union, the military insists on maintaining a strongly centralized, unitary state. Symptomatically, when the Democratic Alliance of Burma (DAB)—an alliance of ethnic nationalist groups and exile political organizations based on the Thai border—in the early 1990s drew up a draft constitution explicitly calling for a federal state, military writers rejected it in the strongest terms: "The DAB constitution . . . is but a visualisation of a confederation of independent, sovereign states, each with its own administration, legislature, judiciary and army. Taking such a constitution together with the present state of political schisms and prevailing world situation, it will be seen to be heading straight towards national disintegration. . . . Myanmar has more than once come to the brink of national catastrophe and another approach to a similar position is not acceptable."[19] The government has also categorically refused to entertain demands for federalism within the National Convention. Even though several smaller ethnic groups under the new constitution will be granted new "self-administered areas," neither these nor the seven existing ethnically designated states, it appears, will have more than nominal autonomy.

Although the fires of insurgency have been doused, military leaders still equate local autonomy for ethnic minority groups with instability and heightened danger of foreign interference. Until this issue is resolved, ethnic tensions are likely to remain high and a second generation of armed conflicts could emerge. Paradoxically, this would revive the direct threat to the union and thus reinforce the perceived need for military rule to hold it together.[20]

National Solidarity

The third dimension of the military government's national security ideology is an internally oriented focus on national unity, which transcends the distinction between core values and more strategic objectives and in many ways has come to define the positions and actions of the post-1988 regime: "Our program of democracy is secondary. Our fundamental program is national unity. Given the fact that we have so many races living together, if we are not united, there will be no chance of survival. A new government can emerge, but unless we have solved our problems of national unity, it will not last long."[21]

Military leaders and ideologists identify disunity among Burma's diverse peoples as the main cause of the country's woes, from the loss of independence in the nineteenth century to the failure to develop the country following independence:

> Besides lacking a leader who could unify all national forces for a common cause, there was disunity and mutual distrust within the country. This ultimately led to our loss of independence. This is a lesson which must be taken to heart and forever remembered by us and by all future generations of our national people.[22]

> Myanmar has more than once come to the brink of [national disintegration] and another approach to a similar position is not acceptable. These occasions [have] already sapped and drained national energy for constructive work and the nation has already suffered in lack of development. It is time now that the whole nation united and concentrated its efforts on trying to upstage the nation to the world level.[23]

Since the military's external threat perceptions are closely linked to internal instability, the country's security dilemmas are seen ultimately to require political solutions. Yet, these are perceived in terms diametrically opposed to those proffered by the National League for Democracy (NLD) or ethnic nationalists. Rather than accommodate demands for pluralism, the military has set out to build a monolithic state by suppressing political and, to some degree, ethnic differences. The military demands absolute commitment by all people and organizations to the state's ideology and programs. Following the socialist model, the Revolutionary Council in 1963 disbanded all independent political parties and civil society organizations, replacing them with a single state party, the BSPP, and an extensive system of auxiliary mass organizations. The ruling council also abolished the free press and introduced a draconian system of censorship of all public expression, from news media to fiction. The SLORC/SPDC officially favors a multiparty system, but has continued to wield a wide array of laws and regulations that effectively denies political parties and other organizations any space to promote alternative visions of society or in other ways challenge the existing order. It has also set up a new set of state-sponsored mass organizations that, although usually referred to as welfare organizations, are used primarily for mobilizing the people around state goals and preempting the formation of a genuine civil society. Censorship remains tight, particularly on political subjects, although discussion of socioeconomic issues is somewhat more tolerated than before 1988.[24]

In Burma's multiethnic society, the campaign to enforce orthodoxy across political and civil society poses a more fundamental challenge, however—that of nation building. The country's multitude of disparate ethnic groups is exhorted to show "union spirit," defined by Senior General Than Shwe as "the spirit that binds all citizens in unity no matter in which . . . region they may reside. Union spirit is built on the spirit of nationalism that engenders nationals to love, cherish and value a single motherland . . . and work for its prosperity. In a way, union spirit is that of oneness and unity of nationals who have descended from kin who have lived together with affection, in weal and woe on the same land, drinking the same water for a very long time."[25]

In practice, the military government is engaged in an ambitious program of social engineering, aimed at breaking up ethnocentric identities and constructing a new overarching "national" identity. This involves elements that appear relatively superficial, such as the numerous new historiographical projects celebrating the common history and exploits of the "national peoples" and the large investments in restoration of ancient cultural heritage and promotion of traditional arts and sports. There are, however, also more intrusive efforts underway to inculcate patriotism within state-sponsored mass organizations and through the broader education system, which have the potential over the long term to radically transform people's sense of what it means to be Burmese, as well as their attitudes toward the state on the one hand, and outsiders on the other. The regime's primary mass organization, the Union Solidarity and Development Association (USDA), for example, has among its main aims "promotion and vitalization of national pride" and emphasizes cultural training of its members. School curricula at all levels, similarly, have been revised to "disclose and preserve Myanmar cultural traits" and "strengthen the patriotic spirit and Union consciousness of the youth."[26] Although token gestures are made to minority cultures, for example, in cultural shows on Union Day where each ethnic group dresses in traditional clothes and performs local dances and songs, the attempt to define an overarching national identity revolves around a common language (Burmese), a common religion (Buddhism), and a common culture (Burman). Rather than integrate the ethnic minorities in a union based on "unity in diversity," the aim, it would appear, is to assimilate them into the dominant culture of a monolithic state.[27]

The common element in the government's programs of national unity is their absolutism. The military leaders do not perceive of unity in terms of mutual cooperation and compromises among different actors and interests, but—like their socialist predecessors (and other one-party states)—expound a notion of society as a harmonious, unified whole. Collective action must be of "one blood, one voice, one command,"[28] or as another official publication expresses it, "a nation may be deemed to have been reunified only when the entire nation, all national races, all classes of people and all political persuasions have been brought together into a single fold."[29] This leaves little room for concessions to popular calls for pluralism, whether in the form of democracy, federalism, or any other form of organization involving a differentiation of society, its values, or its ideas. Rather, the military with its strict hierarchy, discipline, and strong corporate ethos is presented as a model of unity, and the main vehicle for attaining it.

It is perhaps unsurprising that the generals in their double role as rulers and soldiers would emphasize national security. But that national sovereignty, territorial integrity, and national solidarity are elevated to top priorities of governance on a day-to-day basis speaks volumes about a sense of threat, which those promoting change overlook at their peril. The military leadership remains steeped in rigid notions of nationalism and exhibits a siege mentality that strongly influences policy and its responses to outside pressure.

Strategic Objectives

While the quest for national security continues to define the government's policies and programs as it has done since 1962, the military leadership does have a broader national development agenda. In broad terms, this involves three strategic objectives—*economic growth*, *international cooperation*, and *constitutional government*—each of which is seen to contribute toward national security, but also aims at ending decades of conflict and stagnation, and restoring Burma's once proud position in the world. It is in these areas that the break with the past and opportunities for the future are most apparent. Yet, it is also here that the inherent contradictions of military rule are most evident and misunderstandings about its nature have been most acute.

Economic Growth

The SLORC/SPDC's commitment to developing the economy is expressed, generally, in its oft-repeated claim to be building a "modern, developed nation" and, more specifically, in the four national economic objectives, which emphasize the need to develop a market-oriented economic system based on agriculture and foreign direct investment. The large increase in military expenditures since 1988, coupled with continuing heavy state intervention in the economy that is manifestly detrimental to economic growth, has led many observers to question the veracity of these claims.[30] Some have even suggested that the generals prefer Burma to remain undeveloped as it facilitates continued military control.[31] Such conclusions, however, are unconvincing and fly in the face of significant evidence to the contrary.

Burma's military rulers need revenue to fund their expansion and modernization of the armed forces,[32] as well as for the government's extensive infrastructure development program, which plays a vital part in their efforts to build a politically, socially, and economically integrated nation. They are also acutely aware that popular economic discontent fuels social unrest. This lesson was driven home to them by the 1988 uprising, which was rooted in the abysmal failure of the socialist economy. In fact, they appear convinced that political aspirations are much less a source of popular resistance than is resentment of poor living conditions: "The majority of people in Burma are not obsessed with politics. They do not see freedom in terms of the right to vote or express their views freely. The demands for such rights will only come when . . . the more fundamental needs of the people have been fulfilled."[33] Thus, the regime's attempts to pacify the population and establish political legitimacy are, at least in principle, heavily focused on improvements in the economy.

There is significant evidence that the military uses the economy, mainly, in the service of power. Certainly, the government's redistributive policies, including price controls, trade restrictions, and the broader system of patronage, serve political functions rather than promoting broad-based growth. Military officers, however, reportedly have been shocked by the realization upon arrival in neighboring countries of just how far Burma has fallen behind in economic development,[34] and often talk about the need to catch up with the rest of the world. With increasingly frequent trips overseas, such comparisons are becoming a stronger motivation for turning the economy around.[35] Some ministers and local commanders, in informal conversations, will also quietly express concern about the broader welfare of the people and are actively supporting social programs in the poorest areas.[36] As in other areas of governance, the overall picture is more nuanced and complex than many critics allow for and, inevitably, has contradictory elements.

The SLORC made a serious attempt in the early 1990s to jumpstart the economy by ending the socialist economic policies and economic autarky of the Ne Win era (although the leadership may not fully have appreciated what this would require). Key economic reforms, such as exchange rate unification and privatization of loss-making state economic enterprises, however, stalled over fears of social dislocation, which raised the specter of another 1988 uprising. As the former minister of national planning and economic development, Brigadier General David Abel, subsequently explained, "We feel that the currency is overvalued, and so we have to devalue it. Not having a unified currency is one of the major issues foreign investors feel uncomfortable about. In 1988 our finance minister talked to the IMF [International Monetary Fund] and asked for a cushion to devalue our currency so that the poor would not be affected, but they refused us. So we cannot move ahead. We need a cushion like Indonesia is getting, like Thailand is getting, like South Korea is getting."[37] When the "Asian crisis" hit in 1997, old fears of economic vulnerability and foreign exploitation "kicked in" and any remaining reform drive dissolved as the government scrambled to fence off Burma from the chaos raging elsewhere in the region. Yet, the regime continues its efforts to develop the economic infrastructure. This program dominates the schedule of all the top leaders, who travel extensively around the country to oversee the construction of bridges, dams, irrigation systems, and new industrial plants. With so much time and resources put into economic projects, it is simply not tenable to argue that they do not want development.

The reasons for the obvious contrast between the government's commitments and accomplishments lie not in a lack of desire for economic growth, but in its economic priorities and mismanagement. The preoccupation with national security, particularly as it is conflated with maintenance of military control over power and resources, dictates economic policies and public investments, and greatly constrains growth. The military rulers not only appropriate the lion's share of government budgets for the armed forces and other security-related programs, but also shy away from any reforms that could disrupt military unity or social stability in the short term, whatever their economic rationale and long-term benefits. Traditional economic thinking is another major constraint. Although the post-1988 government has adopted the language and, to some extent, the form (laws and institutions) of a market-oriented economy, this shift was motivated more by economic necessity than by an intellectual endorsement of capitalism. Today's generals were tutored in the peculiar brand of socialism pursued under Ne Win and in many ways remain trapped in the thinking of that era. Many continue to believe that people and markets must be controlled to protect national interests. In addition, the conception of development among many military and civilian officials remains old-fashioned and simplistic, characterized by a focus on physical infrastructure and an excessive belief in the country's ability to develop based on its natural resources. Any real vision of a modern economy is widely lacking.[38]

It is certainly true that the prospects for economic development are dim under the current political and policy regime. Yet, many of the government's failures in the economic sphere (and elsewhere) are due less to a lack of desire for progress than to a peculiar mind-set and acute lack of capacity. This problem, unfortunately, is only deepened by Burma's continued isolation from international experiences and developments.

International Cooperation

Burma, traditionally, has shied away from international economic, political, and cultural exchanges. Every government since independence has adhered to a policy of self-reliance that under the Revolutionary Council became isolationism and economic autarky. Ne Win once asserted that "all of Burma's problems could be solved if the country were chiseled free of its Asian neighbors and floated out into the middle of the Bay of Bengal."[39] By closing Burma's borders, the early military governments sought to decrease the country's external vulnerability and ensure that it would develop on its own terms. The present leaders, however, have seen the consequences of three decades of isolation and understand, at least in principle, the necessity of opening up to the world. While military discourse still maintains that "the strength of the nation lies within," the twelve national objectives reveal a strong concern with international relations and a repositioning of Burma to exploit the benefits of globalization (while avoiding its potential pitfalls). As Khin Nyunt once stressed, "Myanmar does not wish to remain an island among other states. It wants to develop relations with its neighbors, the international community and international organisations."[40] Indeed, some officials envision Burma as a future mediator or "friendship bridge" between Southeast Asia, China, and India.[41]

There are clear pragmatic reasons why the government has revised the foreign policy of its predecessors. Already by the mid-1980s, it was obvious that Burma, despite its rich natural and human resource base, was unable to develop on its own. The level of state revenue and domestic savings was too low to support the investments necessary to propel the country onto a sustainable growth path. Although official development assistance from Japan, West Germany, and the international financial institutions kept the economy afloat in the face of growing domestic inefficiencies, there was an urgent need to attract foreign investment and expand exports. This, in turn, required a shift not only in economic policy, but in the overall positioning of the country in international affairs. Burma joined both the Association of Southeast Asian Nations (ASEAN) and the Bangladesh, India, Myanmar, Sri Lanka, and Thailand Economic Cooperation scheme (BIMSTEC) in 1997 and has acceded to their respective agreements on economic integration. The government has also signed a large number of bilateral economic agreements, including the Economic Cooperation Strategy (ECS) with Thailand, which involves an extensive list of Thai assistance projects, including plans for joint industrial and farming zones on the Burmese side of their common border.[42] Border trade with Thailand, China, India, and Bangladesh has been liberalized and is booming after the cessation of hostilities with most of the former insurgent groups who previously controlled the borders. In addition, there are plans underway for new infrastructure links with all of these countries, which over time looks likely to realize the government's vision of Burma becoming an important transportation hub for interregional trade, as well as a major source of energy for its neighbors.

As in other areas, it is easy to overestimate the degree of change in political attitudes and beliefs. The recent opening to the world is tempered by traditional suspicions of foreigners and fears of foreign influence, as well as by more personal character traits and values of the top leaders. Many military officers still equate external dependency with vulnerability to interference and exploitation. This, rather than any theory of economic development paths, probably explains the government's emphasis on agriculture and import substitution, which aims to ensure self-sufficiency in food and other strategic products. Meanwhile, many of the top generals remain hesitant to step onto the international stage. Even today, few have ever traveled outside of Asia. Burma's leaders are more likely to be found consulting an astrologer or practicing meditation than on shopping sprees overseas, although they are now keeping a tab on world affairs through satellite TV and the World Wide Web. Nonetheless, the break with past isolationist policies has been both dramatic and decisive. As much as the generals fear globalization and are trying to manage it, they have accepted the inevitability of embracing the world. There are likely to be setbacks along the way when old fears of foreign interference and exploitation are triggered, but the overall trend is toward increased international engagement. Forty years ago the Revolutionary Council closed the door to a region, which in many ways lagged behind Burma in development. By contrast, Southeast Asia today—despite the Asian economic crisis and sociopolitical unrest in some countries—is one of the most dynamic regions in the world and has much to offer. In the long run, the broader regional dynamics are likely to pull Burma along, even if the mindset of particular leaders may cause some delays. Indeed, this is one of the most powerful forces for change in the country today.

Constitutional Government

The political pillar of the government's national agenda is at the center of international controversy about Burma. It is therefore all the more important not to let our beliefs about what "ought to be" cloud our vision of what "is" or "could be." While the continued militarization of governance structures since 1988 could suggest a desire to maintain direct military rule, that is unlikely ever to have been the intention. Despite its long-standing hold on power, the Burmese military has never claimed a right for itself to rule the country, except as a transitional government. The self-image of the armed forces, engineered by Ne Win and his cohorts, is that of an institution "above politics," which intervenes only according to "national duty" and "historic necessity" to save the country. Although the present leadership, by trying to institutionalize a leading role for the military in politics, has taken a step further than its predecessors, the generals recognize that the general "mood" both within and outside the country is hostile to military rule and that any stable long-term political system must at least be nominally civilian. The question is how much civilian autonomy will be permitted.

The first chairman of SLORC, Senior General Saw Maung, initially seemed committed to allowing a democratic government to take office in accordance with the results of the 1990 election (much like his role model, Ne Win, had done after the caretaker government period in 1958–1960): "We have repeatedly said that in relation to the governing power, you can have it back after the elections in accordance with law. . . . Some people may say that the principal point is not the elections, but the constitution, and that power should be transferred to a temporary government while a new constitution is drawn up. As far as this is concerned, do as you please."[43] The overwhelming victory of the NLD, however, alarmed the military, and the commander-in-chief either reassessed the situation or was persuaded by other officers to revise the plan. Accordingly, two months after the election, which saw the NLD sweep 82 percent of the seats, the SLORC issued Order No. 1/90, limiting the role of the elected parliament to that of a constitutional assembly: "A political organisation does not automatically obtain the three sovereign powers—legislative, administrative, and judiciary—by the emergence of a people's assembly. These powers can be obtained based only on a constitution. . . . Therefore, in today's situation, the representatives elected by the people are responsible for drafting a constitution for the future democratic state."[44]

By January 1993, when the SLORC convened a National Convention to establish the principles for a new constitution, the role of the elected leaders had been further circumscribed. Most delegates were appointed by the government and the procedures of the convention were tailored to ensure that its deliberations and conclusions would not deviate from government guidelines.[45] Thus, the assembly quickly agreed on 104 basic principles, which remain the basis for the constitution that in early 2007 finally appears to be nearing completion, including stipulations that

- the president will be elected by an electoral college with strong military representation and will be required to have extensive experience in political, administrative, and economic, as well as *military affairs*;
- one-quarter of the seats in parliament, at both national and state level, will be military appointees nominated by the commander-in-chief;
- the ministers of defense, home affairs, and border areas will be military appointees nominated by the commander-in-chief;
- the armed forces will have complete institutional and budgetary autonomy; and
- the commander-in-chief will have statutory right to assume state power in a national emergency (defined as any danger to the main causes).

Subsequently, even the notion that parliament would prepare the final constitution has been dropped and the election results thus effectively annulled.[46]

The political transition, as the current military leaders envisage it, will institutionalize essential elements of previous military-controlled systems of government within a framework that they hope will be more acceptable to the people and the world. As Tin Maung Maung Than sums up,

> The president and the commander-in-chief of the armed forces, between them, wield considerable executive powers and all important executive positions at the national and provincial level are ultimately responsible to the president only. The political parties that win national and regional elections face a situation whereby the executive positions may be filled with personnel external to the body politic. Even when elected representatives are chosen to serve in the government they have to forego their party affiliations. It effectively de-links state power from political competition and representation of voting constituencies.[47]

The aim, which has changed little since the early 1990s, is to introduce a system of government that combines the form of democracy (notably regular elections, political parties, and a parliament) with continued executive control by the military and strict limitations on political and civil rights. This system, which military leaders have dubbed "disciplined democracy," supposedly has the advantage of being "in line with Burma's historical traditions, customs and culture" and "compatible with the political, economic and social structures of the state," while "bringing benefits fairly for all nationals within the framework of national security."[48] More to the point, perhaps, it constitutes a compromise between what the military leadership feels it needs to do to gain political legitimacy and what it deems necessary to protect military interests, including national security.

That said, the government's concern about being in line with global standards of governance, even if only in form, holds some prospect for gradual reform. Since both international and regional trends are toward more participatory government and greater respect for the rule of law and human rights, chances are that the Burmese military, too, will gradually—if grudgingly and apprehensively—allow a process of political liberalization, although for the foreseeable future not broader democratic reforms.

Military Attitudes and Beliefs

In order to understand the priorities of the military leaders and their reaction to competing visions of the future, it is necessary to consider their self-image and perceptions of other political actors. These images influence their evaluation of democracy and its likely implications for the country, and thus help explain their resistance to political reform.

Self-Image

Since the late 1950s, the Burmese military has explicitly defined its role and responsibilities in society to include not only defense but also internal security tasks, which in turn have been seen to call for political, social, and economic measures.[49] The three main causes and twelve national objectives constitute the latest phase in the military's ideological development and extend its role even further into the civilian realm than previously. Although this is not the place for a comprehensive analysis of military role perceptions, it is important to consider the "political orientation" of the current leaders (that is, the attitudes, values, and beliefs that predispose them toward a certain form of intervention in political life).

Crucially, the Burmese military was never an apolitical institution. Although the legacy of British colonial rule was evident in the 1947 constitution, which established a parliamentary democracy, the armed forces were not significantly influenced by the standards and ideas of British military "professionalism."[50] On the contrary, the outbreak of multiple insurgencies immediately after independence made the civilian government dependent on the army, which came to enjoy considerable autonomy during the 1950s as it took charge of important state-building tasks, especially in remote areas of the country.[51] These experiences, coupled with the perceived success of the military caretaker government that governed the country for eighteen months from 1958 to 1960, set the stage for the 1962 military coup and subsequent attempts to resurrect central state control under military leadership that continue today. Current military ideologists describe the military as the "father and mother" of the Burmese people[52]—or in a more political formulation, "a neutral institution, a sort of UN organisation in its own country."[53] The military, in other words, is perceived to be "above" popular organizations, including political parties; it is viewed as the overseer and final arbiter of political life, bound by duty to guide the people and regulate their behavior.

The claim to "military supremacy" is based on the political experience of the armed forces, as well as their broader characteristics and achievements. As one government publication notes, "Since Myanmar began its struggle for freedom, the *Tatmadaw* has been the most important organisation. . . . The Tatmadaw has performed not only military duties, but also political duties uniting political elements and organising the masses of the people. . . . The political experience of the Tatmadaw that has stood firm for fifty years is much greater than the political experience of the political parties."[54] This is, of course, a truism since military governments since 1962 have denied independent political parties and civil society organizations any space to function. Still, it is significant for the military's political orientation that senior military officers, in or out of uniform, have been at the helm of the independent Union of Burma for forty-seven of its fifty-nine years' existence, while lower-ranking officers have served in prominent positions throughout the civilian bureaucracy or have had similar extragovernmental roles.

The military leaders did initially adhere to the ideal of civilian supremacy and have always appeared somewhat uncertain about their role as governors. Thus, military governments have traditionally sought refuge in law,[55] while seeking further legitimacy in the achievements of the armed forces in service of the state. During the socialist period, the military's performance claims focused primarily on the role of the Burma Independence Army in the national independence struggle and its lineage with Burma's national hero, General Aung San, who is considered the father of both the military and the modern Burmese state. Since 1988, with a new generation of officers in charge who joined the army after independence, there has been a shift in focus from the military's role in *establishing* the state to its role in *protecting* it. Particular attention is paid to "four political crises" (in 1948–1949, 1958, 1962, and 1988), each of which purportedly presented a grave threat to the survival of the union that was averted only by the intervention of the military. As General Khin Nyunt stressed in his first speech as prime minister in 2003, "A careful analysis of the events of 1988 will show that . . . As the group who was making demonstrations and launching struggles and demands with the aim of getting political gain and the people who were waiting for an opportunity to loot and destroy combined to form the majority, anarchism reigned over the nation and the Union was on the verge of disintegration. The people were facing untold hardship and difficulties and the Tatmadaw which has the responsibility for national defense and security of the nation had to assume state responsibilities."[56] The military hierarchy also takes great pride in the post-1988 cease-fires, which supposedly have brought seventeen and a half out of eighteen insurgent groups into "the legal fold" and established a degree of peace unprecedented in modern Burmese history: "Now that mutual confidence, respect and understanding has been built and regional stability and tranquillity have been achieved, . . . the people are beginning to enjoy the pleasures of a normal war-free life hitherto unknown in the period after regaining independence. . . . The change of heart exhibited by the armed groups and their return to the legal fold is an unprecedented and spectacular accomplishment for internal peace known only during the time of the SLORC leadership."[57]

With reference to the military's achievements and in light of the perceived behavior of other domestic actors to be discussed below, military leaders stake a special claim to patriotism. Official speeches, publications, and exhibitions project the image of soldiers selflessly risking their lives and limbs to serve the country and the national interest: "Our Tatmadaw was the one who fought against the neo-colonialists with weapons they could get hold of when the people could not stand anymore of their cruelties and abuses. . . . Our Tatmadaw men are the ones who didn't expect any privileges, salary, ration, or a uniform. They endured great hardship and lived with many shortages."[58]

In sum, successive generations of military officers have nurtured the belief that the army won Burma's freedom and has protected the union against centrifugal forces threatening to undermine its independence and sovereignty. They have developed a self-image as the "creators" and "saviors" of the modern Burmese state, maintaining their right and duty to play a leading role in its affairs, political and otherwise, rather than simply acting as servants of the government. Governance is perceived as an integral part of the military's professional responsibilities and current leaders are jealously protecting an assumed entitlement, if not necessarily to dominate politics to the extent seen since 1988, then at least to define the acceptable framework for national politics and policies.[59]

Perceptions of "Others"

The military leadership's insistence on maintaining political control is reinforced by a deep distrust of other actors, including politicians, ethnic nationalists, foreigners, and the people at large, all of whom are commonly criticized for acting against Burma's national interest.

Politicians

The disdain of military officers for civilian politicians is rooted in the historical record of parliamentary politics in the 1950s, which suffered from factionalism and opportunistic struggles for personal power and the spoils of office, causing several damaging splits in the ruling Anti-Fascist People's Freedom League.[60] Such sentiments were evident already in 1958, when General Ne Win blamed the political leadership for having brought the country to the brink of disintegration, thus necessitating the establishment of his caretaker government:

> The effects of the political split spread throughout the country like a rampaging forest fire. . . . Former close colleagues and comrades became deadly enemies. . . . The split led to a large increase in the activities of those elements who flout and violate the constitution of the Union of Burma. . . . The government machinery also deteriorated to its present weak position. . . . The political pillar was collapsing. It was imperative that the Union should not drown in shallow waters as it almost did in 1948–49. So it fell on the armed forces to perform their bounden duty to take all security measures to forestall and prevent a recurrence.[61]

Four years later, the Revolutionary Council gave similar justifications for the 1962 coup that ended the period of parliamentary democracy. In particular, the new military rulers blamed the U Nu government for seeking political popularity over national stability in making Buddhism the state religion, and for being "soft" on growing demands for federalism.[62] Whether this was the primary motivation for the coup is contested, but the constant repetition of such criticism over time in military publications and internal propaganda material has ensured that the military's institutional memory of civilian government remains overwhelmingly negative.[63]

Military officers blame civilian politicians for being concerned only with gaining power and promoting party interests. Such narrow concerns, they argue, are evident in the methods of the NLD, which alledgedly defies the authorities and collaborates with insurgent groups and foreign governments, thus undermining the government's efforts to unify the country: "Whenever they have the opportunity, they oppose, attack, denounce and condemn. How can you create grounds where we can stand together. . . . We had a vision we could start our economy moving with tourism, so we put in a lot of effort and money preparing for that. Then they had a campaign not to visit Myanmar. . . . The people have come to understand the real motive of the NLD: just for power, not for the nation-building process."[64] This kind of "party politics" is contrasted with the "national politics" of the armed forces, which ostensibly work to achieve the aspirations of the whole nation: "The Tatmadaw represents no political ideology. It does not represent any particular class of people, any particular national group, or any particular territory. It represents . . . the whole of Myanmar."[65] In short, politicians are seen to lack the patriotism and unity of the military and therefore to be ill suited to manage the multitude of internal and external threats facing the nation.

Ethnic Nationalists

Although military leaders promote the armed forces as a model of national unity, it is in reality an overwhelmingly Burman institution. Since a purge of high-ranking Karen officers in the early 1950s, following the desertion of large numbers of Karen soldiers to the Karen National Union (KNU), the leadership has been almost purely Burman. There are today only a few non-Burman officers with rank above major and none of them are in command positions.[66] This reflects—and at the same time reinforces—an "us" (Burman) versus "them" (non-Burman) mind-set within the armed forces.

Military ethnocentrism is rooted in the era of British colonial rule, but was reinforced by interethnic clashes during the Second World War and more than half a century of civil war. Many Burmans resented the special relationship that developed between the British and ethnic minorities, notably the Karens, Kachins, and Chins, many of whom converted to Christianity and were favored for positions in the colonial army and bureaucracy. As Martin Smith notes,

> Ethnic assertiveness and the expression of ethnic minority views became equated with the divisions of colonial rule. "In order to separate them culturally from the Burmese," claimed U Ba Shwe, president of the Socialist Party and prime minister of Burma (1956/57), "they converted the Karens to their religion and also created a separate literature and privileges for them." This distrust was fuelled by the Karen role in the colonial army and has until today prevented an

> objective assessment of any ethnic minority cause, including the Buddhist Shans and Mons. In harking back to the colonial experience, ethnic nationalists are regarded as stooges and separatists whom it is automatically presumed are being instigated by some foreign power (such as the U.S., China or Thailand). Even in 1987, . . . the state-controlled press was still accusing the KNU of simply "invoking their old owner-masters and craving for colonial servitude, yearning for their distant relative over and above their own mother."[67]

When the Japanese invaded in 1942, several ethnic groups remained loyal to the British and became embroiled in battles with the Burma Independence Army, which collaborated with the Imperial Army. Following independence, unresolved issues of minority rights within the new union sparked numerous ethnic rebellions, which as noted earlier have wrought havoc on the country and have yet to be resolved.[68] Most major ethnic insurgent groups over the course of their long struggle have sought and received foreign support, thus provoking a conflation of ethnic nationalism and state nationalism within the armed forces. Military officers, who have spent their formative years fighting insurgents in the jungle and have seen friends die on the battlefield, are imbued with a strong distrust or even hatred of ethnic nationalists. In the words of one officer, "The KNU would only be too ready to betray the nation as opportunity occurs. Insurgents with such a gene and such a behavioral pattern are ideologists to the bone who would never surrender their objectives."[69] These attitudes go a long way toward explaining the military's insistence on maintaining a unitary state in the face of minority demands for autonomy.[70]

Ten to fifteen years with cease-fires and mutual cooperation, to some degree, have helped improve understanding between the military and armed ethnic groups. The changes, however, were mainly at an individual rather than institutional level, and were limited largely to a small group of military intelligence officers who until recently were in charge of managing relations with the cease-fire groups. The fragility of this situation became evident after the purge of General Khin Nyunt and his coterie of military intelligence personnel in October 2004, which created significant anxiety among cease-fire leaders who did not know or trust the army commanders who replaced them.[71]

Foreigners

The military's perception of foreigners is obscured by the gap between the scathing denunciations in official speeches and the state-controlled press of the "evil machinations" of foreigners who want to "divide the country" and "exploit the people," and the reception of individual foreigners who are normally treated with courtesy. Underneath these contrasting images, however, lies a deep and enduring suspicion among insular army commanders of the motives of foreigners in general and Westerners in particular,[72] which—like the suspicion of politicians and ethnic nationalists—is rooted in factual events, experienced and interpreted by fallible human beings.

The founders of the modern Burmese armed forces, like most Burman elites, were deeply humiliated by the political disenfranchisement, economic exploitation, and social discrimination under British rule, which created a strong backlash against foreign ways and influences and left a collective psychological scar.[73] This set the tone for the development of a peculiarly virulent form of military nationalism, which over the years has been reinforced by the continued insecurity of the modern Burmese state and long-standing isolation of the officer corps from the outside world.

When the British departed Burma in 1948, they left behind a country with a weak government, a fractious society, and an acute sense of strategic vulnerability. Then prime minister U Nu famously said, "Take a glance at our geographical position—Thailand in the East, China in the North, India in the West, and stretching southward, Malaya, Singapore and so on. We are hemmed in like a tender gourd among the cactus."[74] While the government's immediate attention during the 1950s was directed at quelling the ethnic and communist rebellions, which threatened to overwhelm the new state, the threat from these internal challenges was thus usually defined in terms of their external linkages. Not only did organizations like the Communist Party of Burma (CPB) and the KNU receive direct support from the outside, but domestic conflict raised the specter of direct foreign intervention and a possible breakup of the Union. The military coup of 1962 and Burma's subsequent withdrawal from the world constituted, at least partly, an attempt by nationalistic military leaders to take control of their own destiny and protect Burmese sovereignty and national identity.

Twenty-six years of isolation, from 1962 to 1988, reinforced military nationalism and suspicions as Burma's rulers became increasingly alienated from the outside world and uncomfortable about dealing with foreigners. Few military officers traveled abroad and access to foreign views on Burma was greatly restricted by limitations on the import of foreign news and analysis of a critical nature. State officials were even discouraged from interacting socially with foreigners inside Burma.[75] This situation has changed since 1988 with Burma's opening to the outside world. But many military officers still have very limited international exposure; most are educated at home, speak only Burmese, and rarely travel abroad. The alienation of earlier eras is thus sustained and remains an important psychological obstacle to rational assessments of foreigners and international relations.

There are strong indications that the international campaign for democracy and human rights, coupled with the continued failure of the military to forge a stable and prosperous nation, has reinforced this siege mentality. As Senior General Than Shwe once lamented: "In view of the changed geo-political situation following the end of the Cold War, Myanmar has gained more strategic importance. Thus, [Western nations] are now exerting political, economic, diplomatic and social pressures against our government in order to bring about a change so that there would be an administration in Myanmar that would be more amenable to them."[76] From this perspective, even actions of individuals are seen as part of a conspiracy to soil Burma's reputation and undermine the efforts of the government to build a "modern, developed and prosperous nation." In 2001, for example, a *New York Times* article on Burma's HIV/AIDS epidemic elicited a vehement official denial: "It is evident that the data were fabricated. . . . These false allegations are politically motivated and the objective is to defame the government and the people of Myanmar."[77]

It seems probable that the purported "evil mechanizations" of foreigners are exaggerated for strategic purposes, to rally the people—and, particularly, the soldiers—around a nationalistic leadership and justify continued military control of the state. Military fears of the world, however, have regularly manifested themselves in observable behavior. Not only did the arrival of a U.S. Navy vessel in Burmese waters during the 1988 uprising, as noted earlier, cause fear in the War Office of an imminent invasion, but three years later, at the height of the first Gulf War, antiaircraft guns were put up around Rangoon, suggesting that military leaders feared a subsequent attack on Burma.[78] Similar fears appear to have been behind strong Burmese denouncements of subsequent international interventions in Haiti, Kosovo, and East Timor. When asked, in an interview in 1999, about NATO action in Kosovo, Foreign Minister Win Aung explained,

> We deeply deplored it. We do not want this action to be seen as a sort of international precedent for action in other areas too. *You fear interference in Myanmar?* Yes. In the past, because of our very strategic location, we were annexed by the British. Then in the Second World War, the Japanese wanted Myanmar under their control. Even during the Cold War, we suffered—with the Chinese KMT forces, and so on.[79]

Such reactions, coupled with the consistency in military rhetoric over five decades, indicate the existence of a fundamental psychological distortion bordering on paranoia.

"The People"

The concept of "the people" is central to Burmese military discourse and self-perceptions. The army is traditionally defined as a "people's army," military doctrine revolves around the concept of "people's war," and the government claims to be acting in accordance with "the people's desires." This positioning of the military as the vanguard of the people is rooted in the ideas of General Aung San and the mythology of the independence struggle and has been carefully nurtured by subsequent military leaders. In the words of one military writer, "The Tatmadaw and the mass of the people revolted against the fascist Japanese under the leadership of the Anti-Fascist People's Freedom League. . . . The Tatmadaw forged a monolithic unity with the people in the course of the anti-fascist resistance. The Tatmadaw began to get the full support of the people and thus became the People's Tatmadaw."[80]

Yet, even if discursively the armed forces and the people are conflated, in reality, military attitudes toward the general population are exclusive. In tracing the beliefs underlying monarchical Buddhism and socialism in Burma, Robert Taylor points out that the country's political leaders traditionally have assumed "humanity's natural egotism and greed." Thus, they have tried to "reorient the views of the people in order to eradicate fraudulent practices, profit motive, easy living, parasitism, shirking and selfishness."[81] Such views are evident, too, among current military leaders, who frequently lament the failure of business to eschew vested interests and work for the benefit of the country:

> There were allegations against us that we forcibly purchased paddy [at below market prices]. . . . You think that if the private traders buy, the price will be higher? The private traders are preparing to fleece the farmers.[82]

> When the government increased salaries in 1989, private businessmen immediately raised prices. Only the few government shops maintained prices. So who is responsible for inflation?[83]

The general population is perceived, too, as ignorant of its own interests and easily manipulated by demagogues. According to a recent historical account, the defeat of the Stable AFPFL (the faction of the Anti-Fascist People's Freedom League favored by the military) in the 1960 election was due to a lack of political consciousness among the voters: "They were not yet capable of ignoring their immediate inconvenience for the sake of long-term benefits. They were apt to favor indulgent politicians over constructive politicians."[84] Thus, it is claimed that "democracy succeeds better in a country where the people are well-trained in democratic practices and where a majority of people are politically enlightened. People in those countries do not allow themselves to be turned into stooges of politicians . . . they do not fight among themselves as incited and instigated by politicians."[85] The last president of Burma, Dr. Maung Maung, a widely respected civilian lawyer, similarly blamed self-interested political leaders for manipulating the grievances of a long-suffering population for their own ends during the 1988 uprising:

> Here we were trying to organise the transition, every day, every week a step forward by constitutional means, and to end the rule of the BSPP; and there they were trying to get the people to wreck those very steps. The people did not know what was happening, what we were doing, but those self-appointed leaders did. When news of the party congress and its resolutions was announced the people were happy, and demonstrators went home . . . an ex-colonel who was around intervened to say, "No, no, the demonstrations must go on, for an interim government must be formed first." . . . I could only smile, for the ex-colonel whom I happened to know well, was one of those who had nominated themselves for an interim government.[86]

In this way, popular challenges to military rule are put down to misunderstandings by well-meaning but simple people, who do not know any better, and the idea of the people's army is upheld.

Underlying these views is a Hobbesian notion of the anarchic society. According to John Badgley, "U Ne Win once saw Burmese citizens as naturally born to freedom, but gradually came to perceive his people as a threatening mass, incapable of self-government. . . . Thereafter, he governed harshly to save his people from themselves."[87] Current military leaders share these sentiments. More specifically, their attitudes reflect traditional elitist views of the people as an unruly mob, ignorant of their own best interests and thus in need of strong, paternalistic leadership.

Many of the military's attitudes and beliefs are deep-seated and not without some historical basis; others are more ephemeral and based on self-serving interpretations of the past. Either way, they greatly influence objectives and priorities. As Robert Taylor notes, "In this understanding of Burma's political history, the army sees itself as the sole opponent to various enemies of the state since independence—imperialists, communists, secessionists—in the face of the venality and self-seeking of civilian politicians."[88] Democracy is viewed as inherently divisive and parochial, a luxury the country can ill afford, at least while stability and development remain fragile.

Military Prisms

Critics of the the military generally reject its arguments for continued military rule as purely self-serving, and surely there is self-interest involved. Yet we must also consider how the military leaders perceive reality. In English language usage, the term *reality* has acquired a singular quality; we equate *reality* with *fact* and tend to reject presentations of it that deviate from our own as false. Since the reality presented by Burma's rulers in speeches, historical publications, and private talks generally contradicts our own perceptions of the situation, they must—so the reasoning works—be trying to deceive us. But reality is subjective. How we perceive events as they unfold around us is grounded in selectively remembered experiences, filtered by our fundamental values and beliefs, as well as current interests, and strongly influenced by the group we belong to. Each of these factors constitutes a prism through which we look at the world. In other words, perceptions of Burma's present realities, problems, and solutions will genuinely differ among different groups and individuals, including the military leaders, their opponents, and, of course, external observers. In order to understand the military, we need to understand its prisms.

History

The military leaders' perspective is based, first and foremost, on a deeply historical understanding of the country, its politics and national interests. As the late senior general Saw Maung said,

> I base myself upon history when I say things. I study past historical facts. . . . The affairs of the state, which took place in the past, can be forgiven if one wishes to. But we must draw the appropriate lessons from them so that such a thing does not take place in the future. . . . I talk about the lessons of the past in connection with what is to be done in the future so that those who have no experience will come to know and so that they will do what should be done and they will not do what should not be done.[89]

A keen awareness of the past is reflected in the commitment by successive generations of military leaders to the writing of military and political history, starting with *The Origins of the Revolution*, published in 1962, and culminating in a series of volumes produced by the Committee for the Compilation of Authentic Facts, which was set up in 1989 by Senior General Saw Maung to write a "concise history of Burma and the military's role."[90] Critics see these works simply as attempts to rewrite the past to justify military leadership. Yet, whatever its origins and purposes, the project of historiography has a life of its own and reflects as well as influences the way the military perceives reality. For decades, selective lessons from the past have been inculcated in the officer corps in a deliberate attempt to unite the armed forces around a particular vision of the future. Such lessons feed and reinforce the attitudes of susceptible soldiers, providing them with arguments to support perhaps previously unconsciously held images. It also provides them with a powerful justification for seeing things they want to see. We know that this is how they talk about things; it does not require a great leap of faith to assume that it also has become the way they think about them.

The importance of the past to the military leaders is perhaps most evident in the strong continuities in military strategy. While the current government has taken care to present itself as distinct from previous military governments and committed to rectifying their failures, it often appears largely to be reenacting the strategies of its predecessors. When the SLORC first took power in 1988, it emulated many of the policies of the caretaker government (1958–1960), including the relocation of squatters to the outskirts of the main cities and extensive urban beautification programs. The ongoing attempts to create an ideological and constitutional basis for continued military leadership, in turn, have close parallels to the record of the Revolutionary Council, which in 1962 launched the Burmese Way to Socialism to justify its rule and twelve years later sought to institutionalize it through a new socialist constitution. Major initiatives, such as the attempt to mobilize the population in support of military goals through state-sponsored mass organizations and to control the economy by taking over large sections of the private economy, also echo earlier efforts. Thus, while the military leaders blame politicians, ethnic nationalists, and foreigners for the "sins of their fathers," they seem unable themselves to break the links to the past.

There is, of course, nothing unusual about the past influencing current perceptions. This prism, however, is particularly powerful in the case of the Burmese military, whose top leaders personally have taken part in episodes of great significance for Burma's development as a state. Ne Win, who died just a few years ago and has had more influence on military thinking than any other individual, was one of the thirty comrades who formed the nucleus of the Burma Independence Army that fought for independence. The current chairman and vice-chairman of the SPDC, Senior General Than Shwe and Vice-Senior General Maung Aye, in turn, were both commissioned in the 1950s and spent their formative years in the jungle fighting communist and ethnic insurgents. Such personal experiences have had strong influence on the attitudes and beliefs of the top leadership. More generally, as argued above, the identity of the armed forces as an institution is anchored in its role in the national liberation struggle and the earliest years of independence. This, coupled with a belief in the uniqueness of Burma and the absence of wider experience and knowledge of the world, has encouraged military ideologists and strategists to delve into the past—rather than look abroad—to explain current problems and identify possible solutions.[91]

Military Values

Military values constitute another powerful prism. Militaries around the world operate according to principles that differ from those found in the democratic political realm. Studies of military institutions identify a special "military mind," generally seen to encompass features such as nationalism, conservatism, rigidity of thought, and close-mindedness to societal and international affairs, as well as a preoccupation with hierarchy and order and a tendency to influence human behavior by restriction and punishment.[92] The values and principles of this mind-set are rooted in the particular needs of an institution responsible for conducting wars. Yet in Burma, as elsewhere, military leaders upon taking power have continued to do what they know best: centralizing power, eliminating pluralism, and generally emphasizing action over dialogue. These methods of leadership not only provide the framework for military governance, but also become criteria for assessing the needs of society and the behavior of other actors.

Senior Burmese officers draw a clear distinction between "military" and "political" methods. The late senior general Saw Maung, for example, made no excuses about his military approach to governance, which he saw as superior to "politics":

> The military science which we are well versed in is higher than political science. . . . I have said that I will not do politics. . . . The SLORC is not a party organization. It is the government of the country carrying out administrative work. . . . I want to reiterate that we will not tolerate any organization or individual if it is against us. . . . They [the political parties] do not do what they have to do. They ask for a time frame. This is a demanding process. Don't do that. Do what you have to do till you finish it.[93]

Similar views are expressed in recent historical writings by the military on the caretaker government (1958–1960): "The Tatmadaw Caretaker Government was not a political government, not made up of any politicians and therefore . . . was able to pursue a correct and straight administrative policy. It did not have to pander to the whims and fancies of voters and was therefore capable of taking sharp and resolute action that would really serve the interests of the majority of the people."[94]

In practice, the application of military principles is evident in the centralization of power and establishment of a clear hierarchical command structure, which radiates outward from the Ministry of Defense in the capital to most areas of the country, as well as into most spheres of the administration and the economy. The core of this system is a hierarchy of state/division, district, township, and ward/village Peace and Development Councils, which control the administration at their respective levels. The placement of military officers in key positions throughout the civil service and in state economic enterprises serves similar purposes, as do the large investments in military holding companies, military universities, and military hospitals, at the expense of the civilian sector. Unlike civilians, military officers can be relied upon to follow commands without questioning. By expanding the military state within the state—to the extent that the two almost have become synonymous—the generals seek not only to control, but also to improve administrative unity and efficiency. Political parties, ethnic minority organizations, and other nongovernmental actors, in turn, are exhorted to fulfill the roles assigned to them by the state. Failure to follow directions is perceived as disobedience and any form of criticism viewed as confrontation.

The emphasis on firm, top-down leadership reflects an obsession with control, but also a fundamental rejection of the principles of representative government and popular participation. Burma's rulers, generally, do not appreciate that debate and compromises among groups representing different interests lie at the heart of a sound policy process. On the contrary, they equate debate with inefficiency and see the participatory and decentralizing aspects of the democratic process as a threat to hierarchy and order. As one lieutenant colonel complained in 1994, "If we want to get the work done in the future under a parliamentary government, there will be a lot of problems with bureaucracy and we will have to do everything step by step. If we have a parliament they will have to discuss it, and make contracts and so on."[95] Such views go at least some way toward explaining the military's disdain for politicians, as well as its adoption of the concept of "principled democracy," which denotes an imposition of order on the political process. Similar notions underlie its fear of a freewheeling private sector and reluctance to relinquish state control of the economy.

Group Norms

Each of the prisms discussed here functions within, and is amplified by, the social setting in which military officers live and work. Political education classes ensure that the "military perspective" is inculcated into aspiring officers from their first day in the armed forces, and deviating views or behavior are often punished.[96] Andrew Selth notes, "The military leadership harbors deep-seated fears that the armed forces will once again be driven by serious internal dissension, possibly causing the military government to fall. This profound insecurity is reflected in the curricula of all the Tatmadaw's training institutions, which are seen as critical to bringing all members of the armed forces 'into line with its ideological orientation,' the better to 'cement its grip on state and society.'"[97] In an environment of intense rivalry, where mutual trust is lacking and military intelligence is omnipresent, even high-ranking generals are vulnerable to "excommunication."[98] Critical views are therefore rarely expressed, if entertained at all.

At a more basic and often unconscious level, socialization is driven by social comparison and shared experiences. As social animals, human beings are extremely aware of group expectations as to what is appropriate behavior. Attitudes, values, beliefs, and behavior therefore tend to converge toward group norms, particularly within groups with a high level of exclusive intragroup interaction. This dynamic is strong in most militaries, since soldiers live and work closely together for extended periods of time, often away from their families and civilian friends. In Burma, it has been further strengthened by a strong sense of group accomplishment and the need to "stick together" in a hostile environment, as well as by the physical and psychological isolation of the officer corps. Although Burma's links with the outside world are slowly being renewed, this has yet to affect more than a small number of international "liaison" officers. Meanwhile, high-ranking officers have come to constitute a privileged "caste" within their own country, living apart from the rest of society, separated not only by the barbed wire around military compounds but also by socioeconomic inequalities and mutual fear and distrust, which have created a strong insider/outsider mentality. The officer corps at large has limited exposure to alternative views and values. It is therefore particularly susceptible to internal socialization processes and emulation of dominant views and accompanying stereotypes.

The importance of these socialization processes is hard to overemphasize. The strength of internal propaganda and continuance of internal and external threats to the state, real and perceived, coupled with the isolation of the officer corps, serve to integrate political attitudes and militate against significant changes in group outlook. Younger officers are in both an intellectual and cultural sense descendants of the first generation of military leaders who set the tone for the ideological development of the armed forces. They have inherited the historical lessons of their predecessors and share many of the attitudes, values, and beliefs associated with those lessons. This is not to suggest that everyone in the military thinks alike or that the military perspective will forever remain the same, only that there are strong impediments to change. Perceptions, though not unrelated to facts, generally linger long after objective realities have shifted.

Vested Interests

The relative impact of perceived national responsibilities and vested interests on government policy is difficult to assess since they tend to coincide. Yet, generally speaking, the perceived need for military leadership and suppression of autonomous political activity appear to be *reinforced* by corporate and personal interests rather than *dictated* by them.[99] While maintaining power is certainly a core aim of the military leadership, this is linked to a broader national agenda and perception of the threats facing the nation they have sworn to defend and with which their personal lives and careers are inextricably linked. The Burmese military regime does not primarily serve a supreme leader or royal family, or even a social class like the apartheid regime in South Africa. Military privileges are significant, at least for the highest ranking officers, but members of the military are drawn from all segments of society. Few of the current military leaders come from a privileged background, nor do many of their sons and daughters seem to be entering the military. On the contrary, the strident nationalism and threat perceptions of the regime have often seen it act in ways detrimental to the personal welfare of its members. A case in point is the regime's restrictions on foreign investment and aid, which in most other countries are welcomed by authoritarian (and democratic) leaders as a major source of personal wealth.

That said, Burma's military leaders have strong corporate and personal interests in a continuance of essential features of the present system. After almost a half century of military rule, the military as an institution is geared both ideologically and structurally toward government responsibility. It has grown accustomed to dominating all other power structures in the country and having full decision-making and budgetary autonomy in the pursuit of its goals. The economic and social stakes of individual officers in the present system are also considerable. The upper echelons of the military have long constituted a privileged upper class in Burmese society, with superior access to everything from consumer products to education and health care. Such privileges have been further extended since 1988, which has seen a substantial increase in economic opportunities for those who control the state (opportunities linked, mainly, to new foreign direct investment and development of the country's rich natural resources). Most importantly, perhaps, high-level officers fear being persecuted for decades of human rights violations should they lose the protective shield provided by absolute power.[100] Although Aung San Suu Kyi has tried to weaken the specter of retaliation by emphasizing the value of forgiveness,[101] in the early 1990s there were repeated demands from more militant members of the opposition for the responsible officers to be brought before human rights tribunals or tried by the international community in absentia.[102] It seems inevitable that such fears would have been reinforced by international developments, such as the establishment of the International Court of Justice, and actions taken against former dictators such as Chile's General Pinochet, Indonesia's President Soeharto, or Serbia's Prime Minister Milosovic, not to mention the recent referral of Burma to the international courts on the issue of forced labor. What is at stake is no less than a way of life, a threat that is bound to invoke very powerful defense mechanisms, even if it is not the only—or even the primary—determinant of government policy.

Diverging Perspectives

The claim is not made here that all members of the military elite (not to speak of the rank-and-file) share the "military" mind-set to the same extent. There are officers who are more restrained in their fear of external subversion and perceive the intimate links between national security, economic development, and more responsive and participatory government. Several military officials, in talks with this author and others, have indicated a certain empathy with Aung San Suu Kyi or even expressed support for a power-sharing arrangement between the military and the NLD.[103] Some have gone out on a limb to facilitate cooperation with international human rights and development agencies. There are also significant differences between military officers, often commented on by businessmen, when it comes to rent-seeking and broader personal behavior.[104] These divergences within the military hierarchy are multiplied when considering the broader government structure, which represents a broad cross-section of Burmese society, including ardent military loyalists, NLD sympathizers, and highly skilled technocrats committed to public service. Yet, by and large, in a system that places extreme value on unity and conformity, the most powerful leaders—and often the most hard-line views—set the standard. Others play along with the illusion for strategic purposes, or simply to survive.

The most prominent example of diverging views within the top military leadership, which significantly affected the collective behavior of the regime, was the emergence in the 1990s of a parallel authority structure (or at least influential substructure) linked to Khin Nyunt. The former head of military intelligence and short-term prime minister showed a rare willingness to engage with other political forces, although without abandoning the insistence on military leadership or compromising on the core values of national sovereignty, unity, and stability. Working closely with a coterie of high-ranking military intelligence officers, Khin Nyunt was the point man in negotiating the cease-fires with former insurgent groups, as well as in the sporadic talks with Aung San Suu Kyi. He also made significant efforts, helped by a number of internationally savvy ministers and Burmese ambassadors overseas, to improve relations with the outside world, primarily by trying to accommodate selective human rights concerns. Until they were purged in October 2004, Khin Nyunt and his associates were a distinct and competent voice within the military hierarchy, with a prominent role in many aspects of government affairs, although excluding economic policy. While it is hard to say how far they were prepared to go down the reform path, they represented an emerging separation between the military-as-government and the military-as-institution, which held out the promise at least of better governance. Indeed, several governments in the region had high hopes that they would take Burma in new directions and were purposefully cultivating relationships with them at the expense of other parts of the military and government hierarchy.

With Khin Nyunt gone and the entire military intelligence and related structures revamped, speculation on diverging views and possible openings for reform are centering on the next generation of military leaders. Although they have been, and remain, subject to strong socialization and pressures for conformity, their career experiences are different from those of the current leadership. They have had much less combat; they are educated at improved military academies, all having university degrees; and they have spent a significant part of their lives and careers in the very different post-1988 environment in which contacts with the outside world have greatly expanded, if not always for them personally then certainly in the government and society at large. Mary Callahan suggests that the younger generations may be less committed to the nationalist ideals of their predecessors and more concerned about personal power and privileges.[105] Yet, this—together with their growing awareness of the development gap between Burma and its neighbors—may make them more flexible, at least in dealing with economic issues. Personal interests, as seen elsewhere in the region, can be fulfilled through other means than government office.

How this generational gap will play out is a question that can be answered only by time. None of the future leaders will "show their hand" until they reach the top and have consolidated their power base, and all will be concerned to maintain internal military unity. Some of those slated to take over leadership of the armed forces are said, however, to be supporters of Khin Nyunt's approach,[106] and have shown indications of a similar pragmatism in dealing with international and economic issues in particular (even if their influence remains limited for the time being).

The Bottom Line

The national priority of the military government is to establish a stable political order that safeguards national security, while facilitating the development of a modern, developed nation on par with its successful neighbors. While closely interrelated, these objectives, however, form a loose hierarchy that helps explain the regime's policies and resource allocation. Constituting indivisible aspects of its national security ideology, the three main causes—national sovereignty, territorial integrity, and national unity—effectively dictate government priorities. Other objectives are assessed in terms of their impact on these core values. In case of perceived trade-offs, the latter takes precedence.

This prioritization, and the methods and policies applied, correspond closely with the corporate and individual interests of the military hierarchy, which, by insisting on maintaining power, is also protecting its autonomy and very significant personal material privileges. Yet, by reducing the military's program to a personal grab for power, its opponents miss important elements of the subjective basis for military rule. Many military officers do perceive democracy as a recipe for political instability and prescribe continued, though more effectively applied, centralization of state power under military leadership to overcome years of disunity and induce people to work for the benefit of the country. While the opposition argues that the problems and centrifugal tendencies of the past—from political factionalism to ethnic nationalism and imperialism—have declined or at least can be solved by enlightened democratic government, the generals believe they exist in undiluted form, only held in check by firm military leadership. Thus, they continue to see themselves as defenders of the national interest against inept and unruly politicians who allegedly care only about the narrow interests of their parties and constituencies.

The military's self-image is rooted in the past, in a time when militaries were indeed perceived by many, including in the West, as progressive institutions, and their role in cleaning up after inept and corrupt civilian governments was widely accepted. More specifically, the military leaders' perception of reality is shaped by the historical experience of Burma and the problems, actual and perceived, that they have faced since independence. These images do not remain unchanging, and the growing discord between the military's essentially insular perspective and changes in the world around them, which are increasingly impacting developments within the country, is likely to drive a broadening and diversification of outlooks. This was evident with Khin Nyunt and his coterie of military intelligence officers who were at the front line of managing Burma's relations with the outside world and, over time, adjusted their views of foreigners and the challenges facing Burma, thus facilitating a period of surprisingly close cooperation with international actors on sensitive issues. For the time being, however, conservatism remains the dominant value and should be taken at face value. We may feel that the military leaders hold socially deviant values, or that their fears regarding political reform are unjustified. Yet, like many leaders who believe they have a higher purpose, they are largely impervious to criticism and do not expect nonbelievers—foreigners in particular—to understand.

Meanwhile, Western governments should not overlook the military's broader development agenda, which—however weakly and ineffectively implemented—does provide significant areas of converging interests between the regime and its domestic opponents, as well as the international community. Indeed, as will be argued later, this may provide a better framework for national reconciliation and social progress than the assumption of a zero-sum struggle for power that underlies existing confrontational strategies.

Notes

1. Than Shwe, speech on Armed Forces Day, 1996, quoted in Martin Smith, "Army Politics as a Historical Legacy," in *Political Armies: The Military and Nation Building in the Age of Democracy*, ed. Kees Koonings and Dirk Kruijt (London: Zed Books, 2002).

2. SLORC, Order No. 1/88, 18 September 1988.

3. Nawrahta, *Destiny of the Nation* (Yangon: News and Periodicals Enterprise, 1995). *Nawrahta* means "government" in Burmese.

4. Nawrahta, *Destiny of the Nation*, 18.

5. According to military ideologists, the main national causes "have guided the *Tatmadaw* previously without formal announcement and will remain indisputably true in the future." Nawrahta, *Destiny of the Nation*, 21.

6. Nawrahta, *Destiny of the Nation*, 151, 155.

7. The Burmese military regime differs fundamentally from past modernizing military regimes, for example, in South Korea, Thailand, and Indonesia, but also from purely kleptocratic dictatorships such as Togo, Equatorial Guinea, Nigeria under Mobutu, or Haiti under Papa and Baby Doc. It has national interests at heart, *as the military leaders perceive them*—only the military leaders are more concerned with security than development, and more with the state than its people.

8. Ohn Gyaw, "Statement Concerning Developments in Myanmar" (statement given at the UN General Assembly, Third Committee, 51st Session, 1 October 1996).

9. Quoted in *Working People's Daily*, 22 February 1991.

10. General Maung Aye, "Address at the 50th Anniversary Special Commemorative Session of the UNGA," 23 October 1995, in NCGUB, "Report of the NCGUB Delegation on the 50th Session of the United Nations General Assembly," 1995.

11. William C. Johnstone, *Burma's Foreign Policy: A Study in Neutralism* (Cambridge, MA: Harvard University Press, 1963); Maung Maung Gyi, "Foreign Policy of Burma since 1962: Negative Neutralism for Group Survival," in *Military Rule in Burma since 1962*, ed. F. K. Lehman (Singapore: Maruzen Press, 1981).

12. Wedged in between China and India, Burma is relatively small in size and population, as well as in economic and military strength. Military leaders frequently express concern that the country's favorable land-people ratio and rich natural resources make it a potential target for its overpopulated neighbours. See, for example, interview with Foreign Minister Win Aung, *Time* magazine, 15 November 1999. They must also take account of the possibility that rivalry between China and India could draw Burma into a future regional big power war.

13. Nawrahta, *Destiny of the Nation*, 152. The idea of a U.S. invasion may seem far-fetched given the absence of any vital U.S. national interests in Burma and the proximity of China, which has strong strategic interests in the country. Yet, it is not uncommon to hear it expressed among antigovernment forces and the population at large.

14. Military "insider," interview by author, Rangoon, December 2000.

15. The most extreme policies were relaxed in the early 1970s when foreign aid and investment in certain sectors were invited back to salvage a stagnating economy. Further steps toward a normalization of foreign relations have been taken since the late 1980s, as exemplified by the new foreign investment law, which on paper is one of the most liberal in the region. These steps, however, remain partial and do not appear to reflect a lessened sense of vulnerability to foreign influences.

16. Nawrahta, *Destiny of the Nation*, 135.

17. Ne Win specifically blamed the civilian government for fueling ethnic disunity by making Buddhism the state religion and being "soft" on alleged Shan secessionists. Tatmadaw Researcher, *A Concise History of Myanmar and the Tatmadaw's Role, 1948–1988* (Yangon, 1991), 6.

18. Andrew Selth, *Burma's Armed Forces: Power without Glory* (Norwalk, CT: EastBridge, 2002), 35.

19. Mya Win, *Tatmadaw's Traditional Role in National Politics* (Yangon: News and Periodicals Enterprise, 1991), 77.

20. Ironically, the current cease-fires give some of the former insurgent groups more de facto autonomy than they would have within a federal system, while allowing their leaders to maintain control and prosper from state-sanctioned and state-supported

commerce. This reflects a broader pattern of concern with form over substance within the government, which is partly explained by a lack of capacity and resources, but may also have cultural roots.

21. Interview with Foreign Minister Win Aung, *Time* magazine, 15 November 1999.

22. Senior General Saw Maung, "Address to the Academy for the Development of National Groups," 21 February 1990, in *Senior General Saw Maung's Addresses, Vol. III*, 5 (Yangon: News and Periodicals Enterprise, 1991).

23. Mya Win, *Tatmadaw's Traditional Role*, 77.

24. This approach, so much in evidence over the past forty years, is usually interpreted as a quest for absolute power, but the deeper purpose may be to enforce absolute political orthodoxy and thus, in a sense, to eliminate the very need for exercising power. This fits with the military's self-image, discussed below, which presents the armed forces not as a contestant for power, but as the embodiment of the national "will."

25. Than Shwe, quoted in Maung Aung Myoe, "Building the Tatmadaw: The Organisational Development of the Armed Forces in Myanmar, 1948–98" (Working Paper No. 327, Strategic and Defence Studies Centre, Australian National University, Canberra, 1998).

26. Secretary-1 Khin Nyunt, quoted in Gustaaf Houtman, *Mental Culture in Burmese Crisis Politics* (Tokyo: Institute for the Study of Languages and Cultures of Asia and Africa, Tokyo University of Foreign Languages, 1999), 56. The top leadership is personally involved in the formulation and supervision of these projects. Senior General Than Shwe, for example, is the patron of the USDA and chairman of the Committee on Special Projects. General Khin Nyunt, before his removal in 2004, chaired most committees on social and cultural affairs and regularly attended even low-level conferences, openings, and so on.

27. For an extensive discussion of these issues, see Houtman, *Mental Culture*, 59–120. Racial or religious discrimination does not appear to be a matter of official policy, but occurs to varying degree in different areas of life and in different parts of the country, the latter depending on the personal idiosyncrasies of local officials, as well as the overall security situation.

28. Nawrahta, *Destiny of the Nation*, 31. These words are borrowed from Aung San and often repeated by military leaders and ideologists.

29. Mya Win, *Tatmadaw's Traditional Role*, 74–76. The emphasis on "unity of mind and purpose" is found, too, in historic writings on ethnic unity by Burmese scholars and government officials. See, for example, Tun Aung Chain, "The Broken Glass: Changes in the Perception of the Myanmar Past," *Myanmar Historical Research Journal* 6 (December 2000).

30. For example, NCGUB, "Report of the NCGUB Delegation on the 50th Session of the United Nations General Assembly," 1995, 22.

31. For example, Donald Seekins, *The Disorder in Order: The Army State in Burma since 1962* (Bangkok: White Lotus, 2002), 269.

32. The military's first claim on state budgets, coupled with its control of large sections of the "private" sector, secures minimal, necessary funding even in a stagnant economy. High economic growth, however, is necessary to fund the lavish modernization program that the junta is aiming for. Since the late 1990s, the military's recruitment drive has slowed down, and there appears to have been a decline in arms procurements. Military battalions have even been ordered to grow their own food. Evidently, military budgets are under strain.

33. Mya Win, *Tatmadaw's Traditional Role*, 40–42.

34. Businessman, interview by author, Rangoon, December 2002.

35. Alas, the superficial trappings of modernity represented by new infrastructure projects and the increasing availability of luxury consumer goods in the main cities may create a false belief among some military leaders that this is already happening.

36. Aid officials, interviews by author, January 2002, February 2004.

37. Interview with David Abel, *Leaders' Magazine*, April–June 1998.

38. There are some capable economists and technocrats in the government, who understand the limitations of current policies. Governance in Burma's strongly hierarchical, military-run system, however, is strictly top-down, highly personalized, and generally unresponsive to advice from subordinates.

39. James F. Guyot, "Burmese Praetorianism," in *Tradition and Modernity in Myanmar*, ed. Uta Gartner and Jens Lorenz, 142 (Münster: LIT, 1994).

40. Quoted in Eric Miller, "Forced Labour Blues—ILO Action," *Burma Issues* 10, no. 3 (August 2000).

41. *Asian Wall Street Journal*, 6 November 1998.

42. The ECS, which was signed by the four heads of state in Bagan in November 2003, revives the long-held Thai dream of turning mainland Southeast Asia's "battlefields into market places" by providing an engine for economic growth in its poorer neighbouring countries.

43. Senior General Saw Maung, quoted in NLD, "Statement No. 52," August 1998.

44. SLORC Order No. 1/90, 27 July 1990.

45. See, for example, Jeanelle M. Diller, "The National Convention: An Impediment to the Restoration of Democracy," in *Burma: The Challenge of Change in a Divided Society*, ed. Peter Carey, 27–54 (Houndsmills, England: MacMillan Press, 1997).

46. Most observers speculating about why the SLORC would hold elections and then effectively cancel them have suggested that it miscalculated the degree of support for the NLD, were under pressure from the international community, or simply wanted to "flush out" their opponents. While at least the first of these answers is credible, an alternative—or complementary—one may lie in the hierarchy. The senior general's speeches before the election suggest that he genuinely saw himself as following in the footsteps of his former commander, General Ne Win, who in 1958–1960 temporarily assumed state leadership as head of a military caretaker government but returned power to an elected parliament after organizing peaceful elections. Other high-ranking officers, including Khin Nyunt, were less sanguine about

this prospect, however, and may have moved to change the script once the landslide victory of the NLD was a reality, raising the specter of the military losing all influence over the political process. This idea of diverging views within the top leadership would explain why there was a delay of two and a half years before the constitutional assembly was convened. It also squares with reports that Saw Maung's replacement by Than Shwe in 1992 essentially constituted an internal leadership coup.

47. Tin Maung Maung Than, *The Dilemmas of Stalled Reform* (Singapore: ISEAS, 2000), 10.

48. Secretary-1 Khin Nyunt, address delivered at the closing of the ceremony of the Special Refresher Course No. 3 for officers of the Development Department, Central Institute of Civil Service, Phaunggyi, 21 November 1997 (quoted in Houtman, *Mental Culture*, 25).

49. "The National Ideology and Our Pledge," issued by the armed forces in 1958, stated that "man's endeavour to build a society set free at last from anxieties over food, clothing and shelter, and able to enjoy life's spiritual satisfactions as well . . . must proceed from the premise of a faith only in a politico-economic system based on the eternal principles of justice, liberty, and equality. . . . In order to achieve the establishment of such a society, we have resolved to uphold this belief forever." This was followed in 1959 by "The National Ideology and the Role of the Defence Forces," which stipulated that "our national objectives should be: to restore peace and the rule of law—first; to implement democracy—second; and to establish a socialist economy—third." Both documents quoted in Maung Aung Myoe, "Building the Tatmadaw," 12.

50. The armed forces of the new Union of Burma began as an amalgam of mainly ethnic-minority colonial forces that stayed loyal to the British through the war and the largely Burman liberation forces, which collaborated with the Japanese before switching sides in 1944. However, following the desertion of several ethnic minority battalions to the rebel side in 1948–1949, Ne Win and his fellow Burman officers purged all high-level minority officers. The modern Burmese military was thus shaped by men who were freedom fighters and anti-British.

51. See Mary P. Callahan, *Making Enemies: War and State Building in Burma* (Ithaca, NY: Cornell University Press, 2003).

52. Mya Win, *Tatmadaw's Traditional Role*, 37.

53. Nawrahta, *Destiny of the Nation*, 23.

54. Nawrahta, *Destiny of the Nation*, 6–7, 10–11.

55. Military leaders, for example, insist that the military caretaker government in 1958 was established according to law on request of Prime Minister U Nu. Their abrogation of the constitution four years later in 1962, in turn, has been justified as a historic necessity, since the constitution itself threatened the union. The 1962 Revolutionary Council and the 1988 SLORC both committed early on to drafting a new constitution.

56. Khin Nyunt, "Developments and Progressive Changes in Myanmar Naingngan" (clarifications at the Pyithu Hluttaw, Rangoon, 30 August 2003). For a detailed discussion of all the four "crises," see Nawrahta, *Destiny of the Nation*, 8–16.

57. Kyaw Thein, "An Analysis of the Return of Armed Groups of National Races to the Legal Fold and the Renunciation of Armed Insurrection" (paper presented at the Symposium on Socio-Economic Factors Contributing to National Consolidation, Rangoon, 9–11 October 1996). For an official elaboration of the government's efforts for peace, see Yan Nyein Aye, "Endeavours of the Myanmar Armed Forces Government for National Reconsolidation," Yangon, 4 January 2000. While the present leadership readily admits that mistakes were made by previous military governments, they blame these on individuals and do not appear to perceive any inherent structural constraints in military rule. This may explain their apparent self-confidence and belief in the righteousness of their programs despite the failures of military governance that seem evident to external observers, such as the continuance of ethnic tensions and depressed economic conditions.

58. Than Shwe, speech at the graduation of the 49th Intake of the Defence Services Academic, Naypyidaw, 15 December 2006, http://mission.itu.ch/MISSIONS/Myanmar/statement&speech/speech_SGTS/SGTS_%2049%20DSA%20Intake%2015%20Dec%2006.htm (accessed 27 April 2007).

59. Military ideologists admit that successive interventions by the armed forces in politics have made the institution gradually more unpopular among the people. Yet, they shrug this off, claiming that national leaders faced with the responsibility to make tough decisions for the common good must expect to be criticized, even hated, by some. Nawrahta, *Destiny of the Nation*, 10, 31, 35.

60. For a detailed discussion of this period, see Mary P. Callahan, "On Time Warps and Warped Time: Lessons from Burma's Democratic Era," in *Burma: Prospects for a Democratic Future*, ed. Robert I. Rotberg, 49–68 (Washington, DC: Brookings Institution Press, 1998); also Callahan, *Making Enemies*, 172–206.

61. Ne Win, quoted in Maung Maung, *Burma and General Ne Win* (Bombay: Asia Publishing House, 1969), 247–48.

62. Maung Maung, *Burma and General Ne Win*, 291.

63. Most historians, including foreign scholars, support the military's bleak account of the political situation in the 1950s. There are divergent views, however, on what the implications were for democracy as a system of government. Mary P. Callahan, for example, points out that high voter turnout for the 1947, 1951, 1956, and 1960 elections (often higher than 70 percent), coupled with the emergence of a loyal opposition and the victory of U Nu over the military-backed candidate in 1960, "represented clear steps toward institutionalizing a competitive parliamentary system." Callahan, "On Time Warps," 50.

64. Interview with Foreign Minister Win Aung, Reuters, 27 April 1999.

65. Nawrahta, *Destiny of the Nation*, 110.

66. Retired Burmese army officer, interview by author, Washington, DC, July 2001.

67. Martin Smith, *Burma: Insurgency and the Politics of Ethnicity*, 2nd ed. (London: Zed Books, 1999), 45–46. For a comprehensive analysis of the adverse effects of colonial administration on traditional Burmese society, see J. S. Furnivall, *Colonial Policy*

and Practice: A Comparative Study of Burma and Netherlands India (New York: New York University Press, 1956). For some interesting indigenous comments on these effects, see Aung San Suu Kyi, "Intellectual Life in India and Burma under Colonialism," in *Freedom from Fear, and Other Writings*, 82–139 (London: Penguin Books, 1991); and Michael Aung-Thwin, "1948 and Burma's Myth of Independence," in *Independent Burma at Forty Years: Six Assessments*, ed. Josef Silverstein, 19–34 (Ithaca, NY: Southeast Asian Program, Cornell University, 1989).

68. SLORC chairman General Saw Maung in 1990 estimated that the death toll since independence "would reach as high as millions," including soldiers, paramilitaries, and civilians. *Working People's Daily*, 10 January 1990.

69. Tatmadaw Researcher, *Concise History*, 11.

70. It is unclear to what extent this hostility extends to minority groups at large, but one cannot but suspect that the brutality of the army during military operations in minority areas reflects preexisting animosity toward the population, probably compounded by perceptions of ethnic superiority, although fear is likely to be a factor as well.

71. This mistrust of the infantry commanders was emphasised by a high-level Wa official several months before the purge of Khin Nyunt, who also expressed concern that the head of military intelligence was losing power. Interview by author, Wa Special Region, March 2004.

72. A high-level, military official in the Burmese Foreign Ministry in early 2005 revealed to an Asian colleague, "I do not like Westerners. I do not trust them." Asian ambassador, interview by author, March 2005.

73. The late senior general Saw Maung emphasized this theme in 1990: "Some of our grandparents are old enough to have experienced the life of servitude. . . . They will tell you that it was a nightmare, how they had to live in subhuman conditions under many controls and restraints." "Address to the Academy for the Development of National Groups," 21 February 1990, in Saw Maung, *Senior General Saw Maung's Addresses*, 365. For a broader discussion of this theme, see Aung-Thwin, "1948 and Burma's Myth of Independence."

74. U Nu, speech delivered in Parliament, 5 September 1950, in U Nu, *From Peace to Stability: Selected Speeches*, 95–105 (Rangoon: GOB, 1951).

75. Harriet O'Brien, who spent her teenage years in Rangoon where her father served as a British diplomat, explains, "In Rangoon, permission had to be granted before any army or government members could come to our house. When they did come, they were never alone. Officials would arrive in a bunch, nervously watching over each other and keeping a check on what was said or revealed. It was only in the rarest of circumstances that we could visit their homes." Harriet O'Brien, *Forgotten Land: A Rediscovery of Burma* (London: Michael Joseph, 1991), 86.

76. Than Shwe, letter to Thai prime minister Thaksin, dated July 2003 [copy in author's possession].

77. Myanmar Information Committee, "Information Sheet," 27 June 2001.

78. Selth, *Burma's Armed Forces*, 41.

79. Interview with Win Aung, *Asiaweek*, 3 September 1999. A Western ambassador in Rangoon confirms that military officers not only were "obsessed" with what was happening in the Balkans in 1998, but also expressed concern in connection with the international intervention in East Timor that a similar force might come through Thailand. Interview by author, Rangoon, August 2001.

80. Nawrahta, *Destiny of the Nation*, 4–5.

81. Robert H. Taylor, "Political Values and Political Conflict in Burma," in Rotberg, *Burma: Prospects for a Democratic Future*, 35–39.

82. Senior General Saw Maung, "Address in Taungoo," in Saw Maung, *Senior General Saw Maung's Addresses*, 168–69.

83. Nawrahta, *Destiny of the Nation*, 138.

84. Mya Win, *Tatmadaw's Traditional Role*, 34–35.

85. Mya Win, *Tatmadaw's Traditional Role*, 59.

86. Maung Maung, *The 1988 Uprising in Burma* (New Haven, CT: Yale University Southeast Asia Studies, 1999), 189.

87. John Badgley, "Remodelling Myanmar," in *Myanmar Dilemmas and Options: The Challenge of Economic Transition in the 1990s*, ed. Mya Than and Joseph L. H. Tan, 268 (Singapore: ISEAS, 1990).

88. Robert H. Taylor, "The Evolving Military Role in Burma," *Current History* 89 (March 1990): 105–8.

89. Senior General Saw Maung, "Address in Taungoo," in Saw Maung, *Senior General Saw Maung's Addresses*, 119, 145, 196.

90. In addition, the Burmese military wrote several "in-house" histories during the 1970–1980s. Andrew Selth, personal communication, February 2001.

91. There has been much talk about which regional models might appeal to the military. But the most influential ones are probably domestic. As Senior General Saw Maung once said, "Myanmar is a country which is quite different from other countries in the world. We cannot compare the situation of another country with ours and say that something is happening in another country and that the same thing should happen in our country." Saw Maung, *Senior General Saw Maung's Addresses*, 229.

92. See, for example, H. W. Tromp, "The Assessment of the Military Mind: A Critical Comment on Methodology," in *The Perceived Role of the Military*, ed. M. R. Van Gils (Rotterdam: Rotterdam University Press, 1971).

93. Saw Maung, *Senior General Saw Maung's Addresses*, 54, 89, 121.

94. Mya Win, *Tatmadaw's Traditional Role*, 24.

95. Quoted in David Mathieson, "Burma: A State of Cachexia" (honors diss., Flinders University, Adelaide, Australia, August 2000).

96. See Maung Aung Myoe, "Officer Education and Leadership Training" (Working Paper No. 346, Strategic and Defence Studies Centre, Australian National University, Canberra, 2000).

97. Selth, *Burma's Armed Forces*, 88.

98. For example, the deputy minister for national planning and economic development, Brigadier General Zaw Tun, was fired in 2000 after giving a speech at the Institute of Economics in Rangoon in which he spoke candidly about the economic problems facing the country and criticized the government's economic policy. The director of the institute was also fired for allowing this to happen. Zaw Tun, speech delivered at the Seminar on Myanmar Economy, Institute of Economics, Rangoon, 7 July 2000, www.ibiblio.org/obl/docs/zaw_tun%2007-07-2000.htm (accessed 26 April 2007).

99. Exceptions are at the micro-level, where individual interests in the form of corruption often run counter to the general thrust of government priorities and programs, not to mention the welfare of the Burmese people at large.

100. *Burma Digest*, "Interview with Former Malaysia Prime Minister Mahathir Mohamad," 16 November 2006, http://burmadigest.wordpress.com (accessed 10 January 2007).

101. Aung San Suu Kyi, *The Voice of Hope: Conversations with Alan Clements* (London: Penguin Books, 1997), 86–89.

102. Selth, *Burma's Armed* Forces, 266.

103. Several lower-level military officials in private conversations have indicated that they see the opposition leader as someone they could work with. Interviews by author, Rangoon, March 2003, December 2004. See also Pricilla Clap, "Can the Generals Face Their Demons?" (paper presented at the U.S. State Department Bureau of Intelligence and Research [INR] Workshop, Washington, DC, 16 September 2003).

104. Burmese and foreign businessmen, interviews by author, Rangoon, June–July 2004.

105. Mary P. Callahan, "Cracks in the Edifice? Changes in Military-Society Relations in Burma since 1988," in *Burma/Myanmar: Strong Regime, Weak State*, ed. Morten B. Pedersen, Emily Rudland, and R. J. May, 22–51 (Adelaide, Australia: Crawford House, 2000).

106. Burmese diplomat, interview by author, Rangoon, March 2006.

CHAPTER THREE

Domestic Balance of Power

> Ten years after the movement began, we have made almost no real progress toward democracy. More people are in jail, countless others are suffering from the effects of sanctions, and the military government seems stronger than ever. The NLD may have won the moral battle, but it is losing the war.
>
> —former NLD member[1]

The issue of power has been given more attention in Western policy circles than the military's priorities and perceptions, but superficial images of a regime fighting a rearguard action against massive popular demands for change, international isolation, and a crumbling economy have created unrealistic expectations regarding the process of change. Nearly twenty years after the 1988 uprising, leading advocates of the core strategy continue to predict the impending collapse of the military regime, from either its own internal contradictions or another popular revolt.[2] Any assumption, however, of inexorable forces of change clashes with the fact that military rule has persisted for forty-five years through much worse isolation and instability than exist presently. It also runs counter to popular perceptions on the ground among those who face the reality of military rule on a daily basis. While, in the mid-1990s, many people in central Burma talked with enthusiasm about Aung San Suu Kyi and the next student uprising that would sweep the military from power, today such hopes have largely dissipated. Ethnic minority groups around the country's periphery have also become less inclined to wait for a resolution in Rangoon, as reflected in their cease-fire agreements with the government and participation in the ongoing National Convention.

In assessing the prospects for regime change (distinct from its desirability), the aspirations of the general population are less important than the relative ability of elites and counter-elites to tap relevant bases of political power and build winning coalitions. This chapter examines the unceasing battle between the military regime and the opposition along these dimensions, the outcome of which reflects the leadership exercised and strategic choices made, as well as the "objective" resources of each side. The first section provides a dynamic account of the ebbs and flows of opposition politics since 1988, with particular focus on the fate of the National League for Democracy (NLD). This is followed by a comparative assessment of the bases of power of the military regime and antiregime groups, including violence, organization, finance, and legitimacy. The concluding section assesses the prospects for regime change in the short to medium term, and thus—indirectly—the extent to which international efforts to promote human rights in Burma will have to take into account the priorities and perceptions of the military leadership as discussed in the preceding chapter.

Opposition Politics

Such is the unpopularity of the military regime that most of the country's citizens could in some sense be categorized as part of the opposition. Opposition politics, however, has taken four main forms: party politics, popular activism, armed struggle, and cease-fire agreements. The most common strategy—that of passive resistance—is not considered here as it does not directly seek political ends, but is addressed in the subsequent discussion of sources of power.

Party Politics

The eighteen-plus-year struggle for control of the state between the State Law and Order Restoration Council/State Peace and Development Council (SLORC/SPDC) and the NLD has followed a cyclic pattern of liberalization, mobilization, and repression. The NLD persists, but the extended war of attrition with the regime has left deep marks on the organization, which has lost much of the pluralism and dynamism of the early years. Having long been largely synonymous with its leader, Aung San Suu Kyi, limited to small islands of activity in her immediate physical proximity, the main opposition party is floundering under her current forced absence.

The 1988 Uprising

The seed of the NLD was sown on 26 August 1988 when Aung San Suu Kyi in her first public appearance, speaking to hundreds of thousands of people in front of the Shwedagon Pagoda, called for a "second struggle for national independence."[3] Coming from the daughter of Burma's independence hero, Aung San, to whom the armed forces trace their lineage—and ultimately their legitimacy in national politics—these were poignant words, containing a direct challenge to the legitimacy of the military, which since has become the hallmark of the NLD's strategy.

A few weeks earlier, the army had crushed a general strike. However, as if reproving itself, the Burma Socialist Programme Party (BSPP) government on 12 August had appointed a new, civilian president, former supreme court chief justice Dr. Maung Maung; martial law had been lifted; and the army had withdrawn from the streets. This relaxation had sparked an upsurge in protests, effectively bringing the administration and the economy to a standstill as professionals, workers, civil servants, and even members of the military (mainly from the air force and navy) took to the streets in cities and towns all around the country. It was into this space that Aung San Suu Kyi and other political leaders now stepped, transforming the amorphous mass of disaffected people rejecting the existing order into a more purposeful movement with an alternative vision for the future. Allied with a number of experienced politicians, including several ex-military officers purged by General Ne Win in the 1970–1980s, Aung San Suu Kyi quickly gained the trust and support of the students and monks who had spearheaded the protests until that point. For the first time, there was thus an authoritative leadership for the movement, which was able to negotiate with the government and specify its demands.

On 10 September, President Maung Maung offered to dismantle the one-party system and hold a general election within three months. He also appointed an election commission of respected elders. This, however, was rejected by the new political leaders, as well as the students, who demanded that the BSPP government step down immediately and establish an interim administration to oversee the election. The demonstrations continued and grew increasingly violent as protesters began attacking the security forces and government buildings, and criminal elements took advantage of the general breakdown of law and order to loot and destroy. A number of policemen and suspected informers were killed by angry mobs. It is not clear whether any of the future NLD leaders encouraged this escalation of the protests, but few appear to have called for moderation, as they were focusing instead on the modalities for a transition to democratic rule that now seemed in sight.

The initial cycle of resistance was brought to an abrupt end, however, on 18 September when active duty military commanders, headed by commander-in-chief of the armed forces General Saw Maung, took control of the government and quickly crushed the uprising. Several light infantry divisions were redeployed from the battlefields in the border areas to Rangoon, Mandalay, and other cities where they dispersed the protesters by firing into the crowds, killing large numbers of people.[4] This was followed by systematic "mop up" operations lasting several weeks, which targeted individual student leaders and other activists, resulting in further killings and hundreds of arrests. Civil servants and other state employees were given an ultimatum—return to work or lose your jobs—which was heeded by most.[5] The universities were closed to preempt further mobilization against the regime, and remained so until 1991. Thousands of activists fled to the border areas to launch an armed insurrection, resulting in a major loss of both talent and numbers for the democracy movement in central Burma.

The Election Campaign

Once in control, the new military rulers invited political parties to form in preparation for multiparty elections to be held once law and order had been restored.[6] The NLD was among the first to register on 30 September 1988, with Aung San Suu Kyi as general secretary, Brigadier Aung Gyi as chairman, and U Tin Oo as vice-chairman.[7] Intended as an umbrella organization for the democracy forces, it quickly became the focal point for continued resistance to the SLORC as professionals, artists, and students flocked to the party or formed close alliances with it.[8] By early 1990, its membership reportedly had reached 2 million.[9] The NLD's official program was: "To organise unity among the democratic forces, to protect the democratic rights of the people, and to create conditions for holding a free and fair general election in order to form a genuine democratic government in conformity with the will of the majority of the people."[10]

Although the SLORC officially supported the goal of multiparty democracy, it did not allow free debate and broader political freedoms. The new parties—a total of 235, of which 93 eventually contested the election and 27 won seats—were constrained by a series of martial law regulations and other security laws, which among other things stipulated that "gathering, walking, marching in procession, chanting slogans, delivering speeches, agitating, and creating disturbances on the streets by a group of five or more people is banned."[11] Some allowances were made for election campaigning. But all political speeches and publications, including party programs, had to be preapproved by the authorities, and any criticism of the military, the government, or other parties was prohibited.

While most parties conformed with these conditions, the NLD embarked on an election campaign, which deliberately tested the boundaries of political space. Between October 1988 and July 1989, Aung San Suu Kyi traveled all over the country and delivered hundreds of campaign speeches. The SLORC at first allowed this, perhaps out of respect for her lineage. Yet, as the crowds at the NLD's political rallies grew to tens of thousands, military intelligence began harassing and arresting local party organizers, and the official media launched a smear campaign to defame Aung San Suu Kyi. The authorities also suppressed the political activities of other groups, such as the Democratic Party for a New Society (DPNS), which represented the student movement and was closely aligned with the NLD. The only exception was made for the National Unity Party (NUP), the successor party to the BSPP, whose leaders had close personal connections with the new military rulers and were allowed to campaign freely around the country.

During the spring of 1989, Aung San Suu Kyi's speeches became increasingly strident. While she initially talked mainly about democracy and people's role in it, she now began publicly attacking the military, which she described as "fascist" and "an obstruction to peaceful change." She accused Ne Win of being "the real leader of the SLORC," "the source of the people's hardships," and "the man who destroyed everything her father stood for and tried to achieve."[12] In June, soldiers opened fire on an NLD gathering, killing one, and with tensions rising Aung San Suu Kyi called off a planned celebration on the anniversary of her father's assassination on 19 July, reportedly fearing that it could end in another bloodbath.[13] This, however, failed to mollify the military leaders who the following day detained both her and NLD chairman Tin Oo. Aung San Suu Kyi was subsequently barred from running in the election and put under house arrest until July 1995. Tin Oo was formally charged with disturbing the peace and sentenced to three years of hard labor, later extended to ten years.

The 1990 Election

The arrest of its leaders effectively ended the NLD's election campaign. Yet, the powerful image of Aung San Suu Kyi calling for a return to the ideals of her father, who forty years after his death remained a mythical figure in the country, had settled in the popular consciousness. Thus, on 27 May 1990, when the SLORC, to the surprise of many, not only fulfilled its pledge to hold elections, but also allowed the voting to go ahead without any interference, the NLD registered a landslide victory, taking around 60 percent of the vote and 82 percent of the seats.[14] The NUP, which was closely associated with the old regime (and, by extension, the military), took 25 percent of the vote but only 2 percent of the seats.

The election result was never implemented, however. While the SLORC formally acknowledged the NLD's victory, it insisted that a new constitution had to be written before the transfer of power legally could take place (something which seventeen years later has yet to happen).[15] A proposal by the NLD to adopt an interim constitution based on the 1947 constitution was rejected, as were the party's calls for dialogue with the military.[16] On 27 July, the ruling council instead issued SLORC Order No. 1/90, which laid out the regime's own road map for the transition:

- The representatives elected by the people are responsible for drafting a constitution for the future democratic state.
- Drafting an interim constitution to obtain state power and to form a government will not be accepted in any way, and if it is done, effective action will be taken according to the law.
- During the interim period before the emergence of a government formed under a firm constitution, the SLORC—the Defense Services—hereby announce it will give priority and safeguard its responsibilities toward
  (1) the three national causes of prevention of disintegration of the union, prevention of disintegration of national unity, and perpetuation of sovereignty;
  (2) prevalence of law and order and regional peace and tranquillity, secure and smooth transport and communications, and easing of people's need for food, clothes, and shelter; and
  (3) development of all national people in all of Myanmar.

According to the head of military intelligence Major General Khin Nyunt,

> A party or an organisation should not monopolise or consider as personal the drafting of a constitution. . . . The wishes of the people should be taken into consideration in as extensive a manner as possible in the drafting process. . . . People's representatives are to draft it. . . . The SLORC and the Defence Forces will do everything possible to render help and will also provide suggestions. . . . What we aim for is the inclusion of the full essence of the three National Causes that have been declared since the inception of SLORC. . . . If that is the case, there will be peace of mind regarding the future of the nation. . . . Once the state constitution has been drafted in a systematic, correct and complete manner, and once it has been approved by the people, the SLORC is to

hand over power to a government formed in accordance with the constitution.[17]

In defiance of the order, the NLD on 28–29 July called a meeting of all its elected representatives at Gandhi Hall in Rangoon, which ended with the issuing of a declaration calling on the SLORC "to convene Parliament by 30 September, enter into political talks with the NLD, release Aung San Suu Kyi and all other political prisoners, and withdraw all restrictions on people's freedom."[18] A few weeks later, the main opposition party cemented an alliance with the United Nationalities League for Democracy (UNLD)—a coalition of nineteen ethnic-based parties that won the second largest number of seats in the election—and leaders of the two groups pledged to work together in a new government.[19] The SLORC responded with a wave of arrests of NLD leaders and members. It also launched a scathing attack on the party, accusing it of being unprepared to take office and having no real policies on how to run the country.[20]

As it became clear the SLORC was going to ignore the September deadline, the NLD made plans to establish a parallel government at a monastery in Mandalay where the monks could provide protection.[21] The arrangement was leaked, however, resulting in a series of raids on NLD offices and several monasteries. Resorting to an alternative plan, the NLD instead sent a group of elected representatives to the "liberated areas" on the Burma-Thai border where, on 18 December 1990, they set up the National Coalition Government of the Union of Burma (NCGUB), headed by Aung San Suu Kyi's cousin, Dr. Sein Win.[22] The new exile government pledged "to eliminate the SLORC," "to call a National Convention with the elected representatives, as well as members of ethnic nationalist organisations and other democratic forces," and "to establish a genuine democratic government."[23] It also called on all "fraternal nationals" in the union "to work as one united front under the slogan 'Revolution by All Towards Victory for All' in the struggle to liberate the Union of Burma from fascist dictatorship."[24] Initially, the NCGUB was based at Manerplaw, the headquarters of the Karen National Union (KNU) near the Thai border. In 1992, however, its members were denied access through Thailand and had to move to Washington, DC, where they have struggled to maintain relevance for the struggle inside Burma.

In central Burma, the military continued to arrest elected representatives, other party members, and dissidents, and also began deregistering political parties. By 1992, there were only ten legal parties left of the ninety-three that contested the election. The NLD avoided disbandment, but many of its elected representatives were arrested, disqualified, or pressured to resign, and strict regulations barred the party from recruiting new members or making any kind of public statements. Under coercion, the interim leadership expelled Aung San Suu Kyi and Tin Oo from the party and, along with all other parties, signed a statement of support for SLORC Order No. 1/90, formally accepting the regime's transition plan. For the next several years, the NLD thus adopted a less confrontational line.

The National Convention

The period from 1992 to 1995 saw a slight widening of the political space. In April 1992, SLORC chairman Senior General Saw Maung was relieved of his duties, supposedly for medical reasons, and replaced by his former deputy, General Than Shwe. This was followed in quick succession by a number of reforms, including the rescinding of martial law, release of hundreds of political prisoners, and reopening of the universities. The regime also declared a nationwide, unilateral cease-fire and began preparations for the National Convention, which was eventually convened in January 1993 to deliberate on the principles for a new constitution. In 1994, the top generals met twice with Aung San Suu Kyi, and in July 1995 the opposition leader was finally released after six years under house arrest.

The NLD had joined the National Convention in 1993, its leadership unwilling to risk provoking a more serious backlash by further challenging the regime. Yet, the release of Aung San Suu Kyi from house arrest became a turning point. Resuming her place as general secretary of the NLD, the charismatic opposition leader had a galvanizing effect on the fledgling party. Together with her two closest associates, Kyi Maung and Tin Oo, both of whom had been released as well after long prison stays and were reinstated as cochairmen, she began rebuilding the party's organizational structure. She also held regular public meetings on weekends outside her house on University Avenue, where she spoke about political and socioeconomic issues and answered questions from the audience. The crowd soon grew to several thousands, and videotapes from the meetings were circulated all around the country. When the National Convention reopened in November 1995 after the customary rainy season break, the NLD delegates further upped the ante by walking out from the proceedings, which they criticized for being undemocratic (they were subsequently expelled for breaching convention regulations regarding attendance).[25] A few months later, the party resumed its calls for convening the elected parliament, and at the sixth anniversary of the 1990 elections in May 1996, a party conference resolved to draw up an alternative constitution. For the first time, Aung San Suu Kyi also personally started calling for international sanctions to put pressure on the regime.

The SLORC responded to the NLD's direct challenge to its constitution-drawing process by aggressively stepping up its propaganda against the party and further cracking down on party activities. In June–July 1996, mass rallies organized by the pro-regime Union Solidarity and Development Association (USDA) were held all around the country, at which the NLD was denounced as "internal destructionists" and "stooges of Western neo-imperialist powers."[26] The government also enacted a new law, imposing harsh penalties for anyone seeking to disrupt the National Convention.[27] This time, though, rather detaining the top leaders of the NLD, the authorities targeted the next echelon in the party structure, thus cutting off their contacts to the grass roots. Hundreds of people were arrested ahead of the party conference in May 1996 and again before planned celebrations of the seventh anniversary of the formation of the party in September. The same month, Aung San Suu Kyi's weekend talks were effectively banned when the military erected blockades around her house, and the opposition leader's movements were further restricted. In December 1996, her motorcade was attacked by members of the USDA, the first in a series of incidents where this organization has been used to physically disrupt opposition activities.

The Committee Representing People's Parliament

The intense repression of 1996 was followed by a period of relative quiet. Having regained control, the authorities allowed hundreds of NLD members to congregate for the party's anniversary celebrations in September 1997, which they had thwarted the year before. Tensions, however, escalated again in May 1998 after the NLD reiterated its long-standing call for convening of the parliament and set a public deadline for 21 August. When the government moved to preempt the threat being carried out by detaining scores of NLD elected representatives, the NLD responded by setting up the Committee Representing People's Parliament (CRPP). Comprising ten members (mainly from the NLD, but including one representative from a small ethnic political party), the CRPP was charged with acting on behalf of the parliament until a parliamentary session attended by all the elected representatives could be convened. Aung San Suu Kyi appealed directly to elected parliaments overseas to recognize the CRPP as the legitimate government. In its first act of "office," the new committee declared all laws and regulations passed by the government since 1988 null and void. It also called for the immediate release of all political prisoners.[28]

This outright rejection of the authority of the ruling council—by then renamed the SPDC—was met with a massive crackdown on the NLD, which continued for two years and decimated the party. Having condemned the CRPP as illegal and a threat to national unity, the authorities launched a nationwide campaign which saw tens of thousands of NLD members coerced to resign from the party and scores of local party branches forcibly dissolved. In yet another round of USDA-led mass rallies, no-confidence motions were passed against locally elected representatives. The state media began publishing almost daily editorials and op-eds, ridiculing and condemning Aung San Suu Kyi. By mid-2000, the NLD's organizational network had collapsed and only 110 of its original 392 elected representatives were still active.[29] A few months later, Aung San Suu Kyi was put back under house arrest after she had several times attempted to leave Rangoon and travel up-country.

The Release of Aung San Suu Kyi

By this time, Western diplomats in Rangoon were speculating that the SPDC was preparing to deregister the NLD and eliminate political opposition altogether.[30] Yet, in an apparent U-turn, the military leadership in October 2000 instead initiated a series of "secret talks" with Aung San Suu Kyi, which included two face-to-face meetings between the top generals and the opposition leader and were supported by confidence-building measures, including release of more than two hundred political prisoners and relaxation of the constraints on NLD political activities. The content of the talks was never revealed by either side, but nineteen months later, in May 2002, Aung San Suu Kyi was unconditionally released and, for the first time since 1989, was allowed to travel freely around the country to meet with party members and reopen party offices.

In talks with UN officials before her release, Aung San Suu Kyi had indicated that she believed the two sides could work together.[31] Echoing these sentiments, the government issued a statement at the time of her release saying that "we shall recommit ourselves to allowing all our citizens to participate freely in the life of our political process."[32] Yet, the professed spirit of reconciliation only lasted a few months. While the SPDC stalled on further substantive talks, Aung San Suu Kyi embarked on a series of party organizational tours, which soon came to resemble her campaign tours in 1988–1989 with frequent stops and impromptu speeches to large crowds of people who turned out to see her in cities, towns, and villages along the way. The first few trips went peacefully, but in December 2002 in Rakhine state and Irrawaddy division, local chapters of the USDA on several occasions sought to disrupt party activities, harassing NLD supporters and onlookers, and distributing pamphlets criticizing the party. In a particularly tense encounter in the town of Mrauk-Oo, the authorities threatened to disperse the crowd with high-pressure fire hoses.

On her return to Rangoon from the northwest, Aung San Suu Kyi abandoned two years of no criticism of the government and at a press conference accused high-level officials of being behind the harassment. Although she emphasized that some local authorities had been very cooperative, she went on to complain publicly for the first time since her release that the reconciliation process was in a state of limbo and that there had been no further dialogue with the government.[33] A few days later, on Burma's Independence Day, the NLD issued a statement on the party's policies, which reiterated a number of its long-standing "principled positions" and thus seemed to mark the end of its more pragmatic search for compromise and common ground:

- The NLD will not accept the holding of another election without first honoring the results of the 1990 election.
- The NLD will not accept any provisions in a constitution written by the current National Convention.
- Economic sanctions impact negatively only on a section of the community.[34]

Over subsequent months, frustrations within the opposition became increasingly apparent. On Union Day in February, the NLD issued a highly critical statement concerning the nonexistent talks and called for increased international pressure to overcome the deadlock.[35] Two months later at another press conference, Aung San Suu Kyi directly accused the government of not wanting change: "We have been forced to question the integrity of the SPDC and their sincerity in achieving national reconciliation. . . . They do not want change. . . . If the SPDC is truly interested in the welfare of the country, they should be prepared at least to cooperate with the NLD in matters of humanitarian aid."[36] At this time, the opposition leader in private meetings with foreign missions had also begun asking for more sanctions, although she did encourage donors to support specific "humanitarian" projects.[37]

Government spokesmen maintained a conciliatory, optimistic tone. Yet, behind the façade, darker forces were building up. At a USDA meeting in Pegu (Bago) in late January, Lieutenant General Soe Win, who was soon after promoted to secretary-2 of the SPDC—and in October 2004 to prime minister—publicly stated that the government had no intention of negotiating with the NLD.[38] A few weeks later, the authorities arrested seven members of the NLD in connection with an alleged plot to attack Insein Jail in Rangoon and blow up the railway station in Thazi on the main line from the capital to Mandalay. In early May, in an apparent last-ditch effort by "moderate" elements in the government to save the reconciliation process, head of military intelligence General Khin Nyunt offered to meet with Aung San Suu Kyi, which would have been the first high-level meeting in more than six months. But since she was about to leave on another trip, the meeting was postponed.[39]

On 6 May 2003, Aung San Suu Kyi embarked on what was to be her last trip, a month-long tour of Kachin state, and Mandalay and Sagaing divisions. The authorities issued public orders for people not to welcome her,[40] but with little effect. The opposition leader continued to attract large crowds of supporters and onlookers, and extended her tour by several days. An escalating pattern of confrontations and low-level violence between NLD security personnel and members of the USDA ensued. Abandoning a year-long "truce," the government press started accusing Aung San Suu Kyi and the NLD of causing "havoc in peaceful communities." In the third week of May, a message went out from the Ministry of Defense in Rangoon to local commands around the country to be prepared for further unrest.[41] Finally, on the evening of 30 May, as the NLD motorcade was passing through the small village of Depayin in Sagaing division, it was attacked by a mob of supposed government supporters who brutally beat up NLD members and onlookers, killing a number of people.[42] This was followed by a countrywide crackdown on the NLD, which saw Aung San Suu Kyi detained, all members of the party's Central Executive Committee put under house arrest, and party offices closed. The opposition leader was charged under section 10(a) of the 1975 State Protection Act for endangering the security of the state,[43] which legally allows the government to hold her in jail for five years without trial. Initially held in a VIP room in Insein Jail, she was later moved back to her house where she has remained since, almost totally isolated from the outside world.

The "Road Map to Democracy"

The violent crackdown on the NLD left the military leadership divided and seemingly uncertain about how to proceed.[44] Yet, after three months of almost daily high-level meetings, the government under much publicity announced a new seven-step "road map to democracy," beginning with a reconvening of the National Convention, which had been adjourned since March 1996. The convention, supposedly, would finish its deliberations on the remaining principles for the drafting of a new constitution, which would then be put to a referendum, finally paving the way for new elections and the transfer of power to an elected parliament.[45]

The initial announcement of the road map was followed by a series of political meetings between the government and the main cease-fire groups, most of whom did not participate in the first convention but now agreed to join. In early 2004, these contacts were expanded to include the NLD, most of the party's top leaders were released, its head office was reopened, and the Central Executive Committee was permitted to meet with Aung San Suu Kyi at her house several times. Both Aung San Suu Kyi and ethnic leaders told UN officials in private that they believed the government's main negotiator, Prime Minister Khin Nyunt, was sincere and genuinely trying to move the process forward.[46]

Against the backdrop of apparent rapprochement between the government and the NLD, many observers speculated that a deal was being hammered out and that Aung San Suu Kyi, too, was due to be released. Although the NLD put forward several conditions for participating in the National Convention, party leaders seemed confident that the remaining issues would be resolved and until just a few days before the convention was due to convene were making preparations to participate. In the end, however, the government backed away, refusing to comply with the NLD's demands, and the party responded—as it did in 1995—by boycotting the constitutional proceedings.[47] It was joined by the Shan National League for Democracy (SNLD), which won the second biggest number of seats in the 1990 election, while the government proceeded with the National Convention on its own terms.

In July 2004, the remaining members of the NLD Central Executive Committee launched a nationwide signature campaign, calling for release of their leader as well as other political prisoners and reopening of party offices. The government, however, ignored them and instead reiterated calls frequently made over the years for the NLD to abandon its "confrontational tactics" and support the ongoing national reconciliation process.[48] An unprecedented offer by the NLD in February 2006 to recognize the military as the legitimate transitional government if it agreed to convene the parliament elected in 1990 was similarly ignored.[49] The country, party leaders argued later, faces a serious humanitarian situation requiring urgent action and international assistance, which only a legitimate government can effectively address.[50] Instead, the authorities have stepped up their efforts to force remaining members of the party to resign. When Malaysian foreign minister Syed Hamid Albar in March 2006 sought a meeting with Aung San Suu Kyi, he was told by officials that "she has no more influence, the NLD has no more influence."[51] Information minister Brigadier General Kyaw Hsan subsequently warned, at a government press conference, that the government had enough evidence to declare NLD an unlawful association because of its ties with "terrorist groups."[52]

While the cycle of confrontation and repression continues, now in its nineteenth year, the spiral for the NLD has been downward. Each crackdown has left the party weakened, its membership diminished, and internal cohesion under increasing pressure as hopes for victory have subsided. Since the 2003 crackdown, in particular, cracks have begun appearing. Without Aung San Suu Kyi, the aging leadership appears rudderless and ineffective. Internal dissent has been growing among members, who are calling for a rejuvenation of the party and a new strategy.[53] In the Burmese exile community, which generally has been among the NLD's most faithful supporters, some have begun questioning whether the democracy movement needs a new vanguard party.[54] This is all symptomatic of growing perceptions of a crisis within the NLD, which is looking increasingly unlikely to assume a future role in government, at least in its present form.

Popular Activism

The NLD was born of a social movement, which brought together a wide cross-section of Burmese society. Yet, while the party continues to promote the population's aspirations for regime change, popular activism has largely disappeared. Notwithstanding the masses of people, which turned out to see Aung San Suu Kyi during her trips around the country in 2002–2003, the level of political activity has declined as people have returned to passive strategies of resistance or simply given in to the reality of military rule. This development is evident within the two primary forces of political resistance in Burmese history, the students and the monks, as well as among the general population, although the new 88 Generation Students group since 2006 has brought a certain new vitality to the opposition.

The Students

The 1988 movement originated in student activism, and students provided the core leadership until older politicians stepped onto the scene at the height of the uprising. Many students subsequently became active members of the NLD or joined DPNS, the official student party, which campaigned for the 1990 election on behalf of the NLD before being disbanded. Others went underground to organize the people for further resistance against the regime or fled to the border areas to launch an armed insurrection. In August 1989, the old All-Burma Federation of Students' Unions (ABSFU) was revived with a reported membership of thirty thousand before that, too, was disbanded.[55] As for the NLD, however, the spiral of student activism has been downward, both inside the country and on the border.

The 1988 student protests followed a long tradition of student activism going back to the 1930–1940s when university students were at the forefront of the anticolonial movement and later provided most of the political leadership of the new independent state. During the parliamentary period (1948–1962), students were active and well organized, constituting an important forum for political action that both the political parties and the insurgents sought to exploit. After 1962, the Revolutionary Council took steps to bring the student body under control by banning any further political activity and seeking to "redirect student energies and interests into wholly educational and socially constructive activities."[56] Yet, while student activism declined sharply as a result, hundreds of students joined informal political discussion groups, forming a loose network of underground cells—some organized by the Communist Party of Burma (CPB) or affiliated with it, others independent—which on several occasions mobilized against the BSPP government. It was such groups which again in 1988 took the lead in organizing other students and, ultimately, mobilizing the broader public.[57] Until the late 1990s, many Burmese continued to view the students as a potential vanguard of political change, although that does no longer appear to be the case.

The military, of course, is acutely aware of the potential threat the students pose and has gone to great lengths to ensure that the events of 1988 will not be repeated. In June 1988, the authorities closed the universities. They were reopened in May 1991, but closed again from December 1991 to June 1992 and from December 1996 to July 2000, both times in response to renewed unrest. Since then, in a deliberate move to isolate the students from the socialization and uniting experience of campus life, the government has closed down the main city university campuses, except for postgraduate studies, replacing them with numerous smaller campuses in the suburbs and around the country. It has also shortened each term and pushed distance education as an alternative to traditional forms of study. Tight security is maintained on all campuses, and university teachers have been made personally responsible for maintaining discipline among their students, as have the parents of the students.[58] Arrests of politically active students as young as high school age, sometimes followed by harsh jail sentences, serve as an example to their peers who today, unsurprisingly, show significant anxiety about the dangers of becoming involved in political activities.

The effectiveness of these policies has become increasingly evident over time. Sporadic political protests by students and monks continued until the early 1990s but were quickly broken up, and—as the military's supremacy became increasingly evident—mobilization against the regime slowly faded away. Although student protests erupted toward the end of 1996 in both Rangoon and Mandalay, and again briefly in 1998, these events focused on internal student affairs. Since then, the student movement inside the country appears to have gone dormant. Kyaw Yin Hlaing, in December 2001, was unable to find anyone engaged in informal student groups.[59] A more detailed follow-up survey by the same author in 2004, involving in-depth interviews with forty-five students, revealed that none of them had been approached by any political group for recruitment purposes. The great majority, he observed, exhibit very limited knowledge of the country's history of student politics and show clear signs of political apathy.[60]

The parallel student front, represented by those who fled to the border, has also petered out. More than ten thousand young activists are reported to have gone during the army's crackdown in 1988; smaller waves followed after the election in 1990 and the student protests in 1996 and 1998, but the numbers have slowed to a trickle since then as the fortunes of the border-based groups have waned. Many student activists arrived in the jungle expecting that the Americans were ready to supply them with weapons and it would only be a matter of months before they would topple the military regime.[61] The reality proved different, however. Upon arrival, they formed an uneasy alliance with the ethnic nationalist armies, particularly the KNU and Kachin Independence Organization (KIO), which helped set up a new student army, the All-Burma Students' Democratic Front (ABSDF).[62] Yet, like their new allies, the students found themselves stuck in the border areas, too weak to launch attacks on the main cities and towns, not to mention the capital. Many were killed in battles in the jungle or died of malaria or other illnesses in the new and unhealthy environment, while others moved on to exile life and politics, which has had weak links to the opposition inside Burma. By 2005, the ABSDF battalions counted less than eight hundred soldiers, and some of those are currently in the process of resettling as refugees in the West, along with large numbers of other border-based activists.[63]

In sum, while one should never discount the possibility of further political protests by the students who have always opposed authority, it seems all but impossible for them under the present circumstances to recreate the spirit of 1988 among themselves, let alone among the wider population. By quelling the student movement, the SLORC/SPDC may in fact have scored one of its most important victories and considerably diminished the risk of broader mobilization against the regime.

The Sangha

Like the students, Burma's monks have a long tradition of resistance to "unjust" rule going back to the colonial period when Buddhist religious organizations were among the first to confront the British authorities over their disregard for the local population and culture.[64] The *Sangha* (Burmese monk order) does not have the institutional influence of, for example, the Catholic Church in the Philippines or the main Muslim organizations in Indonesia, reflecting the more individualistic orientation of Theravada Buddhism, which makes for a much looser hierarchy. Yet, Buddhism is a pervasive force in Burmese society and individual monks are held in great respect and veneration as religious leaders and teachers, placing them in a position of authority often surpassing that of local government officials and other leaders. With three to four hundred thousand monks nationwide, including novices,[65] the *Sangha* is a force to be reckoned with.

During the 1988 uprising, monks played an important role alongside the students in helping organize the demonstrations and maintaining security in local communities after the breakdown of the state apparatus. Even after the SLORC's take-over of power, outspoken monks continued to actively support the NLD during the run up to the 1990 election. In August 1990, demonstrations commemorating the killings of 8 August 1988 led to clashes between soldiers and Buddhist monks in Mandalay, where two monks were killed. As a result, monks all over the country imposed a religious boycott of the regime, refusing to receive alms from or provide other religious services for military officers and their families. Since then, however, the SLORC/SPDC has reestablished state control of the *Sangha* hierarchy and "wayward" monks have suffered heavy reprisals from the authorities no less harsh than other activists, resulting in the near disappearance of open opposition by the monkhood.

The military, since the establishment of the Revolutionary Council in 1962, has attempted to gain control of the *Sangha*, and in 1980 succeeded in imposing a single structure under the patronage of the state and supervised by the State Sangha Maha Nayaka Committee, a council of thirty senior monks. The new structure allowed only nine traditional sects and, for the first time in Burma's history, all monks in the country were forced to register. This hierarchy broke down temporarily during the 1988 uprising when even members of the supreme council supported the protestors and several new Buddhist associations emerged outside the structures authorized by the state. The SLORC/SPDC, however, has reconstituted the State Sangha Committee with forty-seven senior monks considered loyal to the state and reconfirmed that there shall be only one *Sangha* organization in the country, encompassing the nine original sects. Any monk found to be a member of an illegal sect is subject to imprisonment for six months to three years.[66] In addition, the regime has made extensive efforts to co-opt the *Sangha* leadership. Lavish gifts and other favors are bestowed on senior monks to induce their loyalty, ranging from religious titles to donations and personal gifts, including luxury goods such as Land Rovers or TVs, which are technically prohibited by the monks code of conduct.[67]

The strategy of cooptation has not fully succeeded in disciplining the monks, many of whom disapprove of current policies and human rights abuses, and therefore are sympathetic to the demands for fundamental political reforms. But while previous governments have hesitated to physically restrain members of the *Sangha*, the SLORC/SPDC has shown little restraint in this respect. Faced with a growing religious boycott, the army in September 1990 raided several monasteries and arrested hundreds of monks. Subsequently, all monks were forced to sign a declaration of endorsement of the government and pledge not to disrupt the stability of the state. Informers were placed in monasteries and a campaign was initiated to suborn "disloyal" monks. Similar tactics were applied when political agitation by monks resurfaced toward the end of 1996 in response to rumors that a military officer had stolen a precious gem from a Buddha statue. This time barbed wire and barricades were erected by the police around several monasteries to keep the monks inside, and more than four hundred monks were arrested and forcibly disrobed.[68] After the outbreak of anti-Muslim riots in 2003, the authorities further curtailed the activities of the *Sangha* by limiting the population of each monastery at any given time to three hundred monks.[69]

The government remains hesitant to challenge the authority of the most senior monks, whose standing among their followers, including high-ranking military officers, provides some protection. Individual *sayadaws* have thus sought from time to time to engage directly in the political process. In 1999, for example, two venerated monks from Pegu (Bago) and Mandalay issued separate appeals to both the regime and the NLD, urging them to work together for national reconciliation. One even offered to mediate between the two sides and called on the government not to go against the will of the people.[70] But such relatively moderate acts of resistance notwithstanding, most senior monks have taken steps to discipline their followers, some expressing concern that activism—and the disruptions it causes to monastic life—undermines the *Sangha*'s ability to undertake its primary responsibility of promoting Buddhism.[71] As a result, open activism today is rare and largely limited to individual acts of defiance by lower-order monks who do not have wider responsibilities but also lack wider followings. While there is little doubt that should another uprising erupt, monks will again be an important source of moral support and leadership, it is unlikely that they would initiate or be able to sustain a broader challenge to military rule. In recent interviews, even veterans from the 1988 movement expressed doubts that the *Sangha* could again become the driving force in an antigovernment movement, at least under the current political conditions.[72]

The General Population

Lacking leadership, popular activism has become infrequent and largely limited to individual acts of resistance. Most civil servants returned to work within days of the SLORC's take-over in September 1988, and the last workers' strikes were broken up by early October. Significant numbers of people have continued to turn out to see Aung San Suu Kyi at public events such as her weekend talks in 1996–1997 and during her tours around the country in 2002–2003. But while the opposition leader remains a symbol of hope among the general population—and an object of great curiosity and exaggerated rumors—at no time since 1988 has there been any indication of broader mobilization against the regime. On the contrary, many people have lost faith in the promises of change and have become increasingly disillusioned with all sides in the political process, including the NLD.

Some foreign observers were quick to draw a parallel between the student protests in December 1996 and the initial stages of the 1988 uprising.[73] Yet, a repeat of those fateful events was never "in the cards." The demonstrations remained largely peaceful and there were no signs of broader segments of society joining in (although some people encouraged the students from the sidelines and helped them escape after encounters with the riot police).[74] Three years later, there was an attempt by activists on the border to bring the struggle back into central Burma by organizing a "political defiance" movement. The plan was for agent provocateurs trained in KNU-controlled areas to filter back into the country where they would mobilize the people behind a countrywide general strike and civil disobedience campaign.[75] A target date was set for 9 September 1999 (9/9/99)—a deliberate reference to the last general strike which was launched on 8 August 1988 (8/8/88)—and, as eleven years earlier, foreign radio stations were used to deliver the message to the general population. Exile activists went on the air, confidently claiming that the days of military rule were numbered. Yet, reflecting the state of resistance at the time, the movement failed to gain any significant momentum and in the end simply fizzled out. The military made a few dozen preemptive arrests in the main cities and, apart from a few lone protestors in Rangoon, nothing happened on the specified date, or afterward.

Some border-based dissident groups continue to work to organize the population inside the country, mainly under the cover of nonpolitical activities. But as one of the organizers of the 9/9/99 movement commented after the failed resistance, "It would seem that people are too poor to devote time and resources to political activism; they struggle for daily survival."[76] Two other long-time activists express similar sentiments: "Instead of politicizing and channeling their discontent into revolutionary activities, the public is adjusting to the economic demands of living under military rule. The popular culture and society is shifting toward cooperation with the regime in order to improve their lot."[77] Symptomatically, most outbreaks of social unrest over the past decade have been directed at specific economic grievances, such as in 1996 when one thousand farmers demonstrated against the government's rice procurement policies, or in 2002–2003 when several state-owned rice storages were raided by hungry villagers. In early 2007, demonstrators during a series of small demonstrations in Rangoon called on the government to urgently address the deteriorating socioeconomic situation.

The Burmese people continue to resist the regime in numerous small ways. But as Monique Skidmore observes, "Undoubtedly the most common reply of Burmese of all social classes and ages to the question of resistance is 'I resist in my mind only.'"[78]

88 *Generation Students*

The year 2006 saw the emergence of a new, independent force in opposition politics. The 88 Generation Students group, formed by former student leaders from the 1988 uprising, enjoys widespread respect in the general population and has also impressed foreign diplomats, who describe its leaders as gifted and pragmatic (although some local activists complain they are still "too much in the NLD mould").[79] The group initially took a fairly low-key, conciliatory approach, but after five of its six leaders were detained in September 2006, second-tier members swung into action, launching a countrywide petition demanding the release of its leaders and all other political prisoners, which reportedly garnered more than five hundred thousand signatures. This was followed up, first, with a "White Expression" campaign, for which the students called on the public to wear white clothes as a mark of honesty and purity and, subsequently, by a multidenominational prayer week involving candle vigils at monasteries, churches, and mosques around the country, where prayers were offered for a peaceful resolution of the country's political crisis. In early 2007, the group called on members of the public to write letters to Senior General Than Shwe to urge him to undertake political, social, and economic reform. According to one of the group's leaders, "Our aim is to have the military authorities hear the feelings of the people."[80]

How much of a factor the 88 Students will become is difficult to say. Their "quiet" resistance has drawn significant numbers of people out of their long-standing passivity, prompting comparisons with the early days of the NLD's campaign. Whether there is scope for another mass movement in this polity dominated by fear and violence is doubtful. Although the police so far have done surprisingly little to stop the former students' public campaigns, the detention of their five leaders sent a clear warning signal, and few people in Burma doubt that the military leadership would use violence again if it felt it was losing control. In that way, the fundamental dilemmas of the opposition remain. Yet, the 88 Students may prove an important addition to the movement for other reasons—less for their similarities to the NLD than for their differences. Independent of the main opposition party, yet supportive of its aims, they present an opportunity for a broader reassessment of opposition politics. Compared to the main opposition party, they also carry less baggage with the authorities and thus stand a better chance of bridging the political schisms in society. Much, however, depends on the strategic choices the former student activists make over the coming months and years.

Armed Struggle

The influence of the insurgent forces, which by 1988 had seemed marginalized as a factor in mainstream Burmese politics, was revived by the events of that year and subsequent developments. With new political pressure for regime change from Burman-based opposition groups in the cities, several insurgent leaders judged that their best chance of realizing their political goals lay within the framework of a new democratic state.[81] This decision fueled a brief renewal of insurgent activity from 1988 to 1992, but since then has mainly been expressed in rhetorical support for the NLD and the democratic cause.[82]

The new "link" between insurgents and political opposition groups was reinforced by the large outflow of democracy advocates from the cities to the "liberated areas" in the aftermath of the 1988 uprising, which also added a new dimension to the armed struggle itself. In November 1988, these meetings in the jungle led to the establishment of the Democratic Alliance of Burma (DAB), which included most of the major ethnic nationalist groups, as well as the ABSDF and other Burman democracy groups, representing the broadest coalition of political forces seen in Burma since the Anti-Fascist People's Freedom League (AFPFL) liberation movement in the 1940s. The new alliance helped ethnic nationalists reform their image as armed rebels, which was problematic in the West, and associate themselves with the more "legitimate" democratic cause. Indeed, a prominent scholar referred to the emergence of a "new politics" in the border areas, suggesting that Burma now had two capitals, one in Rangoon and one in Manerplaw, the joint headquarters of the KNU and the Burman democracy groups.[83] The political significance of the DAB was underscored by its close cooperation with the exile government, which included joint efforts to draft a new constitution for Burma.[84]

While these developments, however, at first seemed to herald a new beginning for the insurgent forces, subsequent military and political setbacks have greatly diminished their strength and, in many respects, make it more appropriate to talk about the end of an era. In 1989, the CPB after forty years of fruitless rebellion disintegrated when Kokang, Wa, and Shan forces, who made up 90 percent of the rank-and-file, mutinied against the largely Burman party leadership and subsequently entered into cease-fire agreements with the government. This development more or less overnight reduced the insurgent forces by more than one-third of their combined manpower and set a precedent for other ethnic nationalist groups, which over the next five years went on to negotiate individual cease-fire deals with the government, thereby undermining the potential and cohesiveness of the insurgent front. This proved particularly disastrous in 1994–1995, when a Buddhist faction, the Democratic Kayin Buddhist Army (DKBA), broke away from the Christian-dominated KNU and subsequently helped the army capture Manerplaw, until then the impregnable base camp of this the strongest of the nationalist groups and, at the same time, the physical and symbolic center of the democracy movement in the "liberated areas."[85] Since then, the few remaining insurgent groups have been fighting a largely defensive guerrilla war against the expanding control of the army with little apparent hope of reasserting their authority over significant areas. The KNU, in December 2003, agreed with the government to a cessation of hostilities, raising the possibility that it might join the political process and leave the smaller armed groups with little choice but to follow. The peace talks stalled, however, after the purge in 2004 of Khin Nyunt, who was the main government negotiator.

The fading away of insurgency reflects a number of changes in the external environment. The massive expansion of the armed forces undertaken by the SLORC/SPDC has allowed the government to apply much stronger and more consistent pressure on the insurgents. The army now has the capability to attack on more fronts at one time, as well as to keep up its maneuvers during the rainy season, which used to be an important time of respite and reorganization for the ethnic forces.[86] The military regime has also succeeded to a large extent in undermining the economic base of the insurgencies. By applying a double strategy of attacking insurgent strongholds on the Chinese and Thai borders and liberalizing border trade, it has cut off much of the lucrative black market trade that traditionally financed the insurgent armies. At the same time, ethnic insurgents in the southeast have been weakened by a shift in Thai foreign policy. Until the late 1980s, the Thai government tacitly allowed groups like the KNU to retreat into Thailand when they were under attack from government forces. This served Thai interests since the KNU and other anticommunist forces provided an important buffer between the CPB and Thailand's own communist insurgency. Yet, since SLORC assumed power and the communist parties disintegrated on both sides of the border, Thai leaders have found it more advantageous to seek an improvement in their relations with the government. The insurgent groups have thus come under significant Thai pressure to reach peace with Rangoon. Indeed, during a critical period in the mid-1990s, the Thai authorities not only moved to stop the Burmese insurgents from retreating into safety across the border, but on several occasions allowed the army to cross into Thailand and attack them from behind.

It may be too early to proclaim the end of insurgency in Burma. Although the SLORC/SPDC in negotiating cease-fires have shown more political finesse than its military predecessors, like them, it has refused to enter into genuine political negotiations with the ethnic nationalists and no solutions have been found to the fundamental grievances of the minorities regarding local autonomy and ethnic rights. On the contrary, there have been frequent complaints by some cease-fire groups that the government has failed to follow up on its promises of economic aid and is violating the cease-fire agreements through economic activities and forcible recruitment of porters and other labor in their areas. With cease-fire groups expected to come under pressure to give up their arms once a new constitution is confirmed—but having got few concessions on their core claims for political, cultural, and economic rights—it is possible that some of the cease-fires will splinter and hard-line leaders will take their troops back to armed struggle. Yet, even if a new generation of conflicts were to emerge, the ethnic armed groups do not pose a serious threat to the military regime. The army today enjoys a massive superiority in both manpower and firepower, and without support from and access to neighboring countries, any sizable insurgent group would find it difficult to secure funding and supplies. It is also questionable whether they would find support from local communities, which have suffered immeasurable harm from five decades of armed conflict and, by and large, appear to appreciate the normalization of life brought about by the cease-fires, even if structural violence continues.

Cease-Fire Agreements

The cease-fires opened an alternative avenue for ethnic nationalists to pursue their goals. In fact, the cease-fire groups over the past decade have emerged as a significant political force, due partly to their potential for providing an alternative source of legitimacy for the military's transition plan, but also to their success in building new links and an emerging consensus among previously divided ethnic groups on their position within the Union. Since the launch of the government's road map in August 2003, the central negotiations over the future of the country have taken place not between the SPDC and the NLD, but between the SPDC and about twenty cease-fire groups, which joined the National Convention in May 2004 seemingly willing to accept a continuance of military control of the central state, provided they would be granted significant autonomy in their own areas along with guarantees of ethnic social, economic, and cultural rights. The significance of this was overlooked by many Western policy makers, who failed to recognize that an agreement between the military and the ethnic armies would lead to further marginalization of the NLD. Although the prospects for such a compromise, like for the KNU peace talks, have dimmed significantly after the removal of Khin Nyunt as the "new" leadership has retracted earlier promises made to the ethnic groups, the question is whether mainstream ethnic leaders see any real alternative to cooperating with the military regime. In many respects, developments over the past decade and a half have served only to emphasize to ethnic leaders the overwhelming dominance of the military among the Burmans and thus the need for them to find a way to work with the regime in order to avoid being lost in the political wilderness for another half a century.

The "legalization" of former insurgent groups created the potential for a new opposition alliance between Burman- and minority-based organizations, based not on armed struggle but on political cooperation at the center of national politics. Having set up liaison offices in Rangoon, the cease-fire groups over the past decade have operated in some ways like political parties. The NLD, however, has never fully recognized the legitimacy of the former insurgent groups, which on their part have remained skeptical about the commitment of the main opposition party to their cause. The reconvening of the National Convention in May 2004 provided an unprecedented opportunity for the two opposition fronts to present a common front, but the NLD's decision to boycott the proceedings underscored the gap between them and preempted further interethnic networking and confidence building. On their own, the cease-fire groups have provided a weaker counterbalance to military interests than would otherwise have been possible.

Overall, while the aspirations of the Burmese people for a better government are evident and many continue to work individually or in small groups for the betterment of their country, there is no evidence of the kind of organized mass movements that brought down, for example, President Marcos in the Philippines in 1986, the Thai generals in 1991–1992, or President Soeharto in Indonesia in 1998. As one of the most influential Burmese exile activists from the 1990s wrote in 2004, "The picture that emerges by comparing the NLD-led Burmese revolution and other active political struggles around the world depicts a Burmese public resigned not to support the dissidents or join in any revolutionary effort."[87] For the time being at least, the military regime has the upper hand on all fronts.

Bases of Power

The waning influence of a movement, which brought down the BSPP government and went on to secure a landslide victory in Burma's first free election in three decades, naturally raises questions about leadership and strategy. Yet, while the NLD may be criticized for being too confrontational—or too passive, depending on one's theory of transition—the huge, underlying power gap between military and civilian institutions in Burma, which is one of the contemporary world's most militarized societies, should remind us that removing the military from power always was going to be a very difficult and long-term process.

The modern Burmese state has been built through war and for the purpose of warfare, giving the military a unique role in society. The emergence of multiple insurgencies within the first few years of independence in 1948, compounded by the invasion of Chinese nationalist forces in 1949, impelled a period of rapid institutional development within the armed forces, which far outpaced improvements in civilian bureaucratic capacities. The result, as Mary Callahan shows in her unique study of the origins of military rule, was "military aggrandizement of resources, responsibilities, and powers in traditionally non-military realms," which eventually led General Ne Win to push aside the increasingly ineffectual parliamentary government and take full control of the country, at first temporarily under the caretaker government (1958–1960) but then more permanently with the 1962 coup and establishment of the Revolutionary Council.[88] Although Ne Win and other top military leaders in 1974 discarded their uniforms to head the nominally civilian BSPP government, the military remained the backbone of the state, with military officers dominating the party and other government institutions. Since 1988, the SLORC/SPDC has accelerated this process of military-led state building, diverting an ever larger proportion of the state's resources into the military and military-controlled institutions at the expense of autonomous civilian organizations.

The history of the military's state-building exercise is well covered in the scholarly literature, yet its implications for the struggle for democracy and human rights are often ignored by international policy makers and democracy activists alike. The NLD may be fighting a "just" cause, but the opposition is outmatched in several core dimensions of political power, including *violence*, *organization*, and *finance*. While the main opposition party clearly has broader *legitimacy* than the military regime, legitimacy is essentially a passive resource that needs to be "actualized" somehow in service of the organization or cause to which it relates. An examination of the distribution of these four bases of power tells us more about the prospects for regime change than any moral assumptions about "right" or "wrong."

Violence

The state in Burma, historically, has lacked the monopoly on the means of violence enjoyed by more consolidated states. In the early independence period, the national army was heavily outnumbered by the numerous insurgent groups, political pocket armies, and private security forces operating outside government control, and had to rely on an elaborate set of military alliances with local leaders to maintain peace.[89] By the mid-1970s, the Burmese heartland had been cleared of such autonomous, armed groups. Yet, the army lacked the manpower, as well as the mobility, firepower, and logistical support necessary to defeat the major insurgent groups, which held sway over large parts of the border areas. As Andrew Selth observes, the army was in fact often "out-gunned and out-maneuvered by its opponents," who generally "enjoyed better sources of supply, shorter lines of communication and greater support from the local population."[90] Although the insurgents no longer presented a direct threat to the government, the existence of some two dozen armed groups with a combined force of around forty thousand soldiers around the country's periphery remained a source of instability, as well as a major drain on the military's limited resources.[91]

The 1988 "crisis" highlighted the unsustainability of this situation. The strength of antigovernment sentiments among the majority Burmans evident at the height of the popular uprising, coupled with the renewal of communist underground activity in the cities, raised the possibility that urban opposition could develop into armed insurrection and link up with rebel forces in the border areas.[92] As if to underscore this, the three main insurgent armies—the CPB, the KNU, and the KIO—all launched major military offensives within months of the SLORC's take-over, resulting in some of the hardest fought battles the country had seen in years.[93] Insurgents even began filtering back into parts of central Burma, from whence they had been displaced twenty years earlier. At the same time, the emergence of a Western alliance vocally backing the democracy forces raised anew the specter of external intervention in the country's internal conflicts, which had haunted the country's leaders since independence.

If Burma's military leaders in 1988 had reasons to feel insecure about their ability to stem the tide of revolution, armed or otherwise, this is much less the case today, however. Immediately upon taking control of the state, the SLORC embarked on a major expansion and modernization of the armed forces, as well as the police and other auxiliary security forces, which continues under the SPDC although at reduced pace. Over the past eighteen years, the regime has more than doubled the size of the armed forces from 186,000 to around 400,000 soldiers.[94] It has also greatly increased Burma's defense imports from $18 million per year in 1970–1988 to $138 million per year in 1988–1997[95] and expanded the indigenous defense industry, thus vastly improving the firepower and logistical capacity of the previously underresourced armed forces. This expansion has benefited all services, including military intelligence (MI), which since 1962 has been responsible for surveillance of the civilian population as well as members of the armed forces and is responsible for most arrests of political suspects (on the recent changes to MI, see the next section). The police force has also been strengthened from 50,000 to about 72,000, including 4,500 combat police stationed in strategic areas of the main cities,[96] and has been brought under direct military control. In addition, the regime has stepped up military training of civilians, including members of the civil service, the USDA, the Myanmar Fire Brigade, and the Myanmar Red Cross. These paramilitary forces are integral to the army's plans for defense against a foreign invasion, but have also been used to intimidate potential opposition and break up any signs of mobilization against the regime.

The implications of this strengthening of the security forces for the balance of political power are threefold. First of all, the military since 1988 has consolidated its control of the main population centers. This is not so much a matter of conventional troop strength. Although several new army battalions have been established in and around the main cities to ensure that sufficient soldiers are at hand to quell any renewed unrest, the SLORC/SPDC since taking power has rarely used military force against the political opposition and only in very limited form.[97] The key to the regime's control of the population in central Burma is the intelligence apparatus, which together with its liberal use of a range of national security laws enforced by a pliant judicial system has turned Burma into what Trevor Wilson describes as "one of the most effective police states in the world."[98] The military leadership controls a massive surveillance network, which incorporates both military and (nominally) civilian intelligence agencies, as well as tens of thousands of informers and an increasingly sophisticated electronic monitoring system. There are few organizations in Burma today which have not been infiltrated by military intelligence. Monitoring of private phones, faxes, e-mails, and even normal mail is used routinely to keep tabs on people who are suspected of antigovernment activities. The police and local government organizations, such as the neighborhood warden system, which patrols urban and rural neighborhoods to ensure that people are not staying away from home without official notification, also report to military intelligence. Although the surveillance may be broader than it is deep, the common perception among Burmese that "MI knows everything" creates an atmosphere of fear and distrust in which people essentially police themselves. This makes organizing by dissident groups, whether above- or underground, extremely difficult. As Christina Fink observes, "No one knows whom they can or cannot trust, so activists find it hard to expand their organisations or activities beyond a small group of sure friends."[99]

Little information has as yet emerged about the changes since the purge of Khin Nyunt in 2004 and subsequent dismantling of his military intelligence apparatus. The new Office of Military Affairs Security, which has been brought back into the army command structure directly under control of the army hierarchy, appears to be much smaller than the former MI and to have had its responsibilities significantly reduced. By contrast, the Police Special Branch, under the Minister of Home Affaires, has been expanded and seems to have taken over much of the surveillance of political groups, as well as international agencies. It has also been hosting and participating in various seminars, for example, on peace building and economic reform, much like MI used to do under Khin Nyunt. These changes are likely to have reduced the overall ability of the intelligence agencies, both to monitor the population and provide timely information to the government. Indeed, activists outside the country have suggested that this would be a good time to launch a revolution. No doubt, though, the authorities are working overtime to redress any weaknesses and—apart, perhaps, from the triple bombing in Rangoon in May 2005, which killed over twenty people, the most deadly such attack in recent times—there have been no signs that the regime's control is slipping dangerously.

In addition to tightening its stranglehold over the urban population, the SLORC/SPDC has significantly increased the territorial reach of the state, leaving only some small "islands" in the most remote areas under full control of antigovernment forces. The regime was helped in this respect by a number of fortuitous developments, notably the collapse of the CPB in 1989, which removed the strongest of the insurgent groups (and the only one with a significant potential constituency in the main cities). The growing power projection capability of the army, however, has been a crucial factor as well, and has decisively altered the balance of military power in the country. According to Andrew Selth, during the 1991–1992 dry season, the army—for the first time—was able to "conduct concurrent campaigns against ethnic and religious minorities along the borders with Thailand, Bangladesh and India."[100] In the mid- to late 1990s, further large-scale military operations were undertaken against nearly all remaining major insurgent bases, which were overrun one by one, forcing the last insurgent groups to retreat into the most remote areas from where they have been limited to small-scale guerrilla warfare. Since then, roads have been built into many previously insurgent-controlled or contested areas. Numerous new, permanent army bases have also been established, greatly increasing the government's physical control of local populations and ensuring that the army can respond quickly to any signs of rebellion. The twenty or so cease-fire groups have varying degrees of authority over local areas, but only the Wa enjoy near full autonomy. Several of these groups, in fact, serve as government militias and have engaged in battles against the remaining insurgent groups alongside or on behalf of the army. Although some of the cease-fires are under growing strain, the now overwhelming military superiority of the national army means that future armed challenges to the regime are likely to be of little consequence at the heart of the state. Any risk that a broader antigovernment movement could emerge bridging the traditional center-periphery divide thus also appears to have been removed.

Finally, as an important corollary to the expansion of the army's presence up-country, the central government—for the first time since the Union of Burma was formed in 1948—has established control of the country's borders. A significant part of the post-1988 military buildup is concentrated along the borders with Thailand, China, India, and Bangladesh. A new border administration—generally known by its Burmese acronym *Na-Sa-Ka*—has also been established, incorporating army and military intelligence personnel, as well as emigration and customs. As evident from the large-scale illegal population movements in and out of the country, as well as the existence of cross-border aid programs not sanctioned by the Burmese authorities, the length and remoteness of many parts of Burma's borders make absolute control all but impossible. Yet, the central government today has much greater control, among other things, over external trade flows and thus a stronger claim to be treated by foreign countries as the sole authority of the country (whether that authority is considered legitimate or not). This further strengthens the regime and diminishes the prospects of a return to large-scale rebellion.

Organization

While the military regime's repressive capabilities provide the all-important backdrop, the true measure of its political power, however, is its organizational reach. The Burmese military since 1962 has dominated all elements of the state, including the legislative, executive, and judicial branches; it has controlled the media; it has established a range of mass organizations, which populate the space normally filled by civil society; and it has run a wide network of state-owned, as well as joint-venture and nominally private enterprises. Although the collapse of the BSPP government in 1988, superficially, saw the disappearance of most of the institutions established during the socialist period, many were quickly resurrected under new names but with much of the same personnel and similar purposes and responsibilities. In fact, the SLORC/SPDC has further extended the military's control over traditionally civilian institutions through the systematic placement of military officers at increasingly lower levels of the state and promotion of state-organized mass organizations at the expense of traditional civil society. The demands on the general population for participation in and support of the state's activities through mass organizations, political rallies, and miscellaneous compulsory "donations" have also increased. Through these institutions, the military leadership is able to mobilize at will a large proportion of the population and the country's resources in support of its objectives and activities, while preempting the emergence of alternative power structures.

The executive arm of the central government has four tiers, all controlled by the military—the ruling council, the cabinet, a dozen policy coordination committees, and about forty ministries. At the apex, the ruling council (the SPDC) consists entirely of generals at the lieutenant general level or above.[101] The full council meets only half a dozen times a year, including regular quarterly meetings and at times of national crisis and major political decisions. Its chairman, Senior General Than Shwe, however, concurrently serves as de facto head of the cabinet and defense minister.[102] The top generals also head key policy committees, such as the Committee on Implementation of Special Projects (Than Shwe), the Trade Policy Council (SPDC vice-chairman Vice-Senior General Maung Aye), and the Central Committee of the National Convention (secretary-1 Lieutenant General Thein Sein), which supervise and coordinate ministerial activities in their respective areas. The cabinet includes a few civilian ministers, but none are in a position of any real influence. In fact, the whole executive system down to and including director generals is stacked with active and retired military officers who are subservient to the military hierarchy.[103] The SPDC also effectively controls the judicial system through the appointment of the attorney general, as well as senior judges, and frequently intervenes in the judicial process, particularly in "political" cases.

From the center, political authority radiates outward through three partly overlapping administrative networks. The most powerful of these is the four-tiered structure of *Peace and Development Councils* (PDCs) under the SPDC—state/division, district, township, and village/ward. Composed of local military commanders, police, and civil service officers from the relevant levels of administration, the main responsibilities of the PDCs are to "enforce law and order, to pass on the directives of the central state to the subordinate structures, and to coordinate the activities of the subordinate political organs as well as other state departments and economic agencies."[104] State/division PDCs are chaired by the regional commanders, who since 1988 have been given extensive autonomy in the general administration of their regions and thus effectively act as governors. Township and village/ward PDCs have civilian leaders—in fact some of the latter are elected locally—but nonetheless are an integral part of the system of state control. The village/ward PDCs, for example, are responsible for enforcing state policies, such as agricultural production quotas, at the individual household level, as well as for organizing communities to provide labor and financial contributions for state projects. They also serve a control function through their surveillance of community life, including the monitoring of people's movements, which must be reported to military intelligence.[105]

The *civil service* forms a parallel administrative structure throughout the country down to the township level, but is under double military control, subservient to a military minister as well as to the local commander. As Ardeth Maung Thawnghmung observes, "Each national ministry and department has its functions-based specialization, field-staff of specialists, and performs its particular functions, and yet none of its subordinate organs can implement their own policies without consulting and getting approval from the [PDC] at their parallel levels."[106] Although the large majority of officials outside the top levels of the central government are civilians, the power gap between them and the soldiers among them ensures that all defer to the military hierarchy. Moreover, most civil servants are rotated around the country every two to three years in order to ensure that they do not form loyalties that conflict with the needs of the state.

The third arm of the SLORC/SPDC's politico-administrative structure is the state's mass organizations—usually referred to as government-organized nongovernmental organizations, or GONGOs—which serve to mobilize support for the government's objectives and policies, implement specific programs, and disseminate official orthodoxy around the country. The largest and most powerful of these is the USDA, which officially boasts 21.6 million members[107]—more than one-third of the entire population—and has sections at the state/division, district, and township level, as well as in many wards and villages. Other prominent GONGOs, with a nationwide structure, are the Myanmar Women's Affairs Federation (MWAF, 1.6 million members), the Myanmar Maternal and Child Welfare Association (4.4 million members), the Myanmar War Veteran's Organization (136,000 members), the Myanmar Fire Brigade (104,000 members), and the Myanmar Red Cross Society (260,000 members). While all of these are classified by the government as civil society organizations, they are usually run directly by senior military officers—or, in the first two examples, by their wives—and benefit from the use of public buildings, as well as privileged access to economic monopoly activities.

The USDA was formed explicitly to support the national objectives of the military, including the three national causes.[108] Its patron is Senior General Than Shwe and the Central Committee includes a dozen high-ranking officers and ministers. Established within a few weeks of the convening of the first National Convention in 1993, it is an overtly political machine intended among other things to secure a favorable outcome in a future constitutional referendum and subsequent elections. Although most of the GONGOs serve developmental roles as well,[109] they operate top-down through rigid hierarchies and their fundamental purpose is to serve the state (rather than represent community interests). They figure prominently in the state-controlled press, where they are presented as the "voice of the people," invariably expressing support for government objectives and denigrating antigovernment forces, both at home and abroad.[110] Moreover, they work closely with the PDCs in mobilizing communities for participation in mass rallies, state development projects, and other activities seen to benefit the national interest.

Membership of the GONGOs is ostensibly voluntary. Yet, the incentives for participating are deliberately structured to swell the ranks, and many people do not perceive that they have any choice but to join. This is particularly the case for the USDA, which has been expanded aggressively, seemingly as a sort of statistical counterweight to the NLD.[111] The benefits of membership range from power and prestige to better business and educational opportunities, social welfare benefits, and greater freedom of travel, as well as protection against state demands for labor and other contributions. Conversely, some of those who have resisted joining or participating in required activities have lost their jobs, been failed in school exams, or otherwise denied access to scarce resources.

Although the military's ability to mobilize the population may seem "sterile" in some respects, the role of the GONGOs in regime maintenance should not be underestimated. Significant numbers of people are attracted by the power that comes with leadership positions in the state's organizations and willingly participate in the subjugation of other members of their communities. The GONGOs are also used for the distribution of the rewards and punishments, which lie at the heart of the broader system of social control. In addition, the demand on people's time and resources that comes with participation in these organizations leaves less space for participation in genuine civil society organizations. Monique Skidmore has found evidence that "the formation of GONGOs is, in a very short period of time, significantly changing the community structure and forms of association that existed prior to their introduction. A clear pattern emerges here despite the diversity and character of individual wards within the relocated townships. As the townships become more established, non-governmental community groups such as Buddhist organisations and community social groups are slowly losing influence as GONGOs aimed at specific demographics rise in prominence."[112] The extensive membership of the GONGOs—along with that of the armed forces, civil service, and other state organizations—means that nearly every family, at least in central parts of the country, has one or more members who work for, or in one form or another represent, the military state. Even if people resent the regime, this has important implications, for example, for the exposure to military orthodoxy and the sense of autonomy from the state, which would be respectively lesser and greater without such organizations.

The prevalent assumption is that the USDA will be turned into a political party before the next elections. This has reportedly been denied by its secretary-general, Major General Htay Oo,[113] and would run afoul of at least two clauses in the new constitution.[114] But whatever model the military leaders have in mind, there is no doubt that the USDA, along with the more recently established MWAF[115] and other state-sponsored mass organizations, will be used as "electoral machines" to secure support for loyal candidates, as well as to maintain central government control at the local level. Since 2004, local USDA chapters have been directed to step up their recruitment drive and support for local development projects (the latter seemingly in an effort to gain increased legitimacy in local communities). Individual members have also increasingly been given formal administrative roles, for which they are provided training by military and government officials in such matters as the management and control of local communities.[116] It seems likely that USDA members in the future will be favored for local leadership positions as a means of securing continued centralization of power through strict hierarchies, much like was the case under the BSPP regime.[117]

Burmese society is not devoid of organizations outside the state. Compared to the BSPP era, some limited space for independent activity has opened up under the SLORC/SPDC. Yet, political and civil society remains tightly regulated and, after twenty-six years of the Burmese Way to Socialism, there has been almost no institutional legacy to draw upon. In the absence of a constitution, the political parties have yet to be given any role in the governance of the country and most consist almost solely of a small number of leaders based in Rangoon. Only the NLD ever established a countrywide organizational structure, but repression and underachievement has seen it fall into disrepair. Community-based organizations engaged in social welfare activities continue to expand both in numbers and, more slowly, in capacity, encouraged by deteriorating socioeconomic conditions and international support.[118] There are also a growing, if still limited, number of more substantial nongovernmental professional and development organizations today. The emergence and continued operation of such organizations, however, depend on their remaining strictly apolitical.

In some respects, since the cease-fires, the greatest space for civil society has opened up in parts of the border areas. In addition to the cease-fire groups, which in the future may convert into political parties, several cultural and development organizations have emerged or stepped up their activities to address the long legacy of conflict and central government neglect.[119] The churches, which are a vital element of community life in large parts of Kachin, Chin, and Karen state, also generally maintain greater autonomy than the *Sangha*. Such anomalies, however, reflect perceptions—probably correct—on part of the military leadership that the influence of these organizations on the struggle for state power is minimal. In political terms, the military's organizational dominance remains near absolute.[120]

Finance

Most analysts view the economy as a major weakness of the military regime. Advocates of sanctions, in particular, have argued that the SLORC/SPDC's economic failures must eventually force it to compromise with the opposition in order to revive international trade, investment, and aid. Yet, what matters for regime maintenance is not so much the health of the economy as the distribution of economic resources in society (more specifically, the relative capacity of different groups to finance their political activities and underwrite core support groups). From this perspective, the economy, far from being a "weakness" of the regime—never mind a likely source of its demise—emerges as another important base of power.

The Burmese military has a long history of economic control. The first military economic enterprise, the Defense Services Institute (DSI), was established already in 1951. Originally designed as a nonprofit enterprise to provide basic necessities such as food and clothing for the troops, under the caretaker government (1958–1960) it was registered under the Companies Act and granted a number of economic privileges, such as exemption from sales tax, customs duties, and port fees.[121] As a result, it expanded rapidly to become the largest company in the country with interests in a wide range of companies, setting an important precedent for the future. Although the DSI was nationalized after the 1962 coup, along with about fifteen thousand other businesses, the military-as-government continued to expand its economic control. Under the cover of socialist economic priorities, the state took control of most of the formal economy, including use of the country's abundant natural resources, both above- and underground. Since 1988, the SLORC/SPDC has again opened up the economy to private economic activity, including foreign direct investment, but as David Steinberg concludes, "Although there is a growing set of private business interests ostensibly outside of state control, the iron glove of the military envelops the invisible hand of the private sector."[122]

The SLORC/SPDC controls the state, and the state controls large parts of the economy. Under the current system, the top generals set both economic policy and national budget priorities. The military-as-government dictates key economic signals including interest rates; foreign exchange rates; and prices of strategic goods such as electricity, transport, and petrol, as well as rice and other agricultural products, although the latter is increasingly done indirectly through trade controls. It also determines the allocation of public investments, state loans, land, electricity, export/import licenses, foreign exchange, and other scarce resources—and it does so with no accountability or countervailing power.

In addition to controlling economic policy, the military leadership makes production decisions for a large number of companies, including state economic enterprises (SEEs) and a number of military-owned "private" enterprises, most of which not only are subject to the dictates of the senior military leadership, but actually are run by lower-ranking officers (usually at the lieutenant colonel level). The SEEs, despite official government commitment to privatization, still account for 25 percent of gross domestic product (GDP) and 30 percent of external trade,[123] as well as being the primary partners for foreign investors. Most are managed by ministries such as Industry I, Industry II, and Energy, but others are directly under the military's Directorate of Procurement.

The military-as-institution also participates directly in the "private" economy through a number of military-owned economic enterprises, including the Union of Myanmar Economic Holding (UMEH) and the Myanmar Economic Corporation (MEC). The UMEH, which was established in 1990, mainly to serve the welfare needs of military personnel, is jointly owned by the Ministry of Defense, various regimental funds and veteran's organizations, and individual serving and retired officers. It has a total authorized share capital of 10 billion kyatt of which Kt3.8 billion was paid up in 2000, making it the largest holding company in the country.[124] Like its forerunner, the DSI, in the 1950s, it is involved in a broad range of sectors, including trading, banking, hotels and tourism, property development, and manufacturing. The MEC is a similar, but more strategic, company, set up in 1997 to decrease the military's dependence on state budgets by providing additional funds and producing militarily relevant products.[125] Wholly owned by the Ministry of Defense, with the quartermaster general acting as chairman of the board, it has strong interests in heavy industry such as steel and power generation, as well as communication technology. The two companies, like their private counterparts, generally appear to be responding to economic policy rather than influencing it. Yet, they have privileged access to sectors otherwise monopolized by the state, along with free use of military personnel, land, facilities, and transport, which gives them a distinct advantage over private businesses in the same fields. Not surprisingly, they are said to be making large profits, benefiting the military-as-institution as well as individual members of the armed forces at the expense of civilian businesses.[126]

With a stranglehold on the economy, the military possesses numerous tools of political control. In addition to funding military and civilian organizations, as already discussed, the generals make extensive use of their economic authority and resources for patronage purposes. The SLORC/SPDC through the diversion of resources to the military and its officer corps seeks to ensure that its core support base is isolated from the economic depression affecting the general population. This includes direct support in the form of subsidized consumer goods,[127] access to exclusive military educational and health facilities, jobs for military family members, and so on, but perhaps more importantly a tacit tolerance of personal rent seeking by military and civilian state personnel, which has made some high-ranking military officers very wealthy, while allowing others to at least supplement their incomes.

Government largesse is used also to co-opt potential opposition. As noted, prominent monks have received generous donations and personal gifts from military leaders in order to enlist their support in controlling the *Sangha*. The cease-fire groups similarly have been given licenses for economic activities as well as support for infrastructure development in their areas in return for their cooperation with the government. At an individual level, members of the NLD have been offered rewards for quitting the party, while the population at large is enticed by economic and other perks to join government organizations such as the USDA. More subtly, the imperative of maintaining access to scarce resources such as jobs and business licenses controlled by the military ensures that the business, middle, and working classes are less inclined to "rock the boat" than they might otherwise have been. This control of economic goods and opportunities is a critical factor in ensuring that large segments of the population comply with government directives rather than march in the streets, and may well be used also to ensure a favorable outcome in future elections. Until such a time, as in 1988, when regime change seems imminent, most members of the general public are likely to continue to follow a course that maximizes their short-term welfare, whatever their feelings about the government or its policies. For the individual at least, this is rational, utility-maximizing behavior.

The failure of the SLORC/SPDC, like previous military regimes, to mobilize Burma's rich economic resources in support of broad-based economic growth ultimately inhibits it from fully realizing its vision for the country and its armed forces. Yet, the resources available are undoubtedly sufficient for maintaining power as long as the generals agree on prioritizing this objective. Burma may be one of the world's poorest countries, but there are numerous ways for the military to mobilize the necessary financial resources. When foreign exchange reserves run low, it barters or buys arms on credit instead. When normal tax revenue is insufficient to cover outlays, the government prints more money, effectively passing the bill on to the general population through inflation. In 1998, when the SPDC faced problems in resourcing its massive army, the Ministry of Defense simply ordered local commanders to find what they needed locally. For an organization that controls most of the resources in a country, even one as poor as Burma, there are always ways, and the economic pain—whether internally created or externally imposed—is often pushed on to the general population. As with the use of violence—and indeed this is a form of structural violence—there may be a limit to how long this strategy can work. Yet, with the opposition decimated and the population cowed, the breaking point could be long in waiting.

Importantly, the cash crunch, which faced the SLORC/SPDC throughout the 1990s, has been significantly alleviated. The government since 2000 has been bringing in up to $400 million annually in shared revenue and taxes from two offshore natural gas fields, Yadana and Yetagun in the Gulf of Martaban, its single largest source of income.[128] New massive finds in three fields in the Gulf of Bengal—Shwe, Shwe Phyu, and Mya, the first two already under development and expected to start production in 2010—have sparked an intense bidding war between New Delhi, Beijing, and Bangkok, all of which are seeking sole rights to the gas. The three fields, which are known jointly as the Shwe project, hold 5.7–10 trillion cubic feet (TcF) of gas, estimated to be worth another $600–800 million annually for the Burmese government over the next twenty to twenty-five years.[129] State-owned companies from the same three countries are competing as well with Malaysian, Japanese, South Korean, and Russian companies for further exploration and extraction rights, with more significant finds already confirmed, notably in another block (M9) in the Gulf of Martaban currently being explored by Thailand's PTT Exploration and Production. According to official estimates, Burma has total gas reserves of 88 TcF, only slightly less than Indonesia.[130] Moreover, Thailand and China are both planning massive investments in a series of hydropower plants on the Salween and other rivers, Thailand's MDX Group having in 2006 inked a $6 billion contract for the largest one at Ta Sang.[131]

By selling off the country's natural resources, the powers that be will be able to secure their own financial position for decades to come. The key question therefore may no longer be whether the regime can survive economically, but whether the windfall from these concessions—through the institution of economic reforms—could come to benefit the wider society as well. Paradoxically, by limiting policy dialogue and capacity building, existing Western policies make economic reform less likely.

Legitimacy

The main Achilles heel of the military is its lack of legitimacy. Yet, even in this area, the weakness of the regime is easily overestimated (as is the strength of the opposition). Research indicates that—at least among the rural population—negative assessments of the top leaders in the capital are less pervasive than often assumed. Many farmers convey positive—or at least ambiguous—sentiments about senior leaders, who are credited, for example, for beneficial programs such as the expansion of summer paddy, or for disciplining local officials who are held directly responsible for daily abuses, including corruption and the enforcement of harmful policies.[132] In a similar vein, Ingrid Jordt argues that the regime's propagation of Buddhism may give it a certain support among the country's many devout Buddhists.[133]

In the meantime, the depth of support for the NLD appears to be waning. Considerable numbers of Burmese, particularly within the intelligentsia, today criticize the main opposition party for having contributed to the country's problems by unnecessarily confronting the generals and calling for international economic sanctions. Such people support the quest for democracy, but are less certain that Aung San Suu Kyi or her coleaders in the NLD are going about it the right way.[134] Others are simply getting frustrated with the political elites on all sides, none of whom have delivered on their promises to help them. Trevor Wilson sums up this ambiguity regarding the NLD: "Internationally, the NLD is seen as enjoying enormous popularity across Burma. To a great extent this is certainly true, but it is a simplified perception. Some Burmese support the NLD perhaps because there are few alternatives; others support the NLD's allies rather than the NLD itself. But some Burmese, who do not support the military at all, are not sure the NLD is the answer."[135]

The more important question though, in assessing the balance of power, is how much legitimacy matters. Clearly, a lack of legitimacy on the part of the military increases the costs of maintaining power and generally carrying out the functions of government as many people simply ignore or actively circumvent government directives, requiring more resources to be spent on surveillance and coercion than would otherwise have been the case. It also presents an obstacle to the institutionalization of military control under a new constitution, as evident from the fact that the constitution-drafting process has taken fourteen years. The value of legitimacy for the party in opposition, however, is more difficult to ascertain. It is not evident that the rejection of the regime—or even a more positive commitment to the NLD—by large segments of the population provides much practical support for the opposition in its struggle to force the military out of power. As noted, popular activism is at a very low level—and has been so historically, except at times of regime crisis such as in 1988 when the balance of power seemed to be shifting and hopes for political change escalated. Most people in Burma expect Aung San Suu Kyi personally to bring about change and do not see themselves playing a direct role in this. In Kei Nemoto's words: "The people seem to have little interest in her philosophy of democracy or her precepts relating to the making of a future democratic Burma. . . . What the ordinary people expect from Suu Kyi is to become the political leader and change Burma promptly to the 'golden age of democracy' where the nation enjoys peace and prosperity."[136] This may be linked to widespread beliefs that the opposition leader has mystic powers, as well as to people's own sense of disempowerment and helplessness in changing their situation.

The crucial point here is that, while the military leaders would like to gain the support and admiration of the population—for self-esteem as well as more practical reasons of authority and control—they do not need it to maintain power. All they need is the acquiescence of enough people to make it possible for them to maintain control and isolate the activists (as they have done successfully over the past nineteen years). Faced with the military's superior means of violence, organization, and finance, not only has the great majority of the population remained passive, but many are also cooperating with the regime, to varying degrees. For these reasons, for the NLD or other opposition groups to rely on their legitimacy alone is likely to be a losing strategy. They need to somehow reverse the current imbalance in other bases of power.

Prospects for Regime Change

The outpouring of popular discontent during the 1988 uprising and 1990 election was widely perceived as a decisive moral victory for the democracy forces. The timing of these events, which coincided with the fall of the Berlin Wall and revolutionary regime changes in Eastern Europe, not to mention democratic breakthroughs in Latin America, Asia, and Africa, further fueled perceptions that Burma's military rulers were destined for the dustbin of history, thus establishing an analytical prism that emphasized regime weaknesses. Indeed, during the 1990s, it often seemed as if analysts were expected to "prove" the impending collapse of the military regime and thereby justify existing hopes and strategies for democratization. Yet, for all the speculations about military disunity, economic collapse, or a final international push that would bring the regime to its knees, no significant cracks in the armor of the regime have emerged.[137] On the contrary, the military seems more dominant than ever.

The generals who rule Burma today may have taken power relatively recently, but the structures of control on which their power rests have been built over more than half a century. The Burmese military has played a leading role in the building of the state since independence in 1948, and has ruled the country directly for more than half of that time. Since 1962, military authority has been strengthened through the deliberate militarization or dismantling of civilian institutions within the state as well as in the broader society. Indeed, the long history of internal security problems has created a gulf between the general population and the military, which has come to see the Burmese people not as citizens but as potential enemies of the state and therefore has worked to ensure that no centers of power develop outside its ambit. Although the 1988 uprising revealed the residual power of civil society, the underlying structures of power withstood the onslaught and once the military leaders were back in full control of the government, they redoubled their efforts to immunize the state against any future threats. Having discarded the socialist framework for state policy, the SLORC/SPDC over the past nineteen years has used the country's resources unsparingly to build an armed forces—and a regime—that is significantly stronger today than it was then, both militarily, organizationally, and, despite the economic "crisis," economically.

The NLD, by contrast, is a newcomer on the political scene, born literally in the dying days of the BSPP government, and operates in a narrow political space almost devoid of any other politically relevant civil society groups. The main opposition party—and the movement it leads—was, and remains, institutionally weak, made up of a disparate set of actors with widely varying backgrounds and ideas about how to carry the struggle forward. It has had a trump card in the legitimacy and global recognition of Aung San Suu Kyi, but while dissatisfaction with military rule in the general population is pervasive, popular mobilization behind the party's program has proven to be ephemeral. Although the 1988 uprising in Burma saw evidence of the kind of mass movements that have brought authoritarian regimes down elsewhere in Asia and the wider world, democracy activists ultimately have failed to build lasting, functional coalitions with other segments of society that could create the consistent critical mass of opposition necessary for regime change. This may partly reflect the failure of individual leaders and organizations to devise effective strategies suitable to Burma's unique political environment. Underlying this, however, are also several deep-seated structural obstacles to effective opposition in the country's undeveloped political society.

One of the greatest challenges for the democracy movement is the lack of autonomous organizations. It is nearly impossible to achieve a sustained social movement without effective organizations. As Sidney Tarrow argues, activists need to create formal organizations "that are sufficiently robust to structure sustained relations with opponents, but are flexible enough to permit the informal connections that link people and networks to one another to aggregate and coordinate contention."[138] The NLD today faces the same problem the students did in 1988. Burmese society lacks organizations that can carry the struggle into the realm of institutional bargaining and on which the regime depends for the maintenance of the existing order. The fundamental fragmentation of society may be overcome temporarily in times of crisis when people are drawn together by common frustrations and the excitement of the moment. Yet, challenges to the regime that result in widespread social unrest provoke a knee-jerk response from the military leaders and ultimately are no match for an army prepared to shoot.

The absence of political organizations reflects another structural problem at the individual or household level. For people to participate in sustained opposition, they need certain resources and outlooks. Yet, the large majority of the Burmese population live at subsistence level, preoccupied with the daily needs of survival. They may well share the aspirations of democracy activists for a better government, but they have little time to engage in noneconomic activities and cannot take the risk of losing their freedom or jobs on which their families depend for survival. Aung San Suu Kyi and the NLD have tried to persuade people that democracy is about them and their daily lives, but in practical terms that is simply not the case—not in the short term anyway, and for the poor there is no other time perspective that matters. As Ardeth Maung Thawnghmung concludes, based on her research in Burmese rice farming villages,

> Paddy farmers are more likely to use passive resistance and individual contacting, which present the most clear, direct, and immediate link between actions and results. The option for voice through peaceful protests, not to mention violent actions or rebellions, is usually non-existent, since the results of exercising voice are often uncertain, risky, and dangerous. . . . The goals of paddy farmers' resistance against the state is directed towards changing particular policies and practices that have a detrimental impact on their lives, and it is seldom aimed at changing those responsible for peasants' economic stress and disaster, or the government in power.[139]

Students, monks, and other young activists are often freer to engage in antigovernment activities since they do not have the same family responsibilities. The military's extensive use of collective punishment of family members and other people associated with activists, however, appears to have succeeded in its goal of enlisting parents, teachers, senior monks, and so on, in disciplining the younger generations.

In addition to these general problems of mobilization, the opposition to the military is divided by ethnicity. While the establishment of the DAB in the aftermath of the 1988 uprising was seen by some observers as an indication that the traditional gap between majority Burman organizations at the center of the state and ethnic minority groups could be bridged, comments by ethnic leaders suggest that the experience of living and working together with Burman activists may in fact have reinforced existing prejudices.[140] Martin Smith, similarly, suggests that negative perceptions of the democracy groups that formed on the border were partially responsible for the decision by groups such as the KIO to seek common ground, through the cease-fire process, with the military regime instead of the opposition.[141] Although ethnic minority leaders have generally expressed support for the democratic cause, their primary concerns are with local issues of autonomy, identity, and development. Aung San Suu Kyi and the NLD, on the other hand, seem to view the issue of ethnic rights and aspirations as secondary to democracy. On both sides, decades of armed conflict and propaganda have left deep scars of distrust.

Aung San Suu Kyi has often stated her conviction that time is on the side of the democracy movement, a view shared by many activists and proponents of the core strategy. This is not, however, borne out by developments on the ground over the past nineteen years, which have seen a steady weakening of the opposition in both relative and absolute terms. While the military leadership has consolidated its hold on the government, the state, and society, the NLD has fractured under pressure from the authorities and lack of political progress, and today faces a serious crisis of leadership as well as waning public confidence. Both sides suffer from overreliance on aging leaders. Yet, while the military regime has in place the institutional mechanisms for leadership succession, the NLD is totally reliant on Aung San Suu Kyi for both policy direction and popular support, which leaves the party acutely vulnerable to exigencies over which it has no control, such as her continued detention. This problem has been reinforced by the NLD's failure to rejuvenate and replenish its top ranks, which are currently dominated by octogenarians.[142] In the absence of effective leadership and organizations, despair dominates among the general public. More and more people seem resigned to the reality of military rule and inclined to work within the system to maximize their personal benefits rather than work to change it. At the same time, growing criticism of the NLD's strategies for change from both dissidents inside the country and activists abroad threatens to splinter the opposition (although that may turn out to be a blessing in disguise if new groups can emerge and reenergize the movement).

It is important to recognize the aspirations of the Burmese people for regime change, as well as the many committed and courageous individuals who continue to work to make it a reality. But effective strategies for change must take account of objective conditions. Given the current balance of power, realistically, the only chance for a breakthrough in the short term is a negotiated solution between military and civilian leaders emphasizing common concerns, which would remove the element of confrontation and thus neutralize the massive power imbalance that exists. Failing that, a longer-term process of military-controlled reform may over time allow the civilian counterelites to develop the organization and support necessary to become a more viable alternative to military rule. Either way, the military is likely, for the foreseeable future, to maintain control of—or, minimally, a veto over—all aspects of government and policy.

Notes

1. Ma Thanegi, "Sanctions Don't Bring Burma Democracy," *International Herald Tribune*, 20 March 1998.

2. See, for example, ALTSEAN, "Pressure Works: Burma Backs Off from ASEAN Chair," 6 August 2005; Zaid Ibrahim, "Losing Patience with Burma," *Wall Street Journal*, 13 January 2006 [op-ed].

3. Aung San Suu Kyi, "Speech to a Mass Rally at the Shwedagon Pagoda," in *Freedom from Fear and Other Writings*, 193 (London: Penguin Books, 1995).

4. The official number of deaths was 451, but most independent sources quote from several thousand to ten thousand fatalities. See Amnesty International, "Burma: The 18th September 1988 Military Takeover and Its Aftermath," December 1988; Bertil Lintner, *Outrage: Burma's Struggle for Democracy* (Bangkok: White Lotus, 1990).

5. Several thousand civil servants were later fired anyway for their role in the uprising or failure to denounce the democratic opposition in mandatory questionnaires distributed by the military authorities.

6. SLORC, Order No. 1/88, 18 September 1988.

7. Aung Gyi was expelled a few months later after accusing Aung San Suu Kyi of being influenced by communist members of the party. Tin Oo took over as chairman, while U Kyi Maung became vice-chairman.

8. Several veteran politicians from the period of parliamentary democracy in the 1950s formed their own parties, including former prime minister U Nu, who was deposed by the military in 1962. The people of Burma, however, were looking for something new and gave them little support.

9. Tin Maung Maung Than, "Myanmar: Military in Charge," in *Government and Politics in Southeast Asia*, ed. John Funston, 232 (Singapore: ISEAS, 2001).

10. Myanmar Ahlin Aung Than, *Record of Multi-Party Democracy General Election* (Rangoon: Aung Sitthi Sarpay, 2002).

11. SLORC, Order No. 2/88, 18 September 1988.

12. Josef Silverstein, "Aung San Suu Kyi: Is She Burma's Woman of Destiny?" *Asian Survey* 30, no. 10 (October 1990): 1012.

13. Stephen R. Heder, "The Struggle for Democracy and Human Rights in Myanmar: Opposition Politics in a Situation of Severe Repression," in *Human Rights in the*

Asia-Pacific Region, ed. John Girling, 56 (Canberra: Australian National University, 1991).

14. The NUP, which in the popular mind was closely associated with the military, got 25 percent of the vote but only 2 percent of the seats, while the remaining votes/seats were divided among twenty-five other parties, most of which ran on ethnic nationalist platforms in minority-dominated constituencies in the border areas.

15. Many foreign observers have, wrongly, described this as a turnaround in the military's position. Whatever its moral or legal merits, it was basically in line with comments made by several military leaders before the election who had argued that the first responsibility of the elected parliament would be to draw up a new constitution. See, for example, SLORC, 43rd News Conference, 9 June 1989; SLORC, 90th News Conference, 11 May 1990.

16. See comments by Secretary-1 Khin Nyunt, SLORC, 100th News Conference, 13 July 1990.

17. SLORC, 104th News Conference, 11 September 1990.

18. NLD, "Gandhi Hall Declaration," 28 July 1990.

19. NLD and UNLD, "Bo Aung Kyaw Street Declaration," 30 August 1990.

20. NLD, "Update: September 1990," in *Democracy and Politics in Burma: A Collection of Documents*, ed. Marc Weller, 197–98 (Manerplaw: NCGUB, 1991).

21. Khin Nyunt later claimed that military intelligence had confiscated documents from the NLD, which revealed that the party's youth group had recommended that the NLD take more drastic action and call for "initiating a general boycott, making the public service personnel join the boycott, halting government operations, destroying machinery and vital goods at factories and mills, and cutting all communications throughout the country." SLORC, 107th News Conference, 7 December 1990. Most of the other information provided in this briefing is corroborated by NLD sources, so the claim appears credible.

22. NCGUB, "The Birth of NCGUB," in Weller, *Democracy and Politics*, 236–38.

23. NCGUB, "Declaration of the National Coalition Government of the Union of Burma, 18 December 1990," in Weller, *Democracy and Politics*, 238–40.

24. NCGUB, "Statement to the People of Burma, 18 December 1990," in Weller, *Democracy and Politics*, 241–42.

25. NLD, "Observations of the National League for Democracy on the National Convention" (statement given at NLD press conference, NLD Headquarter, Rangoon, 22 November 1995).

26. BurmaNet editor, "Analysis of the USDA," *BurmaNet News*, 2 November 1996, www.burmanet.org/bnn_archives/1996/bnn1196n557.txt (accessed 26 April 2007).

27. SLORC, Order No. 5/96, "Law Protecting the Peaceful and Systematic Transfer of State Responsibility and the Successful Performance of the Functions of the National Convention against Disturbances and Oppositions," June 1996.

28. CRPP, Notification 1/1998, 16 September 1998.

29. Tin Maung Maung Than, "Military in Charge," 232.

30. Trevor Wilson, "An Australian Perspective on a Transitional Period in Myanmar: May 2000–May 2002," in *The Illusion of Progress: The Political Economy of Reform in Burma/Myanmar*, ed. David S. Mathieson and Ron J. May, 68 (Adelaide, Australia: Crawford House, 2004). Wilson was Australian ambassador in Burma from 2000 to 2003.

31. UN official, interview by author, Rangoon, June 2002.

32. *Myanmar Times*, 13–19 May 2002.

33. *Agence France Presse*, 2 January 2003.

34. NLD, "Statement on the 55th Anniversary of Independence Day," 4 January 2003.

35. NLD, "Statement on the 56th Anniversay of Union Day," 12 February 2003.

36. *Radio Free Asia*, Burmese language news broadcast, 23 April 2003.

37. Western diplomats, interviews by author, Rangoon, March–April 2003.

38. *Democratic Voice of Burma*, "No Plan to Talk to the NLD," 28 January 2003, www.burmanet.org/bnn_archives/2003/20030130.txt (accessed 26 April 2007).

39. International official, interview by author, Rangoon, May 2003.

40. *BBC*, Burmese language news broadcast, 10 May 2003.

41. According to a Western journalist, this order was confirmed by intelligence sources in Thailand. Interview by author, Bangkok, June 2003.

42. The actual events of 30 May are contested. According to the government, there was "a clash" between local supporters and opponents of the NLD, which left four dead and forty-eight injured. Military spokesmen denied all responsibility for the incident, which ostensibly resulted when Aung San Suu Kyi and her entourage tried to drive through a crowd of anti-NLD protesters. *New Light of Myanmar*, "Press Conference Clarifies Instigations to Cause Unrest," 1 June 2003. Members of the NLD reported that their motorcade was ambushed by hundreds of men, who also attacked local villagers with wooden clubs, pointed bamboo sticks, and other weapons, killing scores. Thai Senate Standing Committee on Foreign Affairs, "Affidavits by Eyewitnesses of the Depayin Massacre," 4 July 2003. Several dissident and activist groups abroad accused high-ranking officers of planning the attack, which they alleged was carried out by members of the USDA and prisoners from local jails who had been instructed in training sessions at local schools during the previous week. Ad-Hoc Commission on Depayin Massacre, "Preliminary Report," 4 July 2003. Some reports claimed that more than one hundred people were killed and secretly cremated at an army base. NCGUB, "Statement," 1 June 2003. Given the politicization of reporting on all sides, it is unlikely that the exact course of events will ever be known.

43. Information about the charge, which has never been made public by the government, was given to UN envoy Razali Ismail by Aung San Suu Kyi herself during his visit in mid-June 2003. International official, interview by author, Rangoon, 5 July 2003.

44. According to some sources, the commander-in-chief of the army, Vice-Senior General Maung Aye, and the head of military intelligence, General Khin Nyunt,

were not consulted about the attack and were "very upset." Interviews by author: military "insider," Rangoon, September 2003; international official, Rangoon, June 2003.

45. Prime Minister Khin Nyunt, "Developments and Progressive Changes in Myanmar Naing-ngan" (clarifications at the Pyithu Hluttaw, Rangoon, 30 August 2003).

46. UN official, interview by author, Rangoon, April 2004.

47. The government agreed to a demand that the NLD could choose its own delegates for the convention, but failed to offer firm promises that the constitutional principles adopted in 1993–1996 would be open to discussion. It also turned down demands that Aung San Suu Kyi and her deputy, Tin Oo, be released from house arrest and party offices allowed to reopen. The government's negotiators asked the NLD to be patient, arguing that the release of Aung San Suu Kyi could create unrest and undermine the convention. The party, however, did not feel that they were acting in good faith and therefore decided to boycott the assembly. International official, interview by author, Rangoon, May 2004.

48. See, for example, *New Light of Myanmar*, 25 May 2005.

49. NLD, "Special Declaration No. 1/02 (2006)," 12 February 2006.

50. NLD, "Special Statement," 20 April 2006 (copy in author's possession).

51. Associated Press, "NLD No More Influence," *BurmaNet News*, 27 March 2006, www.burmanet.org/news (accessed 27 March 2006).

52. *Irrawaddy* (online ed.), "NLD Under New Threat," 27 April 2006, www.irrawaddy.org (accessed 27 April 2006).

53. Nandar Chann, "Opposition Blues," *Irrawaddy* (print ed.) 13, no. 2 (February 2005).

54. See, for example, Aung Zaw, "Regrets: The Residue of the 1990 Election," *Irrawaddy* (online ed.), 27 May 2005, www.irrawaddy.org (accessed 27 May 2005); Zarni and May Oo, "Common Problems, Shared Responsibilities: Citizens' Quest for National Reconciliation in Burma/Myanmar," a Free Burma Coalition report, October 2004.

55. Interview with student leader Min Ko Naing, *Asiaweek*, 28 October 1989.

56. Josef Silverstein, "Burmese and Malaysian Student Politics: A Preliminary Comparative Enquiry," *Journal of Southeast Asian Studies* 1, no. 1 (1970): 3–22.

57. Kyaw Yin Hlaing, "Myanmar in 2004: Why Military Rule Continues," *Southeast Asian Affairs*, 2005.

58. For a detailed discussion of student activism and the regime's response, see Christina Fink, *Living Silence: Burma under Military Rule* (Bangkok: White Lotus, 2001), 174–90; Kyaw Yin Hlaing, "Burma: Skirting the Regime's Rules," in *Civil Society and Political Change in Asia: Expanding and Contracting Democratic Space*, ed. Muthiah Alagappa (Stanford: Stanford University Press, 2004).

59. Kyaw Yin Hlaing, interview by author, Singapore, February 2004.

60. Kyaw Yin Hlaing believes repression is an insufficient explanation of the disappearance of student activism. The difference between the pre-1988 and post-1988

period, he points out, is that none of the leading political groups in the country today have actively attempted to mobilize the students:

> Student activism survived the harsh repression of the previous socialist regime. However, since the collapse of the BCP [CPB], no new organization has made an attempt to help students organize informal student groups. It appeared that the NLD and other democracy organizations spent more time on attracting international attention than strengthening civil society and organizing underground political organizations. Due to political constraints the NLD did not approach students; it only worked with the students who came and joined the party. Likewise exiled organizations including the ABSFU did not try to mobilize the students in the way the BCP had done. Kyaw Yin Hlaing, "Skirting the Regime's Rules."

61. ABSDF official, interview by author, Bangkok, 20 June 1997.

62. The move to the border is often described as an attempt by the mainly Burman students to link up with the ethnic insurgent groups and form a national front against the military regime, and in practice this is to some extent what happened. Yet, for many Burmans the model for taking up arms was not the struggle of their ethnic cousins, but the independence struggle fifty years earlier when Aung San together with twenty-nine other young leaders left Burma for Japan and returned with the Japanese Imperial Army to push out the British. The students in 1988 saw themselves as the new generation of liberators.

63. Kyaw Zwa Moe, "Farewell to the Liberated Areas," *Irrawaddy* (print ed.) 13, no. 2 (February 2005).

64. Buddhism is often perceived to be preoccupied with otherworldly affairs. Dressed in their yellow or—as in Burma—red robes, Buddhist monks everywhere symbolize the quest for inner knowledge and peace and harmony. Like other religions and ideologies, however, Buddhism reflects the societal context in which it is imbedded and the modern history of Burma shows a record of monks participating in secular politics going back to the advent of colonial rule in the late nineteenth century. See Melford E. Spiro, *Buddhism and Society* (Berkeley: University of California Press, 1982).

65. Most writers in the 1990s referred to a number of three hundred thousand monks and novices, but the Burmese government in 2005 quotes four hundred thousand. *New Light of Myanmar*, 14 July 2005. If these figures are correct, the increase may reflect deteriorating socioeconomic conditions that motivate more people to seek solace and refuge in the monasteries.

66. SLORC Order No. 20/90, "Law Concerning Sangha Organisations," 31 October 1990.

67. Fink, *Living Silence*, 216.

68. Monique Skidmore, *Karaoke Fascism: Burma and the Politics of Fear* (Philadelphia: University of Pennsylvania Press, 2004), 16.

69. Kyaw Yin Hlaing, "Skirting the Regime's Rules."

70. The offer for mediation reportedly was accepted by the NLD, but rejected by the SPDC. Fink, *Living Silence*, 221–22.

71. Kyaw Yin Hlaing, "Skirting the Regime's Rules."
72. Kyaw Yin Hlaing, "Skirting the Regime's Rules."
73. Economist Intelligence Unit, "Myanmar: Quarterly Review," 1st Quarter, 1997.
74. Burmese political analyst, interview by author, Rangoon, 8 June 1997.
75. ABSDF official, interview by author, Washington, DC, July 2000.
76. ABSDF official, interview by author, Washington, DC, July 2000.
77. Zarni and May Oo, "Common Problems," 70.
78. Skidmore, *Karaoke Fascism*, 175–76.
79. Interviews by author, Rangoon, October 2006.
80. Quoted in *Irrawaddy* (online ed.), "Activists in Burma Start New Campaign," 3 January 2007, www.irrawaddy.org (accessed 3 January 2007).
81. All the main groups by this time had abandoned earlier claims to independent statehood and were committed to join "a new federation based on the principles of equality, autonomy, liberty, and self-determination." Josef Silverstein, "Civil War and Rebellion in Burma," *Journal of Southeast Asian Studies* 11, no. 1 (1990): 118.
82. See, for example, "Report from Ethnic Nationalities Seminar held at Mae Tha Raw Hta, 7–14 January 1997," n.d.
83. Josef Silverstein, "The Civil War, the Minorities and Burma's New Politics," in *Burma: The Challenge of Change in a Divided Society*, ed. Peter Carey, 129 (Houndsmills, England: MacMillan Press, 1997).
84. The DAB first appointed a constitution drafting committee in 1990 and a draft was approved at the first congress of DAB in July 1993. Democratic Alliance of Burma, *(Future) Federal Union of Burma Constitution* [draft] (n.p.: NCUB, 1995). A more recent draft was published in March 1996. National Council of the Union of Burma, *Future Constitution of the Federal Union of Burma* [proposed draft] (n.p.: NCUB, 1996).
85. Behind these developments lay a dramatic shift in the military's approach to the ethnic insurgents. During the four preceding decades the military leaders had consistently insisted on their unconditional surrender.
86. Andrew Selth, *Transforming the Tatmadaw: The Burmese Armed Forces since 1988* (Canberra: Strategic and Defence Studies Centre, Australian National University, 1996).
87. Zarni and May Oo, "Common Problems," 37.
88. Mary P. Callahan, *Making Enemies: War and State Building in Burma* (Ithaca, NY: Cornell University Press, 2003), 18.
89. Callahan, *Making Enemies*, 114–44.
90. Andrew Selth, *Burma's Armed Forces: Power without Glory* (Norwalk, CT: EastBridge, 2002), 163–64.
91. For details on the size of the insurgent groups in 1988, see Martin Smith, *Burma: Insurgency and the Politics of Ethnicity*, 2nd ed. (London: Zed Books, 1999), xiv (chart 1).
92. At the height of the uprising, demonstrators attacked police and army units. According to President Maung Maung, some of their leaders wrote to Western

countries requesting arms. See Maung Maung, *The 1988 Uprising in Burma* (New Haven, CT: Yale University South East Asia Studies, 1999), 167, 224–25.

93. Smith, *Insurgency*, 19.

94. Selth, *Burma's Armed Forces*, 79.

95. Selth, *Burma's Armed Forces*, 133–34.

96. Selth, *Burma's Armed Forces*, 81.

97. Contrary to popular perceptions in the West, the army is not usually much in evidence on the streets of Burma's cities, but remains in its barracks. This point is often commented on by visitors, who arrive expecting to see soldiers with guns on every street corner.

98. Trevor Wilson, "Some Reflections on Three Years in Burma" (paper presented at the Australian Institute of International Affairs, Canberra, 6 August 2003).

99. Fink, *Living Silence*, 129.

100. Selth, *Burma's Armed Forces*, 92.

101. The membership of the ruling council has changed several times since 1988, but at any given time has been limited to the highest levels of the Ministry of Defense, at times complemented with the regional commanders. The SPDC in March 2007 is headed by the commander-in-chief of the armed forces, Senior General Than Shwe, who also serves as defense minister, and his deputy commander-in-chief of the army, General Maung Aye. They are the only two left from the original SLORC and, at seventy-four and sixty-nine respectively, are fifteen to twenty years senior to most of the other members of the council. Most of the latter were included while serving as regional commanders when the council was reconstituted in 1997, but in November 2001 were recalled to Rangoon and promoted to senior positions in the Ministry of Defense. The most influential is joint chief of staff General Thura Shwe Man. Lieutenant General Soe Win serves as prime minister, but does not appear to have corresponding influence within the council.

102. Than Shwe in August 2003 handed over the post of prime minister to Khin Nyunt, who was later replaced by Soe Win. Yet, despite the awkward arrangement of having a lower-ranking military officer act as prime minister while Than Shwe is defense minister, the senior general in practice is recognized as the preeminent authority in all areas.

103. There have always been a few civilian ministers and more at lower levels, some of them brought in for their technical competence. They would not have been appointed, however, unless they were considered to be loyal to the top leaders, and often suffer from an acute sense of vulnerability in a military-dominated system.

104. Ardeth Maung Thawnghmung, "Paddy Farmers and the State: Agricultural Policies and Legitimacy in Rural Myanmar" (PhD diss., University of Wisconsin–Madison, 2001), 162.

105. In principle, the location of each person in Burma must be recorded by the village/ward PDC each evening, although in practice this is not done in many places.

106. Ardeth Maung Thawnghmung, "Paddy Farmers and the State," 165.

107. The Union Solidarity and Development Association (USDA), "Talking Points for the Discussion of the General Secretary of USDA with the Special Representative of the UN Secretary-General," August 2005.

108. For a detailed official exposition of the objectives and activities of the USDA, see USDA, "Talking Points."

109. While their essentially political nature is a serious constraint, some GONGOs do serve important welfare functions, which supplement—or in many cases have replaced—the formal government system. The Myanmar Red Cross Society and the Myanmar Maternal and Child Welfare Association, for example, include many midwives, nurses, and other committed health workers, who work as volunteers and make significant contributions to public health and welfare.

110. The last few years have seen a major upsurge in these activities with near daily meetings of one mass organization or another. This seems to reflect a difference of style between Senior General Than Shwe, who has always preferred socialist-style mass mobilization activities, and former head of military intelligence General Khin Nyunt, who favored political dialogue (or at least communication) with the main political groups.

111. As noted, USDA mass rallies, for example, were used in 1998–1999 to pass motions of no-confidence against elected NLD members of parliament. Similarly, Senior General Than Shwe in meetings with foreign ambassadors has pointed to the USDA as evidence of popular support for the regime's programs. European ambassador, interview by author, Rangoon, July 2005.

112. Skidmore, *Karaoke Fascism*, 108.

113. Former Western ambassador to Burma, interview by author, Singapore, July 2006. When this author inquired about the plans for the USDA at a meeting in February 2007, Htay Oo responded rather more cryptically: "We will follow the people's wishes."

114. According to the basic principles for the new constitution, public servants cannot be members of political parties and parties are forbidden from receiving any support from the state, including use of state property. The USDA has hundreds of thousands of government officials among its members, including its entire leadership, and enjoys substantial state support, including in many places the use of state property.

115. The MWAF, headed by Prime Minister Soe Win's wife, Daw Than Than Nwe, appears to have taken over the role of Myanmar Maternal and Child Welfare Association, which was previously headed by Khin Nyunt's wife, as the primary focal point for the organization of women, although the latter still exists.

116. For a critical description and analysis of the evolving role of the USDA by opposition groups, see Network for Democracy and Development, "The White Shirts," May 2006; *Mon Forum*, "USDA: The Organization Strengthening Military Rule in Burma (Myanmar)," no. 4 (2005): 6–16.

117. The growing power of the USDA is said to have irked many military officers and other officials, who have experienced a corresponding loss in authority and

influence. It is, however, backed strongly by Senior General Than Shwe, its official patron.

118. For a systematic study of local nongovernmental organizations (NGOs) and community-based organizations in Burma, see Brian Heidel, *The Growth of Civil Society in Myanmar* (Bangalore, India: Books for Change, 2006). The research for this unique study was conducted while Heidel served as representative of Save the Children (UK) in 2003–2004.

119. Ashley South, "Ceasefires and Civil Society: The Case of the Mon," draft paper, 2002.

120. The emergence of civil society organizations in the cease-fire areas, however, is potentially important for the demilitarization and, long-term, democratization of local politics. See Ashley South, "Roadmaps and Political Transition in Burma: The Need for Two-Way Traffic," *Irrawaddy* (online ed.), 16–17 October 2003, www.irrawaddy.org (accessed 17 October 2003).

121. "The Role of the Tatmadaw in the Economy," confidential report, 2000.

122. David I. Steinberg, "Burma/Myanmar: The Role of the Military in the Economy," *Burma Economic Watch*, no. 1 (2005).

123. "Role of the Tatmadaw."

124. "Role of the Tatmadaw."

125. Military "insider," interview by author, Rangoon, August 2002.

126. The accounts of UMEH and MEC are not public, but, according to a military "insider," those who were allowed to buy shares in the UMEH doubled their investment in the first year alone. Interview by author, Rangoon, April 2000.

127. Military officers, for example, have access to subsidized gasoline, which is sold openly on the black market at several hundred percent profit.

128. The Yadana field is operated jointly by Total (France), Unocal (United States), the Petroleum Authority of Thailand (PTTEP), and Burmar's Ministry of Gas and Oil (MOGE), while Yetagun is a partnership between Petronas (Malaysia), Nippon Oil (Japan), PTTEP, and MOGE. Gas from the two fields currently is sold exclusively to Thailand, covering 20 percent of the country's total supply. The new Shwe fields are currently being developed by a consortium led by Dawoo International (South Korea) and including also South Korea Gas Cooperation, the Gas Authority of India, Oil and Natural Gas Corporation (India), and MOGE.

129. Shwe Gas Movement, "Burma's Military Dictatorship to Gain over US$12 Billion Profits from Western Burma Gas Finds" (media release, 12 July 2006), www.shwe.org/media-releases/statements/July_12_press_release.pdf (accessed 12 January 2007).

130. *Straits Times*, 2 February 2006.

131. Associated Press, "Myanmar, Thailand Sign US$6 Billion Hydropower Plant Agreement," *BurmaNet News*, 4 April 2006, www.burmanet.org/news (accessed 4 April 2006).

132. Comments by participants in the Workshop on Myanmar Issues and Myanmar Views: Searching for a Unified Perspective, organized by the Institute of South-

east Asian Studies (Singapore) in Rangoon, 1–5 February 2004. See also Ardeth Maung Thawnghmung, "Paddy Farmers and the State."

133. Ingrid Jordt, "Mass Lay Meditation and State-Society Relations in Post-Independence Burma" (PhD diss., Harvard University, Cambridge, MA, May 2001), 273–74.

134. Interviews by author, Rangoon, 2000–2005. This observation is echoed by several scholars: David Steinberg, for example, observers that "Aung San Suu Kyi's position opposing most humanitarian assistance . . . is causing some deterioration in her standing among those who, although opposed to military rule, want compromise of some sort, and wish to improve the population's well-being." David I. Steinberg, "The Burmese Conundrum: Approaching Reformation of the Political Economy," in *Burma: Political Economy under Military Rule*, ed. Robert H. Taylor, 52 (New York: Palgrave, 2001). Similarly, Martin Smith argues that "not all citizens welcomed or understood the notion of further isolation as a method to bring about internal reform. In fact, many would welcome international aid and investment within the country if this speeds up improvements in living standards and socio-political change." Martin Smith, "Burmese Politics after 1988: An Era of New and Uncertain Change," in Taylor, *Political Economy*, 30.

135. Trevor Wilson, "Some Reflections."

136. Kei Nemoto, "Aung San Suu Kyi, Her Dream and Reality" (Discussion Paper No. 1, Kansai Institute of Asia-Pacific Studies, Osaka University of Foreign Studies, April 1996).

137. While the purge of Khin Nyunt and military intelligence in 2004 shows that the military—like most organizations—suffer from internal rivalries and "disunity," the decisiveness of this move from the army and the relative ease with which it was carried out seem only to prove the fundamental stability of the regime.

138. Sidney Tarrow, *Power in Movement*, 2nd ed. (Cambridge: Cambridge University Press, 1998), 124.

139. Ardeth Maung Thawnghmung, "Paddy Farmers and the State," 322–23.

140. In an interview in 2004, for example, KNU leader Bo Mya strongly criticized the student soldiers:

> We thought that it would be good to have Burmans in the revolution and fighting against the military regime, a common enemy. So we helped them in every way. We had to feed the 5,000 of them for at least one and a half months. We gave them weapons and they formed the students' armed force. And when they formed, I told them, all of you fled our country because of the government's ill behavior, so be united and stand together, do not get divided and scattered here and there. But my words lasted only for a few moments. They start fighting among themselves, and I had to solve their problems.

He also criticized the NCGUB: "Before the coalition government came, we the KNU had done all the [government] seals. We wanted to form a government with all nationalities. We had done all the seals and also selected the people. When they arrived, they made requests to participate. We agreed and allowed them and gave them all seals and everything. Previously we thought we would be included, but we were not. As we are rebels and they are 'government,' they said, 'both the government and the rebels cannot work together' so they rejected our group altogether." *Mizzima News*, "Interview with Karen Leader Saw Bo Mya," 15 March 2004, www.mizzima.com/Interview/15-mar04-03.htm (accessed 26 April 2007).

141. Smith, *Insurgency*, 435.

142. The average age of the NLD's eight-man Central Executive Committee, excluding Aung San Suu Kyi, is about eighty-three years. The party leader herself celebrated her sixty-second birthday in June 2007, under house arrest.

CHAPTER FOUR

Transitional Challenges

> [In the West], there was a general feeling that a decisive moral victory had been won by the military government's opponents during the pro-democracy protests of 1988-90. . . . Such a perspective takes little cognisance of the institutional and socio-political difficulties that exist in achieving a modern process of transition in such a divided society. In this respect, Burma presented a striking example of the much-discussed phenomenon in the modern political world known as "strong societies but weak state," where post-colonial governments have been unable to achieve or countenance effective action across all ethnic and social sectors.
>
> —Martin Smith, writer[1]

Since the fall of the Berlin Wall in 1989, policy makers and political scientists alike have celebrated the large number of countries that have introduced competitive elections for national government office and thus supposedly become "democracies." In the case of Burma, the refusal of the military regime to hand over power to the winners of the 1990 election similarly became the focus of a one-dimensional Western human rights policy, which viewed recognition of the election as the sine qua non of progress in other areas. Although Western governments no longer demand that the 1990 election results as such be implemented, policy—particularly in the United States—remains rooted in that event, in particular the notion that Aung San Suu Kyi is not only the rightful leader of Burma, but also the sole legitimate representative of the Burmese people. Both U.S. policy makers and activists have regularly argued that international policy ought to follow the requests of the charismatic opposition leader and a subtle struggle has been waged among groups abroad over representation and interpretation of her views.

As demonstrated, however, by the immense problems many of the world's new democracies are facing in making democracy work, the mere fact of elections—and elected leaders—says little about the actual distribution of power and even less about the quality of governance or broader development of the countries in question. Democratization is a complex, multifaceted, and open-ended process, involving shifts in many aspects of governance and social relations, including not only the possibility of turning political leaders out of office but also, for example, an end to violence, improved communication between state and society, a strengthening of civil society, and improvements in economic and educational opportunities for the general population. It is the totality of these processes that matters, both for the quality of democracy as a system of government and for progress in human rights more broadly.

When considering the challenges of transition in Burma, it is important to keep these complexities in mind. There is no question that four decades of repressive and often inept military rule have contributed greatly to the country's social, political, and economic malaise. The military's top-down, authoritarian approach to governance, compounded by failed economic policies, distorted budget priorities, and widespread human rights abuses, has devastated a country once rich in both natural and human resources. Yet, military rule is itself a symptom of deeper conditions in Burmese society, which weaken the prospects for democratic transition and consolidation. Moreover, many of the effects of military rule over time have become causes of underdevelopment in their own right. Burma's problems, in other words, are structural and will not be resolved—or even necessarily alleviated—simply by replacing the military government with one established through elections, a process that has its own dangers, pitfalls, and limitations in this deeply divided, poverty-ridden society.

This chapter discusses five key aspects of any meaningful transition in Burma, all of which present their own unique challenges while simultaneously being closely interlinked: national reconciliation, strengthening state capacity, nurturing civil society, reviving the economy, and developing the border areas. The picture presented is a depressing one, but it is not intended to suggest that there is no hope for progress. The aim here is to provide an antidote to the one-dimensional perspective underlying the core strategy and the often simplistic representations by its most ardent supporters of Burma's prospects for social, political, and economic development. Only by owning up to the obstacles can they be effectively addressed.

National Reconciliation

While the struggle for power between the military government and the pro-democracy forces continues, Burma arguably faces its biggest challenge in ending its long-running civil war and addressing the debilitating legacy of violence, destruction, and distrust. The armed conflicts, which have afflicted Burma since independence, were a major factor in the political crisis that led to the emergence of military rule in 1962 and continue to impede a transition to democratic government today. More than fifty years of fighting have caused a systematic redistribution of power and wealth in favor of those who control the guns, resulting in a breakdown of normal public administration and the rule of law, and contributing to a system that normalizes violence and human rights abuses. This is evident both at the central level and in local areas outside of state control. For half a century, too, the imperative of security has dominated economic policies, the essential feature of which has been the diversion of public resources into the armed forces and away from productive use. The ensuing battles have destroyed or closed access to large parts of the country, and have fostered destructive exploitation of its rich natural resources, which have been sold at "fire sale" prices by armies on all sides to neighboring countries. Most damaging perhaps, the conflicts have led to extreme political and social polarization of society.

The cease-fires, which began in eastern Shan state in the late 1980s and subsequently spread to other areas of Shan, Karenni, Kachin, and Mon states, have much reduced the level of armed conflict. Sporadic fighting, however, continues along the Thai and, to a lesser extent, Indian borders, and the cease-fire groups are still armed. The failure to develop the cease-fires into genuine political settlements, combined with the continuing poverty of former conflict areas, is sustaining conditions of political and social instability and impeding efforts to address the structural legacies of the civil war. Although the odds today are strongly against armed challengers to the central government, growing disillusionment among local populations could see a second generation of conflicts break out.

Ethnic Grievances and Aspirations

Burma's ethnic conflicts are rooted in real and perceived discrimination by the Burman-dominated state against minority groups, particularly in the border regions. While the military seems intent on centralizing political control and forging a homogeneous Burman-Buddhist culture, ethnic nationalists are fighting for autonomy, equality, and the right to maintain their own languages and traditions. In order for the country and its diverse peoples to move forward together, these grievances and aspirations must be acknowledged and addressed.

Political Autonomy

The most fundamental grievance of ethnic leaders in Burma is their lack of influence on the political process and thus on policy decisions that affect their communities. Since independence, all the main national political institutions, including the army, have been dominated by Burmans. As political centralization has ensued, traditional ethnic leaders gradually have been excluded from power in local areas as well. Many have thus accused Burman-dominated governments of having betrayed the promises made at the 1947 Panglong Conference, which paved the way for the new Union of Burma, by denying them a role in national political life and influence over conditions in their own areas. As Khaing Soe Naing Aung, the current vice-chairman of the National Democratic Front (NDF), lamented some years ago, "The Panglong Agreement, to a certain extent, could have drawn all the ethnic nationalities to live together within a Federal Union, having the rights of equality and self-determination for each of them. But in practice, 50 years of bitter experiences have convinced [us] that the so-called Union of Burma has been a total lie."[2]

To redress this situation, ethnic groups have called for a "new" Panglong conference to renegotiate the basis for the Burmese state and establish a "genuine federal union" with substantial autonomy for the ethnically designated states. In private, some minority leaders admit to harboring aspirations for outright independence, while others indicate that they would accept a unitary, but decentralized, political and administrative system that protects the human and ethnic rights of minorities wherever they reside in the country. But for the purpose of unity and establishing a clear negotiation position vis-à-vis the government, most groups since the early 1980s have formally framed their political objectives in federalist terms.

The ongoing National Convention, in principle, has offered an opportunity to discuss such constitutional issues (and has been accepted as such, at least by representatives of the cease-fire groups). Yet, since the actual debate in that arena has been greatly circumscribed and few concessions have been forthcoming from the government, feelings of exclusion remain high among many ethnic leaders and communities.

Economic Equality

The belief that the minorities need formal political control of their "homelands" has grown due to economic and other discrimination by successive

Burman-dominated governments against ethnic groups and areas. Many of the early insurgencies arose, at least in part, due to perceptions of economic neglect, which has only worsened over time. While five decades of civil war and economic mismanagement have undermined economic development and fed a deepening humanitarian crisis across the country, ethnic minority areas generally have suffered the worst. According to the United Nations Children's Fund's (UNICEF's) "Child Risk Index,"[3] most of the border regions, for example, fall significantly below the national average on twelve socioeconomic indicators of household income; health status; and access to health care, education, and safe water and sanitation. Chin, Arakan (Rakhine), eastern Shan, and Karen states are considered particularly "high-risk" areas for children, followed by southern Shan, northern Shan, and Karenni states (in descending order). Only Mon and Kachin states are better off than the least developed parts of central Burma.[4]

The post-1988 government has stepped up budgetary allocations to (some) ethnic minority areas, but the assistance has mainly gone to infrastructure of questionable value for local populations and has hardly made a dent in the needs. Instead, growing numbers of army bases in minority areas have led to escalating demands for land, labors, food, and other contributions from local people. Improved access to former conflict areas has also attracted new investors, who are plundering the natural resources, closing access for local communities, and rapidly exhausting the potential for future development (see section on Border Areas Development later in this chapter for more details). Although, overall, livelihoods have improved for many communities in former conflict areas as a result of the end to armed hostilities, which has allowed more "normal" life to resume, such exploitative practices are reinforcing long-standing perceptions of discrimination and thus laying the basis for further resentment and conflict.

Ethnic Rights

Burma's ethnic minorities lament, too, their inability to maintain and practice their own cultures, including language, literature, and religion, all of which are crucial to ethnic identities. After the 1962 military coup, the use of ethnic minority languages in the education system was curtailed, and the publication of non-Burmese language newspapers and books was banned.[5] Ethnic minority communities have come to see this as a deliberate policy by the central government to Burmanize them. As one (illegal) publication by the Mon Unity League states, "The ethnic non-Burman communities of the country have systematically been deprived of their birth right to teaching their own ethnic languages and literature and to preserving their own cultural heritage, under a policy of Burman ethnocentrism and Burmanization traditionally exercised by the successive Burman-dominated governments in Rangoon."[6]

The situation has improved somewhat since 1988. There is more tolerance today at the local level for ethnic minority language classes run by Mon, Shan, Karen, Kachin, and other minority groups outside the government education system.[7] In 1999, Mon monks were allowed to take most of their exams in Buddhist literature in the Mon language (a right taken away from them in the early 1980s).[8] Yet, there are still no legal newspapers available in ethnic minority languages, and the curriculum at colleges in minority states remains heavily Burmanized.[9] Many of Burma's non-Buddhist ethnic minorities also resent the central role of Buddhism in the regime's nation-building project, including the construction of Buddhist structures in their areas, which they view as a new attempt to destroy and assimilate their cultures.[10]

Human Rights

In addition to discrimination based on race or geography, Burma's ethnic populations have suffered disproportionately from the human rights situation in the country overall. This is mainly due to the counter-insurgency campaigns that for decades have been carried out by the army in ethnic minority regions. Forced depopulation of large areas has been accompanied by severe abuses, including extrajudicial killings; rape; looting; and widespread destruction of fields, property, and livelihoods. Ethnic people in these areas have thus come to see the army as an institution (not just its leaders or specific officers or soldiers) as "the enemy," causing even deeper alienation from the government and the state than that felt by Burmans and ethnic minorities in central parts of the country.

Many of these grievances reflect an underlying layer of center-periphery tensions found in many countries. Yet, they are caused also by racial arrogance on the part of many Burmans, and have been exacerbated by the behavior of the Burman-dominated national army in minority areas, particularly in heavily militarized zones of conflict. Not all of Burma's ethnic groups are equally alienated from the central state or the Burman majority population, and not all "ethnic" struggles are truly nationalist in nature. Yet, the fact remains that many of the country's minorities have little reason to feel that they are part of the union or owe any allegiance to it.

Democracy and National Reconciliation

Democracy activists, both inside Burma and abroad, have tended to conflate the quest for national reconciliation with that for democracy. The National League for Democracy (NLD) has essentially taken the position that dialogue between all groups and interests in the country can ensue once democracy is in place, and any further issues can be resolved then.[11] The main opposition party has thus worked primarily for a "bilateral" solution to its disagreements with the military government, expecting the ethnic minorities to wait their turn.[12] Democracy, however, does not provide an infallible solution to conflict, whether in Burma or elsewhere. As Robin Luckham warns, while democracy in principle poses an alternative to violence by encouraging the resolution of disputes through the political process, "in practice, democratic institutions have often failed to resolve conflicts and in some cases have even aggravated them."[13] The challenge is to ensure that political institutions and processes are as inclusive as possible for all ethnic groups and at all levels of authority. This will require genuine interethnic empathy and willingness on all sides to compromise, qualities that are not evident in Burma's polarized sociopolitical landscape.

Although the NLD is formally committed to establishing a federal union, some ethnic minority leaders feel that the NLD—by giving priority to democracy before ethnic rights and equality—is showing the same arrogance and insensitivity to minority issues exhibited by other Burman-dominated organizations throughout history.[14] Most support the general call for democracy, if for nothing else, because it would provide them with a chance to renegotiate their position in the union. Their priority, however, is securing local autonomy, safeguarding their cultures, and getting their fair share of the country's economic wealth (much of which is located in the border areas).[15]

Questions also arise about the capacity of any government to broker the necessary compromise between majority Burman and ethnic minority groups. Many ordinary Burmans share the attitude of successive military leaders that the Burmans are the rightful leaders of the state. As the Crisis Group observes, "Many who identify themselves as majority Burmans consider their needs take precedence over minority demands. Many also consider Burman historical achievements and culture superior to that of minority groups. In part due to regime propaganda, Burmans tend to understand unity as requiring homogeneity and oppose any attempt by ethnic groups to break that unity. There is implicit tolerance for regime attempts to Burmanise minorities by discouraging the practice of other religions and the use of minority languages."[16] Such attitudes present a latent problem for future democratic leaders who ultimately will be constrained by their ability to secure electoral majorities.

Similarly, many ethnic minorities who have suffered from decades of brutal counterinsurgency campaigns and other abuses by what they perceive as an invading army have come to view all Burmans as "the enemy." Much like in central Burma, these sentiments have been reinforced by strident nationalist propaganda by ethnic leaders seeking to rally local populations behind their counterhegemonic wars. Even the cease-fire groups do not necessarily seek cooperation with a Burman-led state, but rather want to be left alone. The United Wa State Army (UWSA), for example, currently enjoys almost full autonomy in large parts of eastern Shan state, something it is unlikely to give up easily (and it has around twenty thousand well-armed soldiers under its command to help defend its interests).

Military officials believe ethnic nationalists would take advantage of the installation of a weaker democratic government in Rangoon to push demands for wider autonomy, possibly by returning to war.[17] Whether such concerns are justified or not, continuing deep-seated ethnic divisions and concerns over identity among both majority Burmans and ethnic minorities provide fertile ground for nationalist politicians and agitators to push ethnocentric agendas, which could overwhelm immature democratic institutions.[18] This poses another dilemma for a future democratic government, which could well come under pressure to adopt strategies of violence or political repression that would undermine its democratic credentials.

Ultimately, national reconciliation depends not on democracy per se, but on the emergence of moderate voices and organizations on all sides that promote peaceful compromise, tolerance, and inclusiveness. This is a major challenge in a country where interethnic prejudices run deep and most groups historically have taken an all-or-nothing approach to politics.

Strengthening State Capacity

Critical to any transition process is how effectively a new government deals with the multiple development challenges facing the country. This is partly an issue of political will, effective leadership, and popular support. Yet, even the most committed, competent, and popular leaders depend on broader state structures for efficacy. In order to execute policies and deliver services, a government requires a coherent administrative structure, covering the length and breadth of the country, which both follows directions from above and responds to the needs of local communities. It needs a skilled and honest civil service that can support policy makers and effectively implement their decisions. Moreover, it must have the ability to generate sufficient revenue to pay for salaries and carry out public investments. Each of these requirements is problematic in Burma where state capacity is extremely low and will remain so under any new government, which in the short to medium term will have to rely, to a significant degree, on existing state structures and personnel.

Political Leadership

Political leadership is a sensitive and contentious issue. Most observers agree that Burma suffers greatly from the unbridled power of military officers who lack relevant experience and skills for running an effective government. Opinions diverge, however, on how much better an elected government would do. While it appears to be an article of faith among many Western politicians and activists that the NLD, if given a chance, would deliver competent governance, others have criticized its failure to develop a detailed policy platform.[19] Party leaders blame this on the repressive environment in which they function, arguing that they cannot reveal their cards too early.[20] Yet, foreign diplomats and officials, as well as other Burmese elites, who regularly interact with the NLD, commonly express concern over the perceived inability or unwillingness of its leaders to engage in detailed policy discussions, for example, about aid and constitutional provisions.[21]

It would be unfair to judge too harshly an organization that has never been given the chance to prove itself. Still, it is important to distinguish between popularity and effective leadership.[22] The NLD does share with the military and other organizations in Burma a tendency to focus on issues of power rather than policy.[23] While many groups claim to know what is best for the country, few have well-developed visions, not to mention operational plans, for how to deal with the development challenges discussed in this chapter. Much depends on how willing future government leaders are to give up some measure of personal influence to bring in technocrats who can help formulate effective policies. For the time being, comments made by Josef Silverstein fifteen years ago still ring true: "The Burmese people have been in search of leadership since the death of Aung San and many believe that they have found it in his daughter. So long as she remains untried in a responsible position and isolated from the people, they will continue to believe that she is the one who can set them on a new course. But until she is given the chance to use her new-found skills at democratic politics . . . and bears the responsibility of her decisions, no one will know if she is destined to lead Burma toward a new and better life."[24]

If this is true for Aung San Suu Kyi and the NLD, it is equally so for political leadership in the country in general, which—as will be discussed further—has long been growing in infertile soil, with little nourishment or encouragement.

Authority

Leaving aside the issue of leadership, the Burmese state suffers from several structural weaknesses, starting with its inability to exercise authority across its territory. Despite significant progress since the early years of independence when the U Nu government, faced with a plethora of mutinies and insurgencies, controlled only the main cities and towns, the authority of the central government is still contested in many parts of the country. Moreover, the state itself is fragmented, lacking clear lines of authority between central and local authorities. This undermines the ability of the government to implement policies effectively across the country and thus to initiate and guide appropriate development efforts.

While the cease-fires in the 1990s, along with military conquest, have extended the central government's authority further into the border areas than at any time in history, seventeen "special regions" remain formally under the administration of ethnic nationalist armies or militias. The degree of autonomy varies from group to group, but in parts of eastern Shan state under control of the UWSA, government officials cannot enter without permission. These and other regions along the Chinese border are for most intents and purposes part of China rather than Burma. The common language is Chinese; the currency is the Yuan; they use the Chinese telecommunication system; and most trade and investment come from China. In other conflict-affected areas, there is no clear demarcation of authority at all, which may be claimed by several armed groups or by no one. The primary organizing principle in many parts of the border areas is competition for control over natural resources, which frequently causes clashes between army battalions, local warlords, and at times even security forces of private companies.

The situation is further complicated by unclear demarcations of authority among state agencies. Since 1988, there has been a de facto devolution of power to local army commanders who have almost unlimited authority over military, political, economic, and social affairs in their areas. This system works fairly well for security purposes but greatly limits the state's development capacity. While some commanders are efficient managers, others are not, and there is little oversight or coordination among them. They act largely with impunity and routinely override ministerial directives from the capital. Although line ministry personnel are present in local areas, they have little authority.[25] A similar pattern is evident in areas under control of cease-fire or insurgent groups, where individual commanders and battalions often act independently of the central leadership, reflecting the traditionally decentralized nature of insurgent warfare in these regions.

Given the multiethnic character of Burmese society and strong demands for local autonomy, a more effective central government structure ultimately must be complemented by decentralization. But how to do this in ways that facilitate rather than undermine effective governance remains a major challenge.

The Civil Service

These macro-level obstacles are compounded by the weakness of the civil service. Many of Burma's problems are created not by policy as such, but by administrative rigidities and inefficiencies. Since the military coup in 1962, the administrative structure has been greatly weakened by the appointment to leadership positions of military officers with little relevant experience and the dismissal of thousands of competent civilian officials accused of disloyal behavior. The military culture of top-down decision making has further stifled creativity and independent thinking at all levels, while the erosion of real wages has fueled corruption and absenteeism. There is still a significant number of well-educated civil servants (although many are close to, or beyond, retirement age), and in some areas reasonable technical and professional skills have been maintained, even if there is limited scope for applying them. Yet, the capacity of the civil service as a whole has been severely compromised. There is no transparency or accountability, no culture of reform and improvement, and weak commitment to public service.[26] Even if there is a democratic transition, a new government initially will have to work with the existing personnel, which likely will resist any reforms that challenge existing hierarchies or seek to curb opportunities for rent seeking. Many civil servants will have to be replaced or retrained, a major task given the scarcity of human and financial resources and the political dangers of alienating large numbers of state personnel.

Adding to the administrative problems is the acute lack of capacity at the local level. As noted, an effective future democracy will depend critically on decentralization of both power and administrative responsibility to the fourteen states and divisions. Indeed, support for a democratic government by the country's ethnic minority groups will depend on such decentralization. Yet, the experience of the cease-fire groups, which currently have authority over the special regions, stems from wartime administration and economics only. Few, if any, are familiar with modern government methods. Some, such as the Kachin Independence Organization (KIO) and the New Mon State Party (NMSP), have formal administrative systems with departments for health, education, development, and so on. Others are little more than loose networks of warlords whose essential purpose is amassing wealth for themselves and their clients. Everywhere, however, soldiers or ex-soldiers remain in control. Although the traditional extractive, tributary nature of relations with the peasantry is softened in some areas by emerging civil society structures (or, in the case of the Pao, by the influence of a benevolent leader), the exercise of authority generally is top-down, "command style" with little attention to local community needs.[27] Even those groups with more modern, rational governance structures have limited capacity for public administration or development beyond maintaining control of their territory.

Most of these weaknesses are a direct result of decades of war, but they also reflect broader issues of administrative culture and expertise. In many parts of the country, ways of political organization have changed little over the centuries and few people have any formal education or experience with modern administration.[28] The establishment of effective local governance structures necessary to sustain demands for increased local autonomy is thus a major task in itself and likely to take decades. Minimal steps required include demilitarization and a clearer division of authority and responsibility between the center and the regions, complemented with a comprehensive training program for new administrative personnel of all nationalities.

Revenue Generation

The weakness of the administration has created another structural problem. The Burmese government today generates only 6 percent of its gross domestic product (GDP) in (official) revenue, around five times less than most Western states and one of the lowest levels in the world.[29] This greatly limits its capacity to make necessary social investments and contributes to corruption and other abuses of power. Increased international assistance to a new democratic government would ease the burden, but the need to rebuild public confidence in the government, revamp the tax system, and root out deeply ingrained structures of corruption will be a major challenge for inexperienced civilian leaders subject to electoral pressures, just as it is for the current military regime.

The fundamental point here, to paraphrase Mary Callahan, is that any transition to an elected government, while possibly necessary to jumpstart a long overdue process of reform, will place new leaders in the difficult position of having to run a "low-income democracy" with little state capacity to rely on.[30] This will place major constraints on their ability to undertake the kind of administrative and economic restructuring required to turn the country around and fulfill popular demands for change.

Nurturing Civil Society

As much as Burma needs stronger state institutions, it also needs an active civil society that can challenge, support, and complement the state. Civil society organizations (CSOs)—those formally or informally organized groups of people, autonomous of the state, that act collectively in the public sphere—serve multiple purposes and tasks crucial to transitional societies. In the words of Thomas Carothers, "Civil society is the connective tissue that transitional countries need to join the forms of democracy with their intended substance, to ensure that new democratic institutions and processes do not remain hollow boxes and empty rituals."[31] CSOs fulfill this function primarily by keeping the state accountable to, and informed about, the needs of its citizens. But they are not only important for the quality of democracy. In deeply divided societies such as Burma, people banding together across existing social, ethnic, and religious fault lines, for example, is a crucial aspect of peace building. CSOs also play a vital role by complementing the state in delivering services and helping the weakest members of society, all the more important the weaker and poorer the state is. Of course, civil society—like state institutions—can have harmful effects on governance and public welfare, too, depending on the values and behavior of the people and organizations that populate it.[32]

The challenge facing Burma begins with the fact that the military after 1962 largely succeeded in crushing civil society by disbanding or co-opting any autonomous organizations and setting up its own, tightly controlled network of mass organizations. The post-1988 regime to some extent has acknowledged that the state has neither the capacity nor the resources to do everything, and thus has allowed some new space for autonomous organizations to develop. These include a narrow range of political parties (which have been kept on a very short leash), but also a growing number of professional associations, low-key advocacy organizations, development NGOs, and, particularly, community-based organizations that serve various social welfare needs. Yet, all of these new sectors are in the early stages of development. The growth in civil society is limited geographically, mostly to the main cities and two or three cease-fire areas. Moreover, the pervasive influence of the military—and the extremely difficult and limiting circumstances under which any independent grouping continues to function—greatly hamper the development of organizational capacity. According to civil society organizers themselves, as well as aid officials interacting with these organizations, most of them have a long way to go before they can fulfill the roles expected of them in a future democratic system or required to help unite and develop the country on a significant scale.[33] The political parties are particularly weak, largely consisting of a few leaders based in Rangoon with few links to their supposed constituencies.[34] Welfare organizations have had somewhat more space to function—and some have received external support and training—but even the oldest and best organized (typically the church groups) generally lack planning and management as well as implementation skills.[35] Cooperation among such groups is also very limited.

Of all the transitional challenges Burma faces, the civil society "deficit" is perhaps the one most dependent on prior regime change. Authoritarian rulers are inherently fearful of activities outside their control, making it extremely difficult for most types of CSOs to form and for a broader capacity building and socialization process into democratic behavior to get underway. Yet, it is important not to ignore the deeper structural conditions for the emergence of a constructive civil society in a country that has a long history of violent conflict and deep social divisions; whose political culture evinces strong authoritarian tendencies; and where key organizational resources such as wealth, communications infrastructure, and education are available only to a narrow urban elite.

Historical Experience

One of the most difficult challenges facing future civilian leaders is the lack of experience in Burma with peaceful means of dealing with disagreement. From the independence struggle, through a democratic period marred by high levels of political violence, followed by more than forty years of military stewardship, arms have been the primary means used not just in the pursuit of power but also to settle differences over state policy and direction. It is no historical coincidence that the mobilization of supporters during Aung San Suu Kyi's party organizational tours around the country in 2003 was quelled by violence, or that dissident groups overseas subsequently renewed calls for a U.S. invasion and armed struggle.[36]

The talks between long-standing enemies, which have taken place over the past decade and a half—however limited and often unsuccessful—demonstrate a perception among moderates on all sides that violence holds no solutions. Yet, so far, the perceived need to break the political deadlock has not been matched by sufficiently widespread confidence that a satisfactory outcome can be reached through cooperation and compromise. Five decades of continuous conflict, compounded by the often confrontational positions assumed by both the military government and pro-democracy groups since 1988, have created an atmosphere of alienation, distrust, and a lack of basic understanding and empathy.

These conflicts are not just an elite-level phenomenon. Racial, ethnic, and religious tensions run high in the general population, worsened by an intensifying struggle over scarce resources. Many people in Burma identify strongly with their own group against outsiders, and prejudices against other groups are often strong. Pervasive discontent over tough economic conditions and frustration in the absence of any real prospect for change fuel conflicts between insiders and outsiders. The situation in many ways is comparable to India or Indonesia, although it has yet to result in the same levels of communal violence. The 1988 uprising, which had a dark underside in lynchings and extensive looting, as well as the religious violence between Buddhists and Muslims that has rocked several towns in recent years, reflect these tensions.

This fragmentation of society and resultant psychological resistance to cooperation constitutes a fundamental obstacle to political and economic progress that transcends the nature of the political system.

Political Culture

History, together with deeper, traditional values and beliefs, has left a strong mark on Burma's political culture. While it is generally recognized today that the political values, orientations, and behavior of a society are tendencies only, subject to change over time,[37] there is little doubt that certain "cultural" predispositions affect the ease and speed with which broader system changes are likely to occur and, particularly, take root. A liberalization of Burmese politics will not magically see the springing into life of a constructive and efficient democratic civil society. Indeed, it is likely that many new organizations will be highly elitist, even antidemocratic, and that their influence on broader democratization and development processes will be ambiguous.

David Steinberg, among others, warns against assuming that just because Burma experienced a period of democratic rule in the 1950s, democracy as a type of governance is well understood today. Modernists, he argues, "fail to understand the profound influence of a residual traditional political culture, which any new administration must overcome or function within."[38] This view is generally supported by Mary Callahan who in examining the ambiguous legacy of the "democratic era" finds a number of deep-seated obstacles to the establishment of democratic governance in Burma, including an institutionalized intolerance for dissent.[39] Ashley South similarly emphasizes, "Although most armed ethnic nationalist groups claimed to be fighting for 'democracy' . . . this ideal was often not reflected in their practices. Rebel leaders discouraged the expression of diverse opinions, and socio-political initiatives beyond the direct control of militarized insurgent hierarchies were generally suppressed."[40] No major recent studies on popular political values and attitudes in Burma are available. But everyday observations and discussions with mainly educated, urban Burmese over the past decade, by this author and others, reveal several general orientations and associated organizational behaviors, which are likely to impede the development of an efficient—or indeed democratic—civil society in the short to medium term, whatever the political space available.[41]

Among the most salient values or beliefs when it comes to political life in Burma are the hierarchical nature of social relations and the low levels of interpersonal trust.[42] Burmese society is status based and as such strongly hierarchical. Relative status may be determined by age, position, occupation, wealth, ethnicity, or gender, but few people interact with each other as equals. This may simply be acknowledged subtly in speech, but it often plays out as arrogance or aloofness on the part of superiors—and corresponding submissiveness by subordinates—which makes cooperation difficult and obstructs communication and the flow of information within organizations as well as in society at large.[43] Similar difficulties arise from the widespread lack of interpersonal trust. Many Burmese find it difficult to trust anyone outside their closest circle of family and friends. Lucian Pye has explained this by Burmese child-rearing practices, arguing that "infants are not given predictable security, and children are routinely subjected to fear."[44] Others—more convincingly perhaps—point to the debilitating impact of living in a society ruled by repression where surveillance and informers are omnipresent. As Monique Skidmore observes, "Their fear of surveillance, of being 'crushed' . . . culminates in inaction and in alienation for the Burmese who have become a nation of individuals unable and unwilling to trust each other. . . . These breakdowns in interpersonal relations inhibit the formation of, and trust in, community organisations. . . . The military dictatorship thus effectively manages to isolate Burmese people into small knots of friendship."[45] Whatever its cause(s), this generalized lack of trust in society makes it hard for people to come together and work for common objectives.[46]

These general orientations are clearly reflected in Burmese associational life as it exists today, both inside the country and among exiles. Most Burmese organizations are dominated by strong, charismatic leaders who tend to make decisions with little consultation or participation of the rank-and-file. Ambitious subordinates often leave in frustration over their lack of influence, but typically only to form rival organizations that function according to the same patterns. Like the military, political parties and insurgent groups tend to be platforms for the pursuit of power by their leaders rather than vehicles for the aggregation and promotion of broader community interests.[47] Political participation and debate are further stifled by a seemingly systemic intolerance for diverging views. Many observers have commented that this feature is no less evident within pro-democracy groups, which are commonly described as "mirror images" of the military regime.[48] Even the NLD, whose stated objective is to work to spread democratic norms into society, has shown a disconcerting tendency to expel party members who disagree with the official line or act independently of the party leadership.[49] This inability to accommodate, and work through, disagreements is evident also in negotiations between different organizations, which as noted often turn confrontational, reflecting the unwillingness on all sides to compromise on maximalist positions, even when it would seem to serve their underlying interests. Symptomatically, the cease-fires came about through a series of unique bargains in which neither the government nor the insurgent groups gave up significant ground (but therefore also made little progress in overcoming their differences).

The implications of these orientations and behaviors for collective action are only too evident in the paralyzing divisions that historically have seen Burmese organizations divide internally around rival leaders and have prevented groups from coalescing around common national goals. The issue of ethnicity has created particularly deep fault lines, but factionalism is rife also within ethnic and other communities. The persistence of these traits today is reflected in the inability of opposition groups—both inside the country and exile groups abroad—to build a broad antiauthoritarian front, despite the presence of a common "enemy" and the clear imperative of working together.[50]

The point here is not that the Burmese, if given the chance, would not embrace organizational activities, or that they are somehow less capable of democracy than other peoples. Broad popular participation in politics is a relatively new phenomenon even in the most advanced, industrialized democracies and remains a major challenge in most developing countries. It is dangerous, however, to assume that the introduction of a formal democratic system would necessarily lead to the flourishing of democratic politics. The obstacles to organizational life in Burma go beyond the constraints imposed by the military regime, and democratic attitudes and behavior are weak even within parts of the democracy movement. Although there are many exceptional individuals, who rise above these limitations, they face an uphill struggle.[51]

Reviving the Economy

The poverty of the Burmese state and society alike produces several other obstacles to progress in politics, governance, and human rights. First, the weak economy complicates political reform by increasing the perceived need by military leaders to maintain power,[52] while diminishing the resources available to the country's counter-elites and civil society at large.[53] Second, the lack of economic progress in the border areas threatens the cease-fires, which were presented by both the government and key cease-fire groups as a new, development-first approach to peace building that would help overcome long-standing hostility and provide a win-win path to national reconciliation but have delivered less than expected. Third, the low revenue base of the state, compounded by its weak revenue-generating capacity, lies at the root of an arbitrary and coercive system of taxation and corruption, as well as the deteriorating quality of the country's health and education systems. It also contributes to human rights abuses, as military battalions with insufficient budgets take what they need from local populations. Finally, abject poverty is a serious human rights issue in its own right, affecting millions of households. While the human rights community focuses on political freedoms and physical violence, many Burmese perceive the daily stress arising from their inability to afford sufficient food and other basic needs as the greatest limitation on their lives. This is not just a matter of hunger or illness, but also of drug abuse, prostitution, domestic violence, and other social problems that are less evident to outsiders but often cause immense pain and humiliation to those affected.[54]

Burma's underdevelopment is ultimately a political problem. Armed conflict, economic mismanagement, and international isolation have impoverished a country which at the time of independence was widely considered to have perhaps the most promising economic prospects in the region.[55] Without the political will and necessary external support to carry through with comprehensive macroeconomic and structural reforms and to address the serious humanitarian situation, the outlook is bleak and longer-term political and social stability in danger. Yet, as in other areas, it has long since stopped being just about political leadership. Even if we assume that a future democratic government is sufficiently committed and able to build broad consensus for undertaking the necessary reforms, it faces a Herculean task in building the necessary institutions for economic development and overcoming the legacy of decades of economic stagnation and unsustainable demands on the country's natural and human resources. While this is not the place for a comprehensive assessment of the Burmese economy, a brief overview of some of its key structural weaknesses serves to emphasize the deep-rooted problems the country faces, which pose a serious challenge to any government, present or future.

A Traditional, Agricultural Economy

Burma has the highest share of agriculture in GDP of any country in Asia, 57 percent compared to 9 percent in Thailand, 23 percent in Bangladesh, and 24 percent in Vietnam.[56] Moreover, its exports are heavily dominated by primary commodities, including oil and gas (30 percent), teak and hardwood (12 percent), and agricultural products (17 percent).[57] The industrial sector is small and stagnant. According to official figures, the share of industry in GDP has in fact fallen over the past two decades, from 13 percent in 1980–1981 to 10 percent in 2001–2002, further evidence of the lack of structural change in the economy.[58]

Weak Linkages to the Global Economy

The Burmese economy, despite the post-1988 opening to foreign trade and investment, remains inward looking and only weakly connected to the world economy. Even during the economic "boom" in the mid-1990s, Burma's actual foreign direct investment (FDI) per capita was less than one-sixth of Vietnam's.[59] Foreign trade flows, although growing, also remain a fraction of those of its neighbors. The total value of recorded Burmese exports in 2001–2002 ($2.4 billion) was only 3.5 percent of Thailand's ($65 billion) and 4.5 percent of Indonesia's ($56 billion).[60] In addition, Burma has only very limited access to the international capital market.

Underdeveloped Physical Infrastructure

Clearly Burma needs major structural reforms, but even with the right policies serious bottlenecks exist in the economy that must be overcome to put the country on a sustainable growth path, starting with its debilitated physical infrastructure, which is poor even by developing country standards. The post-1988 regime has made substantial investments in infrastructure, including roads, bridges, irrigation, power generation, and telecommunication, but it started from a very low level and serious deficits remain. Land transport is slow and expensive as even many intercity roads are in poor condition and need repair after each rainy season. Most of the secondary road network is still unsealed, and many of the country's forty thousand villages do not have any road access, making commercial agriculture all but impossible. The rail system provides an important alternative, particularly for freight, but both the tracks and the rolling stock are seriously outdated, leaving the Irrawaddy River as a major transport corridor, subject to seasonal variations in the water level. Power is another major constraint. Even at the current low levels of industrialization and electrification, consumption of electricity greatly exceeds the available supply, resulting in frequent black- or brown-outs, even in the main cities. Most industries, hotels, and better-off households rely on individual diesel generators to ensure a steady power supply. Much of the population in rural areas do not have access to electricity at all.[61] The telephone system is similarly underdeveloped, with only eight lines per one thousand inhabitants (the lowest ratio in Asia), and is unreliable outside the main cities.[62] Internet access was unavailable until just a few years ago, and even today private users number only in the hundreds.[63] Weak infrastructure thus imposes major constraints on both industrialization and agricultural development.

Rudimentary Financial System

The financial services sector, including banking, insurance, and capital markets, is crucial for private sector development, yet it too is grossly underdeveloped. Although the current government has allowed the establishment of private banks, Burma today has only twenty banks, about half of which are government owned or controlled. Branches are generally limited to the main cities and towns, and the level of computerization is low, making transactions slow. There are only two insurance companies in the country, both military controlled, and essentially no capital market (plans for the opening of a securities exchange made in 1995 never got off the ground). The weak banking sector, compounded by negative real interest rates, contributes to low savings levels. Bank deposits per capita in Burma ($8) are only about one-fourth of Vietnam's ($28), one-thirtieth of Indonesia's ($224), and two hundred times lower than in Thailand ($1,737).[64] Both deposits and loans grew rapidly in the late 1990s, driven by private bank expansion. A major private banking crisis in 2003, however, wiped out much of the progress made and private banks have since been under tight regulations, which effectively stop them from developing any further.[65] Not surprisingly, informal surveys indicate that access to credit—especially access to foreign exchange credit—is the single biggest problem facing private business.[66] Limited availability of credit is also a major constraint in the agricultural sector where small-scale farmers receive less than one-tenth of the normal bank credit available to farmers in neighboring countries, forcing them to rely on informal moneylenders who charge exorbitant interest rates.[67]

Growing Land Concentration

The nationalization and land reform policies of the Burma Socialist Programme Party (BSPP) government, aimed at distributing land from foreign land owners to Burmese peasants, ensured that the overall distribution of agricultural land toward the end of the socialist period was fairly equitable. Since 1988, however, the abandonment of social equality concerns, compounded by aggressive government promotion of commercial agriculture and growing poverty in some rural areas, has changed the situation significantly. Although the evidence is anecdotal, large companies and wealthy farmers appear to be taking control of increasing amounts of land, while many small holders are losing theirs due to indebtedness or inability to fulfill production targets.[68] This process of concentration is opposite to that of successful economies such as South Korea and Taiwan and instead resembles the situation in Bangladesh, the Philippines, and Latin America, which have much less dynamic agricultural sectors and higher levels of poverty.[69]

Declining Natural Resource Base

Burma's high forest cover and relatively low ratio of population to arable land is one of the country's main economic advantages, and perhaps the only reason it so far has avoided a major humanitarian crisis.. Yet, these natural resources are rapidly diminishing as pressures on forests and agricultural land reinforce each other, causing serious problems of deforestation and land degradation. According to the World Bank, deforestation rates have doubled since the late 1980s, from 0.7 to 1.4 percent per year, as a result of a number of factors, including large-scale illegal logging, growing demands for fuel wood, and land clearing for agriculture and infrastructure development. This, in turn, has caused serious ecological problems in many agricultural areas where increased erosion, local climate changes, and sinking water levels, coupled with growing population pressure and inappropriate technology, have seen soil quality deteriorate. Growing poverty completes a vicious circle as people seek to complement their income by gathering wood and other "free" resources. Already ten years ago, a UN report warned about the tensions between environmental decline and economic progress, arguing that Burma was nearing a threshold from which point recovery would be difficult and increasingly expensive.[70] This may now be a reality, presenting a serious challenge to future sustainable growth.

Low and Falling Education Levels

One of the most troubling aspects of Burma's economic stagnation is the extent to which the country is running down its human assets. Under pressure from dwindling government budgets and falling disposable household income, the education standards of the Burmese population are deteriorating at all levels. The current regime has built a significant number of new schools, hospitals, and other health facilities, including in the border areas, which were previously outside central government control. It has also trained and employed a larger number of new teachers, doctors, and health workers. Yet, with increasing outlays on physical and human infrastructure under dwindling budgets, the quality of services has deteriorated and user payments have increased, resulting in lower participation and educational outcomes (see section on Humanitarian Situation in the introduction). This has serious implications across the range of transitional issues discussed here. Low levels of education not only limit the pool of qualified political leaders, civil servants, economic managers, and skilled labor; they also have serious effects at the individual level, where low education is generally associated with lower income, weaker health, and a deepened sense of powerlessness. Even if some of the many Burmese citizens who have left the country over the past four decades to study or work overseas and constitute a significant pool of talent can be enticed to return under a more open political system, it will take decades to lift the education of the general population to the levels needed in a growing, modern economy.

Deepening Health Crisis

The problem of human capital is compounded by Burma's poor health situation, which is further depressing economic productivity at both the household and national level (as well as negatively affecting educational outcomes).[71] The country's HIV/AIDS epidemic, in particular, has emerged as a serious threat, which could undermine the basis for economic development and health services in the country for decades to come if it is not halted soon. Although no surveys of the socioeconomic impact of the epidemic in Burma are available, comparative research shows the far-reaching socioeconomic implications of HIV/AIDS elsewhere in the world, particularly in poor agricultural economies (such as Burma) that depend critically on physical labor for production.[72] Poor health is, in some respects, easier—or at least quicker—to reverse than poor education, given sufficient investments. Yet, as Emily Rudland emphasizes, comprehensive progress depends on "flows of income and recurrent expenditure on health, in combination with stocks of knowledge, infrastructure and social institutions that are built up over decades."[73] Thus, there is no question that health will continue to be a serious drag on economic development in Burma for some time to come, under any policy regime.

The solutions—or at least responses—to many of Burma's socioeconomic problems are generally known from experience elsewhere in the world, and, in some respects, it would not be too difficult to improve the situation. The task would be further eased under an elected government, which—at least initially—would be able to count on greater popular support and international assistance. Yet, even under the best of circumstances, turning the situation around will be a massive undertaking, particularly in light of the weakness of state and civil society institutions, including the private business sector. Importantly, there is growing urgency in several key areas, as the country's natural and human resource base is being run down at alarming rates. Any further hesitation in addressing these problems will make it all the harder for future governments to manage what is bound to be a difficult and volatile transition process.

Border Areas Development

The underdevelopment of the border areas and their diverse mainly ethnic minority populations present a particularly intractable challenge for would-be reformers, and one especially critical to peace and democratization. More than half a century of armed conflict since independence has uprooted many communities, fueled a litany of human rights abuses, and undermined normal economic activities, not to speak of longer-term development efforts. The affected areas, already remote and disadvantaged, have thus fallen far behind the rest of the country. This development gap, compounded by the damage done to local governance and community structures, is not only of serious humanitarian concern but also has grave implications for the political future of the country if left unaddressed.

Although Burma's long-standing ethnic conflicts, as noted, have diverse roots, economic neglect is at the heart of the matter. The failure of postindependence governments to fulfill the promise—"if Burma receives one kyat, you [the border areas] will also get one kyat"—made by independence leader Aung San before he was assassinated in 1947 was a significant factor in the second and third rounds of insurgencies in the late 1950s and 1960s.[74] Similarly, the failure since the early 1990s to genuinely develop the cease-fire areas has been emphasized by several armed groups as a reason not to stop fighting. Continued poverty fuels antigovernment sentiments, obstructs the broader process of nation building, and could fill the ranks of future insurgent groups as well. A brief examination of conditions affecting most border areas serves to emphasize just how big the challenges are.

Economic Opportunities

The large majority of the population in the border areas are subsistence farmers who rely on shifting upland cultivation and foraging for forest products for their livelihood. Yet population growth, worsened by conflict-induced population movements, is putting increased pressure on already marginal lands and the number of landless and land-poor is rising. Some jobs are available, mainly in the valleys where better-off farmers grow paddy and other commercial crops. Several cease-fire groups have also established large new plantations, as well as some industrial projects. Labor demand is seasonal, however, and with few off-farm job opportunities outside the main trading towns, many families today rely for their survival on members migrating to the cities, the mining areas in Kachin state, or neighboring countries for work.

Infrastructure and Social Services

Limited economic opportunities are compounded by the lack of physical infrastructure and social services outside the few towns. Since the cease-fires, both the central government and former insurgent groups have made significant efforts to expand the road network and, to a lesser extent, improve the health and education systems. However, remoteness, difficult terrain, and low population density make this a huge task. Many villages are still inaccessible except by foot or water and lack both government services and access to markets. They have no schools or health centers, no electricity, no improved water or sanitation, no agricultural extension services, and little commerce except for visiting traders who supplement otherwise self-sufficient and largely cashless subsistence economies.

Since the 1960s, generations of school children in the border areas have had their education severely disrupted by the effects of civil war. In many remote or conflict-affected areas almost no schools exist—and where they do, teachers are often absent or the teaching is of very poor quality.[75] Some communities establish their own schools and hire independent local teachers, but under increasing economic pressure, their ability to maintain these is weakening. The prohibition on use of ethnic minority languages in the state school system—apart from its political implications and effects on the vitality of minority cultures—also acts as a constraint on the achievements of students whose first language is not Burmese. The situation in terms of health facilities is no better, with coverage in the border areas still ten times lower than the national average.[76] Most facilities are seriously underresourced and understaffed. Language barriers and the high cost of treatment, including unofficial service fees and expenses for travel over long distances, further limit access to health services for the poverty-stricken, primarily ethnic minority populations.

The isolation of many border areas from central Burma contrasts with their proximity to more developed neighboring countries. All along the country's periphery, transient populations cross the international borders regularly for work, business, or to access health facilities. Yet, most of the regions in Thailand, Laos, China, India, and Bangladesh that Burma borders are remote in their own right and thus offer limited development opportunities.

Displacement

The decades of war have not only impeded normal development, but have also caused great destruction and uprooted many communities. Since the 1960s, large numbers of people have been displaced by fighting or forcibly relocated as part of the government's "four cuts" counterinsurgency campaigns, which seek to deny the insurgent groups access to food, funds, recruits, and intelligence by moving the civilian population into areas under government control.[77] The situation improved somewhat after the cease-fires in the early 1990s, but then deteriorated again in the mid- to late 1990s after the army defeated the last major insurgent bases in the southeast and stepped up its efforts to "secure" areas previously controlled by ethnic armed groups, causing a spike in the numbers of refugees as well as internally displaced persons (IDPs).[78] According to Amnesty International, the army continues to launch regular patrols across large swaths of the countryside, aimed at seeking out noncompliant villagers and destroying their shelters and rice supplies to deny support for the remaining insurgents.[79]

The Internal Displacement Monitoring Centre estimates that, as of October 2006, around half a million people were internally displaced in eastern Burma.[80] This is in addition to 150,000 official Burmese refugees in Thailand, as well as large numbers of de facto refugees who are treated by the Thai government as illegal immigrants. According to reports from humanitarian agencies based in Thailand,[81] most families in the relocation sites have no access to land and are therefore left to forage or beg for food; health and education services are usually minimal or nonexistent; and demands for forced labor are invariably high. Outside the relocation sites, other families are hiding from government troops, living in temporary shelters, and eking out a precarious living from the forest. Some are reportedly forced to move from place to place every few days or weeks to avoid discovery, a situation that further limits their livelihood options.

The notion of hundreds of thousands of IDPs living in hiding or effective captivity is questioned by some international agencies in Burma, which point out that many of those displaced essentially have resettled and, although facing harsh conditions, cannot meaningfully be separated from the general population in conflict-affected areas.[82] What is not in dispute though, is that the situation facing many ethnic minority people and communities affected by war and displacement is extremely serious and poses major challenges. Although some resettlement has taken place in the cease-fire areas, only minimal relief activities have been possible in the remaining conflict zones along the Thai and Indian borders. The resettlement and rehabilitation of IDPs, refugees, and other displaced populations will require major postconflict reconstruction efforts to establish the basis for longer-term development in areas that have effectively been depopulated and destroyed. Many villages literally will have to be rebuilt; new infrastructure must be put in, fields rehabilitated, and social services established. Before any of this can proceed, it will be necessary to locate and begin to remove the thousands of landmines, which have been laid by combatants on all sides.[83]

Militarization

The cease-fires have brought a stop to fighting and counterinsurgency activities in many regions but have not led to a demilitarization of the former war zones. On the contrary, the government has been moving numerous new battalions in to establish control over "insecure" areas. Underfunded and often insensitive to local populations and their needs, the army has expropriated large land areas for the establishment of new bases, including fields for growing food and commercial crops. Demands for forced labor and other "contributions" to the army have also increased around these bases.[84]

In northern Arakan (Rakhine) state, local army commanders have taken control of all commerce by establishing an "agent system" that requires licenses for any trade in livestock, crops, or other produce, including in village markets. The licenses are sold by the army through a system of middlemen to the highest bidders, thus creating a major source of rent seeking. The system squeezes out small-scale traders and creates monopolies, which allows price manipulation at the expense of both producers and consumers.[85] Frequent, arbitrary openings and closures of international as well as internal state borders further disrupt trade.

In the absence of the rule of law, militarization fuels exploitative behavior by soldiers who act with impunity. Most of the armed ethnic groups, cease-fire and non-cease-fire, engage in similar "feudal" practices, although their ethnic and social bonds with local populations tend to limit the most extreme types of abuses. Indeed, in some areas villagers are subject to "taxation" from several different armed groups, sometimes from different sides of the conflict lines. The inevitable result is further impoverishment and, in some cases, displacement as families flee to areas with a less pervasive military presence.

Commercialization

Improved access to former conflict areas has also attracted new investors who are plundering the natural resources, closing access for local communities, and rapidly exhausting the potential for future development. Most of those involved are "outsiders," including military officials and entrepreneurs from central Burma, drug warlords, and foreign companies. They often collaborate, however, with local elites, including leaders of cease-fire groups and wealthy villagers, to the exclusion of the general population, thus also contributing to widening inequality.

The nature of these new commercial activities varies. In Mon state, large-scale agribusinesses have driven small farmers off the land, in a government-supported program of privatized agricultural expansion.[86] Similar trends are visible also in eastern Shan state, where former insurgent groups in cooperation with Chinese investors are establishing large rubber and fruit plantations as part of their top-down drive for development. While often presented as crop-substitution activities for poor opium farmers, it is unclear how these plantations benefit local communities. In fact, their commercial sustainability is often questionable, as access to markets is lacking.

Yet, the greatest problems are occurring in connection with natural resource extraction, including mining and logging. In Kachin state, large mining companies have displaced local people engaged in small-scale gold panning and digging for jade, rubies, and other gems. The mining companies generally operate in isolation from local communities, bringing in everything they need from the outside and taking away the minerals for sale elsewhere. The industrialization of mining has also been accompanied by increased mechanization (at the expense of jobs both locally and for migrants from other poverty-stricken parts of the country) and is causing great damage to the environment.[87]

Logging of teak and other commercial wood has also increased dramatically over the past nineteen years, primarily along the Thai and Chinese borders with areas of operation gradually expanding as new roads improve access. Concessions are sold by the government and the army, as well as cease-fire groups, mainly to Thai and Chinese companies that have large resource-hungry markets at home. In some cases, local communities have been given minimal compensation, but often they are simply denied access to forests where they traditionally have been foraging for firewood, food, and other products, or at best are hired for labor. They are also hurt more indirectly by the massive deforestation, which causes soil erosion and falling water levels, thus undermining the basis for local agriculture.[88]

Militarization and commercialization are closely linked as those in power control access to all land, forests, and minerals. In principle, all natural resources are owned by the state and thus managed by the central government, but the relevant ministries are routinely overridden by military officials, including high-level generals, local commanders, and individual army battalions and military intelligence units, who are selling concessions to companies without any apparent accountability or transparency.[89] Most cease-fire groups have been granted extensive concessions by the government to fund their operations and local infrastructure projects, while the remaining insurgent groups continue to sell logs and other resources to fund their armies as they have always done. For all of these groups, the income from natural resources is vital for maintaining power, as well as a source of personal wealth for their leaders. Very little of the income is funneled back into the local economies or used for genuine development purposes. The result is widening inequality and a growing potential for social unrest.

Opium Eradication

Since the 1950s when production was put on a commercial footing by remnants of the Chinese Nationalist Army (the Kuomintang), supported by the U.S. Central Intelligence Agency (CIA), Burma has been one of the two largest producers of opium and its derivate heroin in the world. Over time, opium has become the primary means of survival for an estimated four hundred thousand farming households, primarily in Shan state east of the Salween River, who grow it as a cash crop to buy rice and cover food deficits.[90] Yet, since the mid-1990s national and local authorities, under pressure from the international community, have begun enforcing an opium ban, which has resulted in a sharp decline in production in some areas.[91]

Opium eradication activities, to some extent, have been accompanied by efforts to introduce alternative crops and income opportunities, but the effectiveness of military law enforcement has far outpaced any development activities. While poor opium farmers are jailed for failing to comply with the ban, many alternative development activities have focused on big infrastructure projects and commercial plantations, which have questionable or at best only long-term benefits for the farmers.[92] In the Kokang region, where a total ban on opium production was enforced in 2002, a significant increase in poverty was observed among farmers who were already among the poorest in the country. Some families lost up to 80 percent of their annual income, forcing them to cut meals, borrow food, or sell their livestock and other assets. In some villages more than half the parents had to take their children out of school, and two out of three private pharmacies closed due to a fall in customer demand.[93] According to some reports, a third of the population left the region in search of alternative income opportunities. Even then, intensifying cultivation to make up for lost income and food shortfalls has greatly increased the pressure on marginal land, causing soil degradation and other stresses on the environment with serious long-term implications for development.[94]

Breaking the shackles of the opium economy is critically important for longer-term peace, stability, and democratization in the border areas and the country at large. It would also have significant social benefits as growing abuse, in particular of injecting heroin, is destroying the lives and earning potential of increasing numbers of primarily young men and fueling the HIV/AIDS epidemic.[95] Yet, most communities have lost the knowledge and traditions which sustained them before opium was introduced, and today are weaker and more vulnerable than they were before.[96] In the absence of sufficient alternative income opportunities and support for the affected communities, the short-term implications of forced eradication are therefore hugely damaging. Ultimately, more than 2 million people that currently depend on opium for their survival could be affected.

Overall, while conditions have improved in many parts of the border areas as a result of the cease-fires, the challenges and obstacles to development are immense. The continued exploitation of local communities by vested interests—whether military, commercial, or criminal in form—blurs the lines between war and peace and underscores the need to strengthen the rule of law and protect people from the powers that be, whatever their affiliation. This, however, remains a gigantic task in regions that for decades have known only wartime governance—or, in some cases, have never truly been governed by anyone.

Promoting Human Rights (Not Just Elections)

There is a strong tendency in the West to reduce Burma's human rights problems to a simple matter of leadership or regime form. Yet, the underlying assumption that a transition to elected government would deliver national reconciliation, effective governance, economic development, or even democracy is problematic without paying attention to the broader political, social, and economic conditions discussed in this chapter. As experience from other countries such as Pakistan, the Philippines, and Indonesia shows, popularity of individual leaders does not necessarily translate into good governance and social progress.[97] More important is the ability of national leaders to build effective institutions and promote consensus among key stakeholders for reforms that may entail significant costs to vested interests. These goals have proven illusive for both military and civilian governments in Burma since independence, and remain a tall order in a deeply divided and impoverished society. Indeed, past failures are likely to foreshadow future problems.

In the excitement about political personalities and headline events, the seriousness of the long-standing conflicts dividing Burmese society and the complex crises that flow from them is easily overlooked. Burmese politics historically lacks the qualities of moderation and compromise that lie at the heart of the democratic process. The intolerance for diverging views and inability by organizations on all sides of the political divides to work through differences without fragmenting constitute serious obstacles to the kind of compromise-seeking, bridge-building politics needed to overcome the deep divisions in Burmese society. Meanwhile, the central state has neither the authority nor the institutional capacity to effectively implement policies across its realm. The success of the military in co-opting or destroying most of Burma's civilian institutions, compounded by general underdevelopment and a massive brain drain, greatly diminishes the prospects of a smooth transition from military to democratic rule. As a local analyst puts it, "Our country is like an old house. The foundation has long since crumbled. It is only held together by the creepers [the military]. If you remove them, the whole house will collapse."[98] Even if a pact could be established between military and civilian leaders, the weakness of the civil service and near absence of effective nonstate organizations reduce the ability of the country to respond to the challenges presented by the growing HIV/AIDS pandemic and other social crises, as well as to the opportunities created, for example, by the new global information order. The installation of an elected government would be an important step forward, but even getting to that transitional event—not to mention overcoming the long legacy of autocratic rule, social fragmentation, international isolation, and deep-rooted structural poverty—requires serious, long-term efforts by all parties to promote change along a range of issues.

None of this is to suggest that Burma is doomed. On the contrary, the country has much "going" for it. The Burmese intelligentsia still counts many well-educated people committed to the betterment of their country, including doctors, lawyers, engineers, and journalists (although many have left the country and will have to be enticed to return). The authoritarian legacy, however deep, is balanced to some extent by traditional Buddhist ideas and values, as well as the influence of international norms that will only grow with an opening up of the country. Most importantly, perhaps, Burma still has economic resources that are the envy of other low-income countries, including fertile land, large oil and gas reserves, and a key geostrategic position in a region that remains the fastest growing in the world. It is important, however, not to be complacent about the scale—or urgency—of the reforms and changes in institutions and behavior that are needed in order to achieve the overarching goal of improving the human rights of the Burmese people, including their freedom, security, and welfare.

Notes

1. Martin Smith, *Burma: Insurgency and the Politics of Ethnicity*, 2nd ed. (London: Zed Books, 1999), 420.

2. Khaing Soe Naing Aung, quoted in "A Brief History of the National Democratic Movement of Ethnic Nationalities," August 2000.

3. UNICEF, "Child Risk Index" (unpublished document, n.d.) [copy in author's possession]. The index measures the relative status of children and women in the fourteen states and divisions based on official government data from 1997 to 2000.

4. A similar picture emerges from FAO, "Food Insecurity and Vulnerability Information and Mapping System" (unpublished document, 2004) [copy in author's possession], which includes proxy measures of local food production, physical access for food imports, and the resilience of the population to periodic food shortages. While most of the border townships are judged to be "highly" or "moderately" vulnerable in food security terms (with Shan, northern Kachin, and Chin states being the worst off), nearly all townships in central Burma are considered to have "low" vulnerability. Even then, the actual disadvantages of the border areas are likely to be even greater than indicated by these data sets since the most remote and conflict-affected areas are not included at all.

5. See, for example, Article 19, "Censorship Prevails: Political Deadlock and Economic Transition in Burma" (London, March 1995), 36–37.

6. Mon Unity League, "The Mon: A People without a Country," n.d. (copy in author's possession).

7. Martin Smith, *Burma (Myanmar): The Time for Change* (n.p.: Minority Rights Group International, May 2002), 26.

8. Ashley South, *Mon Nationalism and Civil War in Burma* (Richmond: Curzon, 2003), 311.

9. Article 19, "Censorship Prevails," 37.

10. Burma's multireligious population enjoys a relatively high degree of religious freedom in central parts of the country. There have been frequent reports over the years, however, particularly from Chin and Kachin states, of villagers being pressured to adopt Buddhism, as well as restrictions on building new churches. See, for

example, U.S. State Department, "International Religious Freedom Report 2002," 7 October 2002. More ominously, many Burmese, both soldiers and civilians, are strongly prejudiced against Muslims, who are commonly accused of harboring aspirations of turning the country into an Islamic state. In February 2001 tensions between the Muslim and Buddhist population of Akyab (Sittwe), the capital of Arakan (Rakhine) state, erupted in large-scale riots in which an unknown number of people were killed and Muslim property was destroyed. Anti-Muslim riots have also taken place on numerous occasions in towns in central Burma, for example, in 2001 in Taungoo (Toungoo), Prome (Pyay), and Pegu (Bago). Human Rights Watch/Asia, "Crackdown on Burmese Muslims," July 2002.

11. See, for example, "Interview with Aung San Suu Kyi," *Far Eastern Economic Review*, 7 May 1998.

12. This order of priorities became a matter of contention during the "secret talks" between Aung San Suu Kyi and the military leadership in 2000–2002, facilitated by UN special envoy Ismail Razali, which led some ethnic minority leaders to express concern that they were being left out. International official, interview by author, Rangoon, December 2001.

13. Robin Luckham, "The International Community and State Reconstruction in War-Torn Societies," *Conflict, Security and Development* 4, no. 3 (December 2004): 481–507.

14. Discussions with representatives of cease-fire administrations and local civil society groups at the Workshop on Myanmar Issues and Myanmar Views: Searching for a Unified Perspective, organized by the Institute of Southeast Asian Studies (Singapore), Rangoon, 1–5 February 2004.

15. It is worth remembering that the insurgencies began during the parliamentary period and spread, at least in part, as a result of the policies of the elected government in the 1950s.

16. International Crisis Group, "Myanmar: The Role of Civil Society," Asia Report, 6 December 2001, 27.

17. Military official, interview by author, Rangoon, March 2003.

18. How bad things might get is, of course, a matter of conjecture. However, the experience from the parliamentary period in the 1950s, when Burma not only was engulfed by insurgency but faced serious problems of general lawlessness as well, provides a stark warning about the potential for internal conflict.

19. For example, David I. Steinberg, "Burma/Myanmar: A Guide for the Perplexed," in "Reconciling Burma/Myanmar: Essays on U.S. Relations with Burma," ed. John H. Badgley, special issue, *NBR Analysis* 15, no. 1 (March 2004): 41–54.

20. ALTSEAN, "Interview with Aung San Suu Kyi," 15 July 1998, www.kyoto-seika.ac.jp/eng/1_intro/altsean.htm (accessed 25 April 2007).

21. Interviews by author: Western diplomat, Rangoon, March 2005; UN official, Rangoon, December 2004; international NGO director, December 2004. Such criticisms, though, tend to be less directed at Aung San Suu Kyi than at other members of the party leadership.

22. This is borne out by the experience in the Philippines under Corazon Aquino and Indonesia under Megawati Sukarnoputri, where other hugely popular leaders failed to deliver effective governance.

23. When asked about their policy program, members of the United Nationalities Alliance, for example, responded that "our policy is democracy—we can make policy when we are in power." Interview by author, Rangoon, February 2004.

24. Josef Silverstein, "Aung San Suu Kyi: Is She Burma's Woman of Destiny?" *Asian Survey* 30, no. 10 (October 1990): 1019.

25. International agencies report arriving up-country with permission from their counterpart ministries to initiate new development projects, only to be told that "Khin Nyunt [the former prime minister and long-term coordinator of most government affairs] has no power here." International NGO director, interviews by author, Rangoon, January 2004.

26. In one of the few relatively recent evaluations of the Burmese bureaucracy, Paul Cook and Martin Minogue conclude that key administrators have little conception of the methods of modern management and lack communication and human relation skills as well as analytical skills. They link this to the lack of job incentives, arguing that low salaries, little delegation to lower levels, and absence of career paths and development opportunities have crippled individual initiative and led to low morale. Paul Cook and Martin Minogue, "Economic Reform and Political Change in Myanmar," *World Development* 21, no. 7 (1993): 1151–61.

27. Workshop on Myanmar Issues and Myanmar Views: Searching for a Unified Perspective, organized by the Institute of Southeast Asian Studies (Singapore), Rangoon, 1–5 February 2004.

28. The United Wa State Army's command style and associated distrust of autonomous community organizations, for example, owes much to traditional Wa political culture and to ideas of the leading role of the party inherited from the Communist Party of Burma (CPB). Ashley South, personal communication, March 2004. These factors are exacerbated by the limited social and economic opportunities in the Wa substate; the minimal quantity and poor quality of education and health services; and the pervasive corruption, political violence, and warlordism associated with the booming drugs trade in the region.

29. IMF, "Myanmar: Recent Economic Developments," staff report for the 2006 Article IV Consultation, 2 March 2004, 23. Latest available figure (2005–2006).

30. Mary Callahan makes this point with regard to the weak capacity of the existing political parties, but the problem extends to the broader state structure. Mary P. Callahan, "Democracy in Burma: The Lessons of History," *NBR Analysis* 9, no. 3 (May 1998): 20.

31. Thomas Carothers, "Think Again: Civil Society," *Foreign Policy* (Winter 1999–2000): 18–29.

32. Needless to say, for civil society to play these diverse roles requires a wide range of different organizations, ranging from political parties and advocacy groups to media organizations, professional associations, business associations, trade unions,

social welfare organizations, parent-teacher associations, and so on. Generally speaking, however, most of these organizations will be either present or absent to a similar degree in any given society, and have a similar quality, depending on the underlying conditions for the emergence of autonomous associational life. Thus, it is possible to discuss them meaningfully as a group, although necessarily at a high level of abstraction.

33. Interviews by author: local NGO director, September 2004; international NGO director, December 2004.

34. The NLD is a partial exception, but even the main opposition party has only a very skeletal organizational structure. It lacks even basic communication tools like computers and fax machines and is largely unable to communicate with its members and the population at large.

35. In a UN seminar for church leaders in June 2004 in which this author discussed the role of civil society, several of those present talked frankly about the novelty of many of the development concepts and challenges they face in their interaction with external aid agencies as well as local communities. One of their primary requests was thus for leadership and management training.

36. See, for example, "The Fort Wayne Declaration" (statement issued by exiled activists after a meeting in Fort Wayne, IN, 30–31 August 2003).

37. See, for example, Larry Diamond, *Developing Democracy: Toward Consolidation* (Baltimore: Johns Hopkins University Press, 1999), 161–218.

38. David I. Steinberg, "The State, Power and Civil Society in Burma-Myanmar: The Status and Prospects for Pluralism," in *Burma/Myanmar: Strong Regime, Weak State*, ed. Morten B. Pedersen, Emily Rudland, and Ron May, 92 (Adelaide, Australia: Crawford House, 2000).

39. Callahan, "Democracy in Burma."

40. Ashley South, "Ceasefires and Civil Society: The Case of the Mon," draft paper, 2002.

41. This is obviously a limited segment of the population, but particularly salient since the urban middle class is expected to serve as the democratic vanguard. The majority group of poor, subsistence farmers is likely to be even more traditional in outlook.

42. Steinberg discusses another core notion, namely, the tendency of Burmese to perceive power as "finite"—or, in other words, a "limited good." This, he argues, makes the sharing of power, whether among individuals or organizations, difficult and impedes the emergence of a truly pluralist system. David I. Steinberg, *Burma: The State of Myanmar* (Washington, DC: Georgetown University Press, 2001), 38–39.

43. For observations on this problem within the civil service, see Ardeth Maung Thawnghmung, "Paddy Farmers and the State: Agricultural Policies and Legitimacy in Rural Burma" (PhD diss., University of Wisconsin–Madison, 2001).

44. Lucian Pye, "Civility, Social Capital and Civil Society: Three Powerful Concepts of Explaining Asia," *Journal of Interdisciplinary History* 29, no. 4 (1998): 774.

45. Monique Skidmore, *Karaoke Fascism: Burma and the Politics of Fear* (Philadelphia: University of Pennsylvania Press, 2004), 51.

46. The widespread lack of trust is observed also by Kyaw Yin Hlaing, who in interviews with twenty Burmese activists from five different exile organizations found that many do not trust their fellow pro-democracy activists whether from their own or other groups. Kyaw Yin Hlaing, "Myanmar in 2004: Why Military Rule Continues," *Southeast Asian Affairs*, 2005.

47. This is not to say that political leaders necessarily are motivated by personal power, but the definition of the public interest tends to be top-down.

48. See, for example, International Crisis Group, "Role of Civil Society," 11–12.

49. The absence of internal democratic structures, as Larry Diamond points out, does not mean that independent sector organizations cannot "represent group interests, check the power of the state, and perform many other democratic functions." But when, in their own patterns of governance, they "perpetuate norms that penalise dissent, exalt the leader over the group, and cloak the exercise of power," one thing they will not do is build a culture of democracy. Diamond, *Developing Democracy*, 228.

50. According to a political analyst close to many exile Burmese pro-democracy groups, "The government did not have to do anything to get rid of these groups. It only had to let the groups undermine each other's position and make them fight over petty things." Quoted in Kyaw Yin Hlaing, "Why Military Rule Continues."

51. It is worth noting that other countries in the region, such as Pakistan and the Philippines, have faced major difficulties in overcoming the authoritarian tendencies and corrupt practices of the past, even if they shared with Burma the apparent advantage of starting out with hugely popular democratic leaders. Even more politically advanced countries like Singapore and Malaysia have yet to leave behind the historical legacy of strong, dynastic leaders and truncated political discourse.

52. The military leadership is very concerned about ensuring that sufficient funding is available to the armed forces to protect its interests, and therefore is less likely to compromise in a situation of poverty than one of affluence. In addition, there may be an issue of pride. According to a military "insider," "The SLORC saw it as one of its primary goals to revive the economy. It would therefore be embarrassing to the current leaders to step back before this goal has been achieved." Interview by author, Rangoon, August 2003.

53. One does not have to accept the "economic development thesis" that democracy comes to countries at a certain GDP in order to recognize that education and socioeconomic welfare is necessary for broad popular participation in politics and gradual reform of authoritarian attitudes at all levels of the state and society.

54. For a description of the impact of poverty on individual lives in the periurban areas of Rangoon and Mandalay, see Skidmore, *Karaoke Fascism*, 147–73.

55. David I. Steinberg, "Myanmar: The Anomalies of Politics and Economics" (Working Paper No. 5, Asia Foundation, November 1997).

56. Asian Development Bank, "Asian Development Outlook 2002," December 2002. Latest available figures (2001–2002).

57. IMF, "Recent Economic Developments," 34. Latest available figures (2001–2002) for recorded trade; excluding border trade, which is likely to be even further skewed toward primary products.

58. By contrast, over the same period, the share of industry in GDP in Thailand rose from 29 to 42 percent, in Vietnam from 23 to 37 percent, and in Bangladesh from 16 to 25 percent. Asian Development Bank, "Asian Development Outlook 2002."

59. David Dapice, "Development Prospects for Burma: Cycles and Trends," in *Burma: Prospects for a Democratic Future*, ed. Robert I. Rotberg, 158 (Washington, DC: Brookings Institute Press, 1998).

60. IMF, "Recent Economic Developments," 34. Comparative Asia figures from "Commodity Composition of Exports," confidential paper, 2 November 2004. Burma has a large unrecorded trade as well, commonly believed to equal recorded trade, but so do its neighbors.

61. According to a Japanese report, in 1998, only about 10 percent of the rural population had access to electricity. Study Group on the Myanmar Economy, *Current Situation of the Myanmar Economy and Its Future Development Strategy* (Tokyo: Institute of Fiscal and Monetary Policy, 1998), 63. Although electrification has expanded since then, rural areas receive low priority and the number of people who have regular access to electricity remains very low.

62. UNDP, "Human Development Report 2006," n.d., 329.

63. Stuart Larkin, "Thoughts on a Pro-Poor Growth Strategy for Myanmar" (report prepared for the United Nations Development Programme/Myanmar, 29 May 2002), 107.

64. Dapice, "Development Prospects," 162.

65. Bank owner, interviews by author, Rangoon, November 2003, May 2004, December 2006. For a detailed analysis, see Sean Turnell and Alison Vicary, "Burma's Banking Crisis: A Commentary," 6 March 2003, www.ibiblio.org/obl/docs/BEW2003-03.htm (accessed 27 April 2007); Sean Turnell, "Burma Bank Update," *Burma Economic Watch*, no. 1 (2004): 19–27; Sean Turnell, "Profiles of Burma's Banks," *Burma Economic Watch*, no. 1 (2006): 3–33.

66. Larkin, "Thoughts on a Pro-Poor Growth Strategy," 107.

67. "Boosting Myanmar's Agricultural Productivity: A Look at Fertiliser, Credit and Rice Pricing Policies," confidential report, February 1998.

68. Burmese agricultural economist, interview by author, December 2004.

69. Dapice, "Development Prospects," 157.

70. "Prospects for Sustainable Growth in Burma/Myanmar," confidential report, 12 September 1995.

71. For a rare discussion of the socioeconomic implications of Burma's current health situation, see Rachel Safman, "Assessing the Impact of HIV and Other Health Issues on Myanmar's Development," in *Myanmar: Beyond Politics to Societal Imperatives*, ed. Kyaw Yin Hlain, Robert Taylor, and Tin Maung Maung Than, 117–39 (Singapore: ISEAS, 2005).

72. In parts of Africa it has been estimated that the AIDS epidemic will set back economic development by twenty to thirty years, reversing gains not only in GDP and per capita income, but also almost all other measures of social welfare. Safman, "Assessing the Impact of HIV."

73. Emily Rudland, "Health, HIV and the State in Myanmar," in *The Illusion of Progress: The Political Economy of Reform in Burma/Myanmar*, ed. David S. Mathieson and Ron J. May, 163–99 (Adelaide, Australia: Crawford House, 2004).

74. Aung San quoted in Smith, *Insurgency*, 78.

75. Most government teachers in the border areas are from central Burma. They are typically new graduates who are assigned to areas far from their homes and families where living costs far outweigh their minimal salaries. Most do not even speak the local language. While some do a heroic job under impossible circumstances, absenteeism and lack of motivation are big problems.

76. UNICEF, "Children and Women in Myanmar: A Situation Assessment and Analysis," April 2001.

77. This strategy is similar to that applied by the British in Malaya and the Americans in Vietnam, who also faced insurgents that were rooted in the local communities.

78. The Burma Border Consortium identified more than 2,500 villages believed to have been relocated, destroyed, or abandoned from 1996 to 2002 in central Shan, Karenni, and Karen states, and Tenasserim division. Burma Border Consortium (BBC), "Internally Displaced People and Relocation Sites in Eastern Burma," September 2002.

79. Amnesty International, "Myanmar: The Lack of Security in Counter-Insurgency Areas," 17 July 2002.

80. The Internal Displacement Monitoring Centre (IDMC) collects information from other sources, primarily human rights groups based in Thailand. "Myanmar (Burma)," www.internal-displacement.org/ (accessed 20 April 2007).

81. See, for example, Burma Ethnic Research Group (BERG), "Forgotten Victims of a Hidden War: Internally Displaced Karen in Burma," April 1998; Thailand Burma Border Consortium (TBBC), "Internal Displacement in Eastern Burma—2006 Survey," 26 October 2006.

82. UNHCR official, interview by author, Rangoon, December 2004.

83. According to the International Coalition for Banning Landmines, the army, as well as fifteen ethnic armed groups are or have been using landmines. Nine out of the fourteen states and divisions are believed to be affected. The total number of mine casualties is not known. International Coalition for Banning Landmines, "Landmine Reporter," 2003, www.icbl.org/lm/2003/ (accessed 26 January 2007).

84. Special rapporteur on the situation of human rights in Myanmar, "Situation of Human Rights in Myanmar," report to the United Nations General Assembly (A/61/369), 21 September 2006; Amnesty International, "Myanmar: Leaving Home," 8 September 2005; Karen Human Rights Group, "Setting Up the Systems of Repression," 7 September 2006.

85. The agent system reportedly is spreading into other parts of Arakan (Rakhine) and Kachin states as well. UN official, interview by author, Rangoon, January 2004.

86. Ashley South, personal communication, Bangkok, March 2004.

87. Images Asia and Pan Kachin Development Society, "At What Price? Gold Mining in Kachin State, Burma," November 2004. See also EarthRights International, "Turning Treasure into Tears: Mining, Dams, and Deforestation in Shwegyin Township, Pegu Division, Burma," 20 February 2007, for information on mining in eastern Pegu (Bago) division.

88. For a detailed perspective on logging and its implications for local communities, see Global Witness, "A Conflict of Interests. The Uncertain Future of Burma's Forests," October 2003.

89. Global Witness, "Conflict of Interests."

90. Joint Kokang-Wa Humanitarian Needs Assessment Team, "Replacing Opium in Kokang and Wa Special Regions," March 2003.

91. The Shan State Army (North) officially had eradicated opium in Shan Special Region 4 by 1997; the Kokang authorities had done so in Shan Special Region 1 by 2003; and the UWSA in Shan Special Region 2 by 2005. Elsewhere in Shan state, the Burmese army has engaged in forced eradication to differing degrees. The results of these campaigns are evident from opium surveys undertaken by both the United Nations Office on Drugs and Crime (UNODC) and the U.S. Drugs Enforcement Agency (DEA), which indicate a major drop in opium production from 1996 to 2006, in terms of acreage as well as output, although production is reported to continue in some of these areas on a smaller scale and to have expanded elsewhere in the country. UNODC, "Opium Poppy Cultivation in the Golden Triangle October 2006: Lao PDR, Myanmar, Thailand," October 2006, 57–118; United States National Drug Intelligence Center, "National Drug Threat Assessment 2007," October 2006, 21.

92. Observations and interviews by the author, eastern Shan state, March 2004.

93. United Nations Country Team, "Presentation on the May 2004 UNCT Mission to the Wa Region" (paper presented at the Mini Dublin Group Meeting, Rangoon, August 2004).

94. International aid consultant, interview by author, Rangoon, May 2004.

95. Heroin injection is responsible for 30 percent of officially reported HIV cases in the country and is a particular problem in the mining areas of Kachin and Shan states. UN official, interview by author, Rangoon, January 2004.

96. UN official, interview by author, eastern Shan state, March 2004.

97. In each of these countries, popular support for new populist civilian leaders shifted within a few years from the reintroduction of elections to former generals, although in the Philippines and Indonesia the principle of elections survived.

98. Interview by author, Rangoon, May 2003.

CHAPTER FIVE

Assessing the Core Strategy

> It is this isolation that kept Burma in poverty; isolation that fuels a negative, almost xenophobic nationalism; isolation that makes the Burmese army see everything as a zero-sum game and any change as filled with peril; isolation that has made any conclusion to the war so elusive, hardening differences; and isolation that has weakened institutions—the ones on which any transition to democracy would depend—to the point of collapse. Without isolation the status quo would be impossible to sustain.
>
> —Thant Myint-U, historian[1]

The value of the core strategy has been subject to growing debate since the late 1990s. Yet, while faith in it is wavering among some previous supporters, others insist it is only a matter of trying harder.[2] Many advocates of the core strategy seem to assume that *any* strengthening of sanctions serves the objective of promoting democracy and human rights (or, conversely, that any engagement that provides legitimacy or material benefits to the regime runs counter to those goals). Such assumptions reflect what Johan Galtung refers to as the "naïve" theory of sanctions: that there is some kind of roughly proportionate relation between the degree of value deprivation imposed on the target regime and the probability that it will comply with what is demanded of it. The idea, as Galtung explains, "is that there is a limit to how much value-deprivation the system can stand and that once this limit is reached . . . political disintegration will proceed very rapidly and will lead to surrender or willingness to negotiate."[3] This may sound reasonable in theory. The dynamics on the ground in Burma, however, tell a different story. While the military rulers are certainly affected, annoyed, and even concerned about their international pariah status and lack of access to Western trade, investment, and aid, the theories underlying the core strategy do indeed appear "naïve." Certainly, they do not take sufficient cognizance of the "psychology of sanctions" (i.e., the way the target in all its complexity responds psychologically to pressure), or of the broader historical, political, and economic context for the ongoing struggle for reform. As this chapter will show, the use of coercion to promote democracy and human rights in Burma has major limitations as well as serious adverse effects, which raise urgent questions about existing Western human rights policy.

Achievements

There is no doubt that the military leadership is affected by international pressure. The State Law and Order Restoration Council/State Peace and Development Council (SLORC/SPDC) has gone to significant lengths to defend itself in the Third Committee of the UN General Assembly, each year sending a team of its most experienced ambassadors to New York to lobby for a softer resolution. Similarly, after the 1997 U.S. investment ban, two Burmese companies linked to the government hired public relations firms in Washington at considerable cost in an attempt to ward off further sanctions.[4] This all shows some measure of apprehension over Burma's international isolation.

In practical terms, international censure and sanctions have had some positive effects in four areas. First, external pressure has encouraged the military government to adopt the language, if not yet the practice, of democracy and human rights. While Burmese officials in the early 1990s rejected the relevance of "Western" concepts of human rights in Burma, Western countries today are accused of obstructing Burma's path to democracy and abusing the human rights of the Burmese people:

> We see their policy [of sanctions] as not very practical. If you do not have a strong economy, if you do not have basic infrastructure, transformation from a one-party socialist system into a multi-party system is not realistic.[5]

> If there is no investment because of sanctions, it is the people who suffer since there will be fewer jobs. If there is no development assistance, it is the people who suffer since such assistance can have a positive impact on their daily lives.

If there are fewer tourists, the people will have less income to improve their standard of living.[6]

The generals still insist that Burma must have its own form of democracy, suitable to the country's political situation and stage of development, but they no longer deny the principle of popular rule. Similar shifts are evident in other dimensions of human rights. The post-1988 government, for example, has ratified a number of international human rights conventions, including the Convention on the Prevention and Punishment of the Crime of Genocide; Convention on the Rights of the Child; Convention on the Elimination of All Forms of Discrimination against Women; Convention against Torture and Other Cruel, Inhuman, or Degrading Treatment or Punishment; and the Slavery Convention. It has also invited institutions like the UN special envoy, the UN special rapporteur on human rights, the UN Refugee Agency (UNHCR), the International Committee of the Red Cross (ICRC), the International Labor Organization (ILO), and Amnesty International into the country. It has even established a human rights committee and supported human rights training for government officials. Although most of these new commitments still lack substance, they provide access points for international dialogue and capacity building, and may begin to build a constituency for change within the military state itself as military and government officials assume formal responsibility for human rights issues.[7]

Second, international censure and sanctions have reinforced the domestic pressure on the military to accommodate Aung San Suu Kyi and the National League for Democracy (NLD). With few material bases of power, the main opposition party derives its influence mainly from the political legitimacy it enjoys at home and abroad. How much the backing of the international community counts in this respect vis-à-vis the support of the Burmese people is difficult to say. The SLORC/SPDC has generally appeared more concerned about domestic stability than international respectability. But international pressure certainly helps explain why the generals have felt the need to negotiate with Aung San Suu Kyi and why they have not, so far, disbanded the NLD (clearly, they do not recognize the opposition party as having any normative or legal right to govern). This, in turn, has helped keep the idea of a different political order on the agenda within the country and sustain some minimal room for democrats to operate aboveground.

A third area in which international pressure has had an impact is in the greater efforts by the regime to address particular human rights concerns such as political prisoners, forced labor, prison conditions, and protection of returnees. The frequent releases of political prisoners ahead of international meetings or after visits by the UN rapporteur on human rights clearly have been motivated by a desire to improve international relations. External pressure has also helped create space for international human rights agencies to work on the ground. The ICRC, for example, from 2000 to 2005, gained near universal access to the country's prisons. Working with the prison authorities, it made significant progress in improving overall conditions for both political and ordinary prisoners.[8] It also gained wide access to conflict-affected areas along the Thai border where local leaders reported that the level of human rights abuses decreased as a result.[9] The ILO, similarly, has made some progress in reducing the use of forced labor on government infrastructure projects.[10] In May 2003, it reached agreement with the Burmese government to establish an unprecedented international ombudsman position to investigate complaints from the public. The mechanism was subsequently suspended by the ILO itself after the attack on Aung San Suu Kyi and NLD members and supporters later that month, but a new agreement was reached in February 2007. Officials from these and other international agencies confirm that efforts by the Burmese authorities to ward off international criticism—or, in some cases, to disprove particular accusations—have helped facilitate human rights work in the country.[11] That the military regime has been more cooperative on highly sensitive human rights issues than on economic reforms, which have been much less a subject of international attention, seems to confirm this.[12]

Finally, Western governments and organizations have provided sustenance for Burmese pro-democracy groups. Due to political sensitivities, direct financial support for domestically based political groups has been small-scale and channeled through nongovernmental entities.[13] Western funding and training programs for exile groups, however, have been substantial. Burmese dissidents also often comment on the importance of the moral support provided by international attention to their cause.[14]

These various concessions by the military regime contradict claims by critics that censure and sanctions are "meaningless" since Burma's rulers prefer isolation.[15] On the other hand, the limitations are obvious. At no time during nineteen years of mounting international pressure have the generals given up important values, nor has such pressure resulted in substantial, lasting improvements in the overall human rights situation. International actors may have helped secure the release of Aung San Suu Kyi in 1995 and again in 2002, but the military has shown little hesitation in re-detaining the opposition leader or anyone else whenever they become a threat.[16] Similarly, although international pressure after the May 2003 attack on Aung San Suu Kyi probably spurred the government to launch its seven-step road map to democracy three months later, this "new" program simply confirmed core features of the military's long-standing transition plan, which has changed little since the National Convention was first convened in 1993. The releases of political prisoners, along with some improvements in forced labor and other aspects of human rights, have had direct benefits at an individual level, but have not fundamentally changed the wider culture of human rights abuses and impunity. Even when the regime plays along with its international critics, it still sets the ground rules for the "game" and decides when it stops. Importantly, the most positive results have been achieved in areas where sanctions rather than being the end of policy have served as a backdrop only for critical engagement through policy dialogue, capacity building, and, in some cases, limited financial assistance aimed at identifying and implementing concrete measures to improve human rights.[17]

Ominously, the receptiveness of the regime to international calls for reform, which appeared to be growing in the early 2000s when the generals accepted UN mediation in its talks with Aung San Suu Kyi and worked constructively with international human rights agencies, has since diminished drastically. The special rapporteur on human rights has not been allowed into the country since November 2003. Any talk of releasing Aung San Suu Kyi or broadening the participation or scope for debate at the National Convention has also ceased. In addition, since late 2004, the UNHCR, the ICRC, and the ILO have all had their movement and programs severely constrained (as have a number of other international aid agencies in the humanitarian or development fields).[18]

Limitations

Many advocates of the core strategy insist that it is only a matter of time and ratcheting up the pressure before the regime buckles. Yet, this view ignores not only the fact that past achievements are now being reversed, but also major structural limitations to the use of coercion, linked to the psychological profile of the military leaders, their material interests, and the relative capacity of the regime and the opposition to exert political pressure. While isolation certainly hurts the military (as well as the general population), the political impact is greatly circumscribed.

The Military Mind

It is important to recognize that the generals do not respond "rationally" to international demands, which would imply a fairly detached, interest-based calculation of the relative costs and benefits of compliance versus resistance.

While the seclusion of the top leaders from society renders any psychological evaluation somewhat impressionistic, their military mind-set clearly presents obstacles to effective international pressure.

Burma's rulers are soldiers, trained in the art of warfare, not politics. They run the government like a military campaign and react to international diplomatic and economic pressure like they would to an invading army. To them, it is war, even if it is fought by different means, and they are not inclined to negotiate with the enemy. If anyone believes the generals might "blink" under pressure, it is worth remembering that all of the current leaders are battle hardened veterans from the long-running guerrilla wars against communist, ethnic, and economic insurgents. They are tough, often ruthless men, not easily intimidated, and seemingly confident—to the extent of arrogance—in their ability to overcome any adversity.

This uncompromising stand is reinforced by a "bunker mentality," the result of half a century of being under attack from real or perceived internal and external enemies. Today's military leaders, despite some openings since 1988, by and large, are still insular and deeply suspicious of a world that they view as threatening. They are more likely to see enemies than friends, or threats than opportunities. Above all, their agenda is essentially defensive. In their own mind, they are still fighting for the survival of the nation they have sworn to defend with their lives, and they may well see the country laid to waste rather than surrender.

In addition, most officers are fiercely nationalistic and proud of Burma's historical record of resisting imperialism in any shape or form. Under no circumstances will they allow themselves to be seen to give in to external pressure. Even asking for outside help or admitting to shortcomings is difficult for them. This attitude is often commented on by the government's friends and enemies alike. According to a former European ambassador, "They exhibit a proud stubbornness which frequently leads them to react in ways detrimental to their own best interests. They know that they are going to be bashed at the [UN] General Assembly for putting the NLD leadership back in custody. Yet they face it with a shrug. Nobody is going to tell them what to do in their own country."[19] A local businessman puts it more prosaically: "They will cut their noses to spite their faces."[20] Even the Chinese, in private, express exasperation with the refusal of their allies in Rangoon to listen to "advice."[21] In fact, this goes to the core of the generals' self-perception (and self-esteem), and affects the regime's response to threats and "bribes" alike. Thus, when the *International Herald Tribune* in 1988 broke the news—mistakenly, as it were—that the UN and the World Bank were offering the Burmese government $1 billion in financial assistance in return for political reforms, the immediate reaction was a scathing comment from Foreign Minister Win Aung: "For us, giving a banana to the monkey and then asking it to dance is not the way. We are not monkeys."[22]

It is conceivable that the military leaders' sense of duty and national pride could be turned into a constructive force for change. As their exposure to the outside world has increased, they have increasingly come to compare conditions in Burma with its neighbors and today often talk about "catching up" with other nations (although they insist on doing so on their own terms and without sacrificing national values and traditions). Ironically, however, Western policy makers and activists in their eagerness to ratchet up pressure on the regime have often managed only to reinforce the reactionary and self-destructive elements of the military's traditional, insular outlook. There are members of the government—quite possibly even a majority—who acknowledge that Burma has to change. Yet, even the most progressive officers are exasperated by the failure of their critics to recognize the major challenges facing the country or acknowledge the progress made since 1988, for example, in establishing cease-fires and developing the country's infrastructure.[23] They are further incensed by being singled out for criticism of their record on issues such as drugs and human trafficking, which they feel they have tried hard to address (even if their methods are crude and they lack capacity to launch an effective response).[24] Many Burmese officials, both military and civilian, feel that the United States, in particular, is simply out to "get" them and will grab any opportunity to criticize and condemn.[25] Not surprisingly, this has reinforced their suspicions that the human rights agenda is driven by self-interest rather than humanitarian concerns and made them less inclined to engage in a constructive dialogue.[26]

Military Interests

Aside from the psychological aspects of the influence process, the impact of international pressure is limited by the disproportion between the demands of Western governments and the sticks they wield. Put simply, the military leadership has more to lose than gain from giving in, in political as well as personal terms.

As discussed in chapter 2, the military leaders are concerned above all else with national security and view continued military leadership as a matter of vital importance to the integrity of the state.[27] Not only do they deeply distrust civilian politicians, but they are strongly opposed to core elements of the NLD's political program, which are seen to threaten long-standing military concerns about national sovereignty and unity. The regime does have important developmental goals, which are gravely affected by international sanctions (in particular, by the near stop to bilateral and multilateral aid, without which the reconstruction of the country's physical and human infrastructure, among other things, is greatly constrained). National security, however, remains the bottom line, simply because it is seen as a precondition for everything else. The generals are not interested in prosperity—whether for themselves or the country at large—*without power*.[28] This, in turn, represents a serious obstacle to any bargain that seeks political concessions in exchange for foreign investment, trade, or aid.

The SLORC/SPDC, of course, needs revenue to pay for the army and its hardware, as well as other security-related programs. The leadership also recognizes the close association between social stability and general economic conditions (as evident, for example, from their efforts to keep the domestic price of rice and other main staples down, even at the expense of much needed foreign exchange export earnings).[29] Yet, unlike their counterparts in countries such as Thailand, Malaysia, Singapore, and Indonesia in the 1960–1980s, the Burmese generals' national security agenda does not substantially emphasize broader development goals but focuses on political and military means of control. Tellingly, although the Burmese economy has been hit badly twice in the past ten years, first by the Asian economic crisis and then by the private banking crisis in 2003, resulting in an overall contraction in economic activity and deepening poverty, the military leaders have not expressed particular concern or accorded priority to redress the situation.

There is some controversy among observers about the importance attached by the military rulers to improving international relations more generally. As noted, some believe that a regime which isolated itself for twenty-six years during the socialist period will not be worried about further isolation. This view may underestimate the shift in the military's international outlook over the past decade and a half, which has brought it into much closer contact with—and indeed, to a significant degree, has made it dependent on—the outside world (more specifically, on its neighbors in the region). Still, it would be a mistake to underestimate the residual power of traditional beliefs. Burma's two top generals were part of the inner circle around Ne Win in the 1980s and are deeply influenced by the thinking of the socialist era. They may no longer actively seek isolation, but they remain wary of external influences—political and economic as well as cultural—that threaten core nationalist values.[30] Moreover, they are convinced that Burma can go it alone *if it has to*. The "fall-back" position of self-reliance is not frightening to them. It may even be comforting in some ways, given that the international stage has proven to be such a hostile place.[31]

In addition to these national interests and outlooks, there is the important issue of self-preservation. Burma's military leaders have strong personal interests in maintaining absolute power. Not only do the top leaders risk retribution for decades of gross human rights violations if they lose the shield of power,[32] but the officer corps at large enjoys socioeconomic privileges—or, in the case of lower-ranking officers, *hope* to enjoy such privileges in the future—that would be lost under a civilian government.[33] By comparison, the personal costs to the military elite of standing up to the West are negligible. While they may be denied the respect and recognition they feel they deserve, they are not hurt significantly financially. Today's high-ranking officers have their own life support system and access to previously unheard of economic opportunities based on seniority, privilege, and patronage, most of which is largely independent of the overall state of the economy. The targeted sanctions imposed by the United States and the European Union are no more than symbolic gestures. The joint asset freeze caught only a few hundred thousand dollars in the United States and nothing in Europe.[34] As for the travel bans, few of the affected officials have ever been to the West, or show any inclination to go. While the wives of some of the top leaders are said to have developed a taste for international shopping and their children, like everyone else in Burma, often seek education overseas, they have access to everything they need in Asia. In essence, Western governments are demanding that the military government commits the political equivalent of collective suicide to avoid what amounts to little more than a slap over the wrist.

The military leaders may be sufficiently bothered by sanctions to make certain concessions that do not threaten vital military interests, but hard-line governments, particularly in the United States, have undercut their own potential influence by repeatedly moving the goal posts and refusing to reward progress. Although the release of Aung San Suu Kyi from house arrest, for example, has been a core demand of Western governments since 1989, in neither 1995 nor 2002 did they offer more than bland words of "appreciation" for her release before demanding further concessions. These snubs became the cause of great resentment among military leaders, who felt that they had gone to significant lengths to accommodate Western concerns only to be told that it was not enough,[35] and they eventually backfired. The final straw appears to have been Washington's decision in January 2003, for the fifteenth consecutive year, not to certify Burma for its antinarcotics efforts—this despite several years of growing cooperation between Burmese and U.S. drugs officials that had given Rangoon hope of being taken off the list of noncooperative countries.[36] According to Burmese officials, this decision—which was made under pressure from Congress and others for transparently political reasons—so upset Senior General Than Shwe that he subsequently admonished government officials not to bother with U.S. demands anymore.[37] It may well have contributed, too, to the general souring of the political environment over the following months that culminated in the attack on Aung San Suu Kyi on 30 May 2003, an act that showed a flagrant disregard for international opinion.[38] Prime Minister Khin Nyunt, together with a group of like-minded ministers and military intelligence officers, continued to cooperate with the UNHCR, ILO, and ICRC, among others, until they were purged in October 2004, but since then the government has largely stonewalled on human rights issues.[39]

Regime Capacity

Given the priorities and perceptions of the current military leaders, the success of the core strategy depends critically on the ability of the "coalition of the willing" to deny the military regime the resources needed to retain the loyalty of its core supporters and suppress its opponents, a near impossible task given the nonparticipation of Burma's neighbors and main trading partners.

Advocates of sanctions have long postulated that Burma's economic isolation is undermining the ability of the country's military leaders to sustain their patronage networks and keep regime supporters "happy."[40] This, however, remains a theoretical proposition for which there is little empirical support. The number of people on whom the top leadership rely to maintain control is relatively small, probably counting no more than a few thousand, mainly high-ranking military officers and a few "national entrepreneurs" (the official Burmese euphemism for cronies) who play a key role in the military economy. Unlike more developed countries, the SLORC/SPDC does not depend on a large class of investors and economic managers, whose support is conditional on continued economic growth and expanding opportunities. There is no question that the inability of the Ministry of Defense to provide adequate salaries and living conditions for its soldiers is hurting morale among lower-ranking officers and the rank-and-file.[41] Yet, like the population at large, they are subject to ruthless discipline and do not present a threat to the regime unless organized by senior officers.

In addition, the privileges of the elite are only weakly linked to the dynamism of the national economy. The major part of the military's income derives from natural resource extraction, notably oil and gas, which is set to expand further in the coming years as several new fields go "onstream." Individual officers, meanwhile, obtain most of their personal income from rent-seeking activities, including the sale of public goods, such as trade licenses or subsidized products, and extortion of private businesses, communities, and individuals, not directly from trade or investments. The wealth that can be siphoned off from private citizens is, of course, a function of the size of the overall economy, but if the goal is to "starve" the military elite, ordinary people will have to suffer extreme deprivation before the regime buckles.

In recent years, there have been growing signs of dissatisfaction among younger and better-educated military officers with the government's economic mismanagement. In Burma's underdeveloped political and economic system, however, there are few avenues of social mobility outside the army and therefore nowhere to "go" for disaffected officers. Thus, rather than desert the regime, they are more likely to conform—or, at best, push for economic reforms. In any case, the prospect of huge revenue from the sale of gas and electricity over the coming decades will much reduce the pressure on the regime in the economic arena.

As for the physical means of control—the guns—international sanctions, again, are largely of symbolic value. The arms embargo, which is limited to Western countries, Japan, and South Korea, is irrelevant in instrumental terms, since there are adequate alternative suppliers in the region and elsewhere who in any case are cheaper and more likely to offer favorable financing terms than Western companies. To the extent that sanctions hurt the economy, they contribute to the budgetary constraints that inhibit a full expansion and modernization of the armed forces. Yet, while this weakens the country's conventional defense capabilities, it does not have much affect on the military rulers' ability to suppress internal political dissent. As noted, the regime's political power depends less on military might than on its organizational reach through military intelligence, police, and other informer and control networks, including mass organizations such as the Union Solidarity and Development Association (USDA). Such controls must be backed up by the threat of force, but as the events of 1988 showed, the effectiveness of force against an unarmed population is largely a function of the willingness of the leadership to use violence, not of the number of guns it owns.

Opposition Capacity

International censure and sanctions may have helped to shore up the morale of dissidents and protect a narrow space for political activities (though not open opposition). In short, it may have kept the NLD on life support. It has not, however, helped build a stronger resistance front. If anything, the personalization of the struggle by Western governments, which have elevated Aung San Suu Kyi to iconic status, has impeded the development of a broader, more diverse democracy movement within the country by disadvantaging other potential opposition leaders and groups (see section on Counterproductive Effects on the next page).

Although most people in Burma are aware that Western powers support their aspirations for a freer and better government, this has not inspired people to join in the struggle for regime change. In the absence of any indications that the military is giving in, the vast majority of Burmese remain politically passive and without hope. In fact, pressure from afar does not seem to inspire action the way direct engagement with people on the ground can do, but perhaps rather to encourage people to abdicate responsibility for their own situation. The weaknesses of the domestic resistance movement further diminish the effect of international sanctions on regime capacity—as well as the consequences that any deterioration in such capacity might have—since little (physical) repression is actually needed to keep the population cowed.

Some hard-line opponents of the military regime argue in private that sanctions, by denying the Burmese people relief from day-to-day suffering, increase the likelihood of another uprising that will bring down the regime.[42] Apart from the serious moral questions arising from any strategy that seeks to capitalize on people's misery (even if it is supposedly in their own "best interest"), there are no signs that the Burmese people are prepared to sacrifice their lives again. The failure of the 9/9/99 movement is illustrative in this respect, as is the later banking crisis and virtual collapse of the private banking sector. A lot of people lost their savings in 2003–2004 and overall economic activity contracted significantly, causing widespread job losses and a drop in trade. Yet, although people complained privately about their economic misfortunes, there were no angry mobs in the streets demanding the departure of the government or any other signs of major political stress. People simply tightened their belts another notch, adjusted, and went on with the business of surviving, like the Burmese have done for so long.

In any case, it is highly doubtful whether increased social unrest—or even another uprising—would be a positive force for change. Since 1988, the military leaders have been highly sensitive to any indication of "disorder," and—as the events of 30 May 2003 show—they remain willing to use extreme violence to maintain stability. In the absence of reform-minded leaders, strong civilian institutions, and a common commitment to the nation by its diverse peoples, the alternative to the current government is more likely to be another military regime than democracy (or, at worst, civil war). Social unrest driven by a deepening socioeconomic crisis is likely only to provoke further repression from the military in an escalating cycle of suffering and violence.

Adverse Effects

If the limitations of coercion as a tool for change in Burma illustrate the need to look for alternative—or at least complementary—measures, the urgency of this is underscored by the adverse effects of current policy on the human rights situation. These include *counterproductive effects* (i.e., responses by the military regime to international pressure that weaken the prospects for democracy and improvements in human rights), *collateral damage* (i.e., the direct costs imposed on the general population by sweeping economic sanctions that affect the government and people alike), and *opportunity costs* (i.e., positive outcomes that might have come from engaging the military government and the Burmese population at large in international exchanges rather than isolating the country).

Counterproductive Effects

By reinforcing the siege mentality of the country's strongly nationalistic leaders and intensifying suspicions of the opposition, external interference in Burma's political affairs has compounded political rigidities and provoked further measures to strengthen the state to the detriment of popular welfare as well as the prospects for effective domestic resistance.

Western criticism and sanctions, as illustrated, have intensified historical fears of foreign intervention and loss of sovereignty, thus confirming the military's belief in the correctness of its cause. Others may feel that such measures are justified by international norms and obligations to protect the rights of the Burmese people. But Burma's insular military leaders view them as yet another attempt by Western powers to control and exploit the country for their own purposes. Some are said to see sanctions as a precursor to a military attack, aimed at weakening the country's defenses.[43] Such concerns, no doubt, have been reinforced by the covert efforts by Americans working in the border areas in the 1990s, with U.S. government funding, to help build a "political defiance" movement.

At the same time, Western political and economic support for Aung San Suu Kyi, the NLD, and dissident groups overseas has tainted the democracy movement in the eyes of many military officers, who have come to see it as a Trojan horse for Western political interests and therefore unnationalistic and untrustworthy.[44] This perspective reportedly originated in the visit by then U.S. ambassador to the UN Madeleine Albright to Aung San Suu Kyi in September 1995, which directly preceded the NLD's decision to boycott the National Convention, as well as the opposition leader's first open calls for international sanctions.[45] Aung San Suu Kyi herself has complained in private to UN officials that the generals view her as being controlled by Washington,[46] a situation that greatly complicates her primary task of building confidence across the military-civilian divide.

The implications of this siege mentality for the stated objectives of promoting democracy and human rights are strongly negative and evident across a range of areas. First of all, heightened security concerns inhibit rational thinking and lessen the confidence needed to experiment with reforms. As Robert Taylor observes, "In a world in which the army felt the country was beleaguered and friendless, and where within the country itself there were perceived to be political and military forces allied with hostile external forces, a huge degree of suspicion led to an inability to consider alternative forms of political behaviour other than armed force, and solidarity within the officer corps took precedence over any other consideration."[47] This is natural human behavior. It is common for insecure people to withdraw into their shells. People who are afraid do not think outside the box. It is notable in this respect that the SLORC/SPDC has made its greatest concessions during periods—specifically 1993–1995 and 2000–2003—when the international community took a *relatively* softer line and sought dialogue with the regime rather than simply condemning it from afar.[48]

Second, by giving conservative military leaders a new enemy, Western powers have handed them a useful tool for reinforcing military unity and counteracting the emergence of opposing voices from within. In a situation of "war," criticism is much more difficult and more harshly punished than under conditions of peace. More fundamentally, the persistence of enemies of the state reinforces the military's esprit de corps and helps avoid a potential "identity crisis" (clearly a concern for the military leadership in the post-cease-fire environment, judging from the efforts made to develop an Indonesian-style *dwi fungsi* role for the armed forces). It is not just propaganda when government officials and state-controlled media rally against "neo-imperialism" and "internal axe handles." This fits a long-standing military mythology—artificially created perhaps, but no less influential for it—of the role of the armed forces in "protecting the nation" against external enemies, self-serving politicians, and ethnic nationalists bent on secession. If the purpose is to encourage splits in the regime, it would likely be more effective to seek to weaken its raison d'être, open alternative avenues of self-identification and income for military officers, and help establish credible, moderate groups outside the military with which disaffected officers might cooperate. Coercion simply feeds the fears and attitudes that have kept the military united for so long.

Third, fears of external intervention and internal subversion have encouraged further efforts by the SLORC/SPDC to expand the state's coercive capacities at great expense to the freedom, security, and welfare of the Burmese people at large. Apart from massive investments in the expansion and modernization of the armed forces themselves, the post-1988 regime has greatly expanded its capacity for political and social control through surveillance, indoctrination, and patronage. Kyaw Yin Hlaing sums up the implications for political activists: "The student activists survived the oppression of the BSPP [Burma Socialist Programme Party] period. Yet the paranoia of the military rooted in the 1988 uprising and subsequent Western pressure has fueled policies that have shattered the students."[49]

Fourth, Western censure and sanctions have pushed the military regime back into isolationist mode. This is particularly evident in the economic field, where growing suspicions of foreign involvement has prompted a reversal of some of the early open-door economic policies. Although the military government continues to engage the region through joint ventures and trade, the period since the mid-1990s has seen a reemphasis on the virtues of self-reliance. In a return to BSPP priorities, agriculture in general, and rice production in particular, has been singled out for expansion along with import substitution industries such as steel and cement. Meanwhile, a new class of "national entrepreneurs" has been promoted as the main means of boosting the economy (these are private companies that essentially follow directions from the government in return for various "favors"). The result is a general loss of economic dynamism, as the military state pursues the means for its own survival first, at the expense of broad-based economic growth.

Finally, the politicization of aid has hampered the work of international aid agencies in Burma. In the generally acrimonious environment, Burmese officials not surprisingly have been suspicious of the activities of both UN agencies and international nongovernmental organizations (NGOs), which as a result have faced greater constraints on their operational activities.[50] When the regime is condemned by governments or organizations overseas, there is often a backlash against aid agencies inside Burma, which suffer disruptions to ongoing activities or simply waste time and resources on rebuilding relations with the authorities.[51] The situation has been aggravated by demands from donors that aid agencies consult with the NLD on their programs, a requirement which the military perceives as open interference in the country's political affairs. This has been a constant source of tension in UN-government relations, which in 2002 nearly resulted in the United Nations Development Programme (UNDP) being thrown out of the country when staff was suspected of taking directions from Aung San Suu Kyi.[52] The Global Fund was the most high-profile "victim" of these dynamics, but aid officials have been struggling with them since 1988, and aid programs, as a result, have been more restricted than might otherwise have been the case, not least in the sensitive border regions.

In essence, external pressure encourages and deepens the military's preoccupation with regime maintenance at the expense of broader governance and development issues. There are officers within the military hierarchy who have been seeking to open up the country through a process of both internally and externally directed reform. But, as a Burmese political analyst points out, "The U.S. overkill strengthens the hand of hard-liners in the regime, make liberals run for cover, and marginalizes those we are cultivating and placing our hopes on for a more user-friendly army that we can cooperate with for a better future."[53] As long as the state of siege ensues, "arguing for change and compromise is much more difficult than arguing for the status quo."[54] This was all too evident when former head of military intelligence General Khin Nyunt, who in the early 2000s oversaw the most "open" period in Burmese politics since the 1950s, lost credibility with hard-liners and eventually was removed. Khin Nyunt was one of the most powerful members of the regime but failed to demonstrate that cooperation with the West would generate positive results for Burma. Just as the SLORC/SPDC's repeated attacks on the opposition silence the voices of compromise internationally, so the West's counterattacks silence the voices of compromise within the military regime.

In addition, there is the question of whether the West has encouraged unrealistic opposition strategies. The near-deification of Aung San Suu Kyi, based on her strong principled stand, has effectively marginalized and delegitimized moderate voices within the opposition, who encourage a more compromising line with the military regime and greater attention to policy issues.[55] Some Burmese exiles, similarly, complain that American political aid goes primarily to groups that are closely associated with the NLD or at least echo Washington's hard-line agenda, thus giving such groups an advantage in the struggle over ideas within the broader resistance movement.[56] It is perhaps illustrative that, of the twenty or so insurgent groups existing in 1988, those most closely linked to Western funded groups in Thailand have maintained the hardest stance against compromise with the regime, while those isolated inside the country have sought common ground through cease-fires and joint development efforts with the government. One can, of course, argue—as many supporters of the core strategy have done—that the former is the "correct" course of action, that the cease-fire groups have simply caved in and abandoned the democratic cause. So far, however, organizations like the United Wa State Army (UWSA) and the Pao National Organization (PNO) have achieved more for themselves—and, particularly in the latter case, for local communities—than have, for example, the NLD or the Karen National Union (KNU), which have maintained an uncompromising line.[57]

The West, of course, is not responsible for the zero-sum nature of Burmese politics that was evident long before 1988. Hard-line stances abroad, however, encourage hard-line positions inside Burma, not only within the government but also in the opposition, thus weakening the prospects for a domestic compromise that would allow the main protagonists to move forward together through a process of gradual reform. Meanwhile, the siege economy is weakening both the regime and the pro-democracy movement, but more so the latter. Under the existing depressed political, social, and economic conditions, the opposition does not have the strength to produce political change. International pressure may provide moral support, but it also contributes to the overall stagnation that keeps people trapped in a daily battle for survival.

Collateral Damage

Advocates of the core strategy, including Burmese dissidents, Western policy makers, and human rights activists, generally claim that international sanctions do no harm. In the words of George Soros, chairman of the Open Society Institute and a major contributor to the Free Burma movement, "Sanctions are said to hurt the population, but the people are already as downtrodden as they could be."[58] Such arguments were given theoretical reinforcement in 2004 by Alfred Oehlers, who argues that the general population is largely unaffected by sanctions since most people rely on the domestically oriented informal economy for their livelihoods.[59] Such arguments, however, not only ignore the costs arising from the adverse political effects discussed above, including increased state repression, general policy paralysis, and the "siege economy." They also pay scant attention to the direct economic costs for large numbers of "ordinary" Burmese who are forced to pay the bill for shortfalls in state revenue, lose their jobs in industries affected by Western boycotts, or are being denied lifesaving support from suspended aid programs.

Any claim that you can hurt the government economically without hurting the people must be rejected out of hand on theoretical grounds alone. In any country, a government that loses vital revenue will pass part of the bill on to its citizens—all the more so in countries where concern for public welfare is weak. More direct costs arise from disinvestment, which inevitably hurts workers—and from trade disruptions, which hurt either producers (if domestic prices fall) or consumers (if domestic prices increase). The pain may be stronger or weaker, and affect larger or smaller groups of people, but some pain is unavoidable.[60]

In the case of Burma, the burden of sanctions to a large extent has been shifted to the general population by the way of money printing (which fuels inflation), cuts in government social spending, and increased demands for forced labor and other "contributions." While the SLORC/SPDC is directly to blame for this, sanctioning governments must take responsibility, too, for provoking responses that gravely affect poverty, health, and education standards—particularly since they, at the same time, have curtailed foreign aid, which otherwise could have been used to protect the most vulnerable groups.[61]

A more specific example of the costs of sanctions is the job losses resulting from trade and investment sanctions, particularly in the garment sector, which have had serious implications for hundreds of thousands of people. Even before the U.S. import ban, factory closures and production cutbacks resulting from consumer campaigns against U.S. and European clothing stores sourcing from Burma had cost tens of thousands of jobs in the garment export industry, one of the few sectors that were actually providing new jobs and comparatively "good" wages.[62] This number multiplied in 2003 after President Bush signed into law a total ban on imports from Burma, primarily affecting garments. A report commissioned by a UN agency estimated that around thirty thousand workers were laid off between June and November 2003, while an undetermined number were staying on at greatly reduced salaries.[63] Another survey by World Vision in September 2003 found that sixty factories had closed as a direct result of the new sanctions, at the cost of forty to sixty thousand jobs, with serious spin-off effects for support industries, including vendors and hostels. It also emphasized that since so many people had lost their jobs at the same time, it had been impossible to absorb them into the broader economy. Many families had been forced to adopt extreme coping strategies, including cutting meals, taking high-interest loans from local moneylenders, selling assets, or migrating.[64] The total job loss from consumer boycotts and the U.S. federal import ban is not known, but according to an industry study, the garment export industry at its peak in 2001 employed more than 150,000 workers.[65] Other figures show that the total revenue from garment exports fell from $455 million in 2002–2003 to $216 in 2004–2005, indicating that at least 50 percent of the workforce, or 75,000 people, had been laid off.[66] With an average family size of five, this means that at least 375,000 people were affected, not counting the spin-off effects in other sectors, which likely doubled that number.[67]

The impact of other economic measures is difficult to estimate. However, the U.S. ban on export and reexport of financial services, which accompanied the import ban, caused major, immediate disruptions to trade in and out of Burma, much of which was conducted using letters of credit in U.S. dollars routed via banks in the United States. Many export and import businesses, which at the time were already seriously affected by the private banking crisis, shut down, creating shortages and price fluctuations inside the country. Most of these disruptions proved temporary as traders found alternative ways of transferring money or shifted to border trade, but the ban has increased transaction costs and—together with the general opprobrium—has made Burma less attractive for foreign trading companies. There is bound, therefore, to be a longer-term, negative impact on both producers and consumers.

The worst collateral damage, however, arises from that which is not being done. Despite being the poorest in Asia in purchasing parity terms, the people of Burma receive less than 3 percent of the aid per capita provided to neighboring Laos.[68] Although the majority of Burma's poor depend on subsistence agriculture, almost no assistance is available for this sector. Even education has received very little funding.[69] Most assistance goes into the primary health sector. Nevertheless, in the 1990s, vital time was lost in responding to the HIV/AIDS epidemic,[70] which may now be the worst in Asia and threatens the future of the entire country, starting with the 620,000 people who are estimated to be infected already (and their families who are impoverished by the direct costs of caring for the sick as well as the loss of income). Efforts to combat this epidemic received an additional blow with the withdrawal of the Global Fund in 2005, although donors outside the United States have resuscitated many of the planned programs by setting up the new Three Diseases (3D) Fund.[71]

Some advocates of sanctions argue that the costs are justified by the law of greater numbers. While acknowledging that people lose their jobs or are being denied lifesaving assistance, they view this as an acceptable price to pay for the larger objective of helping all of Burma's 54 million people get a better government.[72] Any such assertions, however, must address the reality that no apparent progress has been made toward that goal since the first sanctions were put in place nineteen years ago. On the contrary, it would seem that Western policy has delayed political change, caused governance to further deteriorate, and made it more difficult for future governments to turn the situation around.

Apparently, few of those responsible, if any, ever made an attempt to calculate the costs of particular sanctions before they were introduced. If they had done so, they would have discovered, for example, that the military government stood to lose less than $10 million in annual revenue from the 2003

U.S. federal ban on garment imports from Burma.[73] This amount is hardly politically significant (in fact, it is less than half of what was paid out in salaries to the workers who lost their jobs as a result of the ban). A similar conclusion would likely be reached if it were possible to calculate the costs of other limitations on trade and investment, since none of the sectors from which the government makes the most profit—oil and gas, mining, and logging—are significantly affected, if at all.[74] The greatest losses are in sectors, such as tourism and manufacturing, which like the garment sector are dominated by private entrepreneurs and are labor intensive. In other words, the burden falls mainly on those already suffering from government policies.

Opportunity Costs

The real tragedy of the past nineteen years, though, is perhaps the realization that the situation today could have been different. Since 1988, the SLORC/SPDC has moved tentatively to redress several of the historical causes of Burma's political and economic underdevelopment, including the one-party political system, the armed conflicts, the socialist economy, and, more generally, the country's isolation from the outside world, only to be rebuked by its critics. How far the military leadership would have gone if the international community had actively supported these processes of change instead of obstructing them is a matter of conjecture. Important opportunities, however, have been missed because Western policy makers and activists have had an eye only for weakening the government to force a quick regime change, thus ignoring openings on the ground in Burma that might have supported a longer-term, domestically driven process of gradual reform.

Political Reform

One opening from which too little has come too late is the constitutional process, which the SLORC initiated in 1993 in preparation for a transition to parliamentary government and now appears to be wrapping up. It is understandable that democracy activists both inside and outside Burma have had serious misgivings about the nature of the National Convention, as well as about the blue print for the new constitution. Yet, the question that should have been asked (but seemingly was not) is whether this *process* could be a step in the right direction even if the immediate *outcome* is not satisfactory.

The configuration of power and interests in Burma suggests that no transition is possible unless the military is assured that its vital interests are protected. It is for this purpose that the SLORC/SPDC has insisted on controlling the constitutional process and including specific clauses that would guarantee a continued leadership role for the military in a new "democratic" system. This may not satisfy Western governments, the NLD, or other democracy activists, but it is arguably a reality that they will have to come to terms with if they are to have any hope of breaking the deadlock. The proceedings at the National Convention have not been a meaningless exercise. However circumscribed, they have offered an unprecedented opportunity for people from many sectors of Burmese society—notably ethnic minority groups that have had no say at the center of national politics since the 1950s—to meet and discuss their vision for a future Burma.[75] Nor will the introduction of a parliamentary system of government, even if it will be dominated by the military, be a useless outcome. At the very least, it will provide a legal framework for political parties in which they can begin to undertake political party activities and build their capacity for governance. It should also provide somewhat increased space for political debate and help jump-start the long and difficult process of reestablishing regional governments and administrations. Most importantly perhaps, it may take the edge of the zero-sum struggle for power, which would allow all sides to pay more attention to the serious development challenges facing the country.

The opposition understandably is concerned that a constitutional process dominated by the military will simply help enshrine military rule. This process, however, is not the endgame. A constitution is a living document, which in many countries is changed or adjusted regularly as power relations or interests change. Numerous critical issues are not specified in the constitution at all, but will have to be negotiated through a future legislative process. In the meantime, agreement on a set of rules for political competition—even competition subjected to significant constraints—may create new space for political activity, which can be used to work for further reform. The Burmese generals would not be the first to underestimate the processes set in train by what began as closely managed reforms from above. In fact, this may be the most common path to democracy globally—certainly it has been the path followed by several of Burma's neighbors, including Thailand and Indonesia.

Although the military's constitution seems about to become a reality anyway, more than a decade has been lost in getting to this point. Moreover, Burma will be arriving there even more divided than it was in the mid-1990s and quite possibly without the participation of Aung San Suu Kyi and the NLD, who remain important representatives of the Burmese people and would have had a critical role to play in making a "second-best" solution work for the benefit of the country. External actors were never in a position to influence the constitutional process, except at the margins. Yet, if Western governments had encouraged all sides to participate and thus assume a real stake in the process, it just might have helped ensure a quicker and better outcome, which in turn would have made the resolution of other urgent issues easier.

Cease-Fires

If the issue of the constitution leaves some room for interpretation and disagreement, the failure of the international community to support the cease-fires between the government and more than a dozen former insurgent groups is clearly a lose-lose strategy. To quote Martin Smith, the cease-fire movement has been "by any international standards . . . an unexpectedly smooth and stable spread of ceasefires in one of the most conflict-torn countries in Asia."[76] It is a process much too important to be ignored by anyone committed to improving the human rights of the Burmese people.

Yet, Western governments preoccupied with Aung San Suu Kyi and the 1990 election have offered little support for ethnic minority groups in their negotiations with the government, which only partly overlap with those of the pro-democratic opposition.[77] Most donors have also ignored calls by the government, cease-fire groups, and local community leaders alike for assistance for the all-important process of reconstructing war-torn communities and economies in the border areas. The frustrations among many ethnic minority leaders with the lack of international support are palpable.

Like the constitutional process, the cease-fires have had their detractors. Many have accused the cease-fire groups of opportunism, some claiming that by entering into agreements with the military regime they have abandoned the democratic cause. Over time, some of the cease-fire groups, too, have come to express misgivings, partly with the lack of progress toward a more permanent political solution, partly with the lack of development of their areas, which was seen by both government and ethnic minority negotiators as a crucial aspect of longer-term peace building. Nonetheless, the end to fighting is still generally seen by people in former conflict-affected areas as a significant improvement and a crucial step toward peace.[78]

Although the cease-fires have been disappointing in many ways, a return to civil war would end all prospects for political reform, better governance, and economic development. Conversely, if the cease-fires could be turned into effective vehicles for the reconstruction of conflict-affected areas, they could provide a model worth emulating by the remaining insurgent groups and become a force for nationwide peace. This, in turn, would weaken one of the main justifications for military rule—the perceived need to protect the union against internal centrifugal forces.

Economic Reforms

While many of Burma's problems originate in half a century of armed conflict, they have been exacerbated by the country's weak economy, which not only impedes political change, but also feeds a range of destructive practices by state agencies and puts immense pressure on poor communities and households.

In the 1980s, the BSPP government came under pressure from foreign donors to liberalize the economy. Yet when the SLORC after its take-over of power in 1988 began dismantling the socialist system, the same donors had a new, political agenda and were no longer interested. Instead of supporting the new reform push, they withdrew nearly all bilateral and multilateral assistance and took steps to actively block Burma's attempt to reengage with the global economy. Subsequent developments are well-known. Despite an early spurt in private-sector growth, fueled by some foreign direct investment, the reform drive soon petered out, and after the Asian economic crisis the SLORC/SPDC reverted to a strategy of self-reliance based on agricultural expansion and import substitution. Foreign trade and investment, in principle, is still pursued, but has come under increasing government controls.

There are many reasons why the SLORC/SPDC has failed to undertake a comprehensive economic restructuring, not the least of which are fears about upsetting the political economy that keeps the military in power. The damaging effects of the West's isolationist policies should not be overlooked, however. The military government in the early 1990s actively considered key steps, such as unification of the exchange rate and privatization of state economic enterprises, commonly identified by economists as among the most fundamental obstacles to broad-based economic development in the country. Yet, denied assistance from the international financial institutions to cushion the expected negative impact on the poor, military leaders rejected such reforms as potentially destabilizing.[79] In other areas, such as the all-important rice trade, the government has moved ahead with liberalization on its own, but lacking technical and financial resources, it has often failed to sustain new reforms or maximize their benefits. The international financial institutions (IFIs), as well as the Japanese government, have offered ready-made blue prints for reform. However, in the absence of sustained, long-term contacts with the relevant parts of the Burmese government, including the top leaders—and without commitment of complementary financial resources—these efforts cannot be considered to have been serious attempts at promoting economic reform, and not surprisingly came to naught.

Burma's military rulers lack basic understanding of a modern economy. In fact, they may truly believe that the country's economic woes—to the extent that they recognize them—are caused by the sanctions, which ironically have become a scapegoat for government policy failures, minimizing the perceived need for internal reform. Had it been handled without upsetting nationalist sensitivities, the scrutiny and policy dialogue associated with bilateral or multilateral assistance could have been an effective way of putting pressure on an isolated government to move forward with economic reform. Certainly, external exposure and support to strengthen the capacity of the economic arm of government—for example, through statistical support and scholarships for a new generation of Burmese economists—could have helped future leaders gain the knowledge required to inspire, formulate, and implement an effective reform program. Of course, such efforts would have had to be backed up by financial assistance, too. Few developing countries have ever successfully undertaken major economic reforms without large-scale international support.

Critics have argued that economic development only benefits the military. Yet, in attacking the economic ascendancy of military officials, opposition groups have often failed to recognize that ordinary people also benefited from the opening of markets in the early 1990s. As Kyaw Yin Hlaing observes,

> By allowing private businesses to export agricultural products, and villagers to grow whatever they wanted instead of following state directives, local entrepreneurs were making more money. The new system was improving the lives of people not connected to the military. Furthermore, there was a positive social impact. The school drop-out rate at primary and junior high-school in the mid 1990s was significantly lower than in previous decades. Increasing numbers of university graduates were getting jobs with foreign corporations, joint ventures, and private companies, and were drawing higher salaries than employees in the public sector.[80]

In any case, the purpose of supporting economic reforms—which would have been done primarily through official aid flows, carefully monitored and subject to strict technical criteria—would have been exactly to break the military's stranglehold on the economy and thus support broad-based development.

There is no doubt that renewed economic growth would benefit the military, but the politically more relevant question is, Who suffers most from the current depressed economic conditions? The regime may be poor, but it has had no problems in sustaining its core support base or staving off social unrest. In the meantime, continued macroeconomic instability and the lack of structural reforms are obstructing the development of the private sector on which society depends both as a counterweight to the state and as a critical source of jobs and other income opportunities. It is not the generals that go hungry, or any of their key supporters.

By not supporting reformers within the government in the critical period in the first half of the 1990s—before the Asian economic crisis hit and reactionary officers assumed control of economic policy—Western countries lost a golden opportunity to help jumpstart a process of economic liberalization, the sociopolitical benefits of which would have dwarfed the minor concessions the regime has made to counteract the current policy of economic sanctions.

Opening to the World

Of course, the opportunity costs of isolating Burma are not just about missed opportunities for influencing or supporting progressive government initiatives and policies, but arise equally from the failure to engage with the broader society. It is widely recognized that Burma was impoverished politically, socially, and economically by the isolationist policies of the BSPP government, which cut off the country from international ideas and advances in knowledge and technology, as well as from foreign trade and investment. By contrast, the SLORC/SPDC's partial reopening of the country to foreigners and foreign organizations has afforded opportunities for building new linkages with the Burmese people, whether through aid programs, joint business ventures, education and cultural exchanges, or tourism. This potential, however, remains largely unexploited due to the policy of isolation. In trying to isolate the regime, too often the opposition and the general population have been isolated as well.

While discussions on Burma in the West have focused on the insularity and failures of the military leaders, the need for dialogue, new ideas, and training is no less acute within the political opposition or among broader groups in civil and economic society.[81] In political terms, it would have been greatly beneficial if political parties, armed groups, and community leaders had been offered the tools to develop a more nuanced understanding of their strategic options, including comparative experiences with "pacted" transitions, federalist governance, the establishment of civil control of the military, and so on. As Mary Callahan emphasizes, "An opposition that shows a nuanced understanding of these issues—rather than one that simply denounces the military en masse—can lower the costs of compromise for members of the junta who may be leaning toward reform."[82] In addition, greater knowledge about economic and aid issues would have helped the NLD and the cease-fire groups to engage more constructively with the government and international aid agencies alike.

Much has been made of the moral support for the opposition provided by international censure and sanctions. Yet, the limited presence of international organizations and companies in Burma has denied the independent sectors—including political parties, civil society groups, and private entrepreneurs—vital space and more practical support on the ground, and thus has limited their ability to generate internal pressure for change, in turn making external pressure less effective. As Kurt Schock argues, "The more integrated a country is in the international system, and the more integrated its population is into international networks, the more likely that foreign states and transnational social movements will be in a position to promote mobilization and facilitate the success of social movements."[83]

There would have been other, less political advantages to a wider, more aggressive international presence in Burma as well. Local leaders from remote areas of the country, for example, often talk about the protection provided by the presence of international agencies against abuses by the army and other powerful groups.[84] This "protection role" may be as important as operational programs, and in principle can be served by any foreigner, including tourists, who bring with them the potential for exposure. It is unlikely a coincidence that forced labor and other abuses are much less prevalent (although certainly not absent) in Rangoon and Mandalay—the two most internationalized cities in the country—than elsewhere.

More foreign companies and organizations would also have lowered the costs to both individuals and the country from the inability of university graduates to find challenging jobs consonant with their educational level. Many of Burma's brightest leave the country, thus contributing to a hugely damaging brain drain. Those who stay frequently suffer from intellectual stagnation and loss of motivation—or they join the military, which increasingly has become the only avenue for social and professional advancement.

Ultimately, it is likely only to be through international comparisons that many Burmese, whether in government or society at large, will begin to question and challenge the current system, which is all they know. As two Burmese exile activists from the emerging "moderate camp" emphasize, "Resolution of our political conflict should be addressed in ways that do not harm our country's long-term strategic interests. . . . Our governments and political groups will rise and fall, but integration of our country into global trade and cultural associations is in the long-term interests of our people."[85]

Wider exchanges with the outside world, economic liberalization, peace building, and the return to constitutional government would all be important contributions to a long-term process of empowering the Burmese people. Yet, in trying to force change on the military regime according to their own road map and time frame, Western governments and activists have ignored—or even sought to obstruct—important changes underway within Burma that, if they had been encouraged and assisted instead, might well have brought quicker advances in the overall political and human rights situation at less cost to the Burmese people, while improving the longer-term prospects for progress under future governments.

Overall Impact and Prospects

The final assessment of the core strategy, perhaps not surprisingly, falls somewhere between the optimistic claims of its strongest advocates and the cynical conclusions of its harshest critics. Strong international pressure is needed to help motivate reforms. Yet, Western censure and sanctions—on its own, and in the form it has been exercised over the past nineteen years—has not only been ineffectual in producing political change, but in fact has compounded the political deadlock, policy paralysis, and deepening humanitarian crisis, which are imposing immense hardship on the Burmese people.

That sanctions are potential tools of influence is not in question. Even if we cannot always trace the causal processes at work, sanctions give bite to international censure by emphasizing how serious governments and organizations take the breach of international norms, and at the same time create an implicit space for bargaining with the military regime. Since the day it took power, the SLORC/SPDC has been on notice that full acceptance into the international community is conditional on progress on democracy and human rights. Every time Burmese officials participate in international meetings, they are personally subject to embarrassing criticism of their country's human rights record. With such pressure, they have more reason to reappraise the normative basis of military rule or particular repressive behaviors. Certainly, they are forced to consider, for instrumental reasons alone, whether certain concessions to their critics would facilitate achievement of their overall national and personal objectives. The opposition, meanwhile, is reminded that it does not stand alone, but has powerful allies in the international community. These are all important conditions for reform.

That said, there are no indications that international pressure—whatever its psychological or material dimensions—has significant positive political effects. In Burma's undeveloped economy, sanctions and isolation are holding back development rather than undermining the basis of development already achieved. This makes a significant difference. First, there is no apparent sense of failure among the top leaders, who rather seem proud of their achievements in the hostile environment.[86] Second, there are no significant economic groups in Burma which are integrated into the global economy and therefore can be expected to bring pressure to bear on the regime to give in to international demands. Finally, there is no general buildup of expectations of progress in the general population. People may blame the government for the depressed socioeconomic situation, but they have no comparative experience of "good" times that could help to fuel and direct their frustrations.

Over the years, proponents of sanctions have lobbied hard for the final push that supposedly would cause an economic "collapse" (whatever that means in economic terms) and force the military to compromise. This strategy, however, ignores crucial aspects of the link between power and economics. Burma does not have a modern economy. Most people still live at a subsistence level; the informal economy may be as large, or larger, than the formal economy; and most of the upper class, including the generals and their families, makes its money from rent-seeking activities rather than production or services. There is little that can "collapse."[87] Meanwhile, the military government does not depend on external economic linkages for its survival. Burma is self-sufficient in food, and the domestic economy is large enough for the army to extract the surplus it needs to function. The current system, having been designed under conditions of extreme shortages, works at minimum costs and resources for the government. There is much barter trade at the border for which no foreign exchange is needed. Even arms have been bought on that basis.[88] Health and education is largely privatized already, and the tax system works on a "take-what-you-need" basis, unrestrained by the rule of law.

Should the economy deteriorate further, the military may have to cut back on its infrastructure or arms programs, but neither are needed to maintain power. With active assistance from China, India, and Thailand, continuing trade with all regional countries, and another major surge in gas exports expected before the end of this decade, hard-line military leaders can hold out, even if they—and the country—must forego some of the nice things in life. The social sectors may continue to suffer from a lack of public investment and the natural resource base may further deteriorate, causing deepening poverty and an increasing gap between rich and poor. But the "breaking point" for a regime based on violence is very high and quite possibly lies beyond a threshold that, once passed, would make it near impossible for a future, civilian government to restore social stability and deliver broad-based development.

It is important to remember also in this context that military rule in Burma was established largely without external support. Unlike authoritarian regimes in countries such as the Philippines, South Korea, and Chile that were propped up by international (American) support and were therefore vulnerable to the withdrawal of such support, the Burmese regime always rested on its own domestic power base.

Notes

1. Thant Myint-U, *The River of Lost Foot Footsteps* (New York: Farrar, Straus and Giroux, 2007).

2. A typical illustration of this view is U.S. Representative Tom Lantos's comments at a 2004 hearing on Burma at which this author testified in favor of a reassessment of U.S. policy. The congressman insisted that "if we fail, it is not because our approach is wrong, but because the State Department has not pushed hard enough." Tom Lantos, comments at Oversight Hearing, "Developments in Burma," House Subcommittee on Asia and the Pacific, Washington, DC, 25 March 2004.

3. Johan Galtung, "On the Effects of International Economic Sanctions," *World Politics* 19, no. 3 (April 1967), 379.

4. *Washington Post*, "Burma's Image Problem Is a Moneymaker for U.S. Lobbyists," 24 February 1998.

5. Brigadier General Kyaw Win, interview with *Japan Times*, 5 February 1999.

6. Lieutenant General Khin Nyunt, interview with *Asiaweek*, 17 December 1999.

7. The importance of this is confirmed by comparative research, which shows that adoption of the language and instruments of human rights are crucial first steps in a longer-term socialization process into international human rights norms. Thomas Risse, Stephen C. Ropp, and Kathryn Sikkink, eds., *The Power of Human Rights: International Norms and Domestic Change* (Cambridge: Cambridge University Press, 1999).

8. In the words of a former political prisoner, "During my years in prison, the external agency that had the greatest positive impact on prison conditions and the lives of the inmates was the ICRC. With a not too large budget and staff, it has managed to visit nearly all the prisons and a large number of labour camps in Myanmar, and its efforts have resulted in marked improvements in many aspects of prison life. . . . This organisation instituted critical inputs at a critical time, and it has become a presence that is effective and welcomed, even an integral part in the workings of the nation." Khin Zaw Win, "Impoverishment as Freedom: An Orwellian Double-Speak," n.d., www.freeburmacoalition.org (accessed 27 January 2007).

9. International officials, interviews by author, Rangoon, 2000–2005.

10. ILO official, interview by author, September 2004.

11. According to the head of a UN agency, in some instances, government officials appear to have been convinced that the accusations were fabricated by antigovernment groups, and that by allowing international agencies access they would be proven wrong. Interview by author, Rangoon, October 2002.

12. With few exceptions, the boycotts of bilateral and multilateral aid to Burma are based on political criteria, not technical ones, although the latter would present a further barrier to aid resumption, particularly when it comes to lending from the international financial institutions.

13. As Aung San Suu Kyi explains, "We are not allowed to accept donations from foreign sources and we are very careful not to do so. . . . I never accepted [the money from the Nobel Peace Price] or any other prize money for myself. I have used those funds to set up a Burma Trust for Education and this is kept abroad." Aung San Suu Kyi, *The Voice of Hope: Conversations with Alan Clements* (London: Penguin Books, 1997), 169.

14. See, for example, *Far Eastern Economic Review*, "Interview with Aung San Suu Kyi," 7 May 1998; also Aung Zaw, "Burmese Feel That Sanctions Must Stay," *Irrawaddy* (print ed.) 9, no. 4, May 2001.

15. For an example of this view, see Marvin C. Ott, "From Isolation to Relevance: Policy Considerations," in *Burma: Prospects for a Democratic Future*, ed. Robert I. Rotberg, 82 (Washington, DC: Brookings Institution Press, 1998).

16. Mary Callahan points out that while the release of Aung San Suu Kyi in 1995 came a week before the U.S. Congress was due to discuss a new, draconian sanctions bill, the military made no effort to placate Washington two years later when the new Clinton administration threatened a ban on all new investments, suggesting that other factors were at play in 1995. Mary P. Callahan, "Democracy in Burma: The Lessons of History," *NBR Analysis* 9, no. 3 (May 1998): 25–26.

17. Forced labor is a case in point. On several occasions, the Burmese government has been on the verge of withdrawing any cooperation with the ILO in protest over censure and sanctions imposed by other members. This has been averted, however, by a firm commitment by the ILO to engage constructively with the Burmese authorities on practical issues of compliance with its rules and willingness to acknowledge positive steps—sometimes against significant opposition from Western governments and labor organizations.

18. The UNCHR, having gained access to eleven townships on the Thai border in March 2004 in preparation for the possible return of Karen and Mon refugees, had to stop its visits after the purge of Khin Nyunt in October that year. The program has since been resumed, but it has been "on and off" and progress is much slower than hoped for. UNHCR officials, interviews by author, Rangoon, February 2005, September 2005, August 2006. The ICRC has faced even worse and growing restrictions on all its core programs, including prison visits (blocked altogether since December 2005), access to conflict-affected areas along the border, and even basic relief operations. In November 2006, it was ordered by the government to close all of its five

field offices. The order was officially reversed soon after, but by March 2007 negotiations had still to produce a practical agreement on reassuming the work. The ILO appears to have done somewhat better with its February 2007 agreement with the government, which formally allows the ILO liaison officer in Rangoon to resume investigations into the use of forced labor anywhere in the country, but it is too early to judge the substance of this. For a detailed discussion of these new threats to humanitarian space, see International Crisis Group, "Myanmar: New Threats to Humanitarian Aid," Asia briefing, 8 December 2006.

19. Interview by author, Rangoon, July 2003.

20. Interview by author, Rangoon, December 2004.

21. Chinese diplomat, interview by author, Kokang Special Region, December 2002.

22. Quoted in *Asiaweek*, 25 December 1998.

23. Whatever the limitations of these developments, the military itself views them as major achievements. Senior General Than Shwe, for example, has described the cease-fires as the most important achievement of the post-1988 regime. *New Light of Myanmar*, 27 February 1998. Similarly, the state-controlled press almost daily for the past decade has been celebrating the construction of new roads; bridges; dams; and buildings, including factories, schools, and hospitals, all of which clearly in the military's mind symbolize the country's progress toward "a modern, developed nation."

24. Burmese ambassador, interview by author, overseas, September 2003.

25. By contrast, when asked by the author why the government in 2004 invited Amnesty International to visit the country, a military official responded, "Because they report fairly." Interview by author, Rangoon, March 2003. A similar perception initially benefited the ICRC, which—apart from its code of confidentiality—was perceived by military officials to be committed to objectivity.

26. The same conclusion is reached by Zarni, founder of the Free Burma Coalition and a former leading advocate of sanctions, who after a return visit to Rangoon in 2004 made this observation: "Many observers and potential investors believe the current military leaders are happy being shunned as pariahs. . . . We find that not to be true. . . . What drives the 'hard-liners' is their conviction that the West feels nothing but ill-will and hostility toward Burma. For them, the logical choice is to ignore the attacks and seek integration with more supportive powers." Zarni and May Oo, "Common Problems, Shared Responsibilities: Citizens' Quest for National Reconciliation in Burma/Myanmar," a Free Burma Coalition report, October 2004.

27. The attempt by Western governments to dictate the country's political future in itself is perceived as a threat to national security, and thus confirms—from the leadership's perspective—the vital importance of maintaining military control of the government (see further section on Counterproductive Effects in the main text).

28. In fact, a surprisingly large number of high-level officers continue to live quite frugally, evidently driven more by a taste of power—or perhaps a sense of duty—than a taste for luxury. According to a businessman who interacts with them socially, "Many officers as high as the rank of colonel have less than the drivers working for

foreign companies. They live in small bungalows and only just get by." Interview by author, Rangoon, July 2004. Tellingly, a senior aide of General Khin Nyunt, who was arrested for corruption in 2004, was charged only for living in an inappropriately large state-owned apartment and having kept his service revolver after being discharged. Burmese diplomat, interview by author, Rangoon, June 2005.

29. The SLORC/SPDC on several occasions has banned the export of food products to keep domestic prices low, most recently in December 2003. The authorities, at times, have also sought to physically "dissuade" traders from raising the price of key staples. Throughout the 1990s and the early 2000s, the government further provided subsidized rice for state personnel and the urban poor. This program was only terminated after the liberalization of the rice trade in 2003, which ended a long-standing policy of forced government procurement of rice at significantly below-market prices.

30. In 2003, for example, the government began denying foreign companies export and import licenses, supposedly after complaints by local "entrepreneurs" that the foreigners "were making all the money." Burmese businessman, interview by author, Rangoon, June 2004.

31. Symptomatically, the government responded to the Asian economic crisis in 1997 by reversing many of its embryonic open-door economic policies.

32. It seems inevitable that such fears of retribution will have been compounded by recent international developments, including the establishment of the International Court of Justice and actions taken against former dictators such as Chile's General Pinochet, Indonesia's President Soeharto, and Serbia's Prime Minister Milosovic.

33. Unlike in neighboring Thailand, for example, military officers cannot expect to be able to pursue an alternative career in the private sector. In fact, few appear to have any interest in doing so. As businessmen often point out, the Burmese leaders rarely take a direct interest in the running of their companies. They simply take part of the profits. Interviews by author, Rangoon, 2000–2006.

34. Interviews by author: U.S. State Department official, Washington, DC, March 2004; European Commission official, Brussels, December 2004.

35. Burmese ambassador, interview by author, overseas, March 2003.

36. According to a U.S. State Department official, Burma had in fact made "significant progress on five of six specific U.S. demands," including a major drop in opium production. Interview by author, Washington, DC, March 2004.

37. Military intelligence officer, interview by author, Rangoon, March 2003. There was even talk about withdrawing the Burmese ambassador from Washington. Burmese diplomat, interview by author, overseas, September 2003.

38. Even more moderate officers and officials, who had been trying to negotiate Burma's return to the international community and, in private, would express understanding of the need for political liberalization and improvements in human rights, expressed deep frustration. As one intelligence officer lamented, "There is nothing we can do to satisfy Washington." Interview by author, Rangoon, March 2003.

39. In a private conversation, a U.S. State Department official told the author that "historical experience shows that the Burmese military only concedes to gain something—this should not be rewarded." Washington, DC, June 2000. In a similar vein, U.S. assistant secretary of state for East Asia and the Pacific James Kelly once commented, "As welcome as the release of Aung San Suu Kyi and other prisoners has been, these individuals simply should not have been incarcerated in the first place." James A. Kelly, "U.S. and Burma" (dinner talk given at the Paul H. Nitze School of Advanced International Studies Conference on Burma, Washington, DC, 21 November 2002). While perhaps understandable from a moral perspective, this raises the question of how sanctions are supposed to work. Sanctions will never "change the heart" of anyone (in fact, they inevitably produce resistance). So, if bargaining is rejected, the only way forward lies in physically defeating the regime, a much more difficult task and one unlikely to succeed in Burma.

40. For example, Philip S. Robertson Jr., "Sanctions Are Working in Burma," *Irrawaddy* (online ed.), 26 August 2003, www.irrawaddy.org (accessed 26 August 2003); ALTSEAN, "Ready, Aim, Sanction," November 2003, 132.

41. Reports of large-scale desertions by Burmese army soldiers have been frequent since the mid-1990s, with deserters complaining about low pay and brutal treatment by their officers. According to a former Burmese army major, "Many battalions have had large-scale defections, and might be down, for example, from 700 to 300 men. The salaries are too low to support a family. The commanders cannot report this to Yangon though." Interview by author, Washington, DC, June 2000.

42. U.S. State Department official, interview by author, Washington, DC, April 2004.

43. Military "insider," interview by author, Rangoon, March 2004.

44. For example, when commenting on the 9/9/99 movement, Colonel Than Tun from the now defunct Office of Strategic Studies said, "It is found that every time expatriate destructive elements resident abroad conspire to cause destruction to the country in violation of the law, there is a linkage between the incident and the National League for Democracy inside the country. . . . They are acting in a synchronised manner. They are heading for internal riots. Most obviously, they are doing so after accepting material and moral support from the outside." Myanmar Information Committee, "Information Sheet," 19 August 1999, www.myanmar-information.net/ (accessed 12 May 2003).

45. Burmese ambassador, interview by author, overseas, March 2003.

46. International official, interview by author, Rangoon, January 2003.

47. Robert H. Taylor, "Stifling Political Change: The Army Remains in Command" (paper presented at the Conference on the Current Situation in Burma (Myanmar: Background, Prospects and Possible Solutions, Bonn, 24–26 July 1998).

48. Unfortunately, both of these more positive periods were cut short by renewed confrontations between the military and the NLD within the country, to which Western governments responded with new hard-line initiatives in support of the beleaguered opposition party.

49. Kyaw Yin Hlaing, remarks made at a panel on Burma at the Paul H. Nitze School of Advanced International Studies, Washington, DC, 25 March 2004.

50. Contrary to claims by critics of aid to Burma, Burmese government controls on aid activities, at least until recently, do not appear to have been aimed so much at manipulating foreign aid flows for political purposes, but rather at ensuring that aid is not used for political subversion by external actors bent on defeating the regime. In the early 1990s, for example, military officials expressed fear that international NGOs might be used to smuggle weapons to antigovernment groups as has happened in Cambodia and other countries. David I. Steinberg, interview by author, Washington, DC, March 2004. In a similar vein, the director of an international NGO explains that the authorities refused him permission to bring blood samples to Thailand for tuberculosis tests because they thought he would test for HIV/AIDS and use it to denigrate the government. Interview by author, Rangoon, December 2001. Recent efforts by the USDA to co-opt aid programs as part of its effort to build legitimacy is a significant qualitative change, but it is being strongly resisted by international agencies and has yet to become a major problem, except for small local organizations.

51. As a Burmese staff member of an international NGO explained, "Whenever there is criticism from the outside, you get a defensive response from the top leaders and everybody lower down in the government closes the door for a while, afraid of getting into trouble. It is really not helpful." Interview by author, Rangoon, December 2001.

52. UN officials, interviews by the author, Rangoon, December 2002–January 2003.

53. Interview by author, Rangoon, August 2003.

54. Robert H. Taylor, "Myanmar's Political Future: Is Waiting for the Perfect the Enemy of Doing the Possible?" in "Reconciling Burma/Myanmar: Essays on U.S. Relations with Burma," ed. John H. Badgley, special issue, *NBR Analysis* 15, no. 1 (March 2004): 34.

55. Many observers in Rangoon feel that the Nobel Peace Prize may also have become a straightjacket for the opposition leader herself, making it more difficult for her to moderate her stance. This remains speculation, but it is notable that she has been significantly "softer" on many issues, including cooperation with the government as well as foreign aid and investment, in private conversations with international officials than in her public statements.

56. Burmese exiles, interviews by the author, Washington, DC, March 2004.

57. Only the future can tell if this is the final verdict, but that it is cause for concern within the more uncompromising groups is evident from renewed efforts by the KNU since 2003 to get a cease-fire agreement similar to those reached by other groups in the early 1990s, which it had previously rejected.

58. George Soros, testimony submitted for the Hearing on Burma, U.S. Senate Committee on Banking, Housing, and Urban Affairs, 22 May 1996.

59. Alfred Oehlers, "Sanctions and Burma: Revisiting the Case Against," *Burma Economic Watch*, no. 2 (2004): 36–46.

60. It is true, as Alfred Oehlers argues, that most people in Burma live at subsistence level and thus are less affected by sanctions, *in absolute terms*, than would have been the case in a more developed economy—and less than the military/business elite. However, they are still affected. Many small-scale farmers produce a small marketable food surplus or grow some commercial crops, and even the poorest family in the most isolated village in Burma buys essentials such as salt and soap. Most also have significant outlays on health and education. They are not, in other words, isolated from the broader economy—and while their losses may be small in absolute terms, they can be devastating exactly because people live at subsistence level, with little to cushion them against economic shocks.

61. This is not to say that donors should provide budgetary support for a government which may be spending in excess of 50 percent of its budget on its security forces. Yet, all costs of a given policy should be calculated and openly discussed (even if they are seen by some to be justified for moral or political reasons), not hidden behind comments such as "sanctions do not hurt people."

62. The salaries in the Burmese export garment industry in U.S. dollar terms are the lowest in the world, but in purchasing power parity are similar or higher than those in, for example, China, Indonesia, and Bangladesh. More importantly, they are about 30 percent higher than in garment factories producing for the domestic market and provide much better benefits. Moe Kyaw, "Report on the Textile and Garment Industry," Yangon, 2001.

63. "Myanmar Textile and Garment Industry," confidential report, November 2003.

64. World Vision, "Report on US Sanctions on Burma/Myanmar: The Impact on Local Communities in Yangon," 26 September 2003.

65. Moe Kyaw, "Textile and Garment Industry."

66. Official figures from the Ministry of Industry, quoted in *Myanmar Times*, 22–28 August 2005.

67. Defenders of the import ban argued that most of these jobs would disappear anyway by the end of 2004, when the quota system in the United States and Europe was due to be eliminated. This, however, has not happened. On the contrary, there appears to have been a weak revival in the garment sector in 2005–2006. Burmese businessman, interviews by the author, Rangoon, August 2005, October 2006. In any case, such arguments are of little comfort to the many poor families for whom every day's work counts in the struggle to cope with deteriorating socioeconomic conditions. While labor in Burma is among the lowest paid in the world, for many families even the $30–50 a month that an average garment worker earned in 2002 can be the difference between a decent life and daily hunger and illness. Most of the laid-off laborers in the garment factories were unskilled, young women, who had few other job opportunities.

68. UNESCAP, "Statistical Yearbook for Asia and the Pacific 2001," October 2001.

69. Despite the crucial importance of education for both democracy and development, the United Nations Children's Fund (UNICEF) for 2001–2005 received only

30 percent of the funds it needed for its planned education program in Burma, which to begin with only covered one-third of the country. UNICEF official, interview by author, Rangoon, December 2004.

70. In 2000, the combined budget for HIV/AIDS of all national and international organizations in Burma was only about $3 million. According to the Joint United Nations Programme on HIV/AIDS (UNAIDS), "Not one of the priority areas of the national response has sufficient resources, technical or financial, to take activities to the scale required for sustainable impact on the progress of the epidemic." UNAIDS, "The United Nations Joint Action Plan on HIV/AIDS," 2001–2002.

71. At first glance, it might look like the loss of the Global Fund ($98 million over five years) has been compensated for by the new 3D Fund (around $99.5 million over five years). The 3D Fund, however, also replaces the Fund for HIV/AIDS in Myanmar (FHAM). The total funding available through these multidonor funding mechanisms from 2007 will, therefore, be significantly less than before. In addition, there are significant opportunity costs associated with the new commitments to the 3D Fund. It seems inevitable that the need to allocate extra money for HIV/AIDS, malaria, and tuberculosis in Burma (beyond existing contributions to the Global Fund) will take away from programs in other critical sectors. This appears to be happening already with the European Commission's new country strategy paper for Burma. While a draft from March 2005 specified two priority sectors—"social development" (including health and education) and "sustainable livelihoods"—by the time public consultations started in November 2005, the latter had been cut, except for a reference to possible future action. Since new livelihood programs would have been an important contribution, essential for addressing the causes of poverty and putting money in people's hands for health and education, this is a serious loss.

72. For example, Oehlers, "Sanctions and Burma," 42. See also Janelle Saffin, "Comments on Paper by David I. Steinberg" (paper presented at the Conference on NGO Strategy for the Democratization of Burma, Seoul, Korea, 23–25 June 1999).

73. Claims by U.S. congressmen in the lead up to the import ban that it would deny the regime more than $400 million in annual revenue (equivalent to total U.S. imports from Burma in 2002–2003) were wildly distorted. See Senator Tom Harkin, statement in the Senate on introduced bills and joint resolutions, 22 May 2001. Contrary to conventional wisdom, the government/military did not own or control the garment export industry, which accounted for about 85 percent of U.S. imports from Burma. Global Trade Information Services, *World Trade Atlas*, 2001–2003, www.worldtradestatistics.com/state/. The industry was dominated by local, generally small, privately owned companies (88 percent), which employed 72 percent of the workers and produced 62 percent of the export value—the rest was divided between joint ventures and fully foreign-owned companies. Moe Kyaw, "Textile and Garment Industry." Moreover, the garment export industry as a whole had very low added-value as it operated largely on a CMP (cut, make, and pack) basis. According to two independent estimates, the military regime's income from garment exports to the

United States in 2002–2003, including taxes and revenue sharing from joint ventures with military holding companies, was thus only $5–7 million. Interviews by author: U.S. official, Rangoon, July 2003; British market analyst, Rangoon, August 2003. Some individual officers had a stake in private garment factories, but that too was very limited.

74. These sectors are less vulnerable to economic boycotts due to the absence of alternative markets for foreign investors and buyers.

75. The importance attached to being directly engaged in the national political debate by ethnic groups, who for decades have been isolated in the border areas, was apparent at a workshop in Rangoon in February 2004, organized by the Singapore-based Institute of Southeast Asian Studies, in which this author took part. This was supposedly the first time since the 1950s that a group of foreign scholars met officially with a broad cross-section of Burmese political and civil society, including representatives of half a dozen cease-fire groups.

76. Martin Smith, "Ethnic Participation and National Reconciliation in Myanmar: Challenges in a Transitional Landscape" (paper presented at the Burma/Myanmar Update, Australian National University, Canberra, 18–19 November 2004).

77. One way of supporting the cease-fire groups would have been for international actors to engage more constructively with issues concerning the National Convention, which most of these groups have accepted as a useful platform for discussions.

78. Community leaders and aid workers, interviews by author, Burma, 2000–2006. This assessment is confirmed by observations by other scholars, including Smith, "Ethnic Participation and National Reconciliation."

79. The need for international assistance is confirmed by one of Burma's leading independent economists, who argues, "We need a transitional period that does not cause havoc in our exchange market, leading to uncertainty and rapid increases in prices causing serious hardships to the people. To prevent this sort of situation [we need] bridging assistance and establishment of a stabilizing fund." Interview by author, Rangoon, November 2004.

80. Kyaw Yin Hlaing, "Will Western Sanctions Bring Down the House?" in Badgley, "Reconciling Burma/Myanmar," 77.

81. As any educator or trainer in Burma can testify, the thirst for knowledge among the Burmese is insatiable.

82. Callahan, "Democracy in Burma," 25. Callahan refers specifically to the role of militaries in democratic transitions, but the idea obviously has wider applicability.

83. Kurt Schock, "People Power and Political Opportunities: Social Movement Mobilization and Outcomes in the Philippines and Burma," *Social Problems* 46, no. 3 (1999): 368–69.

84. Interviews by author: international official, Rangoon, September 2004; Kachin community leader, Rangoon, December 2004.

85. Zarni and May Oo, "Common Problems," 16–17.

86. An Asian ambassador, who traveled extensively with Than Shwe during a state visit to his home country, concluded that "the senior general remains fully con-

vinced that the regime is successfully developing the country." Interview by author, Rangoon, December 2004.

87. There is probably a limit to how long the government can continue to print money at the current rate to cover its budget deficits. However, as witnessed over the past decade, the first sectors to be shut down are health and education, the near collapse of which has already had hugely damaging and long-term consequences for the country and its people.

88. Andrew Selth, *Burma's Armed Forces: Power without Glory* (Norwalk, CT: EastBridge, 2002), 131. Desmond Ball alleges that this includes drugs-for-arms deals with Chinese officers in Yunnan. "Burma and Drugs: The Regime's Complicity in the Global Drug Trade" (Working Paper No. 336, Strategic and Defence Studies Centre, Australian National University, Canberra, 1999), 7.

CHAPTER SIX

A Better Way to Human Rights

> Undoubtedly, there are many in the US with deep sympathy and concern for the sad plight of the Burmese people. However, all these good intentions will have to be tempered by a clearer understanding and recognition of ground realities and with provisions made for well-thought out plans of action. . . . What concrete plan has the US got to restore normalcy and then to facilitate social and economic progress in Burma, aside from vague roadmaps, wishful thinking and fuzzy ideas about bringing the two camps together?
>
> —Burmese economist[1]

Since the 1988 uprising, the West has sought to promote human rights in Burma primarily by pushing for a democratic transition. Although the exact objectives and methods differ somewhat among governments and organizations and have shifted over time, regime change generally has been seen as a precondition for engagement in other spheres. A variety of sanctions have thus been applied to pressure the military to hand over power to a democratically elected government, while assistance normally available to least developed countries has been withheld.

Nineteen years of mounting Western pressure, however, has had little impact on the will or capacity of the military rulers to maintain power. At the time of writing, the regime is poised to impose a new constitution that institutionalizes the military's dominant role in government, while the main opposition party has been marginalized. Each year, Burma's natural and human resources are further eroding, the HIV/AIDS epidemic is mounting, and poverty is deepening. In short, the trends are in the wrong direction.

Democracy groups are calling for further sanctions to break the political deadlock. But there are no prospects that either the UN Security Council or Burma's neighbors and main trading partners will support the sanctions regime—or, indeed, that more sanctions would accomplish the objectives. Further isolation is likely simply to impede domestic processes of change and punish the general population, for whom the denial of foreign aid, trade, and investment only adds to the burden of decades of domestic conflict and misrule. The situation is not without opportunities. Progress toward constitutional government, despite the obvious democratic deficit in the proposed constitution, may help pave the way for longer-term political change and help direct attention to the country's socioeconomic crisis, particularly if it is accompanied by a leadership succession within the military. Any hope for political progress, however, rests on a combination of confidence within the military about its ability to maintain stability and preparedness by the opposition to pursue less zero-sum objectives—factors that appear to be *inversely* correlated with current Western policies. Absent this, the current policy paralysis is likely to continue, socioeconomic conditions will deteriorate further, and the risk of large-scale social unrest and generalized violence will increase. Even if an outright "state collapse" seems unlikely given the cohesion of the army, any regime change that takes place in the context of elite confrontations and socioeconomic crisis, rather than facilitating a positive transformation of society, is likely to simply see one set of unaccountable and ineffective rulers replaced with another, leaving the general population no better off.

Fallacies of Past Policy Thinking

The core strategy of Western countries, which emphasizes the use of censure and sanctions to isolate the military regime and force it to transfer power to a civilian, elected government, originates in the late 1980s and early 1990s when, to many outside observers, Burma seemed to have moved into a "democratic transition zone." It is based, however, on a number of fallacies or misleading notions about the situation inside the country, which have become increasingly exposed over time.

The Military Perspective

Burma's military regime, contrary to conventional wisdom, is not purely opportunistic. Many officers remain convinced that only the armed forces can keep Burma united, and that democratic government would be harmful for the country. Although they have strong interests, too, in maintaining power and privileges, their preoccupation with national security rules out the type of "bargains" that have been made with authoritarian rulers elsewhere who were persuaded to retire in return for guarantees of personal safety and wealth. On the other hand, the military regime does have a national development agenda and has taken some limited steps toward the goal of building a "modern, developed nation," primarily in the form of cease-fires with more than a dozen armed groups, embryonic market-oriented economic reforms, and a general opening to the world after twenty-six years of self-imposed isolation. Its failures in these particular areas are due less to ill will than fear, weak understanding of development processes, and limited resources. There may, therefore, be more space for cooperation on a social and economic development agenda than commonly acknowledged by Western governments and the Burmese opposition alike.

International censure and sanctions have helped induce some limited cooperation by the government on selected human rights issues. The potential benefits of this, however, have remained untapped due to the rigidity of Western governments, which have hesitated to recognize positive steps by the military regime or fully engage on the issues in question. By early 2003, if not before, the senior general seems to have concluded that no attempt to accommodate Western demands would elicit comparable concessions from Washington, and since then the regime's diplomacy has been directed almost exclusively at its neighbors and other "friendly" countries. Meanwhile, Western sanctions and support for Aung San Suu Kyi have sustained the military's siege mentality and deepened its hostility to the democratic opposition, which has become associated with the "foreign threat." Pressure may also have influenced the government's decision to curb its original open-door economic reform agenda, which would have left the regime more vulnerable to foreign influences. Certainly, Western governments wasted an opportunity to encourage a process of economic liberalization that not only would have had major welfare benefits, but also could have helped to advance pluralism in society.

The Balance of Power

Advocates of the core strategy are guilty also of *under*estimating the durability of the military regime and *over*estimating the influence of the opposition. Claims that the regime is brittle and close to collapsing under intense popular pressure for democracy are wishful thinking and have created unrealistic expectations about how change is going to come about. Given the degree of its military, political, social, and economic control, the military leadership is in a virtually unassailable position—vulnerable, it seems, only to an unlikely, large-scale mutiny. The political opposition looked strong in the late 1980s but has failed to harness the wellspring of popular dissatisfaction for sustained political activism. The National League for Democracy (NLD), in particular, is struggling to maintain its relevance as vanguard of the democracy movement, although Aung San Suu Kyi herself remains the focus of many people's hopes and inspirations.

International attention may have helped protect Aung San Suu Kyi and her party from elimination. Yet, focusing on one person inadvertently impedes the mobilization of additional leaders, and the lack of economic reforms and development—to which isolation contributes, even if it is not the immediate or primary cause—inhibits a process of sociopolitical change, which over time could help build a broader, more substantial democracy movement. By limiting the military's access to foreign exchange, economic sanctions may help curtail military expansion, but this has little effect on the regime's ability to suppress internal dissent, which relies mainly on political and social controls (backed by a proven commitment to use violence), not on high-tech weapon systems or even large numbers of troops. In the long term, Burma's international isolation hurts the regime less than it does the opposition, which ultimately is constrained by the underlying weaknesses of political, civil, and economic society.

Transitional Challenges

The preoccupation with regime change, however, not only disregards realistic scenarios for change, but also ignores the complex challenges Burma faces in breaking the present, self-reinforcing pattern of conflict, repression, and poverty. Although the installation of an elected government would be an important step, it could not function suspended from social realities, nor would it provide a panacea for the country's deep-seated development problems. For democratic politics to work, the necessary infrastructure must be put in place. There is a need for strong political organizations, including political parties and broader civil society organizations, which both uphold and promote democratic values and support good governance. The expansion of government authority and stable, modern governance structures, including the rule of law, into areas that have only recently, if ever, been brought within the orbit of the central state will be a particularly difficult, extended, and sensitive process. Initially, the performance of a democratic system is likely to depend primarily on the skills of a narrow band of elites in the main cities and key ethnic areas. But for democracy to take root and bring about improvements in all aspects of human rights, political and economic resources must be extended to the population at large, along with the spread of a culture of participation, moderation, and cooperation.

While Western governments and activists expound the broad objectives of democracy and human rights, they have tended to define this in narrow terms: implementation of the 1990 election results, release of Aung San Suu Kyi, or similar. The structural causes of authoritarian rule and broader crises facing the country are often ignored. The international democracy movement has done little to promote conflict resolution, institution building, or economic reform. It has limited even humanitarian assistance to mainly "emergency relief," excluding crucial areas such as education and reconstruction of war-torn communities and economies. Continued preoccupation with a narrow political agenda delays urgently needed action in areas such as HIV/AIDS and the environment, a delay that threatens the welfare of future generations. Such omissions are detrimental both to the cause of democracy and to the broader welfare and security of the Burmese people.

Costs of Sanctions and Isolation

While many advocates of sanctions today will acknowledge their limitations, they maintain that the benefits outweigh the costs (some deny that any real harm is done at all). This is a serious misreading of the situation. Although the macroeconomic effects of current sanctions are certainly overshadowed by the regime's own economic mismanagement, external interference increases the sense of threat within the government and encourages allocation of further scarce resources for arms and other security matters. By reinforcing the political deadlock and making the search for domestic compromises more difficult, censure and sanctions also contribute to maintaining the zero-sum struggle for power, which diverts attention away from vital governance and development issues within the government and the opposition alike. In addition, the denial of foreign aid, investments, and trade directly reduces job and training opportunities, as well as provision of social services and broader community development activities, thus diminishing the general population's ability to improve their livelihoods.

The South Africa Comparison

The fall of South Africa's apartheid government is often held up by proponents of the core strategy as "evidence" that sanctions will work in Burma, too, if only pressure is maintained. That analogy is misleading, however. First, South Africa was a functioning, if partial, democracy. This became a crucial factor as the country's leaders could not ignore demands from their support base of white voters. In Burma, the top generals are largely isolated from such broader social interests.

Second, when apartheid became a major international concern in the late 1970s, South Africa was deeply integrated into the international economy and the ruling white elite was substantially modernized. Foreign investment and trade were crucial to the ability of the government to maintain the prosperity of its main constituents, the country's large and growing white middle class. It therefore came under strong pressure from domestic business, which acted as a mediator for international sanctions and so greatly added to their impact. These conditions are absent in Burma's traditional agrarian economy where the capitalist and middle classes are small and often owe their positions to military patronage.

Third, although set apart from the world by its racism, the South African government and its white minority supporters relied on contacts with the West to maintain their social and cultural identity. Its leaders were well connected in Western capitals, and white South African society as a whole, especially the English-speaking business community, was closely tied to Europe and the United States in a myriad of important ways. Burma's military leaders are not isolated from their main reference group. On the contrary, they have been able to tap into a strong tradition of "regional nationalism" that emphasizes the distinctiveness of East Asian societies and cultures and challenges any intervention from outside, although this may now be weakening.

Fourth, sanctions on South Africa supplemented and reinforced strong internal pressures for political change. These included an underground resistance movement aligned with the African National Congress (ANC), a broad-based legal opposition movement led by high-profile figures such as Bishop Desmond Tutu, and a substantial group of white liberals and businessmen who opposed apartheid. In Burma, although most people resent the government, there is only limited active opposition that international actors can support or reinforce. The military's efforts to crush the NLD have left the main opposition party a shell of its former self, while the country's longstanding insurgencies have largely faded away. There is also much less general social unrest and violence than was the case in South Africa. The costs to the government of maintaining control are thus much lower.[2]

Fifth, sanctions imposed on South Africa were substantially supported by all its neighbors, as well as all the country's main trading partners in the West, and were accompanied by multifaceted international engagement with both the government and the antiapartheid opposition. During the 1980s, while conservative governments in the United States and the UK maintained close and constant communication with South African leaders, activist groups provided substantial direct assistance to opposition groups and black communities inside South Africa. By contrast, all Burma's neighbors and main trading partners and suppliers of capital are opposed to sanctions, and links between the democracy movement inside the country and the outside world are weak.

Finally, sanctions worked in South Africa because white leaders ultimately proved to be pragmatists. As Anton Lowenberg and William Kaempfer point out, "South Africa's segregationist policies were inherently pragmatic and malleable in the face of changing constellations of economic incentives. Apartheid policies were never locked into a rigid dogma or ideology. Rather, they were constantly being revised in accordance with changes in both internally and externally imposed constraints."[3] So far, Burma's leaders have yet to show the same kind of intellectual or political flexibility. The national security ideology of the military remains an impediment to rational assessments of international pressure and the needs of the country. Indeed, the generals may feel that they have accomplished their primary objective of maintaining national sovereignty and unity. The high levels of socioeconomic deprivation are of less concern, if they are even fully aware of the situation.

Although international pressure, in the end, helped induce political reform in South Africa, the apartheid regime held out for three decades and only gave in when faced with almost total economic, political, and cultural isolation. Further, sanctions worked through domestic mechanisms that are largely absent in Burma today. This does not warrant optimism when it comes to coercing Burma's military rulers, who are much less susceptible to external pressure.

Another Way Forward

Developments in Burma over the past few years underline the failure of the "democracy paradigm" that has guided Western policy since 1988, based on misleading models from South Africa and, to a lesser extent, Eastern Europe. The removal of Prime Minister Khin Nyunt and ministers loyal to him in late 2004, together with the sweeping purge of military intelligence and related agencies that followed, has not only lessened the prospects for compromise with both the political and armed opposition, but has also increased the risk that governance and economic structures could further unravel. The present government is more insular and has less access to information; fragmentation of state authority appears to have increased on the ground even as it has been further consolidated at the top; and current economic trends—notably the prospect of large gas revenues—are more likely to impede economic reform than encourage it. Although the pervasive, centralizing influence of the military, along with declining international opportunities for rebellion, would seem to rule out a resumption of civil war on the scale seen in the past, widespread social unrest and a further weakening of the state cannot be ruled out. This strongly suggests a need to refocus current international efforts at effecting change by working toward a more gradual transition that maintains, or indeed strengthens, the capacity of the state and society to deal with the country's broader development needs.

To be effective, international approaches must reflect realities on the ground in Burma, *not* be imported cookie-cutter style from other continents. The generals' mind-set must be taken into account, as must the huge power imbalance between the military and the democracy forces and the broader structural obstacles to political and economic development, notably the legacy of more than a half century of armed conflict, deep-rooted poverty, and low levels of education. Burma is one of the poorest, most militarized, and conflict-prone societies in the contemporary world. There is no meaningful democratic culture or institutions to build on, nor much in the way of effective governance institutions of any kind, and they cannot simply be "willed" into existence. Inevitably, the building of a state and society capable of realizing the country's potential will be a prolonged and tortuous process. This requires both a long-term perspective and deep humility regarding the prospects for reform and the influence of external actors. Commitment to principles needs to be matched with a pragmatic search for workable solutions that can begin to move the country forward.

Broaden the Aims

However laudable in principle, the singular pursuit of democracy and refusal to deal with the military regime are not effective strategies for promoting the freedom, security, and welfare of the Burmese people. First, the probability of a transition from military to genuine civilian rule in the foreseeable future is low. Any transition, including important governance and economic reforms, will have to be negotiated and implemented in cooperation with the military leadership. Second, democratization is a long and difficult process, not a one-off event. The establishment and maturation of genuinely democratic institutions in any country—not least one as poor and inexperienced with democratic practices as Burma—requires fundamental changes in attitudes and behavior at all levels of society, which take decades if not generations to evolve and depends on broader socioeconomic transformations. Third, the association between democratic governance and human security is imperfect and not necessarily positive, at least in the short to medium term. To push for a revolutionary transformation of the formal political system without paying attention to important underlying or complementary development processes is shortsighted, less likely to succeed, and could do more harm than good. Finally, the longer debilitating socioeconomic processes such as the HIV epidemic and unchecked exploitation of the country's natural resources are left to fester, the greater problems a future government will have to contend with and the smaller are its chances of gaining the confidence of the population.

Instead of focusing on immediate *outcomes*, international actors should work to promote three longer-term *processes* of change—political liberalization, peace building, and socioeconomic development—which not only would produce immediate benefits for the general population, but also could begin to lay the ground for internally driven, and thus more meaningful and sustainable, reforms. This approach would also create wider space for working with domestic actors who, with the exception of a relatively small number of political activists, do not see democracy as the immediate or even the primary goal for society, but are working, for example, to strengthen national unity (the military), to promote local autonomy and ethnic rights (ethnic nationalist organizations), or simply to reestablish their fields or businesses after decades of armed conflict (border areas communities). These three processes are closely interrelated and mutually reinforcing, which is why they need to be pursued in tandem.

Political Liberalization

The overwhelming power imbalance between the military regime and the opposition virtually rules out a democratic breakthrough at this time, whether through an elite "pact" or a revolutionary challenge from the grass roots. Since 1988, however, the military has allowed some narrow political openings, including the formation of political parties and the convening of the National Convention, as well as a limited expansion in popular access to information and the space for public debate and civil society organizations. Although primarily aimed at shoring up the regime's power rather than facilitating increased popular participation in politics, such changes are slowly transforming public life and, if reinforced and expanded, could fuel a process of "creeping democratization."[4] As experience elsewhere in Asia shows, political liberalization, even when reinforced by comprehensive economic liberalization measures, may not quickly lead to liberal democracy. But it would help strengthen civilian institutions, which gain space to form and exercise at least certain basic political functions, thus improving the prospects for a future effective challenge to authoritarian rule and subsequent consolidation of a meaningful democracy. This particularly would be the case if expansion of political freedom and activity combines with peace building and socioeconomic development that spread the possibilities and resources for civilian political activity to a wider section of the population.

Peace Building

Burma's long-running, internal armed conflicts were a root cause of the military's rise to power in the 1950s and continue to present serious obstacles to any future military disengagement from politics. The spread of cease-fires since the late 1980s has brought a nationwide stop to fighting within reach. Yet, continued political tensions, serious human rights abuses by the army in newly occupied areas, and the lack of development of former war zones suggest that peace is still some way off. While the leadership of most ethnic armed groups, including those still fighting the government, appears committed to stopping the violence, frustrations are mounting among younger generations, who have little prospect for a meaningful future and do not remember the suffering caused by the war. Resistance among hard-line army officers to any cooperation with their former enemies means that even minor flare-ups could quickly escalate into renewed hostilities. This, in turn, would reinforce the military's reasons for maintaining a stranglehold on government and justify even larger budget allocations to the armed forces.

The absence of peace also presents a major threat to a future democracy. Although some believe democratic governance would resolve the ethnic conflicts, it is equally likely to introduce new tensions in Burma's plural society where ethnic and religious identities are deeply felt. Democracy rests on moderate politics with a strong emphasis on mutual trust and accommodation among contending groups. It is vulnerable to extremist politicians using ethnic or other cleavages as a basis for generating support for confrontational positions. A democratic process might facilitate inclusion of excluded groups and interests and allow the healing process to begin. But it could also open the way for demagoguery and agitation based on ethnic and religious identity that would fuel latent conflicts. The search for peace, therefore, is not subsidiary to the quest for democracy, but is central to any meaningful political reform process.

Socioeconomic Development

A truly inclusive, democratic political system that gives all groups a voice in the governance of their areas and protects both individual and group rights does *not* result simply from reform of formal structures of government. Without empowerment of ordinary people, democracy will remain elitist and do little to overcome the root causes of conflict and inequality. Yet, the large majority of the population in Burma are subsistence farmers, often semiliterate, and have limited or no experience of the world beyond their village. Many people in the border areas have had little contact with the central state and thus can hardly be expected to quickly develop commitment to its political arrangements, whatever form they take. Local power structures in many areas remain basically feudal with little space for popular participation. Even if democracy were introduced, the poor majority would remain voiceless and subject to the powers that be. Political and socioeconomic development therefore cannot be separated. Before a future democracy can take root in and be meaningful to many people and communities, they must transcend the barriers created by the daily struggle for survival and the cultural and structural legacy of militarization of society and repressive, autocratic rule. This requires greater economic welfare, broader access to education and information, and stronger local organizations as the foundation for a more vibrant (but moderate), pluralistic civil society.

Revise the Strategic Objectives

Western governments also need to reconsider their strategic objectives. Rather than helping Burma move forward, existing measures to weaken the military regime have deepened the siege mentality of the top leadership and widened the divisions in society, provoking further reactionary measures by an institution whose knee-jerk response to any perceived threat is to strengthen its control over the state and society. Further isolation that undermines whatever limited government capacity and economic activity still exists will simply reinforce current repressive, predatory, and corrupt practices and make it more difficult for any future government to reform the existing system. To avoid such a scenario—and to support the three overarching processes of change outlined above—international actors should work instead to establish the conditions for a gradual transfer of power to a stable and competent civilian government. This requires less focus on defeating the military regime and more on encouraging new thinking within the officer corps, building capacity across the state and society to deal with the country's development needs, and strengthening the nascent democratic infrastructure.

Encourage New Thinking within the Officer Corps

Considering the immense power imbalance between the military and civilian forces and the proven commitment of the generals to crush any open challenge to their rule, progress is all but inconceivable without the cooperation of reform-minded officers. The military, however, is locked into traditional ways of thinking rooted in the country's troublesome past and is so fearful of instability that it perceives any criticism or sign of popular mobilization as a threat to the survival of the state. One of the first steps in any strategy for change therefore must be to lessen the siege mentality of the officer corps and open their minds to more participatory and responsive governance. It is imperative that the next generation of military leaders comes to perceive alternative ways of governing that, while protecting their core interests, including Burma's national sovereignty and territorial integrity, also support broader development objectives.

Strengthen Development Capacity across the State and Society

In order to ensure that the military regime derives minimal legitimacy and financial benefits from international assistance, most Western donors stipulate that contacts with the government should be minimized and aid should be provided outside state structures either directly to the beneficiaries or through civil society organizations. Such requirements, however, limit the impact and sustainability of important aid programs. They also ignore the need to encourage evolutionary change of government structures, which provides, certainly, the most likely and, arguably, the preferable path of transition. Realistically, state power will only gradually move from the military to civilian institutions and only in response to successful development and growing confidence on part of the generals that civilian government will not threaten national security. This requires cooperation between military officers, civilian politicians, and technocrats within a governance framework that engenders the trust and cooperation of a skilled and well-educated population. Donors and aid agencies, therefore, should work to improve the capacity of the existing state to formulate and implement pro-poor policies, as well as legitimately raise revenue for public investment in physical and social infrastructure. Much more also needs to be done to develop the capacity of the general population through improved education, health, and welfare to support and complement the state. Most importantly perhaps, bridges must be built between the state and society, which go beyond a future electoral system to include a dense network of two-way communication structures through which the state may inform its citizenry and elicit information and ideas. Such efforts may reinforce the military regime in the short term, but over time will strengthen the basis for a successful democratic transition and meaningful democracy by building a credible civilian alternative to military rule that can deliver on the population's high hopes for peace and prosperity.

Strengthen the Democratic Infrastructure

While conservative leadership and weak governance present immediate barriers to progress, the greatest challenge for promoters of democracy is perhaps to build the infrastructure necessary to make a future democratic system truly representative and participatory. Burma's experience with democracy in the early postindependence period was short and ended more than forty years ago; no one under sixty years in the country today has any experience of participation in democratic politics. There are no long-standing political parties, no politically relevant civil society, and no widespread commitment to democratic values and behavior in the population at large. Indeed, the strong hierarchy, top-down approach to governance, and inability to deal with dissent associated with military rule are replicated within most civilian organizations, including the NLD and many exile groups. Although present conditions do not determine future outcomes, this democratic "deficit" is likely to persist long after the establishment of electoral democracy and should be actively addressed, even if at this stage it will probably have to be done indirectly within a broader capacity-building agenda.

Get the Policy Mix Right

The framework set out here does not exclude the use of censure or sanctions, but the policy implications of taking a longer-term, evolutionary approach to reform are clear. In order to contribute to social change processes, international actors need to be engaged on the ground in close proximity with the people and institutions they are trying to influence. This requires a shift away from isolation toward "critical engagement." It is necessary to tone down the public condemnation and punitive measures in favor of more constructive efforts to foster policy dialogue and capacity building. Ultimately, pressure exercised within such cooperative relations is likely to be more effective than the current "megaphone" diplomacy, which seems to do little more than solidify resistance to change and inhibit rational thinking.

Diplomacy

Although censure and sanctions exert some pressure on Burma's military rulers to improve their human rights record for instrumental reasons, it has the unfortunate effect of closing minds and freezing social developments, something which contradicts the overriding need to build capacity for participatory government and the rule of law. Coercive diplomacy encourages only defensive measures by the regime, not genuine reforms that depend on fundamental shifts in the perceptions of top military leaders as well as empowerment of civilian institutions.

The aim of a "new" diplomacy should be to improve communication with the military regime in order to allay its fears of foreign interference and establish the basis for critical dialogue about legitimate international concerns. It is crucially important to draw the generals out of their shell, lessen their suspicion about the ultimate intentions of Western governments, and help them embrace international cooperation and interaction. Although this will be a long-term process, it is the only way to make them see the value in, and prudence of, complying with contemporary international norms of behavior. A "new" diplomacy should also encourage the establishment of institutions inside Burma, which over time can become independent agents of change. The ongoing process of drawing up a new constitution, however flawed, is preferable to the alternative, which would see the military continue to govern unconstrained by any legal institutions. The formation of a parliamentary system, even if initially constrained and largely pro forma, would establish a platform for policy discussion which so far has been ignored by all sides in the ongoing power struggle. It would also provide more space for political party activities and, over time, help to build a more credible alternative to military rule. Similarly, the government's establishment of a human rights committee and the ratification of core human rights instruments such as the Geneva Conventions have provided new access points for dialogue and capacity building. Even if such instruments are weak at first, the mere fact of their existence may begin to build a constituency for change within the military state that is currently lacking. Conversely, rejecting them as irrelevant easily becomes a self-fulfilling prophecy as the new structures are left inactive and their domestic supporters abandoned and isolated.

Sanctions will remain part of Western policy for the foreseeable future, but there is a need for clearer, more realistic benchmarks for progress toward agreed international objectives, together with a firm commitment by Western governments and international organizations to reciprocate with concrete, valuable gestures when positive steps are taken. In order to avoid disagreements in one area becoming an obstacle to progress in all other areas, there should be separate road maps for progress toward political liberalization, basic human rights, and economic reform. The incentives associated with each of these road maps should be relevant to the particular issue in question, as this would facilitate dialogue also at the working level of the government where officials may not always see the bigger picture. For example, since the worst human rights abuses are committed by local army units, reciprocal gestures for improvements could incorporate benefits for active army commanders such as bilateral military exchanges and perhaps some forms of training. Similarly, improvements in international aid access to conflict-affected areas could be acknowledged by releasing assistance for road or other infrastructure building, which may not have priority from a humanitarian point of view, but is central in the government's own development plans (and of course has long-term developmental value). Any such assistance should be additional to existing humanitarian assistance, which should be provided according to needs and technical criteria alone, based on fundamental humanitarian principles.

International Assistance

Apart from refocusing their diplomacy, Western governments need to strengthen their engagement with the state and society through a normalization of aid programs. The efficacy of international assistance depends on a comprehensive and coherent package of policy dialogue, selective capacity building, and financial support, including efforts to strengthen state, as well as private, health and education systems. Political restrictions on assistance to Burma, which limit it to purely "humanitarian" programs, constrain efforts in each of these areas and are not conducive to promoting sustainable improvements in popular welfare. Although aid agencies are making a difference in the lives of many poor families through health and livelihood projects, most of these activities leave the policy environment for development untouched and are of questionable sustainability.

While opponents of development aid are correct in arguing that the security priorities and economic policies of the military regime currently limit the sustainability of many programs, the true potential of assistance has never been tested. It is hardly surprising that the military government has rejected sweeping calls for structural adjustment reforms when they are denied support from the international financial institutions that provide the necessary technical and financial assistance and encouragement of such reforms in other low income countries. It is no wonder either that the current leadership is generally suspicious of the activities of aid agencies when the rhetoric and conditionalities of major donors are blatantly partisan and show little concern for the overall development needs of the country.

There is no doubt that the military leaders are hostile to economic and administrative reforms that would directly weaken their hold on power, and less than enthusiastic about community development and other programs that contravene national notions of development, which lag several decades behind current international thinking. There is no doubt either that both the state and society lack the capacity to absorb and effectively apply large amounts of assistance, or that this capacity will have to be built up gradually ahead of any major new financial commitments. The international aid community, however, is hardly unfamiliar with such obstacles, but has a range of strategies and tools available that are used in other countries with arguably less government commitment to development and certainly less potential for long-term progress.

Importantly, the future is not without prospects. The next generation of military leaders, which is likely to take over within the next few years, has different educational and military career backgrounds from the current leaders and has experienced at closer hand the economic progress of their neighbors. Once in charge, like all new governments, they will want to make their mark and improve on the performance of their predecessors. Thus, there will be an important window of opportunity for reviving the economic reform drive—particularly if the international community is prepared to provide the necessary encouragement and technical and financial assistance.

A Final Word

The basic problem with Western policy on Burma is that it freezes a bad situation that does not contain the seeds of its own resolution. The military, despite its many policy failures, has stayed in power since 1962, and there are no indications that nineteen years of external pressure have changed its will or capacity to do so. Perversely, isolation may help sustain military rule. The military has long experience in dealing with domestic dissent and the economics of survival in a poor and strife-torn country, and has become quite adept at it. A greater threat to such reactionary leaders would be engagement with and by the outside world, which would open up both the state and society to new influences and feed popular aspirations and visions for change.

Critically engaging Burma does not mean giving in to authoritarianism or accepting human rights abuses. Rather, it is a rational reorientation of international efforts to facilitate political and economic reform in a country where little progress has been made since 1988 (or seems likely in the foreseeable future, if current policies are maintained). A broader, more process-oriented approach is both *necessary* to overcome military resistance to reform and *prudent* given the difficulty of instituting democratic governance, particularly if it is born out of political or socioeconomic upheaval rather than through an incremental, negotiated transition. In fact, by increasing direct interactions with all parts of the Burmese state and society, and providing new perspectives on the world and Burma's own future, engagement strengthens pressures for change on the ground where it matters.

The opposition generally has resisted efforts to address development issues until an elected government is in place, arguing that it would only strengthen the military regime. While this may be true in the short term, the longer-term effect, however, is to weaken the structures of authoritarianism, strengthen the basis for effective democratic governance, and generally improve human security and welfare. By contrast, continued failure by all sides to deal with the country's complex development challenges is driving Burma ever closer to the proverbial edge, and could well overwhelm any future government and sentence the country and its people to another half a century of conflict and immense human suffering. It is important not to make principles the enemy of the good.

Notes

1. "Impact of US Pressures and Sanctions," confidential paper, 8 August 2003.

2. Maung Zarni, who in the 1990s spearheaded the grassroots boycott movement against companies engaged in Burma based on the South African model, but since has rejected this strategy as ineffectual and counterproductive, makes an explicit comparison between the ANC and the NLD:

> The ANC was categorically different from the NLD, both in its leadership capabilities, its strategic framework which did not rule out political violence as part of its overall work, organizational strength, the level of mass participation (at all costs to the participants), and the wisdom and calibre of South African exiles who operated from Western and northern Europe. . . . The ANC, under an extremely repressive regime, was capable of building its new generations up and created a multi-tier leadership, both within the country and among the exiles. As a result, even when Mandela was locked up and was used initially as the rallying icon, his capable comrades in exile and within the country were able to execute numerous political activities, both violent and non-violent, successfully. Zarni, "Apartheid South Africa and Burma under Military Rule: A Wrong Comparison," 3 June 2005, www.freeburmacoalition.org/ (accessed 28 January 2007).

3. Anton David Lowenberg and William H. Kaempfer, *The Origins and Demise of South African Apartheid: A Public Choice Analysis* (Ann Arbor: University of Michigan Press, 1998), 3.

4. This transformation has perhaps been most dramatic for the armed ethnic leaders, who after decades of isolation in their remote mountain strongholds are now traveling to Rangoon to express their views directly to the government and other Burman-dominated groups, not to mention having more interaction with each other than ever before. Yet, for the general population as well, increased opportunities for organizing and working together for common goals are evident, even if they remain largely nonpolitical, and are slowly building social capital in the wider society.

Bibliography

88 Generation Students. "Statement on Humanitarian Assistance to Myanmar." 6 September 2005.

"Accelerating Progress among the Rural Poor in Myanmar." Confidential report, 15 September 1995.

Ad-Hoc Commission on Depayin Massacre. "Preliminary Report." 4 July 2003.

Agence France Presse, 24 October 1996–3 October 1998.

ALTSEAN. "Interview with Aung San Suu Kyi." 15 July 1998. www.kyoto-seika.ac.jp/eng/1_intro/altsean.htm (accessed 25 April 2007).

———. "Pressure Works: Burma Backs Off from ASEAN Chair." 6 August 2005.

———. "Ready, Aim, Sanction." November 2003.

Amnesty International. "Burma: The 18th September 1988 Military Takeover and Its Aftermath." December 1988.

———. "Myanmar: The Administration of Justice: Grave and Abiding Concerns." 1 April 2004.

———. "Myanmar: Exodus from the Shan State." 10 July 2000.

———. "Myanmar: Justice on Trial." 30 July 2003.

———. "Myanmar: The Lack of Security in Counter-Insurgency Areas." 17 July 2002.

———. "Myanmar: Leaving Home." 8 September 2005.

———. "Myanmar: Travesties of Justice—Continued Misuse of the Legal System." 12 December 2005.

Ardeth Maung Thawnghmung. "Paddy Farmers and the State: Agricultural Policies and Legitimacy in Rural Myanmar." PhD diss., University of Wisconsin–Madison, 2001.

Article 19. "Censorship Prevails: Political Deadlock and Economic Transition in Burma." London: March 1995.

Asian Development Bank. "Asian Development Outlook 2002." December 2002.

Asian Wall Street Journal, 6 November 1998.

Asiaweek, 28 October 1989–17 December 1999.

———. "Suu Kyi Says Australia Hampers Myanmar Democracy." 23 September 1999.

Associated Press. "Myanmar, Thailand Sign US$6 Billion Hydropower Plant Agreement." *BurmaNet News*, 4 April 2006. www.burmanet.org/news (accessed 4 April 2006).

———. "NLD No More Influence." *BurmaNet News*, 27 March 2006. www.burmanet.org/news (accessed 27 March 2006).

Aung Lwin. "The German Connection." *Burma Issues*, January 1994.

Aung San Suu Kyi. "Intellectual Life in India and Burma under Colonialism." In Aung San Suu Kyi, *Freedom from Fear, and Other Writings*, 82–139. London: Penguin Books, 1991.

———. Letter to Gustave Speth, UNDP administrator, dated 14 January 1996. [Copy in author's possession.]

———. Message to the Briefing on Burma. New York, 25 May 1997.

———. "Speech to a Mass Rally at the Shwedagon Pagoda." In *Freedom from Fear and Other Writings*, 192–98. London: Penguin Books, 1995.

———. *The Voice of Hope: Conversations with Alan Clements*. London: Penguin Books, 1997.

Aung Zaw. "Burmese Feel That Sanctions Must Stay." *Irrawaddy* (print ed.) 9, no. 4, May 2001.

———. "Regrets: The Residue of the 1990 Election." *Irrawaddy* (online ed.), 27 May 2005. www.irrawaddy.org (accessed 27 May 2005).

Australian Agency for International Development (AusAID). "Country Information." www.ausaid.gov.au (accessed 20 March 2005).

Australian Embassy Yangon. "Comments by Australian Foreign Minister, the Hon Alexander Downer, MP on Myanmar Made at Media Conferences in Hanoi." Press release, 1 August 2001.

Australian Government, Department of Foreign Affairs and Trade. *Asian Agrifood Demand Trends to 2010*. Canberra: DFAT, July 2004.

Backpack Health Worker Team. "Chronic Emergency: Health and Human Rights in Eastern Burma." 2006.

Badgley, John H., ed. "Reconciling Burma/Myanmar: Essays on U.S. Relations with Burma." Special issue, *NBR Analysis* 15, no. 1 (March 2004).

———. "Remodelling Myanmar." In *Myanmar Dilemmas and Options: The Challenge of Economic Transition in the 1990s*, edited by Mya Than and Joseph L. H. Tan. Singapore: ISEAS, 1990.

Ball, Desmond. "Burma and Drugs: The Regime's Complicity in the Global Drug Trade." Working Paper No. 336. Strategic and Defence Studies Centre, Australian National University, Canberra, 1999.

BBC. Burmese language news broadcast, 10 May 2003.

"Boosting Myanmar's Agricultural Productivity: A Look at Fertiliser, Credit and Rice Pricing Policies." Confidential report, February 1998.

"A Brief History of the National Democratic Movement of Ethnic Nationalities." August 2000.

Burma Border Consortium. "Internally Displaced People and Relocation Sites in Eastern Burma." September 2002.

Burma Campaign UK. "Companies Not Supporting the Regime in Burma." N.d. www.burmacampaign.org.uk/dirty_list/clean_list.html (accessed 22 January 2007).

———. "Pro-Aid, Pro-Sanctions, Pro-Engagement: A Position Paper on Humanitarian Aid." July 2006.

Burma Digest. "Interview with Former Malaysia Prime Minister Mahathir Mohamad." 16 November 2006. http://burmadigest.wordpress.com (accessed 10 January 2007).

———. "Interview with Raluca Enescu." 26 September 2006. http://burmadigest.wordpress.com (accessed 10 January 2007).

Burma Ethnic Research Group (BERG). "Forgotten Victims of a Hidden War: Internally Displaced Karen in Burma." April 1998.

BurmaNet Editor. "Analysis of the USDA." *BurmaNet News*, 2 November 1996. www.burmanet.org/bnn_archives/1996/bnn1196n557.txt (accessed 26 April 2007).

Callahan, Mary P. "Cracks in the Edifice? Changes in Military-Society Relations in Burma since 1988." In *Burma/Myanmar: Strong Regime, Weak State*, edited by Morten B. Pedersen, Emily Rudland, and R. J. May, 22–51. Adelaide, Australia: Crawford House, 2000.

———. "Democracy in Burma: The Lessons of History." *NBR Analysis* 9, no. 3 (May 1998): 5–27.

———. *Making Enemies: War and State Building in Burma*. Ithaca, NY: Cornell University Press, 2003.

———. "On Time Warps and Warped Time: Lessons from Burma's Democratic Era." In *Burma: Prospects for a Democratic Future*, edited by Robert I. Rotberg, 49–68. Washington, DC: Brookings Institution Press, 1998.

Carothers, Thomas. "Think Again: Civil Society." *Foreign Policy* (Winter 1999–2000): 18–29.

Casey, Michael. "Humanitarian Crisis Looming in Impoverished Myanmar." Associated Press, 6 December 2005. Posted on *BurmaNet News*, 6 December 2005. www.burmanet.org/news (accessed 6 December 2005).

Central Statistical Organization. *Statistical Yearbook*. Government of Myanmar, 2001.

Chan Nyein. "Clarifications of Progress Made in the Education Sector." Presentation at government press conference, Naypyidaw, 29 November 2006. http://mission.itu.ch/MISSIONS/Myanmar/pressrelease/Press%20Release%2029%20nov%2006.pdf (accessed 27 April 2007).

Christian Aid. "Burma's Dirty War: The Humanitarian Crisis in Eastern Burma." May 2004.

Christian Solidarity Worldwide. "CSW Calls on UK Government to Ban Investment in Burma." www.csw.org.uk/latestnews/print.php?id+552 (accessed 12 December 2006).

Clap, Pricilla. "Can the Generals Face Their Demons?" Paper presented at the U.S. State Department Bureau of Intelligence and Research (INR) Workshop, Washington, DC, 16 September 2003.

Colignon, Stephan. "The Burmese Economy and the Withdrawal of European Trade Preferences." Briefing Paper No. 97/02, European Institute for Asian Studies, April 1997.

Committee Representing People's Parliament (CRPP). Notification 1/1998, 16 September 1998.

"Commodity Composition of Exports." Confidential paper, 2 November 2004.

Conservative Party Human Rights Commission. "Conservative MP's Call for Debate on Burma." 30 October 2006. www.conservativehumanrights.com/news/october06/30.10.06_burmandebate.htm (accessed 14 December 2006).

Cook, Paul, and Martin Minogue. "Economic Reform and Political Change in Myanmar." *World Development* 21, no. 7 (1993): 1151–61.

Council of the European Union. *Common Position of 25 October 2004* (2004/423/CFSP).

———. *Common Position of 28 October 1996* (96/635/CFSP).

———. "Council Conclusions." 16 June 2003. http://europa.eu.int/comm/external_relations/myanmar/intro/gac.htm (accessed 15 March 2005).

———. *Decision 98/612/CFSP Concerning Extension of Common Position* (96/635/CFSP). 26 October 1998.

———. Press release no. 101-7533/00, 10 April 2000.

Council on Foreign Relations. "Burma: A Time for Change." Report of an independent task force, June 2003.

Craner, Lorne W. Testimony before the House International Relations Committee, Subcommittee on Asia and the Pacific, 25 March 2004.

Cranston, Alan. Statement on the floor of the Senate, 12 March 1992.

D'Amato, Alfonso. Introduction of the *Burma Freedom and Democracy Act* before the Senate Banking Committee, 22 May 1996.

Dapice, David. "Development Prospects for Burma: Cycles and Trends." In *Burma: Prospects for a Democratic Future*, edited by Robert I. Rotberg, 153–64. Washington, DC: Brookings Institute Press, 1998.

Democratic Alliance of Burma. *(Future) Federal Union of Burma Constitution* [draft]. N.p: NCUB, 1995.

Democratic Voice of Burma. "No Plan to Talk to the NLD." 28 January 2003. www.burmanet.org/bnn_archives/2003/20030130.txt (accessed 26 April 2007).

Department for International Development (DFID). "Burma: Country Strategy Paper." July 2000.

Department of Health Planning. *Multiple Indicator Cluster Survey*. N.p.: Government of Myanmar, 2000.

Diamond, Larry. *Developing Democracy: Toward Consolidation*. Baltimore: Johns Hopkins University Press, 1999.

Diller, Jeanelle M. "The National Convention: An Impediment to the Restoration of Democracy." In *Burma: The Challenge of Change in a Divided Society*, edited by Peter Carey, 27–54. Houndsmills, England: MacMillan Press, 1997.

EarthRights International. "Destructive Engagement: A Decade of Foreign Investment." October 1999.

———. "If We Don't Have Time to Take Care of Our Fields." 24 April 2005.

———. "Turning Treasure into Tears: Mining, Dams, and Deforestation in Shwegyin Township, Pegu Division, Burma." 20 February 2007.

Economist Intelligence Unit. "Myanmar: Quarterly Review." 1st Quarter, 1997.

European Commission. "EC-Burma/Myanmar Country Strategy (2007–2013)." Draft, November 2005.

———. "Report on Myanmar." Internal document, November 2003.

Europe-Burma Office. "Aung San Suu Kyi Raises the Stakes for Dialogue." General release, Brussels, 6 August 2002.

Fachett, Derek. "Burma." Speech at the Christian Aid/Burma Action Group Conference on Burma, Regent's College, London, 15 October 1998.

Far Eastern Economic Review. "Interview with Aung San Suu Kyi." 7 May 1998.

Fink, Christina. "An Independent Evaluation of Endowment-Funded Ethnic Nationality-Related Projects in Burma." Report prepared for the National Endowment for Democracy, Washington, DC, May 2000.

———. *Living Silence: Burma under Military Rule*. Bangkok: White Lotus, 2001.

Food and Agriculture Organization of the United Nations (FAO). "Food Insecurity and Vulnerability Information and Mapping System." Unpublished document, 2004. [Copy in author's possession.]

"Food Security in Myanmar: A Proposal to Deal with Natural Shocks." Confidential report, January 2000.

"Food Security in Myanmar: A Review of Issues." Confidential report, May 2004.

"Fort Wayne Declaration." Statement issued by exiled activists after a meeting in Fort Wayne, IN, 30–31 August 2003.

Furnivall, J. S. *Colonial Policy and Practice: A Comparative Study of Burma and Netherlands India*. New York: New York University Press, 1956.

Galtung, Johan. "On the Effects of International Economic Sanctions." *World Politics* 19, no. 3 (April 1967): 378–416.

Gelbard, Robert. Testimony before the Senate Subcommittee on Foreign Operations, 24 July 1995.

Global Fund. "Fact Sheet: Termination of Grants to Myanmar." 18 August 2005. www.theglobalfund.org (accessed 29 January 2007).

Global IDP database. www.idpproject.org/ (accessed 15 July 2005).

Global Trade Information Services. *World Trade Atlas*, 2001–2003. www.worldtradestatistics.com/state/.

Global Witness. "A Conflict of Interests. The Uncertain Future of Burma's Forests." October 2003.

Greg, Judd, Mitch McConnell, and Sam Brownback. Letter to Richard G. A. Feachem, executive director of the Global Fund, dated 28 September 2004. [Copy in author's possession.]

Guyot, James F. "Burmese Praetorianism." In *Tradition and Modernity in Myanmar*, edited by Uta Gartner and Jens Lorenz, 129–48. Münster: LIT, 1994.

Hadar, Leon T. "US Sanctions against Burma: A Failure on All Fronts." *Trade Policy Analysis*, no. 1 (26 March 1998).

Harkin, Tom. Statement in the Senate on introduced bills and joint resolutions, 22 May 2001.

Havel, Vaclav, and Desmond Tutu. "Threat to the Peace: A Call for the Security Council to Act in Burma." September 2005.

Heder, Stephen R. "The Struggle for Democracy and Human Rights in Myanmar: Opposition Politics in a Situation of Severe Repression." In *Human Rights in the Asia-Pacific Region*, edited by John Girling. Canberra: Australian National University, 1991.

Heidel, Brian. *The Growth of Civil Society in Myanmar*. Bangalore, India: Books for Change, 2006.

"Household Livelihood Security Needs in Kokang Region." Confidential report, July 2003.

Houtman, Gustaaf. *Mental Culture in Burmese Crisis Politics*. Tokyo: Institute for the Study of Languages and Cultures of Asia and Africa, Tokyo University of Foreign Languages, 1999.

Hubbard, Thomas C. Testimony before the House Subcommittee on Asian and Pacific Affairs, 28 November 1994.

Human Rights Watch/Asia. "Crackdown on Burmese Muslims." July 2002.

Ibrahim, Zaid. "Losing Patience with Burma." *Wall Street Journal*, 13 January 2006.

Igboemeka, Adeze. "Aid Effectiveness in Burma/Myanmar." August 2005. www2.dfid.gov.uk/mdg/aid-effectiveness/newsletters/burma-report.pdf (accessed 2 December 2006).

Images Asia and Pan Kachin Development Society. "At What Price? Gold Mining in Kachin State, Burma." November 2004.

"Impact of US Pressures and Sanctions." Confidential paper, 8 August 2003.

INEB Reader. Bi-Monthly Newsletter of the International Network of Engaged Buddhists (September/October 1994), 7.

Institute for Asian Democracy. "Towards Democracy in Burma." 1992.

Internal Displacement Monitoring Centre (IDMC). "Myanmar (Burma)." www.internal-displacement.org/ (accessed 20 April 2007).

International Coalition for Banning Landmines. "Landmine Reporter." 2003. www.icbl.org/lm/2003/ (accessed 26 January 2007).

International Committee of the Red Cross (ICRC). "Annual Report—Myanmar." 17 June 2005. www.icrc.org/ (accessed 28 January 2007).

International Confederation of Free Trade Unions. "Doing Business with Burma." January 2005.

International Crisis Group. "Myanmar: Aid to the Border Areas." Asia Report, 9 September 2004.

———. "Myanmar Backgrounder: Ethnic Minority Politics." Asia Report, 7 May 2003.

———. "Myanmar: New Threats to Humanitarian Aid." Asia Briefing, 8 December 2006.

———. "Myanmar: The Role of Civil Society." Asia Report, 6 December 2001.

International Labor Organization (ILO). "ILO Concludes 87th Conference." Press release, 17 June 1999.

———. "ILO Governing Body Concludes 292nd Session." Press release, 24 March 2005.

———. "International Labor Conference Adopts Resolution Targeting Forced Labour in Myanmar." Press release, 14 June 2000.

———. "Myanmar: Forced Labour Convention, 1930 (no. 29)." Report of the Committee of Experts on the Application of Conventions and Recommendations, 74th session, 2003.

International Monetary Fund (IMF). "Myanmar: Recent Economic Developments." Staff report for the 2006 Article IV Consultation, 2 March 2004.

Irrawaddy (online ed.). "Activists in Burma Start New Campaign." 3 January 2007. www.irrawaddy.org (accessed 3 January 2007).

———. "KNLA Commanders Accuse Unnamed KNU Leaders." 31 July 2006. www.irrawaddy.org (accessed 31 July 2006).

———. "The New Word from Washington." 1 May 2006. www.irrawaddy.org (accessed 1 May 2006).

———. "NLD Under New Threat." 27 April 2006. www.irrawaddy.org (accessed 27 April 2006).

Japan Times, 5 February 1999.

Johnstone, William C. *Burma's Foreign Policy: A Study in Neutralism*. Cambridge, MA: Harvard University Press, 1963.

Joint Kokang-Wa Humanitarian Needs Assessment Team. "Replacing Opium in Kokang and Wa Special Regions." March 2003.

Joint United Nations Programme on HIV/AIDS (UNAIDS). "The United Nations Joint Action Plan on HIV/AIDS." 2001–2002.

Jordt, Ingrid. "Mass Lay Meditation and State-Society Relations in Post-Independence Burma." PhD diss., Harvard University, Cambridge, MA, May 2001.

Karen Human Rights Group. "Setting Up the Systems of Repression." 7 September 2006.

"Kayah Needs Assessment Project." Confidential report, March 2003.

Kelly, James A. "U.S. and Burma." Dinner talk given at the Paul H. Nitze School of Advanced International Studies Conference on Burma, Washington, DC, 21 November 2002.

Kessler, Glenn. "U.S. Sees Burma as a 'Test Case' in Southeast Asia." *Washington Post*, 3 January 2006.

Khin Nyunt. Address delivered at the closing of the ceremony of the Special Refresher Course No. 3 for officers of the Development Department, Central Institute of Civil Service, Phaunggyi, 21 November 1997. In *Mental Culture in Burmese Crisis Politics*, by Gustaff Houtman, 25. Tokyo: Institute for the Study of Languages and Cultures of Asia and Africa, Tokyo University of Foreign Languages, 1999.

———. "Developments and Progressive Changes in Myanmar Naing-ngan." Clarifications at the Pyithu Hluttaw, Rangoon, 30 August 2003.

Khin Zaw Win. "Impoverishment as Freedom: An Orwellian Double-Speak." N.d. www.freeburmacoalition.org (accessed 27 January 2007).

Kinnock, Glenys. "Travellers Should Boycott Burma." *Times*, 9 May 2001.

Kyaw Thein. "An Analysis of the Return of Armed Groups of National Races to the Legal Fold and the Renunciation of Armed Insurrection." Paper presented at the Symposium on Socio-Economic Factors Contributing to National Consolidation, Rangoon, 9–11 October 1996.

Kyaw Yin Hlaing. "Burma: Skirting the Regime's Rules." In *Civil Society and Political Change in Asia: Expanding and Contracting Democratic Space*, edited by Muthiah Alagappa, 389–418. Stanford: Stanford University Press, 2004.

———. "Myanmar in 2004: Why Military Rule Continues." *Southeast Asian Affairs*, 2005.

———. Remarks made at a panel on Burma at the Paul H. Nitze School of Advanced International Studies, Washington, DC, 25 March 2004.

———. "Will Western Sanctions Bring Down the House?" In "Reconciling Burma/Myanmar: Essays on U.S. Relations with Burma," ed. John H. Badgley. Special issue, *NBR Analysis* 15, no. 1 (March 2004): 73–85.

Kyaw Zwa Moe. "Farewell to the Liberated Areas." *Irrawaddy* (print ed.) 13, no. 2 (February 2005).

Kyi May Kaung. "Sanctions and Burma: Shades of Grey." *Foreign Policy in Focus: Strategic Dialogue*, 18 January 2007. www.fpif.org/fpiftxt/3917 (accessed 25 January 2007).

Landaburu, Eneko. "Supporting People—Assisting Transition." Paper presented at the Burma/Myanmar Forum, European Institute for Asian Studies, Brussels, 29 March 2006.

Lantos, Tom. Comments at Oversight Hearing, "Developments in Burma," House Subcommittee on Asia and the Pacific, Washington, DC, 25 March 2004.

Larkin, Stuart. "Thoughts on a Pro-Poor Growth Strategy for Myanmar." Report prepared for the United Nations Development Programme/Myanmar, 29 May 2002.

Leaders' Magazine, April–June 1998.

Liddell, Zunetta. "International Policies towards Burma: Western Governments, NGOs and Multilateral Institutions." In *Challenges to Democratization in Burma: Perspectives on Multilateral and Bilateral Responses*, edited by International Institute of Democracy and Electoral Assistance, 131–82. Stockholm: IDEA, 2001.

Lintner, Bertil. *Outrage: Burma's Struggle for Democracy*. Bangkok: White Lotus, 1990.

Los Angeles Times, 27 December 2005.

Lowenberg, Anton David, and William H. Kaempfer. *The Origins and Demise of South African Apartheid: A Public Choice Analysis*. Ann Arbor: University of Michigan Press, 1998.

Luckham, Robin. "The International Community and State Reconstruction in War-Torn Societies." *Conflict, Security and Development* 4, no. 3 (December 2004): 481–507.

Mathieson, David. "Burma: A State of Cachexia." Honors diss., Flinders University, Adelaide, Australia, August 2000.

Maung Aung Myoe. "Building the Tatmadaw: The Organisational Development of the Armed Forces in Myanmar, 1948–98." Working Paper No. 327, Strategic and Defence Studies Centre, Australian National University, Canberra, 1998.

———. "Officer Education and Leadership Training." Working Paper No. 346. Strategic and Defence Studies Centre, Australian National University, Canberra, 2000.

Maung Aye. "Address at the 50th Anniversary Special Commemorative Session of the UNGA." 23 October 1995. In NCGUB, "Report of the NCGUB Delegation on the 50th Session of the United Nations General Assembly," 1995.

Maung Maung. *Burma and General Ne Win*. Bombay: Asia Publishing House, 1969.

———. *The 1988 Uprising in Burma*. New Haven, CT: Yale University Southeast Asia Studies, 1999.

Maung Maung Gyi. "Foreign Policy of Burma since 1962: Negative Neutralism for Group Survival." In *Military Rule in Burma since 1962*, edited by F. K. Lehman, 47–77. Singapore: Maruzen Press, 1981.

McConnell, Mitch. "Sanctions Are the Most Effective Weapon against Burma's Military Regime." *Times Asia*, 23 January 2006.

———. Statement of the floor of the Senate, 8 December 1995.

———. "Statement on the State Department FY'05 Budget Request." Press release, 8 April 2004.

———. Testimony on the *Burma Freedom and Democracy Act* before the Senate Banking Committee, 22 May 1996.

Michael Aung-Thwin. "1948 and Burma's Myth of Independence." In *Independent Burma at Forty Years: Six Assessments*, edited by Josef Silverstein, 19–34. Ithaca, NY: Southeast Asian Program, Cornell University, 1989.

———. "Parochial Universalism, Democracy Jihad and the Orientalist Image of Burma: The New Evangelism." *Pacific Affairs* 74, no. 4 (Winter 2001–2002): 483–505.

Miller, Eric. "Forced Labour Blues—ILO Action." *Burma Issues* 10, no. 3 (August 2000).

Mizzima News. "British MPs, Activists Urge UK to Ban Investments." 3 October 2006. www.mizzima.com/MizzimaNews/News/2006/Oct/index.html (accessed 3 October 2006).

———. "Interview with Karen Leader Saw Bo Mya." 15 March 2004. www.mizzima.com/Interview/15-mar04-03.htm (accessed 26 April 2007).

Moe Kyaw. "Report on the Textile and Garment Industry." Yangon, 2001.

Mon Forum. "USDA: The Organization Strengthening Military Rule in Burma (Myanmar)." No. 4 (2005): 6–16.

Mon Unity League. "The Mon: A People without a Country." N.d. [Copy in author's possession.]

Mowat, Jonathan. "The New Gladio in Action?" *Online Journal*, 19 March 2005. www.onlinejournal.com (accessed 20 January 2007).

Myanmar Ahlin Aung Than. *Record of Multi-Party Democracy General Election*. Rangoon: Aung Sitthi Sarpay, 2002.

Myanmar Information Committee. "Information Sheet." 19 August 1999–30 August 2003. www.myanmar-information.net/.

"Myanmar Textile and Garment Industry." Confidential report, November 2003.

Myanmar Times, 13 May 2002–22 August 2005.

Mya Win. *Tatmadaw's Traditional Role in National Politics*. Yangon: News and Periodicals Enterprise, 1991.

Nandar Chann. "Opposition Blues." *Irrawaddy* (print ed.) 13, no. 2 (February 2005).

The Nation, 23 April 1996–26 July 1997.

———. "Canberra Coalition Will Maintain Burma Policy." 23 April 1996.

National Coalition Government of the Union of Burma (NCGUB). "The Birth of NCGUB." In *Democracy and Politics in Burma: A Collection of Documents*, edited by Marc Weller, 236–38. Manerplaw: NCGUB, 1991.

———. "Bommersvik Declaration." Convention of Elected Representatives, 27 July 1995.

———. "Declaration of the National Coalition Government of the Union of Burma, 18 December 1990." In *Democracy and Politics in Burma: A Collection of Documents*, edited by Marc Weller, 238–40. Manerplaw: NCGUB, 1991.

———. "Report of the NCGUB Delegation on the 50th Session of the United Nations General Assembly." 1995.

———. "Scores Killed in Junta Attack on NLD Motorcade." News desk, 1 June 2003.

———. "Statement on U.S. Aid Policy." Council of Foreign Relations, 28 October 1992.

———. "Statement to the People of Burma, 18 December 1990." In *Democracy and Politics in Burma: A Collection of Documents*, edited by Marc Weller, 241–42. Manerplaw: NCGUB, 1991.

National Council of the Union of Burma. *Future Constitution of the Federal Union of Burma* [proposed draft]. N.p.: NCUB, 1996.

National League for Democracy (NLD). "Gandhi Hall Declaration." 28 July 1990.

———. "Observations of the National League for Democracy on the National Convention." Statement given at NLD press conference, NLD Headquarter, Rangoon, 22 November 1995.

———. "Special Declaration No. 1/02 (2006)." 12 February 2006.

———. "Special Statement." 20 April 2006. [Copy in author's possession.]

———. "Statement No. 52." August 1998.

———. "Statement on the 55th Anniversary of Independence Day." 4 January 2003.

———. "Statement on the 56th Anniversay of Union Day." 12 February 2003.

———. "Update: September 1990." In *Democracy and Politics in Burma: A Collection of Documents*, edited by Marc Weller, 197–98. Manerplaw: NCGUB, 1991.

National League for Democracy (NLD) and United Nationalities League for Democracy (UNLD). "Bo Aung Kyaw Street Declaration." 30 August 1990.

National Nutrition Centre. "National Nutrition Survey." 1997.

Nawrahta. *Destiny of the Nation*. Yangon: News and Periodicals Enterprise, 1995.

Neier, Aryeh. Memorandum to Brad Herbert (Global Fund). 24 September 2004. [Copy in author's possession.]

Nemoto, Kei. "Aung San Suu Kyi, Her Dream and Reality." Discussion Paper No. 1, Kansai Institute of Asia-Pacific Studies, Osaka University of Foreign Studies, April 1996.

Network for Democracy and Development. "The White Shirts." May 2006.

New England Burma Roundtable. "Action Update: Hall Plans Not to Offer Pro-Junta Amendment." 16 July 1999. Posted on BurmaNet List, 16 July 1999.

New Light of Myanmar, 5 January 1998–5 May 2006.

———. "Press Conference Clarifies Instigations to Cause Unrest." 1 June 2003.

Nielson, Poul. "Advocating the Needs of the Vulnerable." Keynote address at Open Burma Day, Brussels, October 2003.

Nu, U. Speech delivered in Parliament, 5 September 1950. In *From Peace to Stability: Selected Speeches*, 95–105. Rangoon: GOB, 1951.

O'Brien, Harriet. *Forgotten Land: A Rediscovery of Burma*. London: Michael Joseph, 1991.

Oehlers, Alfred. "Sanctions and Burma: Revisiting the Case Against." *Burma Economic Watch*, no. 2 (2004): 36–46.

O'Hanlon, David. "Whatever Happened to the ABSDF?" *Irrawaddy* (print ed.) 9, no. 9 (December 2001).

Ohn Gyaw. "Statement Concerning Developments in Myanmar." Statement given at the UN General Assembly, Third Committee, 51st Session, 1 October 1996.

Organisation for Economic Co-operation and Development (OECD). "Geographical Distribution of Financial Flows to Aid Recipients." January 2006.

Ott, Marvin C. "From Isolation to Relevance: Policy Considerations." In *Burma: Prospects for a Democratic Future*, edited by Robert I. Rotberg, 69–85. Washington, DC: Brookings Institution Press, 1998.

"Pattern of Household Consumption Expenditure." Confidential paper, 2 November 2004.

Petrie, Charles. "Speaking Notes." Prepared for the Burma/Myanmar Forum, European Institute for Asian Studies, Brussels, 29 March 2006.

Pollard, William E., and Terence R. Mitchell. "Decision Theory Analysis of Social Power." *Psychological Bulletin* 78, no. 6 (1972): 433–46.

Preeg, Ernest H. "Myanmar: Phasing in Sanctions in Asia." In *Feeling Good or Doing Good with Sanctions*, edited by Ernest H. Preeg. Washington, DC: Center for Strategic and International Studies, 1999.

"Prospects for Sustainable Growth in Burma/Myanmar." Confidential report, 12 September 1995.

Purcell, Marc. "Axehandles or Willing Minions? International NGOs in Burma." In *Strengthening Civil Society in Burma: Possibilities and Dilemmas for International NGOs*, edited by Burma Centre Netherlands, 69–109. Chiang Mai, Thailand: Silkworm Books, 1999.

Pye, Lucian. "Civility, Social Capital and Civil Society: Three Powerful Concepts of Explaining Asia." *Journal of Interdisciplinary History* 29, no. 4 (1998).

Radio Free Asia. Burmese language news broadcast, 23 April 2003.

"Report from Ethnic Nationalities Seminar held at Mae Tha Raw Hta, 7–14 January 1997." N.d.

Reuters, 27 April–23 December 1999.

———. "Australia Defends Rights Visit to Myanmar." 5 August 1999.

Risse, Thomas, Stephen C. Ropp, and Kathryn Sikkink, eds. *The Power of Human Rights: International Norms and Domestic Change*. Cambridge: Cambridge University Press, 1999.

Robertson, Philip S., Jr. "Sanctions Are Working in Burma." *Irrawaddy* (online ed.), 26 August 2003. www.irrawaddy.org (accessed 26 August 2003).

Rohrabacher, Dana. Statement before the House Subcommittee on Asian and Pacific Affairs, 8 May 1990.

———. Statement on the floor of the House of Representatives, 23 May 1996.

"The Role of the Tatmadaw in the Economy." Confidential report, 2000.

Rudland, Emily. "Health, HIV and the State in Myanmar." In *The Illusion of Progress: The Political Economy of Reform in Burma/Myanmar*, edited by David S. Mathieson and Ron J. May, 163–99. Adelaide, Australia: Crawford House, 2004.

Sachs, Jeffrey. "Myanmar: Sanctions Won't Work." *Financial Times*, 27 July 2004.

Saffin, Janelle. "Comments on Paper by David I. Steinberg." Paper presented at the Conference on NGO Strategy for the Democratization of Burma, Seoul, Korea, 23–25 June 1999.

Safman, Rachel. "Assessing the Impact of HIV and Other Health Issues on Myanmar's Development." In *Myanmar: Beyond Politics to Societal Imperatives*, edited by Kyaw Yin Hlain, Robert Taylor, and Tin Maung Maung Than, 117–39. Singapore: ISEAS, 2005.

Saw Maung. "Address in Taungoo." In *Senior General Saw Maung's Addresses, Vol. III*, 119–96. Yangon: News and Periodicals Enterprise, 1991.

———. "Address to the Academy for the Development of National Groups." 21 February 1990. In *Senior General Saw Maung's Addresses, Vol. III*, 1–14. Yangon: News and Periodicals Enterprise, 1991.

Schock, Kurt. "People Power and Political Opportunities: Social Movement Mobilization and Outcomes in the Philippines and Burma." *Social Problems* 46, no. 3 (1999): 355–75.

Seekins, Donald. *The Disorder in Order: The Army State in Burma since 1962*. Bangkok: White Lotus, 2002.

Selth, Andrew. *Burma's Armed Forces: Power without Glory*. Norwalk, CT: EastBridge, 2002.

———. *Transforming the Tatmadaw: The Burmese Armed Forces since 1988*. Canberra: Strategic and Defence Studies Centre, Australian National University, 1996.

Seng Raw. "Views from Myanmar: An Ethnic Minority Perspective." In *Burma: Political Economy under Military Rule*, edited by Robert H. Taylor, 159–64. London: C. Hurst & Co., 2001.

Shan Human Rights Foundation and Shan Women's Action Network. "License to Rape." 2002.

Sharp, Gene. "Exploring Non-Violent Struggle in Thailand and Burma." *Nonviolent Sanctions: News from the Albert Einstein Foundation* IV, no. 2 (Fall 1992): 1–6.

Shwe Gas Movement. "Burma's Military Dictatorship to Gain over US$12 Billion Profits from Western Burma Gas Finds." Media release, 12 July 2006. www.shwe.org/media-releases/statements/July_12_press_release.pdf (accessed 12 January 2007).

Silverstein, Josef. "Aung San Suu Kyi: Is She Burma's Woman of Destiny?" *Asian Survey* 30, no. 10 (October 1990): 1007–19.

———. "Burmese and Malaysian Student Politics: A Preliminary Comparative Enquiry." *Journal of Southeast Asian Studies* 1, no. 1 (1970): 3–22.

———. "Civil War and Rebellion in Burma." *Journal of Southeast Asian Studies* 11, no. 1 (1990): 114–35.

———. "The Civil War, the Minorities and Burma's New Politics." In *Burma: The Challenge of Change in a Divided Society*, edited by Peter Carey, 80–92. Houndsmills, England: MacMillan Press, 1997.

Skidmore, Monique. *Karaoke Fascism: Burma and the Politics of Fear*. Philadelphia: University of Pennsylvania Press, 2004.

Smith, Martin. "Army Politics as a Historical Legacy." In *Political Armies: The Military and Nation Building in the Age of Democracy*, edited by Kees Koonings and Dirk Kruijt. London: Zed Books, 2002.

———. *Burma: Insurgency and the Politics of Ethnicity*. 2nd ed. London: Zed Books, 1999.

———. *Burma (Myanmar): The Time for Change*. N.p.: Minority Rights Group International, May 2002.

———. "Burmese Politics after 1988: An Era of New and Uncertain Change." In *Political Economy under Military Rule*, edited by Robert H. Taylor, 15–40. New York: Palgrave, 2001.

———. "Ethnic Participation and National Reconciliation in Myanmar: Challenges in a Transitional Landscape." Paper presented at the Burma/Myanmar Update, Australian National University, Canberra, 18–19 November 2004.

Solomon, Richard H. Testimony before the House Foreign Affairs Subcommittee for Asian and Pacific Affairs, 20 May 1992.

Soros, George. Testimony submitted for the Hearing on Burma, U.S. Senate Committee on Banking, Housing, and Urban Affairs, 22 May 1996.

South, Ashley. "Ceasefires and Civil Society: The Case of the Mon." Draft paper, 2002.

———. *Mon Nationalism and Civil War in Burma*. Richmond: Curzon, 2003.

———. "Roadmaps and Political Transition in Burma: The Need for Two-Way Traffic." *Irrawaddy* (online ed.), 16–17 October 2003. www.irrawaddy.org (accessed 17 October 2003).

South China Morning Post. "US Lawmaker Rejects Opposition Veto." 18 January 1999.

Special rapporteur on the situation of human rights in Myanmar. "Situation of Human Rights in Myanmar." Report to the United Nations General Assembly (A/58/150), 5 August 2003.

———. "Situation of Human Rights in Myanmar." Report to the United Nations General Assembly (A/61/369), 21 September 2006.

Spiro, Melford E. *Buddhism and Society*. Berkeley: University of California Press, 1982.

Stallworthy, Guy. "A NGO Perspective on Assistance in Myanmar." Paper presented at the European Commission's Burma Day 2005, Brussels, 6 April 2005.

State Law and Order Restoration Council (SLORC). 43rd News Conference, 9 June 1989.

———. 90th News Conference, 11 May 1990.

———. 100th News Conference, 13 July 1990.

———. 104th News Conference, 11 September 1990.

———. 107th News Conference, 7 December 1990.

———. Order No. 1/88, 18 September 1988.

———. Order No. 2/88, 18 September 1988.

———. Order No. 1/90, 27 July 1990.

———. Order No. 20/90, "Law Concerning Sangha Organisations." 31 October 1990.

———. Order No. 5/96, "Law Protecting the Peaceful and Systematic Transfer of State Responsibility and the Successful Performance of the Functions of the National Convention against Disturbances and Oppositions." June 1996.

Steinberg, David I. "Burma/Myanmar: A Guide for the Perplexed." In "Reconciling Burma/Myanmar: Essays on U.S. Relations with Burma," edited by John H. Badgley. Special issue, *NBR Analysis* 15, no. 1 (March 2004): 41–54.

———. "Burma/Myanmar and the Dilemmas of U.S. Foreign Policy." *Contemporary Southeast Asia* 21, no. 2 (August 1999): 283–311.

———. "Burma/Myanmar: The Role of the Military in the Economy." *Burma Economic Watch*, no. 1 (2005): 51–79.

———. *Burma: The State of Myanmar*. Washington, DC: Georgetown University Press, 2001.

———. "The Burmese Conundrum: Approaching Reformation of the Political Economy." In *Burma: Political Economy under Military Rule*, edited by Robert H. Taylor. New York: Palgrave, 2001.

———. "Contested Legitimacies in Burma/Myanmar." Paper prepared for the Myanmar Peace Initiative, Hiroshima Peace Institute, 16–18 March 2005.

———. "Liberalization in Myanmar: How Real Are the Changes?" *Contemporary Southeast Asia* 15, no. 2 (September 1993): *x–y*.

———. "Myanmar: The Anomalies of Politics and Economics." Working Paper No. 5, Asia Foundation, November 1997.

———. "The State, Power and Civil Society in Burma-Myanmar: The Status and Prospects for Pluralism." In *Burma/Myanmar: Strong Regime, Weak State*, edited by Morten B. Pedersen, Emily Rudland, and Ron May, 91–122. Adelaide, Australia: Crawford House, 2000.

Straits Times, 2 February 2006.

Study Group on the Myanmar Economy. *Current Situation of the Myanmar Economy and Its Future Development Strategy*. Tokyo: Institute of Fiscal and Monetary Policy, 1998.

Tarrow, Sidney. *Power in Movement*. 2nd ed. Cambridge: Cambridge University Press, 1998.

Tatmadaw Researcher. *A Concise History of Myanmar and the Tatmadaw's Role, 1948–1988*. Yangon, 1991.

Taylor, Debbie Aung Din. "Signs of Distress: Observations on Agriculture, Poverty and the Environment in Myanmar." Paper presented at Conference on Reconciliation in Burma and the Crises of Change, Johns Hopkins University, Washington, DC, 22 November 2002.

Taylor, Robert H. "External Dimensions of the Myanmar Situation." In *Myanmar and the Wider Southeast Asia—Proceedings of the International Seminar on ASEAN and the Wider Southeast Asia*, edited by Rohana Mahmood and Hans-Joachim Esderts. Kuala Lumpur: ISIS, 1991.

———. "Myanmar's Political Future: Is Waiting for the Perfect the Enemy of Doing the Possible?" In "Reconciling Burma/Myanmar: Essays on U.S. Relations with Burma," edited by John H. Badgley. Special issue, *NBR Analysis* 15, no. 1 (March 2004): 29–40.

———. "Political Values and Political Conflict in Burma." In *Burma: Prospects for a Democratic Future*, edited by Robert I. Rotberg, 33–48. Washington, DC: Brookings Institution Press, 1998.

———. "Stifling Political Change: The Army Remains in Command." Paper presented at the Conference on the Current Situation in Burma (Myanmar): Background, Prospects and Possible Solutions, Bonn, 24–26 July 1998.

———. "The Evolving Military Role in Burma." *Current History* 89 (March 1990): 105–8.

Thai Senate Standing Committee on Foreign Affairs. "Affidavits by Eyewitnesses of the Depayin Massacre." 4 July 2003.

Thailand Burma Border Consortium (TBBC). "Internal Displacement in Eastern Burma—2006 Survey." 26 October 2006.

Than Shwe. Letter to Thai prime minister Thaksin, dated July 2003. [Copy in author's possession.]

———. Speech at the graduation of the 49th Intake of the Defence Services Academic, Naypyidaw, 15 December 2006. http://mission.itu.ch/MISSIONS/Myanmar/statement&speech/speech_SGTS/SGTS_%2049%20DSA%20Intake%2015%20Dec%2006.htm (accessed 27 April 2007).

Thanegi, Ma. "The Burmese Fairytale." *Far Eastern Economic Review*, February 1998.

———. "Sanctions Don't Bring Burma Democracy." *International Herald Tribune*, 20 March 1998.

Thant Myint-U. *The River of Lost Foot Footsteps*. New York: Farrar, Straus and Giroux, 2007.

Three Diseases (3D) Fund. "What Is the Proposed 3D Fund?" Background briefing. 2006.

Time magazine, 15 November 1999.

Tin Maung Maung Than. *The Dilemmas of Stalled Reform*. Singapore: ISEAS, 2000.

———. "Myanmar: Military in Charge." In *Government and Politics in Southeast Asia*, edited by John Funston, 203–51. Singapore: ISEAS, 2001.

———. "Myanmar: The Dilemma of Stalled Reforms." *Trends in Southeast Asia*, no. 10 (September 2000).

———. "Myanmar's Golden Anniversary: Economic and Political Uncertainty." *Southeast Asian* Affairs, 1999: 207–34.

Tromp, H. W. "The Assessment of the Military Mind: A Critical Comment on Methodology." In *The Perceived Role of the Military*, edited by M. R. Van Gils. Rotterdam: Rotterdam University Press, 1971.

Tun Aung Chain. "The Broken Glass: Changes in the Perception of the Myanmar Past." *Myanmar Historical Research Journal* 6 (December 2000).

Turnell, Sean. "Burma Bank Update." *Burma Economic Watch*, no. 1 (2004): 19–27.

———. "Profiles of Burma's Banks." *Burma Economic Watch*, no. 1 (2006): 3–33.

Turnell, Sean, and Alison Vicary. "Burma's Banking Crisis: A Commentary." 6 March 2003. www.ibiblio.org/obl/docs/BEW2003-03.htm (accessed 27 April 2007).

Tutu, Desmond. "Foreword." Burma Sanctions Coalition briefing. March 2002. www.burmacampaign.org.uk/sanctions_briefing.html#foreword (accessed 21 January 2007).

Union Solidarity and Development Association (USDA). "Talking Points for the Discussion of the General Secretary of USDA with the Special Representative of the UN Secretary General," August 2005.

United Nations Children's Fund (UNICEF). "Child Risk Index." Unpublished document, n.d. [Copy in author's possession.]

———. "Children and Women in Myanmar: A Situation Assessment and Analysis." April 2001.

———. "Possibilities for a United Nations Peace and Development Initiative for Myanmar." Draft letter to the UN secretary-general, 16 March 1992. [Copy in author's possession.]

United Nations Commission on Human Rights, 61st session. "Resolution on the Situation of Human Rights in Myanmar," 11 April 2005.

United Nations Country Team (Myanmar). "Country Paper." Internal working paper, January 2000.

———. "Presentation on the May 2004 UNCT Mission to the Wa Region." Paper presented at the Mini Dublin Group Meeting, Rangoon, August 2004.

———. "A Silent Humanitarian Crisis in the Making." Letter to head offices, dated 30 June 2001. [Copy in author's possession.]

United Nations Department of Public Information. "Security Council Fails to Adopt Draft Resolution" (SC/8939). 12 January 2007.

United Nations Development Programme (UNDP) Governing Council. "Assistance to Myanmar" (Decision 92/26). 26 May 1992.

———. "Human Development Report 2004." N.d.

———. "Human Development Report 2006." N.d.

United Nations Drug Control Programme (UNDCP). "Northern Wa Region: Report on Opium Poppy Survey with Socio-Economic Findings." June 2002.

United Nations Economic and Social Commission for Asia and the Pacific (UNESCAP). "Statistical Yearbook for Asia and the Pacific 2001." October 2001.

United Nations General Assembly, 48th session. *Resolution on the Situation of Human Rights in Myanmar* (A/RES/48/150). 20 December 1993.

———, 61st session. Item 67(c). *Recorded Vote* (A/C.3/61/L.38/Rev.1). 22 November 2006.

United Nations Office on Drugs and Crime (UNODC). "Opium Poppy Cultivation in the Golden Triangle October 2006: Lao PDR, Myanmar, Thailand," October 2006.

———. "UNCT Mission to the Wa Region." Paper presented at the Mini Dublin Group Meeting, Yangon, August 2004.

United States National Drug Intelligence Center. "National Drug Threat Assessment 2007." October 2006.

U.S. Congress, 101st, 2nd session. H.R. 1594, *Customs and Trade Act of 1990*. N.d.

U.S. Congress, 103rd, 2nd session. *Foreign Relations Authorization Act, Fiscal Years 1994 and 1995*. 28 April 1994.

———, 104th, 2nd session. H.R. 3540, *Foreign Operations Act of 1997* (Engrossed Senate Amendment). N.d.

———, 105th, 2nd session. H.R. 1757, *US Foreign Affairs Reform and Restructuring Act of 1998*, sec. 1106, "Limitations on the United States Voluntary Contributions to the United Nations Development Program." N.d.

———, 108th, 1st session. S. 1215, *An Act to Sanction the Ruling Burmese Military Junta, to Strengthen Burma's Democratic Forces and Support and Recognize the NLD as the Legitimate Representative of the Burmese People*. N.d.

———, 109th, 1st session. H.R. 3057, *Foreign Operations Act, 2006* (reported in Senate). N.d.

U.S. House of Representatives. H.R. 603. 15 October 1998.

U.S. Senate, 104th Congress, 2nd session. Senate floor discussion of H.R. 3540, *Foreign Operations Act, 1997*, Amendment No. 5019, 25 July 1996.

———, 109th Congress, 1st session. H.R. 3057.RS, *Foreign Operations Act, 2006* (reported in Senate). 24 June 2005.

U.S. State Department. "International Religious Freedom Report 2002." 7 October 2002.

van Aartsen, J. J., and E. L. Herfkens. Letter to the chair of the Commission on Foreign Affairs in the European Parliament, dated 16 October 1998. [Copy in author's possession.]

Voice of America. "Crackdown in Burma." *On the Line*, hosted by Robert Reilly. Aired in May 1997. Transcript posted on BurmaNet List, 31 May 1997.

Wallensteen, Peter, Carina Staibano, and Michael Eriksson. "Routes to Democracy in Burma/Myanmar." Report from the Uppsala Pilot Study on Dialogue and International Strategies, Department of Peace and Conflict Research, Uppsala University, 7 April 2004.

Washington Post. "Burma's Image Problem Is a Moneymaker for US Lobbyists." 24 February 1998.

Weller, Marc, ed. *Democracy and Politics in Burma: A Collection of Documents*. Manerplaw: NCGUB, 1991.

White House. "Executive Order Blocking Property of the Government of Burma and Prohibiting Certain Transactions." Office of the Press Secretary, 28 July 2003.

———. "Executive Order Prohibiting New Investment in Burma." Office of the Press Secretary, 20 May 1997.

———. "Special Envoys on Burma." Statement by the press secretary, Office of the Press Secretary, 7 June 1996.

———. Statement by President Clinton to the United States Congress on Burma sanctions, Office of the Press Secretary, 20 May 1997.

———. "Suspension of Entry as Immigrants and Nonimmigrants of Persons Who Formulate or Implement Policies That Are Impeding the Transition to Democracy in Burma or Who Benefit from Such Policies." Proclamation by the President of the United States of America, Office of the Press Secretary, 3 October 1996.

Wilson, Trevor. "An Australian Perspective on a Transitional Period in Myanmar: May 2000–May 2002." In *The Illusion of Progress: The Political Economy of Reform in Burma/Myanmar*, edited by David S. Mathieson and Ron J. May, 65–84. Adelaide, Australia: Crawford House, 2004.

———. "Some Reflections on Three Years in Burma." Paper presented at the Australian Institute of International Affairs, Canberra, 6 August 2003.

Working People's Daily, 10 January 1990–22 February 1991.

World Bank. "Myanmar: An Economic and Social Assessment." Internal draft, 18 August 1999.

World Vision. "Report on US Sanctions on Burma/Myanmar: The Impact on Local Communities in Yangon." 26 September 2003.

Yan Nyein Aye. "Endeavours of the Myanmar Armed Forces Government for National Reconsolidation." Yangon, 4 January 2000.

Zarni. "Apartheid South Africa and Burma under Military Rule: A Wrong Comparison." 3 June 2005. www.freeburmacoalition.org/ (accessed 28 January 2007).

Zarni and May Oo. "Common Problems, Shared Responsibilities: Citizens' Quest for National Reconciliation in Burma/Myanmar." A Free Burma Coalition report, October 2004.

Zaw Oo and Kai Grieg. "Carrots and Sticks for Democratisation in Burma: Policies of the EU and the ASEAN." In *Human Rights in Development: Global Perspectives and Local Issues*, edited by Hugo Stokke and Arne Tostensen, 91–136. The Hague/Oslo: Kluwer Law International and Nordic Human Rights Publications, October 1999.

Zaw Tun. Speech delivered at the Seminar on Myanmar Economy, Institute of Economics, Rangoon, 7 July 2000. www.ibiblio.org/obl/docs/zaw_tun%2007-07-2000.htm (accessed 26 April 2007).

Index

About the Authors

About the Author

Morten B. Pedersen is a research fellow at the United Nations University, Peace and Governance Programme. From 2000 to 2006, while researching this book, he worked in Burma as a senior analyst for the International Crisis Group and as a consultant on Burmese politics and development affairs for various international organizations. He is the coeditor of the book *Burma/Myanmar: Strong Regime, Weak State* (2000) and has written more than two dozen policy reports and academic articles, mainly dealing with the role of the international community in promoting human rights. He is currently working on a two-year research project called "Engaging Myanmar: The Smarter Way to Human Rights (Lessons and Best Practices)."

About the Foreword Author

Thant Myint-U is a historian and former United Nations official. He was educated at Harvard and Cambridge universities and received his PhD in history from Cambridge in 1996. He has served on three United Nations peacekeeping operations in Cambodia and the former Yugoslavia, in the Office for the Coordination of Humanitarian Affairs, and most recently, as the head of policy planning in the UN Department of Political Affairs in New York. He is the author of three books, including *The Making of Modern Burma* (2000) and *The River of Lost Footsteps: Histories of Burma* (2006).

www.ingramcontent.com/pod-product-compliance
Ingram Content Group UK Ltd.
Pitfield, Milton Keynes, MK11 3LW, UK
UKHW012036150926
475560UK00001B/32

9 780742 55559